Haig's Coup

Haig's Coup

How Richard Nixon's Closest Aide
Forced Him from Office

RAY LOCKER

POTOMAC BOOKS   *An imprint of the University of Nebraska Press*

Frontispiece courtesy of the Richard Nixon
Presidential Library and Museum.

All rights reserved. Potomac Books is an
imprint of the University of Nebraska Press.
Manufactured in the United States of America. ∞

Library of Congress Cataloging-in-Publication Data
Names: Locker, Ray, author.
Title: Haig's coup: how Richard Nixon's closest
aide forced him from office / Ray Locker.
Description: Lincoln, NE: Potomac Books, an
imprint of the University of Nebraska Press, [2019]
| Includes bibliographical references and index.
Identifiers: LCCN 2018046952
ISBN 9781640120358 (cloth: alk. paper)
ISBN 9781640121782 (epub)
ISBN 9781640121799 (mobi)
ISBN 9781640121805 (pdf)
Subjects: LCSH: Nixon, Richard M. (Richard
Milhous), 1913–1994—Resignation from office. |
Haig, Alexander Meigs, 1924–2010. | Presidents—
United States—Staff—Biography. | Generals—United
States—Biography. | Watergate Affair, 1972–1974. |
Nixon, Richard M. (Richard Milhous), 1913–1994—
Impeachment. | Executive power—United
States—History—20th century. | Civil-military
relations—United States—History—20th century. |
United States—Politics and government—1969–1974.
Classification: LCC E861 .L63 2019
DDC 973.924092/2—dc23 LC record available
at https://lccn.loc.gov/2018046952

Set in Sabon Next by E. Cuddy.
Designed by N. Putens.

To Shirley

CONTENTS

ACKNOWLEDGMENTS

The act of writing may be solitary, but writing a book depends on collaboration, and it took a dedicated group of collaborators to make *Haig's Coup* a reality. That group starts with Len Colodny. For more than twenty-five years he has been an advisor, an inspiration, and a trusted friend. No one has keener insights into the world of Richard Nixon and Alexander Haig, and no one has fought the keepers of the conventional wisdom longer and more successfully than Len has. His wife, Sandy, son, John, and daughter, Sherry, fight the good fight with him and are turning Len's work into an enduring gift with the Colodny Collection at Texas A&M University.

Shirley Higuchi gave me the confidence and support to write this book in a calm and friendly environment. I am forever grateful for her love, kindness, and generosity in helping make the book a reality. Her introduction to the Rancho La Puerta in Tecate, Mexico, provided a refuge for writing and reflection.

My daughters, Maggie Locker-Polding and Abbey Locker, were, as always, great sounding boards and supporters, forever patient in their knowledge that sometimes Dad gets distracted and thinks about old figures in history a little too often.

Luke Nichter of Texas A&M University is one of the leading Nixon scholars and a great researcher. He has supplied me with documents from his vast trove, including those about FBI official William Sullivan, Department of Justice official Robert Mardian, reporter Bob Woodward, and Alexander Haig.

Ed Gray, author and son of former acting FBI director L. Patrick Gray, provided years of research materials and encouragement. He was the first to mine the Woodward and Bernstein Watergate Papers at the Harry Ransom Center at the University of Texas at Austin and expose the numerous inconsistencies between their notes and books. His insights led me to dig further into the life and work of William Sullivan, which yielded many of the new details here. He helped make this book what it is today.

Authors, officials, scholars, and advisors essential to the existence of *Haig's Coup* include Robert Gettlin, who put his heart and soul into the book he wrote with Len Colodny, *Silent Coup: The Removal of a President*; James Rosen; John A. Farrell; Brian Robertson; Evan Thomas; Joseph Califano; Martin Lobel; and Fred Graboske.

The resources at the Harry Ransom Center at the University of Texas; the Harold Weisberg Collection at Hood College in Frederick, Maryland; the Lowell Weicker Papers at the University of Virginia; the Richard Nixon Presidential Library and Museum in Yorba Linda, California; the Gerald R. Ford Presidential Library and Museum in Ann Arbor, Michigan; the LBJ Presidential Library in Austin, Texas; the Defense Department; the FBI; the CIA; and the State Department Office of the Historian were incredible aids. No historian writing about postwar America should be without them.

Friends and colleagues provided incredible support and insistence. Much of the inspiration came from more than thirty years of conversations with Lee Landenberger, whose fascination with the events of the Nixon era kept me going. There is no better friend. Michael Fechter helped expose the flaws in earlier collections of White House tapes and provided critical help with all stages of the manuscript. Margaret Talev, as always, provided her keen insights and encouragement. Peter Viles, Mike Casey, Fredreka Schouten, Tom Vanden Brook, Chrissy Terrell, David Jackson, Gregory Korte, David Callaway, Lee Horwich, Susan Page, Julie Mason, and Cooper Allen provided personal and professional assists along the way. Special thanks to Kelly Kennedy for helping to line up my agent, the incredible Scott Miller of Trident Media.

Any long project depends on the help and patience of family. My parents, Bob and Marge Locker, who voted for Richard Nixon for president three times, provided tremendous support and encouragement. They are everything anyone would want in parents. Alan Polding, my son-in-law, weighed in with his perspectives as a citizen of the United Kingdom watching current events in the United States. Finally, to the rest of my extended family—Lauren, David, Julia, and Henry Piper and Marina and Steven Sweeney; Lydia, Steve, Ian, and Paul Josowitz; Debbie and Richard Etchison; Bill, Angie, and Amelia Collier and Adele Collier—thanks for the kind thoughts and help.

INTRODUCTION

"I Am in Control Here"

Emotional and breathless, Alexander Haig faced an anxious press corps and nation in the White House briefing room at 4:14 p.m. on March 30, 1981, to announce who led the nation as President Ronald Reagan lay anesthetized in an operating room at George Washington University Hospital. Haig had scrambled from the State Department to the White House to manage the crisis caused by the assassination attempt on the new president. Reagan, it seemed, would survive, but a nervous, jittery nation that had seen a president killed and another forced out of office in the previous twenty years needed to know someone was capable of making decisions in the White House.

"Constitutionally, gentlemen, you have the President, the Vice President, and the Secretary of State in that order, and should the President decide he wants to transfer the helm to the Vice President, he will do so," Haig said. "He has not done that. As of now, I am in control here, in the

White House, pending return of the Vice President and in close touch with him. If something came up, I would check with him, of course."[1]

Haig's words were clear and simple. He and some of Reagan's closest aides had gathered in the White House Situation Room to determine who had shot the president and why. Authorities soon learned that twenty-five-year-old John W. Hinckley, an unemployed and delusional drifter from Colorado, had shot Reagan with a .22-caliber pistol when the president left the Washington Hilton. Reagan's press secretary, James Brady, had been shot in the head, and a Secret Service agent and Washington cop had also been wounded. But, as so often happens in such attacks, thoughts turned to a larger conspiracy and who controlled the government.

That brief moment in the White House, as he strived unsuccessfully to display calm, marked Haig forever as impulsive and unstable as he grabbed for power and attempted to fill Reagan's vacuum. It was not the first time Haig had assumed authority that was not his to take. Haig believed he was in control that day in 1981 because he knew what it meant to be in charge at the White House. During the fifteen months from May 1973 to August 1974, when he served as President Richard Nixon's chief of staff, Haig was the de facto president of the United States.

During those final months of the Nixon administration, as the president desperately tried to withstand the onslaught of negative press reports, congressional investigations, and federal prosecutions spurred by the Watergate scandal, Haig controlled the president's agenda and determined who met with the president and whether to even tell Nixon about many of the decisions made in his name. Haig stacked the deck against Nixon's legal defense, hiring both Nixon's main Watergate defender and the special prosecutor. He also forced the resignation of Vice President Spiro Agnew, under investigation for bribery and corruption, and engineered the selection of his replacement. With Henry Kissinger, who was first Haig's boss at the National Security Council and then secretary of state, Haig coordinated foreign policy. Together, he and Kissinger put the country on nuclear alert while Nixon slept. And as Nixon careened toward resignation, Haig shaped that departure and the pardon Nixon eventually received from his successor, Gerald Ford. Haig knew crisis management because he had managed the White House through an unprecedented political and succession crisis. He was, in the words of Watergate special prosecutor Leon Jaworski, the nation's "thirty-seventh-and-a-half president."[2]

Haig only did what came naturally to him after Reagan's shooting.

But Haig's rushed attempt to assure calm triggered troubling memories for many who remembered his work for Nixon. Shortly after Nixon's departure, author and reporter Jules Witcover watched Haig in the VIP section of the Capitol after Ford addressed Congress and observed that Haig was "in a sense applauding his own deft achievement of presidential transition never contemplated in quite that way by the Founding Fathers." Witcover witnessed "a bloodless presidential coup engineered by an army general, a man who had gravitated to the very right hand of one president and who, when that president fell, saw to a swift removal of the body."[3]

If only he knew the whole story.

Haig eased Nixon out of office not to save the military or the presidency but to save himself.

Nixon needed to go for many reasons. By his final year in office his mental condition alone justified his removal. He drank too much and was often absent during major crises. But Haig, in concert with White House lawyer J. Fred Buzhardt, made it impossible for Nixon to stay, and then both men did everything to protect themselves. Haig needed Nixon to resign and be pardoned by Ford. A House impeachment and Senate trial would have exposed how Haig had leaked White House secrets, obstructed justice, and abused power. As Nixon's deputy national security advisor, Haig led the White House campaign to have the FBI wiretap government officials and journalists to identify the leakers of White House secrets. Those wiretaps were part of the surveillance techniques included in the impeachment articles, and both Haig and Kissinger had lied to cover their tracks. Haig had also cooperated with military leaders who were stealing secret documents from the White House and then leaking the details to derail his plans, an act the president had described as "a federal offense of the highest order."[4] That cooperation would have cost Haig his job and possibly landed him in prison. If Charles Colson and H. R. Haldeman, both longtime Nixon loyalists and top aides, had known about Haig's betrayal, they never would have recommended that Haig succeed Haldeman as the White House chief of staff.

After Haig saved himself by jettisoning Nixon, he engineered his cover-up. Less than forty-eight hours after Ford pardoned Nixon and eliminated the threat of a nasty criminal trial, Haig repaired to the den of his home in northwest Washington DC and met with the two reporters who had caused much of Nixon's problems: Bob Woodward and Carl Bernstein of the *Washington Post*.[5] Together they would write the inside story of Nixon's final days, aided and abetted by Haig's early and enthusiastic guidance. Haig had betrayed the president he had sworn to protect, and then he engineered his cover-up. For an ambitious and cunning man like this, seizing control of the moment at the White House after a president had been shot was just another routine piece of business.

Haig's Coup

1 The Making of Alexander Haig

The world into which Alexander Meigs Haig Jr. was born on December 4, 1924, was filled with great possibilities. Optimism surged through the U.S. economy as factory production rose and the stock market soared. President Calvin Coolidge had shaken off the scandals left by his predecessor, Warren Harding, and won a landslide a month earlier. In Bala Cynwyd, Pennsylvania, a well-tended suburb eight miles from Philadelphia along the Main Line from downtown, young Alec was the second child of a striving lawyer and his lace-curtain Irish wife, Regina. The Haigs were on the verge of making it. Alexander Sr. was an ambitious young lawyer with a bright future.

But Alexander Haig Sr. developed cancer and died at age thirty-eight, when Alec was ten. Then the expectations for the entire family—Alec, his older sister, Regina, and his younger brother, Frank—turned dark. The nation was mired in the Great Depression, and while Haig's father had managed to surf over the rough patches of the national economy with his law practice, his widow had to depend on the kindness of family members and her job to keep things afloat. Instead of private school, Haig had to attend the local public high school, Lower Merion, a change in status that impeded Haig's dream of attending the United States Military Academy at West Point, New York, and becoming an army officer. "Al is definitely not West Point material," the Lower Merion principal told his mother.[1] So Haig traveled to South Bend, Indiana, to attend Notre Dame, where he waited until he could apply to West Point again.

Haig entered West Point in 1944 at the height of World War II. At the rate the war was going, he would not graduate in time to fight in either Europe or the Pacific. The academy lacked the academic rigor of the years before the war, as too many instructors had left for the battlefield, while the remainder focused more on producing combat-ready officers, not academic achievement. Even so, Haig failed to distinguish himself academically, finishing 214th out of a class of 310 cadets. But the contacts he made during his three years at West Point would remain part of his life for decades. Fred Buzhardt, the son of a South Carolina lawyer, was in the class ahead of Haig; they would work together in the Nixon White House. Brent Scowcroft, a future general and national security advisor, finished 86th.[2]

After graduating in 1947, Haig received the routine postings that many young second lieutenants received after West Point and during peacetime. He was stationed to forts in Kansas and Kentucky for courses in infantry and armor. The war was over, the army was shrinking, and Haig's military career seemed to have little direction.

That changed when the army sent Haig to Japan to join the staff of the imperious Gen. Douglas MacArthur, the American viceroy who ruled over Japan from his offices in the Dai Ichi Insurance Company building. The young lieutenant learned quickly how to ingratiate himself to his superiors by anticipating their commands. He also caught the attention of Patricia Fox, the daughter of Maj. Gen. Alonzo Fox, a top MacArthur deputy. They were married on May 24, 1950, just a month before North Korean forces invaded South Korea to start the Korean War. After allied forces retreated under the North Korean assault, ultimately forming a small perimeter around the southern city of Busan, came MacArthur's true genius stroke as a general: the amphibious assault on the port city of Inchon. Surprised, the North Koreans buckled and fled. Haig carried MacArthur's sleeping bag ashore and remained in the commander's headquarters as U.S. forces moved rapidly north, past Pyongyang, the North Korean capital, and toward the Yalu River, the border between North Korea and China, which had turned communist the previous year after Mao Zedong's ouster of Chiang Kai-shek's Nationalists.[3] The coming Chinese attack, signs of which MacArthur and his team ignored, pushed the U.S. forces south in some of the bloodiest fighting ever seen. Haig saw almost no combat in Korea but witnessed MacArthur's leadership failures, which led President Harry Truman to fire him in 1951.

After Korea, Haig endured a series of uninspiring peacetime postings stateside, including trips to the Naval War College and a stint on the West Point staff. The army sent him to Georgetown University in Washington DC, for his master's degree. It was while he was in the Pentagon in 1962 that he caught the eye of Cyrus Vance, secretary of the army, who added Haig to his staff.[4] In the Pentagon, the Republican Haig acquired his four unlikely Democratic benefactors: Vance; his assistant, New York–born lawyer Joseph Califano; Defense Secretary Robert McNamara; and Chicago lawyer Morris Leibman, a liberal anticommunist who advised the army on multiple issues.[5] They embodied the Kennedy era's vigor and optimism and the belief that they could reshape the world. Haig joined a small group in the Pentagon developing secret plans to overthrow the government of Cuban dictator Fidel Castro, who had whipped an ill-prepared band of Cuban exiles when they tried to invade Cuba at the Bay of Pigs in April 1961. Under the direction of President John Kennedy's brother, Attorney General Robert Kennedy, Haig's group plotted assassination attempts, propaganda programs, and military assault plans.[6] Details of the Kennedys' secret obsession would remain secret until the mid-1970s, long after both Kennedys had been assassinated. Haig also oversaw the army's share of the CIA's Project Moses, the repatriation of the Cuban exile soldiers captured at the Bay of Pigs.[7]

During this time, Haig gained two more influential mentors. William

Sullivan ran the FBI's intelligence division. One of Director J. Edgar Hoover's favorites, Sullivan controlled many of the bureau's most controversial programs, such as the attempt to destabilize civil rights leader Martin Luther King Jr., the sweeping COINTELPRO (Counterintelligence Program) domestic intelligence network, and the fight against domestic communism, on which he worked closely with Leibman.[8] With Sullivan, Haig vetted the returning Cubans to determine who could be absorbed into the U.S. Army. A second guiding light for Haig was army strategist Fritz Kraemer, a monocle-wearing, riding crop–wielding exile from Hitler's Germany. The magnetic Kraemer, who had during World War II discovered a young private named Henry Kissinger, espoused a hard-line theory called "provocative weakness"; he believed any signs of weakness by the United States would invite attacks or maneuvers by its rivals, particularly the Soviet Union and communist China. During the Kennedy administration, Kraemer's vision, emanating from deep inside the Pentagon, was very much in vogue, and Haig fell under his spell. "Kraemer was seen as one of the ultimate wise men, an energetic thinker who had a wide knowledge of history and warfighting and how civilizations rise and fall," Califano said. "He had a lot of fans among the army colonels and lieutenant colonels at the time," including Haig, who remained a Kraemer acolyte for the rest of his life.[9] Kraemer and Sullivan also shared a bond, one close enough so Kraemer felt comfortable warning Sullivan in 1963 that national security advisor McGeorge Bundy was a "Fabian socialist" whose tacit acceptance of Soviet domination of parts of the world weakened American will.[10]

After Kennedy's assassination on November 22, 1963, the obsession with Castro waned. New president Lyndon Johnson soon focused his attention on Vietnam, where an incident in the Gulf of Tonkin in August 1964 provided a false pretext for what became a U.S.-dominated war that eventually saw 565,000 U.S. troops stationed in South Vietnam. Haig received his first combat command in 1967 when he was sent to lead a battalion near the Cambodian border. There Haig led his troops in the battle of Ap Gu, an extensive firefight on March 31 and April 1, 1967, in which Haig's troops ultimately defeated a larger North Vietnamese and Viet Cong force. After flying a helicopter into the thick of mortar and small arms fire at the point of contact, Haig helped push off the enemy, actions for which he received a Distinguished Service Cross, a commendation second only to the Medal of Honor.[11] He returned in 1968 to a post as commander of the Third Regiment of the Corps of Cadets at his alma mater, West Point. There he remained at the end of 1968 and the closing of the Johnson administration and the transition to a new president, Republican former vice president Richard Nixon, who had lost a razor-thin election to Kennedy in 1960.

Perhaps Haig's army career would have ended there. But as his national security advisor Nixon chose Kissinger, whom Kraemer had discovered during World War II. By late 1968 Kissinger had established an international reputation as a leading thinker on nuclear weapons policy as a member of the Harvard University faculty. He seemed destined for a prominent role in the administration of either Nixon or his defeated Democratic rival in 1968, Vice President Hubert Humphrey. As he assembled his national security staff with a host of national security bureaucrats and Johnson holdovers, Kissinger sought the advice of Kraemer and Joseph Califano for the name of a reliable officer to be his chief military aide. They both recommended Haig. "I told Henry that Al would work twenty hours a day," Califano said. Kissinger hired him.[12]

Nixon gave his National Security Council a different look from that of Johnson, who often made policy through ad hoc meetings and lunches with advisors. Nixon's system focused almost all authority in the national security advisor and the president. As established in the secret National Security Decision Memorandum 2, which Nixon signed shortly after being sworn in on January 20, 1969, the various agencies would receive policy questions from the White House. The agencies would supply their recommendations, and then the NSC staff and Kissinger would analyze them before presenting Nixon with a series of options from which he would make his decision.[13]

And Haig was in the middle of it, gathering information from the Pentagon and sifting through the flood of paper in Kissinger's overflowing in-box. Haig's twenty years as a military staff officer, starting with

MacArthur in Japan, served him well. Even before Nixon took office, Haig was sending Kissinger memos about how to manage the paper flow into the White House. He stayed at work when others went home. He watched his peers carefully and slyly undercut them. "I have expressed to you on several occasions my concern that the NSC staff is not properly organized and that the functions of the components of the staff, i.e., the Operators, the Planners and the Programmers have not been sufficiently delineated and formalized to insure the kind of smooth staff work that is essential," Haig wrote Kissinger a little more than two weeks after Nixon took office. "I have no personal ambitions with respect to this problem and am honored to serve in any capacity at this level, providing I have assured myself that you are getting the kind of support which you must have," Haig helpfully added, displaying the brownnosing that was quickly earning him the enmity of his colleagues.[14] Kissinger increased his reliance on Haig.

Soon, however, Haig's Pentagon allies saw signs that Nixon was not the hard-liner they wanted. The Joint Chiefs of Staff opposed Nixon's budding plan to return the island of Okinawa to Japan, from which it was wrested in a 1945 battle that claimed 12,500 American lives. Haig became their conduit to the president, saying in an April 2 memo to Kissinger that "I must emphasize that the price we would pay for [redacted] Okinawa, even after a settlement of the Vietnam War, would be extremely heavy."[15] Haig also used a "dead-key" system on Kissinger's telephone to listen in on his conversations. Once he turned to Charles Colson, a Nixon aide and former marine, and whispered, "He's selling us out on Vietnam!" He later told Colson, "I've got to get hold of Kraemer."[16]

Other problems emerged. Nixon's proposals and other secrets quickly appeared in the press, often just days or hours after they developed. A March 31 *New York Times* article included details from a March 29 memo from the Joint Chiefs of Staff opposing the reversion of Okinawa to Japan, a mere hours after the memo was sent to the secretary of defense from Joint Chiefs chairman Gen. Earle Wheeler.[17] Leaks about Nixon's response to a North Korean attack on a military spy plane, troop withdrawal plans for South Vietnam, alternative Vietnam policies, and a potential sale of fighter planes to Jordan also drew anger from Nixon, who was hearing regularly from Attorney General John Mitchell and FBI director J. Edgar Hoover that he had to start placing wiretaps on the telephones of suspected leakers, starting with Kissinger's nominal deputy, Morton Halperin.[18]

Kissinger resisted until May 9, when the *Times* published a story that contained details of the still "secret" U.S. bombing of targets in ostensibly neutral Cambodia.[19] Nixon had approved the secret bombing campaign, called Menu, in March after military leaders said they needed the air strikes to wipe out the border sanctuaries and an alleged North Vietnamese command center along the border. Kissinger erupted when he read the story by reporter William Beecher at breakfast in Key Biscayne, Florida, where he had traveled with the president and his team.[20] Kissinger called Hoover, who had been steadily prodding him to do something, and asked for Hoover's help. By day's end, after three more calls from Kissinger, Hoover had already ordered the first wiretap on Halperin's home telephone. With Haig's help, Kissinger identified two more wiretap targets on the NSC staff, Daniel Davidson and Helmut Sonnenfeldt, and a surprising fourth target, Col. Robert Pursley, the military aide to Defense Secretary Melvin Laird. A former U.S. House member from Wisconsin, the wily Laird had mastered Washington intrigue. He had also opposed the need to secretly bomb targets in Cambodia, which made him suspect to Nixon, Kissinger, and Haig. Ten days later, they added two more targets, NSC officials Richard Moose and Richard Sneider, who led the staff effort on the reversion of Okinawa to Japan, the details of which were showing up in the press too frequently. Those leaks dealt with the military's opposition to the reversion, meaning they came from the Pentagon or perhaps Haig, the military's representative inside the NSC.

Hoover agreed to the wiretaps but only with the signed authorization from the attorney general, who agreed. While most experts considered the wiretaps legal under the current laws, they remained controversial, and Hoover realized public sentiment had turned against the FBI's freewheeling tactics. Hoover delegated the wiretaps to Sullivan, his trusted lieutenant and Haig's friend. "After a lifetime of service under Hoover, he had the weary air of a man who has been sifting other people's secrets all his life and finding them not particularly interesting," Haig wrote of Sullivan.[21] By February 1971, when the program stopped, the FBI had tapped the phones of seventeen government officials and journalists.

Hoover ordered Sullivan to keep the wiretaps secret and hold the files outside the bureau's legendary central filing system, which held blackmail-worthy information on hundreds of members of Congress and other prominent officials. Sullivan coordinated picking the targets with Kissinger and Haig, who met with Sullivan often. Kissinger told Sullivan, "It is clear that I don't have anybody in my office that I can trust except Colonel Haig here."[22] Hoover, however, had picked the wrong man with Sullivan, who believed the wiretaps gave him the leverage to supplant his boss. For years, Sullivan had used Hoover's authority while quietly exceeding the director's desires. Sullivan bridled at Hoover's earlier edict to curtail surreptitious break-ins by agents without warrants.[23] Sullivan used Hoover's antipathy toward civil rights leader Martin Luther King Jr. to justify bugging King's hotel rooms and writing a threatening letter urging King to kill himself.[24] Sullivan oversaw the burgeoning and highly secret COINTELPRO campaign, which targeted legitimate and illegitimate threats alike. Sullivan also used his good relations with the Central Intelligence Agency, which ran contrary to Hoover's wishes, to promote the creation of a national intelligence service similar to the British MI5, another idea anathema to Hoover.[25] Sullivan also cultivated journalists such as columnists Jack Anderson and Robert Novak with a series of secret tips.[26] Hoover would soon regret putting such a sensitive operation in Sullivan's hands.

The wiretaps, Haig claimed, generated proof that one leaker was Daniel Davidson, a protégé of longtime Democratic diplomat and politician Averell Harriman.[27] Haig quietly told Davidson he had been discovered and had to leave, which he did. Beyond Davidson, however, the taps found nothing, leading Sullivan to tell Hoover they should stop. Hoover refused, saying he would maintain the taps as long as Nixon wanted them. Hoover also believed the taps gave him leverage, the reasons for which were detailed in a 1971 FBI memorandum: "It goes without saying that knowledge of this coverage represents a potential source of tremendous embarrassment to the Bureau and political disaster for the Nixon administration. Copies of the material itself could be used for political blackmail and the ruination of Nixon, Mitchell and others in the administration."[28]

Haig steadily became Kissinger's go-to deputy. By September Nixon was pinning on Haig's brigadier general's star at the White House. During the second half of 1969, Haig made another critical connection. A navy lieutenant, Robert U. Woodward, who worked in the Pentagon communications office for Adm. Thomas Moorer, the chief of naval operations and future chairman of the Joint Chiefs of Staff, started delivering secret messages from the Pentagon to Haig at the White House.

In 1971, after leaving the navy and spending a year on the staff of a small newspaper in suburban Maryland, Woodward became a reporter for the *Washington Post* using the byline Bob Woodward. One year later, Woodward and his reporting partner, Carl Bernstein, would became famous for their reporting on the Nixon administration. Haig and Woodward would eventually deny that they knew each other at this time, but recorded interviews with three top Pentagon officials—Moorer, Defense Secretary Melvin Laird, and Pentagon spokesman Jerry Friedheim—show that Woodward regularly met Haig at the White House.[29] Moorer said Woodward was one of six lieutenants entrusted with keeping the White House informed of Pentagon developments, and Haig was their conduit.[30] While Laird said the Woodward-Haig relationship "bothered" him at the time, he never told Nixon about the connection between Haig and Woodward, not even when Laird was a member of the White House staff in 1973 and 1974 and Woodward's stories were putting Nixon on the defensive.[31]

Woodward was part of a larger operation aimed at ferreting out the secrets the White House kept from the Pentagon. The Joint Chiefs of Staff had a liaison office at the NSC, which concerned Laird, because it let the military brass communicate directly with the NSC staff and go around both Kissinger and Laird. He warned Kissinger early that he would regret keeping the office, but Kissinger had other priorities and left it open, not realizing Haig was already telling the military the secrets

Nixon was trying to hide from them. Adm. Elmo Zumwalt, a future chief of naval operations who knew Haig from McNamara's Pentagon, said Haig frequently told Gen. William Westmoreland, the army chief of staff, about the White House's plans.[32] Navy Rear Adm. Rembrandt Robinson, the head of the Chiefs' liaison office, met often with Haig behind closed doors and was one of the few navy officers to attend Haig's promotion ceremony to brigadier general, along with Haig's hard-line mentor, Fritz Kraemer.

Nixon believed he needed secrecy to achieve his three main foreign policy goals: reduced tensions and an arms control agreement with the Soviet Union, diplomatic relations with the People's Republic of China, and an end to the Vietnam War. If his plans were exposed, Nixon feared that Washington's entrenched interests at the Pentagon and in Congress, the State Department, the intelligence community, and the press would kill them. The secret maneuvers started almost immediately. Just one month after taking office, Nixon authorized Kissinger to tell the Soviet ambassador, Anatoly Dobrynin, that the United States had no intention of trying to win on the battlefield in Vietnam and recognized that South Vietnam's long-term chances of survival were grim.[33] Just as quickly, Nixon began to seek improved relations with the Chinese communists, who had fought and killed thousands of U.S. troops in Korea. Haig learned all these secrets as Kissinger's deputy, and he eventually became one of Nixon's favorite confidants.

Military leaders initially thought Nixon would release them from the restrictions that President Johnson had placed on them in Vietnam, but they soon realized how much Nixon did not tell them. On troop reductions in Vietnam, the 1970 invasion of Cambodia, and then the quick reversal of plans for that invasion, Nixon routinely surprised the brass, so by the middle of 1970 Moorer had begun to seek more information from the Chiefs' NSC liaison office and Robinson's strong relationship with Haig. That effort was boosted by the second half of 1970, when Robinson gained a new assistant, navy yeoman Charles Radford, a young enlisted man who did clerical duties for NSC staffers and also traveled with Kissinger and Haig overseas.

Robinson told Radford to get as much information as possible from the White House, which Radford considered authorization to steal documents from the NSC offices. He took the "burn bags" of documents meant to be destroyed after reading, lifted and copied the documents, and then placed them back into the bags for disposal. On trips to Vietnam and elsewhere with Haig and Kissinger, Radford stole papers from their briefcases and sent them to the Pentagon. The information gap between the White House and Pentagon began to narrow.[34]

Laird oversaw a multilayered intelligence-gathering network beyond the White House spy ring. Whenever Kissinger flew on a military plane, such as to Paris for secret talks with the North Vietnamese, the military pilots told Laird where Kissinger was going. Whenever Kissinger used a CIA communications channel, the National Security Agency intercepted the calls and sent the details to the NSA chief, Gen. Noel Gayler, who passed the information to Laird.[35] Finally, Zumwalt, the new chief of naval operations, had a protégé working directly in Kissinger's office, Lt. David Halperin, who told Zumwalt about Kissinger's activities.[36] When Kissinger met secretly in Palm Springs, California, with Joseph Farland, the U.S. ambassador to Pakistan, in May 1971 to discuss his upcoming secret trip to China, Halperin took the notes.[37] He then told Zumwalt about the top-secret trip. While Nixon routinely bypassed Laird and hid secrets from him, Laird was returning the favor, and with Haig's help. Laird never told Nixon about the Haig-Woodward relationship because doing so would have exposed Laird's own spying on the White House.

By the middle of 1971 Haig's rhythms at the White House were firmly established. He had a closer relationship with Nixon, who often tired of Kissinger's emotional neediness and bypassed him to talk with Haig, who often fed some of Nixon's more aggressive or paranoid instincts. Meanwhile, Haig and Kissinger talked behind Nixon's back, often calling him "our drunken friend."[38] In June 1971 Haig inadvertently threw Nixon into a political crisis that would dog him for the remainder of his presidency. On June 12, the day after Nixon gave away his daughter Tricia at a glamorous wedding at the White House, a concerned Haig alerted Nixon to a story on the front page of that Sunday's *New York Times*.[39] The *Times* had obtained a copy of a massive history of the military's involvement in the Vietnam War that was commissioned by Haig's onetime boss, former Defense Secretary Robert McNamara. Quickly dubbed the Pentagon Papers, the archive showed how successive administrations had lied and exaggerated about the Vietnam War despite their grave doubts. Daniel Ellsberg, a consultant, student, and former advisor of Kissinger, had stolen the study and given it to the *Times*, which spent weeks assembling the documents into a narrative. While Nixon had little to fear from the papers, which detailed previous administrations' decisions and mistakes, Haig had greater risks. He worked at McNamara's side as the U.S. involvement in Vietnam deepened, and Haig also had even deeper secrets that risked exposure, such as the long effort to subvert and overthrow Fidel Castro in Cuba. He told Nixon about "the goddamn *New York Times* expose of the most highly classified documents of the war," a story Nixon had not seen.

Was it leaked out of the Pentagon? Nixon asked. "Sir, it, uh, the whole study that was done for McNamara, and then carried on after McNamara left by [Clark] Clifford, and the peaceniks over there," Haig answered, referring to the Pentagon analysts whose ranks once included Morton Halperin, a Haig rival at the NSC. "This is a devastating, uh, security break, of, of the greatest magnitude of anything I've ever seen." Nixon's first instinct was to find someone to fire, preferably at the Pentagon, to show that leaks were not tolerated. Haig speculated that the papers were stolen during the transition from the Johnson to the Nixon administrations and would damage Democrats, not Nixon: "They're going to end up in a massive gut fight in the Democratic Party on this thing."[40]

Nixon wanted the FBI to investigate and destroy Ellsberg, just as the FBI had helped a young Nixon in the late 1940s when he went after Alger Hiss, a former State Department official accused of once being a communist. But this time, Hoover, stuck in a power struggle with Sullivan, declined to cooperate. Nixon then authorized creating a White House team of investigators to do what Hoover *would not* and Sullivan *could not* do. Under the ostensible leadership of White House aide John Ehrlichman, the team consisted of longtime CIA operative E. Howard Hunt, former Treasury agent G. Gordon Liddy, and White House staffers

Egil Krogh and David Young. Hunt tapped his former CIA colleagues for help, and Ehrlichman also sought aid from the agency's deputy director, marine general Robert Cushman, who agreed to lend technology and assistance. By September the investigations unit, nicknamed the Plumbers because they were supposed to plug leaks, had recruited a group of Cuban exiles with Bay of Pigs connections to travel to Los Angeles and help Hunt and Liddy break into the office of Dr. Lewis Fielding, a Beverly Hills psychiatrist who had treated Ellsberg. The break-in yielded no dirt on Ellsberg, but it ensnared the White House in a criminal conspiracy.[41]

In December the Plumbers appeared again, this time in a case that threatened to expose Haig, Laird, and their allies in the Pentagon. Haig and Laird's need to perpetuate the spy ring cover-up extended through the rest of Nixon's presidency and put Haig's survival over that of the president.

On December 14, 1971, a report in the *Washington Post* by columnist Jack Anderson highlighted the dangers of Nixon's decision to send a task force led by the nuclear-powered aircraft carrier *Enterprise* to the Bay of Bengal near India, which was fighting a war with neighboring Pakistan, whose leader, Yahya Khan, had worked secretly to help Nixon's outreach to China.[42] Nixon professed neutrality in the India-Pakistan war, but behind the scenes he tilted U.S. policy to help Pakistan. Anderson exposed the tilt by citing details from secret White House meetings and highlighted the dangers of moving the *Enterprise* to where it could collide with Soviet forces backing India. In the liaison office of the Joint Chiefs of Staff, Yeoman Charles Radford's new boss, Rear Adm. Robert Welander, immediately suspected that Radford had leaked information to Anderson. After a second Anderson column on December 16, internal Pentagon investigators, led by Donald Stewart, a by-the-book former FBI agent, interrogated Radford, who, instead of confessing to leaking to Anderson, broke down and confessed to stealing White House documents for Welander, who then gave them to Moorer.

An outraged Nixon learned the details in a meeting with John Mitchell, Bob Haldeman, and John Ehrlichman on December 21. Calling the theft and leaks "a federal offense of the highest order," he wanted to prosecute Radford, Welander, and Moorer. Mitchell, however, warned that prosecuting Moorer "would have the Joint Chiefs aligned on that side directly against you." What has been done has been done, Mitchell said, and "the important thing is to just paper this thing over." Nixon reluctantly agreed, deciding to ship Radford and Welander to remote posts outside Washington and have Mitchell warn Moorer that he must never do anything like that again. Moorer would then be, in Ehrlichman's words, a "preshrunk admiral" easily manipulated by Nixon.

Troubling for Haig, however, were Nixon's suspicions that Haig had played some part in the spying. "Haig had to know," Nixon said.[43] Ehrlichman said Haig did not know. Aware of Kissinger's suspicion of Haig, Nixon ordered Haldeman and Ehrlichman that Kissinger must not do anything to Haig. While he did not want a criminal investigation or anything more from the White House, Nixon allowed Ehrlichman and Young, one of the White House Plumbers, to interview Welander. During their December 22 meeting in the White House, Welander declined to sign a confession offered by Ehrlichman but readily acknowledged that Haig routinely shared White House secrets with him.[44] Ehrlichman and Young played the Welander confession to Haig and Kissinger the next day, and Kissinger erupted, saying that Nixon needed to do more to punish the spies or else he would eventually regret it. Haig said little then, but that night he called Young at home and threatened him.[45] Young, who hated Haig, told Ehrlichman, who did nothing, thinking that Young had overreacted out of animosity toward Haig. That ended the White House's investigation into the spy ring.

Ehrlichman admitted that he "missed the boat" on Haig's spy ring connections: "I heard what Welander was saying, but I didn't fully realize its implications in terms of Haig's role as an agent of the Joint Chiefs." Ehrlichman's conclusion, which he did not share with Nixon, was that "Haig had an enormous conflict of interest" between his loyalty to Nixon, who "sponsored him and, and fostered his career on the one hand, and the Joint Chiefs on the other." Haig, Ehrlichman said, was in "an impossible situation, which I guess he resolved in favor of the Joint Chiefs."[46]

Ehrlichman had other difficulties. Nixon wanted him to investigate whether Anderson and Radford had a homosexual relationship. Nixon said he discovered homosexual connections in the Alger Hiss investigation in 1949 and suspected the same with Anderson. At the Pentagon Laird blocked the investigation because he had ordered one of his own, which was essentially aimed at covering for military leaders. Laird knew Haig was sending secrets from the White House to the president. "I was disappointed," Laird said of Haig's role in helping the spy ring. "Well, because I didn't think it was fair to the president."[47] But Laird said nothing to Nixon about what he knew about Haig and instead assigned the task of compiling a Pentagon report to the department's top lawyer, J. Fred Buzhardt, Haig's old friend from West Point. On December 22 Laird told Ehrlichman that he needed to deal with Buzhardt exclusively. The next day, he told Ehrlichman that they could not touch the homosexuality issue because it would become public and expose their cover-up. Laird used the controversy surrounding the Radford case to get the White House to shut down the liaison office. "I knew that there was this channel and I knew exactly what the channel was," Laird told Ehrlichman. "Now, I have no problems with investigating these people to death. I do feel, however, that this will be an embarrassment for the President, for the National Security Council, for this whole system that has been set up and has been used in the Nixon administration. And I don't want it to break on the basis of this guy refusing to answer questions on homosexuality."[48]

As part of the investigation ordered by Laird, Buzhardt called Stewart back home early from a vacation in Florida to interview Welander. Buzhardt never told Stewart about the first interview with Welander during which he admitted getting inside information from Haig. Instead, Welander portrayed Haig in the second interview as Radford's victim, not a collaborator in the military spy ring. This carefully massaged interview ended up in the final report that was passed to Laird, while Young and Stewart's more thorough report was filed away in the White House and buried.[49]

There the matter died, leaving a dissatisfied Stewart to believe he had witnessed an attempted coup against Nixon like the one in the movie *Seven Days in May*, a coup that had been covered up. While Haig had escaped discovery, he still worked for Nixon, who remained fixated on the spy ring and repeatedly complained how he could not trust the military, which he also believed owed him loyalty for not prosecuting Moorer and Welander for treason.

The year after the fall of the spy ring was one of triumph and budding tragedy for Nixon. His secrecy began to pay off as he traveled first to the China and then to the Soviet Union for summit conferences that opened diplomatic relations and cemented a significant arms control deal. Military leaders questioned the result of the Strategic Arms Limitation Treaty (SALT), but Haig persuaded them, despite his personal doubts and earlier feelings that Nixon was selling out to the communists. In Vietnam, where Nixon had reduced the U.S. presence to 24,000 troops by May, the South faced a spring offensive from the North that saw Nixon strike back with a bombing campaign led by B-52 bombers, which rained down 155,500 tons of bombs on targets across North Vietnam.[50] Nixon pressured an unusually compliant Moorer, chastened by the discovery of the spy ring, to maintain the pace of the bombing. The South Vietnamese government held, and Kissinger's still-secret talks to end the war continued.

Then, early on the morning of June 17, 1972, a team of five burglars dressed in suits were caught by local police after they had broken into the Democratic National Committee headquarters in Washington's Watergate office complex. The men included four Cuban exiles who had worked with E. Howard Hunt, the longtime CIA operative who worked with the White House Plumbers team. The fifth member of the break-in team was James McCord, another former CIA agent who was now the chief of security for Nixon's reelection campaign. Hunt and fellow Plumber G. Gordon Liddy watched helplessly from a nearby hotel as police took away their partners, and they scrambled quickly to cover up the White House ties to the break-in.[51] Nixon had no advance notice of the break-in, but by June 23 he and Bob Haldeman, Ehrlichman, and White House counsel John Dean were eagerly working to cover up the White House connections, including the existence of the Plumbers team. Their main cover-up effort involved trying to use the CIA to block the FBI's investigation into the Watergate break-in by claiming it would expose secret operations. Dean led these attempts through a series of meetings and calls with the agency's deputy director, longtime army general Vernon Walters, who rebuffed him.[52]

Haig had no involvement with any of the Watergate mess. He remained focused on Vietnam and the myriad other policy issues that dominated the administration. One of his former associates, the young navy officer Bob Woodward, was gaining a name for himself as a journalist covering the evolving Watergate story for the *Washington Post*. With his reporting partner, Carl Bernstein, Woodward had some of the first stories that tied the burglars to the White House and exposed the existence of a secret fund at the Nixon campaign that paid for political espionage and dirty tricks operations. Their reporting, along with that of reporters Seymour Hersh of the *New York Times* and Sandy Smith of *Time* magazine, would begin to preoccupy the White House.

Haig's time at the White House was winding down. He longed to return to the army, and Nixon obliged him by promoting him over 250 other generals to four stars and naming him the army's vice chief of staff. In that position Haig could resume what now seemed like an inevitable rise to the top of the military chain of command and the chance to take over as chairman of the Joint Chiefs when Moorer's tenure ended.

Nixon, meanwhile, swept to an easy victory that November over Democratic nominee George McGovern, a South Dakota senator and advocate for an end to the Vietnam War. Nixon quickly reshuffled his cabinet and dispatched CIA director Richard Helms to Iran as ambassador. Nixon never forgave Helms for not helping cover up the Watergate break-in. Other nemeses, such as Laird, were also out. Nixon's second term would enable him to rearrange the government as he saw fit, and few impediments remained to stop him. His reelection victory, followed by the completion of the Vietnam peace deal in January 1973, left Nixon at the top of the world, a president with a series of policy triumphs and a world he seemed to have shaped to his liking. This was the White House Haig left for the army that month.

Then it all started to fall apart.

2 May 1973, the General Returns

Richard Nixon stood virtually alone on the morning of May 1, 1973. H. R. "Bob" Haldeman, Nixon's loyal chief of staff, and John Ehrlichman, his chief domestic advisor, had resigned the day before, victims of the growing Watergate scandal. Between the Watergate burglary on June 17, 1972, and April 30, 1973, Nixon's rigorously crafted White House had fallen apart. Not only did Haldeman and Ehrlichman resign that day, but so did Attorney General Richard Kleindienst; his Justice Department had repeatedly faltered in its attempts to prosecute Watergate cases. Nixon also fired John Dean, the White House counsel whose role in the break-in and subsequent cover-up were becoming appallingly clear to Nixon and his associates. Dean had started cooperating with prosecutors and Senate investigators earlier in April, swearing he would not be made the scapegoat for Watergate.

Haldeman and Ehrlichman had stood behind Nixon for more than a decade. They knew Nixon in defeat during his failed campaigns in 1960 for president and 1962 for governor of California, and they helped his triumphs in 1968 and 1972. In the White House they shaped his policies and enforced his rules. "They were men with long ties and easy access to the President, men of loyalty, men who transmitted Mr. Nixon's orders to the bureaucracy and to whom, with few exceptions, Mr. Nixon's Cabinet members were forced to report before winning humble access to the Oval Office," the *New York Times* wrote on May 1. "In giving them their release Mr. Nixon has released part of his own political history. What remains is only a shadow of the old superstructure."[1] Nixon had to rebuild that superstructure from the ground up.

Even though Haldeman had left, Nixon still needed his counsel, and he slipped Haldeman into the Oval Office late in the afternoon of May 2 for an unscheduled meeting that was not recorded in his official calendar.

"The thing is, and he may have raised it with you, but [former cabinet official] Bob Finch had an idea, and I wished to hell I thought of it, and I told him that," Haldeman said. "I stewed over it for two days to find out what's wrong with it, and I can't find anything wrong with it and about five hundred thousand things right with it, and that is as you move, at least on a temporary basis, and it could be done temporarily, that you move Al Haig in here in my place."

"Would he do it?" Nixon asked, sounding somewhat desperate. "God, if only he would do it."

"On a temporary basis, he doesn't have any choice," Haldeman said. "You could simply tell him, direct him. You're his commander in chief. You could direct him that he is temporarily relieved of his duties as vice chief of staff and is chief of staff of the White House."

Other presidents, Haldeman continued, had active-duty military aides, such as Gen. Andrew Goodpaster, who was President Dwight Eisenhower's national security advisor and staff secretary.

"And I'm deeply concerned that you've got the problem now," Haldeman said. "Maybe it's only a week or two. Or maybe for a few months." Nixon needed help, Haldeman continued, because so many of his senior aides, such as Treasury Secretary George Shultz, wanted to see him. "There's all this shit where people are coming up with ideas, and they all want to get to you."

Nixon needed the help. He faced a summit in June with Leonid Brezhnev, leader of the Soviet Union, and the new peace deal in Vietnam was already showing signs of falling apart.

"I think Al knows this place," Haldeman said. "He has your confidence. You're able to sit and talk with Al. You need somebody here you can talk some of this stuff through with, and that worries me."

"I've got no one to talk to," Nixon said forlornly.

Nixon, who rarely let his subordinates know how he felt about them, was moved by Haldeman's personal sacrifice.

"Let me say I miss your strength," Nixon said. "You're always so upbeat. We really miss you around here. . . . I need somebody I can lean on now and then."

"That's why we should get Al over here," Haldeman answered. "He's someone I think you can do that with."

Haldeman said he would call Haig.

"It would save us," Nixon said. "I desperately need someone for the good of the country for temporary additional duty for the next thirty days. We'll do that."[2]

Haldeman reached Haig, who was dining with other generals at the sprawling infantry center at Fort Benning, Georgia. "Al, I'm with the president now, and he has asked me to tell you that he wants you to be his Chief of Staff in the White House." Haig knew he could not refuse and that "this could mean the end of the life I had chosen for my family and myself," he wrote later. He asked if Nixon could reconsider.[3]

Haig knew he could not change Nixon's mind, because the president had few realistic options. He knew and trusted Haig, whom he often used to manipulate Kissinger, who resented Haig's access to Nixon and how he ingratiated himself with the president. Now Nixon was just desperate. Haldeman told Haig that a plane would fly him to Washington the next morning.

Before he left, however, Haig called his old boss at the Pentagon, Joseph Califano, who was now the chief lawyer for the Democratic National Committee. Don't do it, Califano urged. "Don't you know we have this guy?" Califano said of Nixon. Haig risked becoming collateral damage when the Nixon administration inevitably imploded. Then Haig called Kissinger, who had reservations about his former subordinate becoming his boss. Kissinger questioned Haig's loyalty, which he told Nixon early the following morning in the Oval Office.[4]

"Al Haig called me last night about being brought in here for an interim period," Kissinger told the president. "I'll go along with any arrangement, but it's a situation to have both [Secretary of State William] Rogers and Haig to contend with."

Rogers, Nixon's friend since the 1940s, had butted heads with Kissinger since Nixon had rearranged the administration to make Kissinger, not Rogers, the focal point of foreign policy. By restructuring the National Security Council, Nixon intended to sideline the national security bureaucracy, regardless of how long Nixon had known and worked with Rogers.

"I've got to get somebody for about thirty days until I get somebody to replace him with," Nixon responded. "I've got to have somebody in whom I have total trust, and you've got to go along, Henry."

"I will go along," Kissinger said.

"I don't want to bring some total neophyte at the moment," Nixon said. "So it's going to be Haig in here for thirty days, maybe two weeks, but I've got to have somebody in here right now."

"For thirty days," Kissinger responded. "I have high regard for him, and I always thought he'd just be the chairman of the Joint Chiefs, and that would do."

Nixon sensed Kissinger's reluctance and concern that Haig would trample on his turf.

"Henry, I'm having him here for domestic purposes," Nixon said.

"But he did not support me in the last three months," Kissinger responded, referring to the end of 1972, when Kissinger had reached a tentative peace deal with North Vietnam, which then fizzled and caused Nixon to resume bombing the North. Nixon then sent Haig to South Vietnam to persuade its president, Nguyen Van Thieu, that he would not get a better deal from Nixon and needed to take the peace offer.

"Well," Nixon answered, "somebody's got to handle Shultz and [Federal Reserve Board chairman] Arthur Burns."

"But I've got to have someone who's loyal," Kissinger said again.

"He'll be loyal while he's here," Nixon said, adding, "I'm going to handle the war policy myself. I want to get the domestic stuff away from me so I can concentrate on the foreign stuff. That's going to be you. Don't you trust Haig?" he asked Kissinger.

"No, I thought he wasn't loyal to me at the end," Kissinger responded. "I thought he was responsible for a lot of the news stories that I was disarmed in the [Vietnam] negotiations. If not responsible, he certainly made no effort to undo them. I just didn't want it to be a circus here when Rogers starts making another run."[5]

Kissinger's initial suspicion of Haig was well founded. While they would partner often in the coming months to cope with Nixon's growing instability, Haig also destabilized Kissinger by exposing his vulnerabilities, particularly as the FBI wiretapping became better understood. But they also had much in common, such as their policy mentor, longtime army strategist Fritz Kraemer. Kraemer and Kissinger had drifted apart because Kraemer thought Kissinger had sold out his values for power. Meanwhile, Haig would forever remain Kraemer's acolyte. Haig and Kissinger also bonded over the challenges of working for the difficult and mercurial Nixon. They commiserated about some of Nixon's more outlandish behavior, often calling him "our drunken friend." Their relationship, tested during the first term, would be taxed again in new and different ways once Haig returned.

For his part, Haig's account of the morning's event in his memoirs is riddled with the exaggerations and falsehoods that dominate his memoirs. Kissinger, Haig wrote, "even threatened to resign if Nixon went through with it. This rings true; Kissinger's encounters with Haldeman had taught him the power of the White House Chief of Staff, and he knew, like it or not, that he would be taking orders from me."[6] While Kissinger did oppose Haig's return, there is no sign he threatened to resign. He did, as Kissinger wrote in his memoirs, promise to make it work.

Nixon greeted his new chief of staff briefly in the Oval Office the next day before flying to Key Biscayne, Florida, a refuge he sought more often as the Watergate pressures kept building.

"Well, Al, you always get the tough assignments," Nixon said as he tried to reassure Haig that he was thinking of the country and Haig's ambitions. "Can I ask you to in this period of time to be the person who would basically handle my staff work as Bob [Haldeman] does? There are an infinite number of things where folks come rushing to me with a lot of crap that I know should be going through someone else. . . . If you would do it, I'd appreciate it. I don't know how it could be done. I want you to keep your military rank and everything like that. I know [Gen. Andrew] Goodpaster was over here as a general."

"He did it, and I think I can do it," Haig said.

This temporary move would not force Haig to leave the army, Nixon said, but he added: "I don't want to play games with it, but we may have to decide for these next four years that you may have to be here."

"I'm here to do what you think is best, sir," Haig said. "You know that, and I'll give it everything I have."

Nixon asked Haig to spend the weekend planning whatever changes he wanted to make at the White House "because we need a strong man, a loyal man, somebody I can talk to and somebody who can talk to others."

Haig agreed.

"OK," Nixon answered. "We're going to win, if you know what I mean."[7]

Few presidents had ever confronted a month like May 1973, and by joining Nixon, Haig reentered a world of turmoil for which he was partly responsible. In Los Angeles, the administration's case against Pentagon Papers leaker Daniel Ellsberg deteriorated each day. The series of FBI wiretaps that Haig and Kissinger oversaw with FBI official William Sullivan were about ready to burst into full view. The White House would become collateral damage in the fight between Sullivan, jilted in his attempts to become the next FBI director, and Mark Felt, his rival at the FBI, who had initially revealed the existence of the wiretaps to *Time* magazine. Another cover-up—the spy ring inside the National Security Council run by the chairman of the Joint Chiefs of Staff—also threatened to crumble. Nixon and Kissinger started May 3 by discussing the involvement of Kissinger aide David Young in investigating that case, to which Haig had a deep and possibly career-ending exposure. Vice President Spiro Agnew, a willing antagonist of the press for Nixon, also faced an uncertain future, as a federal grand jury had started investigating him for bribery and tax evasion when Agnew was governor of Maryland. John Dean would soon bedevil Nixon with a series of interviews and claims about secret documents he had spirited from the White House on his departure. Haig and Nixon would spend weeks trying to grasp the severity of Dean's impending testimony before the Senate committee investigating the Watergate scandal. Those hearings would start May 17 and rivet the nation's attention, as each witness exacerbated Nixon's problems. All of these pressure points, as well as many spontaneous crises, would test Nixon and Haig, who very quickly realized the president was guilty and most likely not going to finish his second term in office.

Even before Haig landed in Washington on May 3, a story in the *Washington Post* by Bob Woodward and Carl Bernstein caused another crisis for the White House. A "vigilante squad" operating with the approval of then attorney general John Mitchell had conducted wiretaps on two reporters following the leak of the Pentagon Papers, said the story, which was almost entirely wrong.[8] It was tipped off by Sullivan, who spun the story to distance himself from the FBI wiretaps on seventeen government officials and journalists. Sullivan and Woodward, according to Woodward's notes from the interview, now stored at the University of Texas library in Austin, show that the two discussed the wiretaps with an easy familiarity. They met on March 5 near Sullivan's home in Prince George's County, Maryland.[9] Felt's favored target for Watergate-related leaks was not Woodward but Sandy Smith of *Time*.[10] The revelations of the wiretaps confirmed the public impression that Nixon had been spying on his opponents all along, but, more importantly, the *Post* story had immediate repercussions in the Los Angeles courtroom of U.S. District Judge W. Matthew Byrne, who presided over the Ellsberg trial.[11] This was the government's second attempt at prosecuting Ellsberg. Byrne had declared a mistrial in December 1972, which forced the government to try again in January 1973, and federal prosecutors fought not only the defense attorneys but also their own government. Ellsberg's defense read the *Post* story into the record, leading Byrne to ask the acting FBI director, William Ruckelshaus, if Ellsberg or fellow researcher and co-defendant Anthony Russo had been caught by the wiretaps.[12] Byrne already felt used by the Nixon White House. On April 26 the prosecution suffered an almost fatal blow when it was forced to reveal that the White House Plumbers team had burglarized the office of Dr. Lewis Fielding, Ellsberg's psychiatrist. On May 2 Byrne had acknowledged in court that he had met twice in April with Nixon's close aide John Ehrlichman to discuss becoming FBI director, a revelation that caused the defense attorneys to ask Byrne to throw out the case or declare a mistrial. Byrne declined, but he refused to give the prosecution the benefit of his growing number of doubts.

In Washington the White House announced formally that Haig had returned as chief of staff. Initial press coverage was muted; few realized the extensive brief Nixon had given Haig. The *New York Times*, not realizing Kissinger's doubts, called the two men close allies.[13] "I knew that taking this job would mean far more for him than just forfeiting military advancement and perquisites," Nixon wrote in his memoirs. "We were in for a long and bloody struggle, and for Haig it would be like volunteering to return to combat with no guarantee of the outcome and with no medals at the end."[14] Haig knew the dangers of rejoining the White House and feared Nixon was too passive to challenge the newspaper stories and his political adversaries, which, ironically, Haig would urge Nixon not to do repeatedly over the next fifteen months. "But I thought, in one of the least correct judgments of my life, that Nixon's dread of the personal encounter was not important so long as he had made the right decisions and had somebody by his side who was competent to handle the confrontations," Haig wrote later. "The force of circumstances had now decreed that that somebody would be me."[15]

White House press secretary Ron Ziegler led off his May 4 briefing with the official news of Haig's appointment. "The President felt the necessity to have someone assume the many responsibilities of Bob Haldeman at this time while the president considers the entire matter of how the White House operates in the future," Ziegler said.[16] Some details of the announcement would soon turn out to be incorrect. Ziegler said Haig would only assume Haldeman's duties, but Haig quickly consolidated all power in the White House. News accounts also compared Haig's selection to Dwight Eisenhower's pick of Maj. Gen. Wilton Persons in 1957 after his chief of staff, Sherman Adams, resigned in disgrace after the exposure of a scandal. Persons, however, had retired from the army by the time he joined Eisenhower. Also, the scope of Haig's authority remained unclear. "White House officials refused to detail the responsibilities and authority given the general, insisting that 'those matters will have to be developed,'" the *New York Times* reported. If it was not apparent to the public at the time, only two White House officials mattered when it came to determining Haig's role: the president, whose grasp of reality slipped each day, and the general himself. The early accounts showed how little the press understood about Haig. The *Times* reported on the missions Haig had carried out for Nixon in Vietnam and Cambodia but viewed Haig as a potential troubleshooter in the mold of Ehrlichman. Califano gave Haig his benediction. "He'll be superb in this job," Califano said. "He'll get decisions made, orders implemented and papers flowing into the President's office. He'll work 20 hours a day, and he knows how to get along with people."[17]

Haig had barely settled into his new office when Judge Byrne demanded that Ruckelshaus and the FBI determine if any of the bureau's wiretaps had picked up Ellsberg.[18] Ruckelshaus then ordered a complete internal investigation of the wiretap program. If thorough, such an investigation could expose Nixon, Haig, and Kissinger in a scheme that, while ostensibly legal when it was started, showed that the administration's zeal at keeping secrets trampled civil liberties.

With his order, Ruckelshaus stumbled into a years-long war between Felt and Sullivan to succeed Hoover, who had favored each at one time during the last few years of his life. Hoover's official deputy was also his close companion, Clyde Tolson, whose poor health left him in no position to succeed Hoover. In 1970, when Sullivan was the FBI's associate director behind Hoover and Tolson, he angered Hoover by telling a group of newspaper executives that the international Communist Party was not a threat to the United States, a statement that contradicted years of Hoover's messages to Congress. Hoover started to freeze out Sullivan, who responded by leaking negative stories to columnist Jack Anderson and other reporters. Hoover then promoted Felt above Sullivan. By July 1971 Sullivan's status had deteriorated so badly that he told his friend Robert Mardian, the head of the Internal Security section of the Justice Department, that Hoover would blackmail Nixon with the FBI wiretap files.[19] Mardian told his boss, Attorney General John Mitchell, who then told Nixon, who summoned Mardian to California. Within days, a Sullivan subordinate delivered the wiretap logs to Mardian, who then took them to the White House, where Kissinger and Haig inspected them before stashing them in Ehrlichman's office. Sullivan continued to antagonize Hoover, who finally fired Sullivan while he was on vacation and changed the locks on his office door. Sullivan confronted Felt, and the two almost had a fistfight in FBI headquarters. Hoover ordered Felt to get the wiretap files, which Hoover had considered too sensitive to go in the regular FBI filing system, from Sullivan's office. When Felt got to the office, however, he realized Sullivan had taken the files.

Hoover died on May 2, 1972. Felt considered himself the next FBI director, as did Sullivan, but Nixon instead named as acting director L. Patrick Gray, an assistant attorney general. Six weeks later, the Watergate break-in put Gray in the delicate position of running a bureau that aggressively wanted to pursue the burglary while reporting to a president whose top aides wanted to cover up the White House's involvement. Felt started leaking to the press damaging stories about Gray and details of the Watergate investigation, which Nixon discovered in September 1972.[20] Meanwhile, Sullivan rejoined the government as head of the Justice Department's new Office of National Narcotics Intelligence. Haig wanted Nixon to put Sullivan back at the FBI. "Al Haig has called me yesterday and said, Jesus, ya know, get Sullivan back in there. Ah, Haig is very high on Sullivan," Nixon aide Charles Colson, a Haig ally, told the president on February 13.[21] Instead, three days later Nixon nominated Gray as the official choice to run the bureau. Nixon distrusted Felt and told Gray he should make Felt take a polygraph test.[22] Gray declined, naively trusting his deputy, and Felt repaid that trust by leaking the existence of the wiretaps to *Time*.[23]

Haig remained in Washington while Nixon went to Florida. He awoke on the morning of Saturday, May 5, to the news that John Dean had told *Newsweek* magazine about Nixon's involvement in the Watergate cover-up.[24] Dean cited two critical meetings: a September 15, 1972, gathering with Nixon and Haldeman in which Nixon told Dean that he liked his efforts to "keep the lid on" Watergate and that "Bob told me what a great job you've been doing," and a March 21, 1973, meeting in which Dean claimed to have resisted efforts to get him to resign and told Nixon "the problem is that there is a massive cancer on the presidency and it must be cut out." Dean's explanations, *Newsweek* noted, were self-serving and aimed at getting him off the hook with prosecutors, but most readers, as well as those in the White House, did not realize that. Dean had also exaggerated or lied about some of the conversations—there was, for example, no attempt to get Dean to resign on March 21—but since he had told his side of the story first, he changed the template for the cover-up and the upcoming hearings by the Senate Select Committee on Presidential Campaign Activities, which was investigating Watergate. As the first close Nixon aide to break with the president, Dean found the committee willing to listen. Since Nixon and Dean had collaborated in the cover-up, the president justifiably feared Dean's impending testimony.

Haig left Washington for Key Biscayne on Sunday, May 6, arriving there in time to help Nixon reorganize the White House. Haig also urged Nixon to hire a special attorney to represent him on Watergate-related matters and suggested two high-profile Washington lawyers: Edward Bennett Williams, perhaps the nation's leading criminal defense attorney, and Joseph Califano, Williams's law partner and Haig's friend. Nixon, however, bridled at the mention of the two prominent Democrats. Califano represented the Democratic National Committee in its lawsuit against the Nixon reelection committee after the Watergate break-in. "Al, both these men are Democrats," Haig wrote that Nixon told him. "You're right about needing somebody. But I've suffered too much from people who have mixed loyalties. We've got to have a man who's with us, a man we can trust."[25]

If Haig's account is accurate, which is never guaranteed with his memoirs, Nixon's comments are rich in irony. It was Haig who had the divided loyalties, and while he failed to bring Califano into the White House, he would work closely with Califano, a sworn Nixon enemy, for the next fifteen months, usually behind Nixon's back.

To replace Elliot Richardson, the departing defense secretary whom Nixon had named attorney general, Nixon and Haig turned to James Schlesinger, the professorial director of the CIA, Haig ally, and another disciple of Fritz Kraemer.[26] Schlesinger had previously run the Atomic Energy Commission and been the deputy director of the Office of Management and Budget before Nixon picked him in late 1972 to lead the CIA, where Schlesinger ruthlessly carried out Nixon's order to clean house by firing more than one thousand agents and letting much of the top staff resign. Nixon needed more advice than Haig could give alone, so the president turned on May 7 to John Connally, the former Texas governor and longtime associate of President Lyndon Johnson, as a special advisor. Connally flew to Florida to meet with Nixon, who admired Connally's forceful advice and swagger.

Before Nixon and Haig left Florida, they learned of a new problem rising from the Ellsberg trial in Los Angeles. A report in the May 7 *New York Times* by reporter Seymour Hersh showed how Gen. Robert Cushman, then the deputy director of the CIA, had agreed in July 1971 that the agency would help the White House Plumbers team as they prepared to break into Ellsberg's psychiatrist's office.[27] By helping the Plumbers, primarily E. Howard Hunt, a longtime CIA operative, the agency violated its charter by operating on U.S. soil. Nixon did not know that FBI agents had interviewed Cushman the previous week. Now the commandant of the Marine Corps, Cushman had been loyal to Nixon for a long time. When Nixon was vice president Cushman had served as his national security advisor; Nixon then placed him at the CIA as deputy director so that Cushman could watch over Richard Helms, the director, whom Nixon had kept from the Johnson administration. Cushman, Hersh's report said, had admitted that the CIA gave disguises, false documents, and other materials to Hunt before the Plumbers team went to California to burglarize the psychiatrist's office. If Nixon and the White House had known in advance that the FBI wanted to interview Cushman, they could have claimed executive privilege and blocked it. Now, however, they had lost the chance to do it again, and once Cushman testified, it would become more difficult to block the testimony of other administration officials. Meanwhile, the chairmen of two congressional committees, Representative Lucien Nedzi, a Michigan Democrat, and Senator John McClellan, an Arkansas Democrat, said they would ask Cushman to testify before their panels.

Hersh also detailed how much Dean had taken from the White House when Nixon fired him. Dean first told Nixon in March of the Fielding break-in, and then he told federal prosecutors about it on April 15 as Dean looked for insurance to protect him from being made the scapegoat in the Watergate affair. Judge Byrne learned about Dean's revelation on April 27.

Nixon had hoped he could persuade William Rogers, the secretary of state, to join the White House. The two men had worked together since the 1940s, when Nixon was a young congressman and Rogers a congressional aide, and they continued while Nixon was vice president for Eisenhower and Rogers was attorney general. While Nixon had sidelined Rogers in foreign policy, he respected Rogers's political acumen and legal talent. Rogers, however, declined, perhaps realizing the extent of the dangers Nixon faced.[28] Those dangers were hard to miss. Everyone in Key Biscayne that weekend knew the scope of Nixon's peril from both forces beyond his control and events he set in motion. In Washington, Richardson promised the Senate that he would appoint a special prosecutor to handle Watergate cases. That was the price of his confirmation, an issue that Nixon opened by moving Richardson from Defense to Justice. The imminent threat of a special counsel also meant Nixon needed a defense counsel. Nixon had already rejected Haig's suggestions of Williams and Califano, but Haig had another contender.

When they returned to the White House on May 8, Nixon and Haig had already agreed to make Haig's stay permanent, and Haig immediately affected the makeup of the government. They agreed on moving Schlesinger from the CIA to the Pentagon, but Haig shot down Schlesinger's potential replacement, William Casey, a former Office of Strategic

Services agent during World War II and the current head of the Securities and Exchange Commission. Haig called Casey "a little dotty."[29]

"I have a better solution at CIA," Haig said. "Bill Colby," the agency's deputy director of operations. "We've got a superb one with him."

"OK, Colby gets the job," Nixon said, rubber-stamping Haig's choice almost without pausing to breathe.

They had a harder time determining a replacement for Ruckelshaus at the FBI, but Haig dispatched two potential candidates in one breath. Of Cartha "Deke" DeLoach, a longtime Hoover deputy, Haig said, "I think DeLoach is a snake." He was out.

Then Haig killed the dream of his ally, William Sullivan, to lead the bureau. "Sullivan's not a good front man," Haig said.

Nixon wanted his former law partner H. Chapman "Chappie" Rose to lead his Watergate defense, but Haig said Rose "just can't take this on full time."

Nixon asked if Rose could squeeze in some time periodically, and Haig said yes. Then a pause settled over the Oval Office before Haig broke the silence.

"We could bring someone in from another department, if you want to," Haig said. "Maybe the Defense Department counsel. He's a hell of a competent guy. [J. Fred] Buzhardt. He's a competent guy. He's kept Mel Laird afloat for the last four years on a number of tricky ones. Very tough ones."

Nixon murmured his agreement.

"I have great confidence in Buzhardt," Haig said. "He's a hardworking guy, and he knows the town. He knows the Hill."

There was another pause.

"Let's try that," Nixon said. "I'd rather have—"

"A known quantity," Haig said.

"Can you get him?" Nixon asked. "Can you borrow him?"

"He's first-class," Haig said.

"You just get a man you can work with," Nixon said.[30]

Buzhardt was Haig's old friend from West Point who had helped him cover up the military spy ring. Haig wrote in his memoirs that he only suggested Buzhardt "without enthusiasm," but his taped conversations with Nixon show that disclaimer is a lie.[31] Haig wrote that Buzhardt was "hardworking, intelligent, rigorously ethical, self-effacing, and discreet," strong credentials for someone for whom he claimed to lack enthusiasm. Once he proposed Buzhardt to Nixon late in the afternoon of May 8, Haig kept vouching for him, calling him strong, loyal, and skilled in manipulating Congress, where the real battle to save the presidency would be fought.

Buzhardt, just like Haig, had hidden conflicts that compromised his defense of Nixon. First, he would remain the Pentagon's top lawyer while helping Nixon, and his two clients had interests that often diverged. As Pentagon counsel, Buzhardt would have known about Cushman's interview with the FBI and had let it go forward. Second, he and Haig had covered up the military spy ring, as well as Melvin Laird's other intelligence operations that ferreted out White House secrets. That meant Nixon's new defender was complicit in covering up the spying against the president. Even before he stepped into the White House, Buzhardt had already acted against Nixon's best interests.

In less than a week, Haig had put his stamp firmly on the White House. He brought in his former aide from Vietnam, Maj. George Joulwan, to start a series of early-morning staff meetings "over which I presided for the purpose of making the president's wishes on all pertinent issues plainly understood."[32] He had placed Schlesinger at Defense and Colby at CIA, and Buzhardt would lead the Nixon defense. And Haig steadily closed off access to the president.

"I knew that Haig was running the show," said Len Garment, Nixon's former law partner and one of his White House counsels. "Haig trusted Buzhardt and not me. My access was that I basically went in and talked to Haig. I was totally blocked. I mean there were times when I couldn't get in to see" Nixon. And that, Garment said, undermined Nixon. "Obviously these are people who helped undo the vote of the people and who, in my theory, helped to grease the slippery slope."[33]

Nixon and Haig walked in the late afternoon from the Oval Office through the underground passageway to the adjacent Old Executive Office Building, the gray Italianate pile of marble that once housed the War Department. Nixon had an office there that provided the extra privacy he could not get in the West Wing. Nixon immediately ordered a Scotch and soda. Haig continued to praise Buzhardt and take some subtle digs at his rivals. Nixon was receptive, but he also wallowed in self-pity, anxiety, and rage at his circumstances. Nixon knew that John Dean knew too much about the Watergate cover-up to be disregarded.

Dean's betrayal, Nixon said, "isn't like a little goddamn yeoman [Charles Radford, the man at the center of the military spy ring Haig enabled] that did that horrible thing to Henry. This son of a bitch was counsel." Nixon's voice rose almost to a squeal. "This is like [Kissinger aide Helmut] Sonnenfeldt, right, or you? God almighty," Nixon continued, "I think that has got to have some effect on the country. I don't know. Or I guess, is the country all crazy? Is it all crazy?"[34]

Nixon lamented that he had no surrogates to defend him against Dean and the growing number of critics and negative stories. They needed to show that Dean was behind the cover-up, not the president.

Then Nixon shifted from agitation to a more serious tone and made an admission that would alter his future and that of his presidency. "I've got to tell you something you're probably not aware of. There's only one other person who's aware of, and that's Haldeman," Nixon said. "[President] Johnson did this, and before him, Kennedy apparently did. Every conversation that's ever been in this office or the Oval Office or Camp David has been recorded."

Actually, a few more White House aides knew about the taping system. They included Larry Higby, Haldeman's assistant, and Alexander Butterfield, another Haldeman aide and a longtime friend of Haig from their time working for Defense Secretary Robert McNamara. Nevertheless, the circle who knew about the taping system was small and tight-lipped.[35]

"At some point, you may have to tell Henry. Henry's been here and in Camp David. Every one of my telephone calls, Al, has been recorded,"

Nixon continued. "*Every* one. Johnson set it up. I didn't know until Haldeman told me. I said, 'All right, Bob, fine.' I don't want them ever transcribed. I don't believe in this sort of shit. I have ordered that they never be used, unless somebody lies. I want you to know they're all there. You just tell Henry when he starts going on.

"Don't say anything you're not totally sure of," Nixon said, warming to the occasion. "It will scare the bejesus out of him, because he said some very stupid things at times."

"That's right," Haig said.

"You know," Nixon answered.

"I guess we all have," Haig said.

"So have I," Nixon responded. "That's right. So have I. Hell, I have a right to say stupid things. He doesn't have the right to say stupid things and lie about them. Do you get my point?"

Haig agreed.

"It's all recorded," Nixon concluded. "I want you to know."[36]

Nixon had grown tired of Kissinger's whining, because the petulant national security advisor had tried to deny how he first demanded and then tracked the FBI wiretaps. He also denied that his former aide David Young was part of the White House Plumbers.

Nixon also knew the tapes could prove Dean was lying. The president's memory on the details of his meetings with Dean the previous March, just six weeks earlier, were sketchy and self-serving. He remembered that Dean told him about a "cancer on the presidency," the phrase from the *Newsweek* interview that had captured the public's imagination, but the context of that comment was all wrong. Dean made that remark after a week of conspiring with the president to hone the cover-up and bolster their claims that no one in the White House knew about the Watergate break-in in advance. But Dean had already told Nixon on March 13 that Haldeman assistant Gordon Strachan knew about the break-in before it happened, which caused Nixon to speculate that Haldeman must have known, too.[37] By March 21, when Dean told Nixon of the cancer, he meant the growing demands of the Watergate burglars to be paid to stay quiet about what they knew.

Nixon knew the tapes could sort out the truth from the lies; now Haig knew it, too.

Nixon's admission meant Haig could now determine the truth for himself. Haig would say later that he suspected almost immediately after returning as chief of staff that Nixon was guilty.[38] The tapes helped prove it.

Haig would also spend the rest of his life lying about when he knew about the tapes, and those lies masked what Haig did to force Nixon from office.

In his memoirs, *Inner Circles*, Haig explicitly wrote that he learned about the tapes "on Monday, July 16," when Butterfield told the Senate Select Committee on Presidential Campaign Activities, commonly known as the Watergate committee, about the taping system. "This was the first I had heard of the existence of an eavesdropping system that recorded every word uttered in the presence of Nixon, and it came as a total surprise to me."[39]

Haig also wrote that he advised Nixon to destroy the tapes once Haig learned they existed in July. However, the recorded conversations between Haig and Nixon from two months earlier reveal no such warning to the president. Nixon wanted to use the tapes, if necessary, to rebut his accusers. Haig, for reasons that would increasingly become apparent, wanted to keep them for his own purposes.

Nixon only wanted the tapes used to prove that "somebody lies." Haig is that somebody. From the evening of May 8, 1973, until he died in 2010, Haig lied about when he learned about the tapes to cover how he used that knowledge. Haig must have known that from that point late in the afternoon of May 8 every conversation that he had with Nixon would be recorded. Haig knew he had the power to expose Nixon's guilt, and he worked surreptitiously to do it. He also knew the tapes contained the facts about any of Nixon's calls or meetings.

After Nixon's revelation about the tapes, he and Haig circled back to national security, and again Nixon mentioned the military spy ring and Yeoman Charles Radford. Haig said Radford made him uncomfortable, which was another lie, since Haig had requested that Radford travel with him and then wrote Radford's commander, Rear Adm. Rembrandt

Robinson, a letter on March 27, 1971, that said, "Please extend my personal thanks to Yeoman Radford for a job well done."[40]

"He had a style about him," Haig said. "He was obsequious. He moved around in almost an Oriental way. . . . He was always ready to do something."

"My God," Nixon blurted. "What he did was unconscionable. We can't put that out, though. It would destroy the Chiefs."

"Well," Haig answered, "it would destroy the chairman. I'm not sure about the Chiefs."

Nixon said they could not let a flaw in executive privilege expose such information.

"That's what they call bureaucratic espionage," Haig said. "They do it all the time. The army against the navy, the navy against the air force. If you ever put that out in *Time* magazine—"

"Moorer would have to resign," Nixon responded.

"He'd have to resign," Haig said of Adm. Thomas Moorer, the chairman of the Joint Chiefs of Staff. "He might even be indicted. There would be people saying, 'Goddamn it, he was involved.'"

"Let me tell you to stand on executive privilege," Nixon said. "They can impeach the president. Screw them. I'm just not going to let them get into those documents. Now that's all there is to it. We can't do that."

Nixon closed by telling Haig to bring on Buzhardt. "We've got the team," Nixon said. "Get Buzhardt over here."[41]

Buzhardt arrived the next day as Nixon continued to obsess over the spy ring and the threat the revelation posed for Moorer. Haig knew Moorer risked the loss of his job and possible indictment because Haig too shared that risk.

The events of May 9 created a ripple effect that would cascade through the rest of Nixon's presidency. At the FBI, Acting Director William Ruckelshaus's investigation into the wiretaps on the seventeen government officials and journalists gained pace. Haig's associate in the wiretaps, William Sullivan, knew the investigation was headed in his direction and told agents he would only answer questions in writing. Agents told Ruckelshaus that the taps had picked up Daniel Ellsberg talking to former

NSC aide Morton Halperin, and Ruckelshaus sent a memo to Judge Matthew Byrne, who seemed on the verge of throwing out the government's case as the evidence of White House misconduct accumulated. Sullivan also took another step to protect himself by talking to John Crewdson, the FBI beat reporter for the *New York Times*.[42] No one knew as much about the taps as Sullivan. If Sullivan told the truth instead of the false lead he provided to the *Post*'s Bob Woodward, it would rip down the screen hiding the taps from the public.

In Washington, Schlesinger testified before Senator John McClellan's appropriations subcommittee investigating intelligence abuses and said the CIA was "insufficiently cautious" when it helped the White House Plumbers with psychological studies and materials that were later used in the break-in at the office of Ellsberg's psychiatrist.[43] In closed testimony, Schlesinger said Howard Hunt contacted Cushman, the deputy director, and said John Ehrlichman authorized him to get help from the agency. David Young asked the agency for one of its psychological reviews of Ellsberg. The debacle of the Ellsberg trial was killing anything it touched, and it also raised deeper issues about possible agency misconduct. Schlesinger was outraged, William Colby said, and swore that he would tear apart the agency and "fire everyone if necessary" in order to find out if other similar problems existed in the CIA.[44] Schlesinger ordered all CIA employees to report examples of potential misconduct to headquarters so he and his top assistants could determine the extent of the agency's problems. Eventually, Schlesinger's order would generate a 693-page document that detailed, among other things, the CIA's secret experiments with psychotropic drugs on unsuspecting subjects and subversion of foreign governments. Howard Osborn, the agency's director of security, reported back nine days later with eight separate instances in which the CIA violated its charter, including the hiring of Mafioso Johnny Roselli in a convoluted plot to kill Cuban dictator Fidel Castro.[45] Schlesinger's order had another, more immediate effect: it spurred Cushman's successor as deputy director, Lt. Gen. Vernon Walters, to remember something that would throw the White House into greater turmoil.

As Schlesinger ordered the collection of what would become known as the "Family Jewels," Colby received a call in his office from Haig, who told him Schlesinger was moving to the Pentagon, "and the president wants you to take over as director of the CIA, Bill." Colby blurted out his thanks to Haig, who said Nixon wanted to see Colby the following day at the cabinet meeting, "where he intends to make the announcement of Schlesinger's and your nominations."[46]

Another casualty of the Ellsberg trial was Egil Krogh, the former leader of the Plumbers team. He resigned on May 9 as undersecretary of transportation after he acknowledged he had approved the Ellsberg break-in.

Haig and Nixon spoke often that day as Nixon continued to try to explain himself and wriggle free from his obvious guilt in the cover-up. They ended the day with an almost two-hour meeting in the hideaway office.

Haig brought Buzhardt over for the first time, and from the beginning, Nixon's new counsel and Haig provided Nixon with bad advice. Nixon worried about his exposure to possible criminal charges or impeachment, and Buzhardt said the chances of that were minimal with Haldeman and Ehrlichman. "Most of the evidence is hearsay, somebody down the line," Buzhardt said. But Nixon had unwittingly given Haig the means to prove obstruction the previous night when he told Haig about the White House taping system, meaning Haig could determine if Nixon had said anything to Haldeman, Ehrlichman, or anyone else that bordered on obstruction of justice.

Nixon empowered Buzhardt with control over Nixon's personal fate, asking Buzhardt to "be the personal and confidential role that we have to have . . . ," Nixon said. "I have a very strong feeling about that, not because I am concerned about—I mean, everybody sees [the entire scandal in which he was ensnared] in its entirety—but the problem is, because if you start wading through the notes that Haldeman made or that even Haig has made, let alone Henry Kissinger when I've talked to him, it will be an unbelievable mess. I don't care how carefully they are gone through."

The president knew that the Senate's investigation, as well as those of the grand jury looking into more possible Watergate crimes and the incoming special prosecutor, could venture into his personal files and the notes of his associates. Nixon wanted those notes declared off-limits to investigators. As much as possible, he wanted a blanket executive privilege claim that would narrow the scope of the investigation to the Watergate break-in, about which he knew nothing in advance, while avoiding the myriad problems that would emerge if investigators pulled back the curtain to look at other activities.

"That's the good thing about having Fred working right here," Nixon told Buzhardt and Haig. "But what I want to do, Fred, is to have executive privilege. I don't mind giving up conversations with the president if anything involving illegal activity is involved. Do you know what I mean? You can't—we're not going to hide a damn thing. But I don't want anything too formal."[47]

Buzhardt suggested they seek help from a senator outside the Watergate committee: John Stennis of Mississippi, a conservative Democrat and chairman of the Armed Services Committee. Stennis had helped Nixon before, primarily by keeping quiet on the secret bombing campaign of Cambodia, which he knew about years before it went public.[48]

"I talked to Senator Stennis last Thursday morning for two and a half hours," Buzhardt said, referring to May 3, the day Haig arrived at the White House as chief of staff. "He wanted to talk to me then—let me be very frank—about whether I would be willing to come help you. You don't have a more dedicated supporter."

"There is no more dedicated Stennis man than Nixon," the president said.

The three debated how Stennis could sway his colleagues.

"Now Senator Stennis's history has been in the Senate," Buzhardt said. "It depends on which way you look at it. They call him the conscience of the Senate; others call him the undertaker, depending on which way you look at it. But he has handled almost all of their major problems in the Senate. He's the one voice for their own protection. They've never been in a position to question him when it came to what was the right thing to do for the Senate."

No one, Buzhardt continued, knew more about executive privilege than Stennis. "If Senator Stennis organizes the people in a positive way, to tell

Senator [Sam] Ervin there are some very valid arguments for withhold-ing these hearings, that's why he would be your best bet to pull it off."

Nixon told Buzhardt to contact Stennis immediately.[49]

Stennis, however, remained hospitalized for gunshot wounds he suffered during a January mugging attempt outside his home in Washington. Chairing the committee in his absence was Senator Stuart Symington of Missouri, a longtime Nixon antagonist suspicious of Nixon's chronic secrecy. Stennis kept in contact with his colleagues, but he had limited ability to roam the Senate hallways to seek out fellow senators.

Nixon had a small opening for his argument on the hearings, because tensions had emerged between the committee staff, primarily its chief counsel, Samuel Dash, and federal prosecutors, who feared that any immunity deals from the committee would hurt their cases.[50]

Buzhardt raised another issue: the concern expressed by Richardson, the designated new attorney general, about Buzhardt leaving the Pen-tagon. "Mr. President, I think you should know I think Elliot has some problem with my going on this job," Buzhardt said. Richardson's main concern was that both he and Buzhardt would be leaving the Pentagon at the same time. "We have been very close," Buzhardt said of Richardson. "He has some problem with the two of us coming from there."

"I said we thought it was manageable," Haig said.

"We have the indispensable man here," Nixon said, referring to Buzhardt.

Nixon said they would find someone to do the legal work in the Pentagon while Buzhardt worked at the White House. "We're taking a lot of heat, and we're going to take more."

Nixon said Haig had told him earlier that he might be a target for impeachment. "I don't know for what, trying to obstruct justice, I guess," he said.

"It's conceivable," Buzhardt said. He added that Nixon could win a vote in the House on impeachment, which would be a "vote of confidence" in the president. "It's a hard way to get a vote of confidence, but that may come sometime."

"It may," Nixon responded. "But let me say that that would have, in my opinion, quite a traumatic effect on the country."[51]

That evening, Nixon met for more than an hour with Haldeman, his former chief of staff. He took a call from Haig at 11:07 p.m. and told Haig that he had told Haldeman that his main contact at the White House would be Buzhardt.

"That is what we had to do," Haig said.

"We had to do it," Nixon said. "We're going to get [White House counsel and Nixon colleague Leonard] Garment the hell out of this thing now. I mean, you know, leave him in a lot of other—you know what I mean."

"We'll just keep him out of it," Haig said.

"But let me say this on the executive privilege thing, though. I just talked to Bob, and Al, we can't give an inch on written documents, not an inch. So I don't want Buzhardt or Garment or anybody else to come in to me and say, look, public opinion will be hurt, think we're covering up. All right. We'll cover up until hell freezes over."

Haig said he and Buzhardt discussed that after their earlier talk with Nixon.

"Did he get the point?" Nixon asked.

Haig said yes, adding that Buzhardt should talk directly with Haldeman before talking to Haldeman's lawyers.

"Oh, yes," Nixon said. "He should talk to Bob before he talks to any lawyers. Oh, no, no, no, no, no. This fellow is our friend, and he's my friend and totally trustworthy," Nixon told Haig. "And if he turns out to be a John Dean, we'll fry your ass, too."[52]

Nixon felt optimistic that he could reverse the events of the last month that had gutted his staff. He scheduled a cabinet meeting to announce his moves—Schlesinger to Defense from the CIA, William Colby from head of operations at the CIA to director, John Connally dipping in from his private law practice to advise the president, and Buzhardt from the Pentagon to run the White House legal work on Watergate. Colby thought his promotion was handled too casually. During the meeting, he watched Nixon lean over and whisper into Haig's ear, and then Haig wrote a note and handed it to Colby. "Do you have any connection with Watergate that would raise problems?" it said. Colby looked at Haig and shook his head no. "It seemed to me a poor way of conducting a security check," Colby wrote later, "and if my answer had been different, poor timing, too."[53]

While Nixon hoped his changes would signal an administration moving to right itself in the face of mounting scandal, outsiders raised multiple questions. "No one in Washington, or at least very few people, question the integrity and competence of such men as Mr. Richardson and General Haig," the *New York Times* reported. "But many doubt that Mr. Nixon has really cleaned house." The same article also noted the questions about Haig remaining on active duty in the army and Buzhardt's conflicts of interest. Could Buzhardt "make dispassionate determinations in the Watergate case, with which the Pentagon Papers case is intertwined?"[54]

Richardson left the cabinet meeting for another session of the Senate Judiciary Committee hearings on his appointment as attorney general. Already, Richardson had promised the committee that he would appoint a Watergate special prosecutor. On May 10 he promised committee members that he would pursue any Watergate cases aggressively and that he felt "betrayed by the shoddy standards of morals" inside the Nixon administration. This feeling of betrayal, Richardson said, would "at least compensate or neutralize any feeling I might have arising out of my prior associations" with the administration.[55] Nixon, Richardson continued, had assured him he would stay out of the Watergate investigations, particularly once Richardson picked a special prosecutor.

That word had apparently not reached the president. He and Haig spoke at length about how they could influence Richardson's pick. They discussed two Democratic former governors as possibilities, including Edmund G. "Pat" Brown, who defeated Nixon in the 1962 California governor's race. Haig also raised an idea that Buzhardt had shared with him the previous day: What if Richardson named Senator Sam Ervin, the chairman of the Watergate committee, as the special prosecutor? "He can't do any more damage there than he can anyplace else, and the son of a bitch would be hard-pressed to turn it down," Haig said.[56]

In Los Angeles, the prosecutors in the Ellsberg case continued to self-destruct as they released in Judge Matthew Byrne's courtroom the details of the wiretaps, which had picked up Ellsberg. They also disclosed how the records of the wiretaps and their summaries disappeared from the FBI between July and October 1971. An outraged Byrne ordered both sides to appear the next day to determine if the case should be dismissed because of the revelation of the wiretaps, which, Byrne said, put "a different posture" on the issues in the case. "It appears that Mr. Ellsberg was surveilled during the most crucial period of the indictment." The court also received a memorandum from Ruckelshaus in which he revealed that the internal FBI investigation showed that Ellsberg was overheard on a tap on the home telephone of Morton Halperin, then a member of the National Security Council.[57]

The cabinet meeting and staff changes announced on May 10 provided only a brief respite for Nixon, as the following day brought a new series of crises that threatened to unravel Nixon's multiple cover-ups: the spy ring, FBI wiretaps, and Nixon and Watergate. In Los Angeles, the wiretaps revelation was destroying the Ellsberg case, while in Washington, Kissinger angered Nixon by trying to distance himself from the wiretaps. Kissinger tested Nixon's patience with yet another period of feeling unwanted and unloved as he tried to prevent the new Vietnamese peace deal from melting down. The House of Representatives had just voted to cut funding for the continued bombing of Cambodia, the government of which was under siege by communist guerrillas. "It's a bad move," Nixon said. "It's a bad break." Cambodia, the upcoming summit with the Soviet Union, and the continued challenge of Vietnam all required Kissinger's attention, Nixon said, adding, "It's my intention to make Henry secretary of state" once William Rogers stepped down. But Kissinger, Nixon continued, had to stop acting like a diva. "I'm not going to have him come in here and say he's going to leave," Nixon said. "I'll handle this thing."

"I think he's all right," Haig said.

"The hell with him being all right," Nixon said.

Nixon then reiterated what he had told Haig three days earlier.

"Just between us," Nixon said. "I have a record of everything he has ever said here, at Camp David, the Lincoln Sitting Room, the EOB [Executive

Office Building]. Everything. Everything in the national security area has been recorded. We're not going to fart around."

The president then lapsed into the routine anti-Semitism that marked so many of his conversations but from which he normally spared Kissinger. "We're not going to have that Jewish son of a bitch come in here and complain," Nixon said. "If he walks in here with that kind of crap today, his ass is out!"

Connally, Nixon said, wanted to be secretary of state, and Nixon was inclined to pick him if Kissinger kept complaining. But, he continued, Kissinger is "so intertwined in this nuclear thing" with the Soviet Union.

"I wouldn't make that decision now," Haig said. "I want to see how this thing goes."

Nixon said he would not tolerate Kissinger's continued complaints, which he blamed on the national security advisor spending too much time with his elitist friends in Washington's Georgetown neighborhood.

"You can't do that with anybody," Haig said.

"Because Connally is not a good option," Nixon said. "But he's a hell of a lot better than Henry Kissinger coming in here and bitching and bellyaching and whining. I spent hours with him in this office," Nixon continued. "That's what will kill him with these goddamn tapes, if I ever put them out, which I trust to God will never have to see the day of light, light of day. If he ever writes a self-serving thing, they're going to get out. Understand?"

"It can't be otherwise," Haig said. "It would be good for him to know this."

"Huh?" Nixon said.

"This wouldn't be a bad thing for him to know, maybe in an indirect way," Haig said.

"No, I think you should be the one to tell him. Say everything the president has discussed in this office, if the EOB office—and, oh, the cabinet room was also wired."

Everything, Nixon continued, about national security issues was recorded: "We've got it all there." He had the right, Nixon said, to release the tapes if "anybody tried to distort what he said to the president and so forth. . . . We could kill Henry Kissinger on some of this stuff." Then Nixon made an even more remarkable admission: "It would kill all of us, if that's what you want."

Haig only chuckled.

Nixon said his telephone calls were also recorded.

"They should be," Haig responded. Then he switched tracks and guided Nixon away from telling Kissinger about the massive secret Nixon had just shared. "Well, I recommend, he's not going to say anything at all about this subject. I just wanted you to know his state of mind. We'll work it out."[58]

Nixon was particularly concerned about Kissinger's tendency to weave his own truths because of a *New York Times* article by John Crewdson that fleshed out the story of the wiretaps. Crewdson's main source was William Sullivan. Crewdson's report named three journalists who were wiretapped: *Times* reporters William Beecher and Hedrick Smith and Henry Brandon of the *Times* of London. The story also implicated Kissinger and, to a lesser extent, Haig for their part in picking the targets of the wiretaps.[59] Unlike *Time* magazine's report in February, which first mentioned the wiretaps, and the May 3 story in the *Washington Post* about a bogus vigilante squad of wiretappers, this story had specifics that put the wiretapping squarely in the White House.

Haig and Nixon believed Sullivan could fix the problems posed by the *Times* story, not realizing that Sullivan had leaked the story in the first place. "I'm not at all worried," Haig said, noting that each wiretap had been approved by the attorney general. Sullivan could set things straight, he said. "Oh, I think he'll say that J. Edgar Hoover, there were leaks—looked like they were coming out of the White House staff or someplace in the government and that J. Edgar Hoover authorized those taps. Uh, that the reports of them as they always have been provided to the White House came over memos from J. Edgar Hoover to the president which were delivered initially to, uh, Kissinger. Well, initially he saw them all."

"But, hell, he was reading everything," Nixon said of Kissinger.

After a few months, Haig said, the details of the taps started going to John Ehrlichman. The tapping stopped, Haig said, after the Supreme Court "made tapping a questionable activity."

Haig, freshly reminded again that Nixon was recording this and all his other conversations, did not mention his own involvement in the wiretapping. Instead, he focused on Kissinger, Ehrlichman, and Hoover, who, one year after his death, was an easy scapegoat. Sullivan, Haig said, could help explain the details, even as Sullivan fought his internal battle in the FBI with Mark Felt, his perceived rival to lead the bureau. Nixon suspected Felt.

"And don't you believe Felt leaked this to the *Times*?" the president said.

"That's the report Elliot [Richardson] had, and Sullivan told me that that's what's going on."

"Well, he used to leak to *Time* magazine," Nixon said. "He's a bad guy, you see."

"Very bad," Haig said. "He's got to go."

"He's got to go," Nixon said.[60]

After Haig left the office, Nixon met with Kissinger, who again tried to evade responsibility for the wiretaps. Nixon had anticipated this, which was why he told Haig earlier that all of his conversations had been taped. Now Kissinger was playing into his hands. Instead of hammering Kissinger as he threatened to do with Haig, Nixon tried to console his fretful national security advisor, but he would not let Kissinger escape acknowledging responsibility.

Why did they do the wiretaps? Nixon asked Kissinger.

"To prevent leaks," Kissinger answered.

"Right, and leaks from where?" Nixon asked.

"Well, from here and elsewhere," Kissinger said.

"That's the point," Nixon said, reminding Kissinger that the leaks were in reaction to the work Nixon and Kissinger had done. "We didn't have Congress with us. We didn't have the press with us. We didn't have the bureaucracy with us. We did it alone, Henry."[61]

Haig brought Nixon troubling news just four minutes after Kissinger's departure. In a reaction to Schlesinger's order for all agency officials to report any potential violations of CIA policy, Deputy Director Vernon

Walters brought to the White House copies of eight memoranda of conversations, known in the trade as memcons, highlighting attempts by White House officials to slow down the FBI investigation of the Watergate break-in.

"Walters was called back by Schlesinger from his trip to the Far East about CIA involvement with the White House, primarily through [fired White House counsel John] Dean," Haig said. "Walters came in to me and gave me eight memcons of the meeting here with Haldeman and Ehrlichman in July of last year and a series of subsequent meetings with [former acting FBI director L. Patrick] Gray and Dean. I, when I read them, I thought they were quite damaging to us. I said, 'What are you doing with these, and where are they?' He said that Schlesinger had ordered him to take them over and deliver a copy to me and a copy to the attorney general," Haig continued. "So I immediately called Buzhardt in, and we both read it. And we said, 'These papers can't go anywhere.' We sent him back to the agency, told him not to take any telephone calls, return here immediately with every copy. And these are vital national security matters and cannot go anywhere."

"What did these deal with, Al?" Nixon asked.

"They deal with Dean's efforts to, to get a CIA cover for the Watergate defendants," Haig said.

Nixon knew there had to be more. "But were Haldeman and Ehrlichman trying to do it, too?" Nixon asked.

"Haldeman and Ehrlichman's discussion was in the direction of having Walters go directly to the attorney—or to the director of the FBI," Haig said.[62]

Indeed, Haldeman and Ehrlichman did talk with Walters and Richard Helms, the CIA director, on June 23, 1972, just six days after the arrest of the Watergate burglars. Nixon ordered that conversation after Haldeman had told him earlier that morning that Dean had recommended using the CIA to block the FBI investigation because of suspicions the break-in was a CIA operation. Nixon agreed with Haldeman's suggestion and told him to make it happen, a conversation that was recorded.[63]

Walters, Haig told the president, objected to the plan and said that

Dean, Haldeman, and Ehrlichman were trying to drag the president into the cover-up, not realizing that Nixon had already approved it. Dean then contacted Walters on his own as he tried to get the CIA to provide bail and other financial assistance to the burglars. Walters turned him down flat. "This guy [Dean] did some business for himself," Nixon said to Haig.

Nixon said he remembered talking to Gray on July 6, 1972, when the FBI director told him that members of the White House staff were trying to cover up their ties to the break-in. "And I said, well, Pat, you have got to go out and get the facts," Nixon said.

Walters is clean, Haig said, but the memcons were damaging to Haldeman and Ehrlichman.

"I mean, do they mention the president?" Nixon asked.

Only in terms of the conversation between Walters and Gray, Haig said, adding that he told Schlesinger that Buzhardt would talk to him about what to do with Walters. After they consulted with Haldeman, Ehrlichman, and their lawyers, Haig said, he and Buzhardt told Walters to go to Henry Petersen, the head of the criminal division of the Justice Department, and say, "The agency has been under attack here. I've been called back, and I am prepared to testify. . . . Everything he says is going to help you."

"Huh?" Nixon said in surprise. Having the deputy director of the CIA tell a congressional committee or a grand jury about a cover-up attempt by the White House hardly seemed helpful.

"Everything he says is going to help the president," Haig said. "That I'm sure."

Nixon said he was "a babe in the woods" about the Watergate break-in, which he had always assumed was a CIA operation.

Haig then shifted direction to the collapsing Ellsberg trial, saying Byrne would have to declare a mistrial or throw out the charges, and if he did, the White House should refuse to give him any more information about the wiretaps. Haig said he would tell Ruckelshaus to determine a strategy for handling the wiretap information, which was part of an ongoing investigation. Haig planned to talk to FBI agents about the investigation that afternoon. Nixon and Haig incorrectly suspected that an FBI official had leaked the details of the wiretaps to the *New York Times*.

"His guy, the same fellow I talked about last night, spilling his guts all over the West Coast, the newspapers . . . ," Haig said.

"Felt," Nixon responded, mentioning Mark Felt, who was not responsible for the leak to the *Times*.

"Including the names of the newspaper people, Joseph Kraft and Henry Brandon, and all those people," Haig said. "And Ruckelshaus feels that we've got to make some kind of a statement on this that's got to be associated with Watergate, and it's going to be interpreted."

"Right," Nixon said. "And what did he say?"

"He would say that, yes, J. Edgar Hoover, the attorney general, the reason for taps, one led to another," Haig said.

Ruckelshaus was preparing to put out a statement about the wiretaps, Haig told Nixon, but they needed to be careful. "There have been leaks of this information before the investigation was completed, and among those was this man who's being discharged," Haig said.

"Felt," Nixon responded.

"Fire his ass," Haig said.

"Blame it on Felt," Nixon said.

Haig said Ruckelshaus had not told him directly that he wanted to fire Felt, but Haig believed he did.

Nixon said he knew nothing about the attempts to use the CIA to block the FBI investigation, which was a blatant lie. Haig responded by telling the president that Walters's "testimony is going to help. He's going to say constant pressure from Dean."

Nixon asked if there was a chance that Walters's memcons could get out. "He will testify, and what will he say, though, about his memcons?"

"He's going to say, 'Oh, yes, I made notes,' if they ask him," Haig responded.[64]

Haig's recommendation to allow Walters to testify opened the door to a catastrophe for Nixon. Walters had a reputation for having a photographic memory, and he was on the verge of telling a congressional committee that members of the White House staff, whether directed by the president or not, had tried to obstruct justice. Haig also knew, because Nixon had told him on May 8 and earlier on the morning of May 11, that all of the conversations in his offices and his telephone were recorded. If Nixon had told Haldeman or Ehrlichman to approach Walters about having the CIA block the FBI's Watergate investigation, it would presumably be on tape, which would implicate Nixon directly in an obstruction of justice. If Haig did not realize that immediately, surely the president's new Watergate counsel, Buzhardt, would.

Haig had recommended that Nixon not speak directly with Haldeman, but Nixon did not listen. Within an hour, Haldeman was in the Oval Office with the president and Haig discussing Walters's possible testimony and what happened between them on June 23, 1972. In that meeting, Haldeman inadvertently provided Haig with the lead he needed to prove Nixon had obstructed justice that day.

"I don't care about the Walters stuff with Dean," Haldeman said. "I don't know what Dean's up to. There was concern about the Bay of Pigs coming out—you told us, you know, get in Helms on this promptly because Helms—I think you had some knowledge that I didn't know about—that Helms was concerned about some Bay of Pigs stuff at that point in time because Helms blocked at that meeting and said, 'Well OK, I'm not concerned about the Bay of Pigs, because no matter what comes out' or something. That's the part I remember clearly, is Bay of Pigs stuff."

You told us. By linking Nixon to the conversation before Walters and Helms appeared at the White House to talk about Watergate, Haldeman had tipped off to Haig that Nixon knew in advance about the attempt to block the FBI investigation. That meant he had obstructed justice, and now Haig knew about it, too. Nixon had mentioned the connection of some of the Watergate burglars, four of which were Cubans, to the failed 1961 invasion of Cuba at the Bay of Pigs, which represented one of the CIA's biggest failures. As a young army lieutenant colonel, Haig had worked to repatriate some of the captured Cuban fighters back to the United States and into the army. Haig knew plenty about the Bay of Pigs.

Nixon should have heeded Haig's advice about not meeting with

Haldeman, because as the meeting continued, the president kept digging a deeper hole for himself.

"I suggested getting in Walters and Helms," Nixon said. "I don't know why I suggested it. You think it is the Bay of Pigs?"

Haldeman said he could not think of another reason and that he and Ehrlichman had done everything legitimately. But, he added, "I worry about the implications in each one, 'cause that's what they like. They don't pay any attention to those facts, you know. The implication of there even being such a meeting poses the problem, obviously. But it's perfectly rationalized, what the hell? It looked like—and the FBI—we were told—I was told by Dean, uh, and I think it was in the papers that the FBI was convinced for months that this was a CIA operation."

Watergate, Haldeman lamented, was a nothing scandal, although it had claimed his job and Ehrlichman's and had the White House reeling. "It's broader because it's unraveling," he said. "These are unrelated things, really. Like Krogh's operation [with the Plumbers], they tied that into Watergate. Doesn't have a fucking thing to do with Watergate."

Haig sat silently as he listened to the president and his predecessor as chief of staff discuss the meeting that would eventually force Nixon's resignation. They obsessed over their concerns about the CIA and why they wanted to use the agency to block the FBI investigation. "I told Bob to meet with Helms and Walters to find out" if the CIA was involved, Nixon said. By the way, Nixon asked, "do you think I would call Helms into something that I wanted to screw up?" Nixon's antipathy toward the former CIA director was legendary. Then Nixon addressed Haig directly. "Al," Nixon said, "Walters and Helms were called for the purpose of seeing that the investigation, ah, delved into Watergate but did not get into the covert operations of the CIA."

Nixon asked Haig if any copies of Walters's memcons were floating around Washington. No, Haig responded, they were Walters's personal copies, and he had originally intended to give a copy of them to Attorney General Elliot Richardson. "Thank God, he stopped here first," Haig said, adding that he told Walters not to give them to Richardson because he had not been confirmed as attorney general yet. Richardson cannot see the memcons, Haig said, "because we've got them, and they are under executive privilege, and they'll stay that way. That's the only thing we can do. . . . It would be damaging now because of the sequence of time. First, you have a big, high-level meeting with Helms and Walters. And then suddenly these contacts start with Dean, who is really a bad guy."

Haig said he wanted Walters to testify because it would put the onus for the cover-up on Dean. Nixon and Haldeman were not so sure, because they saw plenty of dangerous implications for the president in the memcons and whatever Walters could say under oath.

"I don't want Buzhardt to have any implications from just reading that goddamn paper that what this is basically a cover-up on the part of—that first paragraph, where it says the president told Haldeman to get the CIA—what did it say to do?" Nixon said.

Nixon saw the Watergate burglary investigation as an entity of its own and not connected to the multiple other cover-ups he had going at the time of the failed break-in, including the FBI wiretaps, the Pentagon spy ring at the White House, and the secret bombing of Cambodia, to name just three. All involved national security; all involved some degree of secrecy and cover-ups.

"But Buzhardt understands that the purpose of that talk had nothing to do with not pursuing the Watergate burglary," Nixon said. "It had to do with not getting into the national security aspects."

Either way, Nixon's order that Haldeman and Ehrlichman talk with the two CIA officials was tantamount to obstruction of justice, because FBI agents looking into the Watergate burglary would have found evidence of other crimes simply by investigating the burglars and their activities, such as the break-in at the office of Ellsberg's psychiatrist.

Haig said Walters would be a great witness, and so would the former acting FBI director, Patrick Gray. Gray and Walters shared the same views about the impropriety of a cover-up, and Gray told Nixon, who responded that Gray should push forward with the investigation.

"He's so bright," Haig said of Walters.

"Well, now, doesn't that hearten you a little about my role, Al?" Nixon asked. "Would you please mark that for Buzhardt so that he sees that part that I told Gray? Or has he seen it? Or do you think Buzhardt needs to see such things?"

"I am not worried about Buzhardt," Haig said.

"Well, I don't care if you're worried," Nixon replied. "I want you to believe."

Haig claimed that he and Buzhardt did believe Nixon's story, although Nixon appeared skeptical. He and Haldeman seemed both mystified and dispirited by the roiling tsunami of problems from the first term that threatened to wash away the administration. "We didn't order a cover-up by the CIA, and you know that," Nixon said to Haldeman after Haig left the room. While Haig provided Nixon with some solace as a sounding board, he could not replace Haldeman, on whom Nixon leaned heavily during this meeting. "They're trying to get at us with thieves," Nixon lamented. "What in the name of God have we come to?"[65]

Nixon needed Walters to know he was not trying to cover up anything. Haig told him the situation "is very damaging to Bob [Haldeman] and John [Ehrlichman]" and that Buzhardt believed the memcons made it appear that Haldeman and Ehrlichman wanted to start a cover-up, most likely with Nixon's approval.

"Buzhardt must not feel that," Nixon said. "By golly, it's not damaging to the president that Bob and John as my agents did something I wanted them to do."

Nixon wanted Walters to generate "sanitized" versions of his memos that would remove mentions of national security issues, but Haig counseled against that. Nixon almost pleaded with Haig, asking him to believe that Nixon did not want his staff to think he had sought a cover-up, even if he had. "I'm not in this goddamn thing," he said. "That's what burns me up."

Nixon's new lawyer, Buzhardt, might not understand why Nixon wanted to contain the FBI investigation, Nixon worried. He moaned that he could have "sunk" Kissinger for what he had said or "screwed" Adm. Thomas Moorer for the military spy ring.

"I could have screwed the whole Pentagon about that damn thing, and you know it," Nixon said. "Why didn't I do it? Because I thought more of the services. You know that. By golly, that's the way I deal. I want you to know that. There ain't going to be any of that. But Buzhardt is not thinking in those terms."[66]

While the president and Haig spent most of the day worrying about the ramifications of Walters's memos, Cushman testified before three congressional committees about how the agency helped the Plumbers.[67] He backed up his testimony with affidavits attesting to what the agency had done. That created a precedent that prevented the White House from stopping the release of other documents, such as the Walters memos. Cushman told each committee that Ehrlichman and Hunt both called him to get the CIA's help. Cushman said the requests did not strike him as particularly strange, that he agreed to help, that he told Helms about the requests he granted after they happened, and that Helms had "assented." Cushman's testimony and documents had nothing to do with the Watergate break-in, but they went to the core of Nixon's ultimate problem: Watergate was just the umbrella term that referred to the myriad other activities Nixon wanted to hide. Any investigator who pulled on the thread that tied together the men involved in the Watergate break-in would unravel the Plumbers and everything they touched, including the Pentagon Papers and the military spy ring.

In Los Angeles, Judge Byrne did what Nixon and Haig had expected and ended the case against Ellsberg and Anthony Russo. But Byrne went beyond declaring a mistrial; he threw out the entire government case and released a written ruling against acts committed in Nixon's name. "The disclosures made by the government," Byrne wrote, "demonstrate that governmental agencies have taken an unprecedented series of actions with respect to these defendants." The White House created a special investigations team, the Plumbers, and "what we know is more than disquieting," Byrne wrote. The CIA violated its charter by helping the Plumbers, while the administration allowed the FBI to tap the telephones of innocent Americans. "Of greatest significance is the fact that the Government does not know what has happened to the authorizations for the surveillance, nor what has happened to the tapes nor to the logs nor any other records pertaining to the overheard conversations," Byrne wrote. "I am of the opinion, in the present status of the case, that the only remedy available that would assure due process and a fair administration of justice is that this trial be terminated and the defendants' motion for dismissal be granted and the jury discharged." With that, Ellsberg and Russo were free.[68]

Byrne's ruling angered Nixon, but at least the end of the prosecution meant that one spigot of bad news for the administration had been turned off. The second Ellsberg trial exposed the Plumbers and cracked the door open to the FBI wiretaps. The case also exposed the lengths to which the president would go to skew justice, particularly Nixon's attempt to sway Byrne by offering him the job as FBI director. The timing of that revelation coincided with Sullivan's decision to leak details of the wiretaps to the *New York Times.*

By the time Byrne threw out the Pentagon Papers case, the internal FBI investigation into the wiretaps was nearing an end. Former attorney general John Mitchell told investigators he had discussed "these wiretaps with either Colonel Haig or Dr. Kissinger at the White House and they (Mitchell, Haig and/or Kissinger) agreed that these wiretaps could become 'explosive' and that this whole operation was a 'dangerous game we were playing.'" Mitchell said Felt leaked the information about the taps in February to *Time* magazine and that he believed Sullivan was leaking, too.[69] Robert Mardian, the former assistant attorney general and a Sullivan ally, told investigators that Sullivan told him in July 1971 that he feared J. Edgar Hoover would use the wiretaps to blackmail Nixon to not fire him. Mardian then went to Mitchell, who told Nixon, who summoned Mardian to California and ordered him to get the wiretap records. Mardian complied, and he told agents that the wiretap logs were delivered to him. Then, Mardian said, he took the materials to the White House and delivered them in person to Kissinger and Haig. "In Kissinger and Haig's presence," the FBI report of Mardian's interview said, "White House correspondence [was] checked against chronological check list which listed all material sent to the White House by date."[70] Sullivan agreed only to give written answers to twenty-five questions from the investigators. He provided a series of minimalist answers in a memorandum directed to Ruckelshaus that never mentioned Haig at all.[71] Finally, as the growing crisis over Walters's memos swirled around him and Nixon, Haig talked to investigators on the night of May 11. He, too, lied. "General Haig said it was absolutely untrue that logs and other FBI records regarding the wiretaps were ever turned over to Kissinger or himself," the FBI report of his interview said. He minimized his involvement in the taps, saying mainly that they had been valuable in tracking leakers and had led to the departures of two NSC officials, Daniel Davidson and Morton Halperin. Haig said he was merely Kissinger's messenger, and, like Sullivan, he blamed the taps on Hoover. While Hoover had suspected some of the targets as serial leakers, primarily Halperin, he had also resisted putting on the taps unless Mitchell approved them in writing. The true impetus for the spying on members of his own staff and the reporters to whom they allegedly told secrets came from Kissinger, with Haig's considerable assistance.[72]

Haig spoke to Sullivan constantly during the course of the FBI investigation. Nixon wanted Sullivan to minimize the seriousness of the wiretaps and to claim that previous administrations, primarily those of Democrats John Kennedy and Lyndon Johnson, tapped people, too. Haig and Sullivan had a shared interest in keeping their part in the taps secret and also distrusted Felt, whom Sullivan gladly blamed for leaking information to the *New York Times*.

Nixon escaped the White House on the afternoon of May 11, driving to the presidential retreat at Camp David, Maryland, with his good friend Cuban-born millionaire Charles "Bebe" Rebozo. His visits to Nixon often included swimming, drinking, and watching movies in the Camp David theater. But Nixon stayed in contact with Haig throughout the afternoon and into the early evening. Haig called at 6:35 p.m. to tell Nixon what he had learned from Ruckelshaus. The good news, Haig said, was that the newsmen bugged by the FBI were bugged not because they were journalists but because they had received leaked information from someone inside the government. Kissinger should take the heat for the wiretaps, since he wanted them so badly, Nixon said.

That's not what Kissinger says, Haig told the president.

"Bullshit," Nixon responded. "He knew all about it. For Chrissakes, he's who was in my office pounding on the desk."

Haig told Nixon that Mitchell had tried to evade his role in the wiretaps. Mitchell told the FBI that he did not know who approved the taps, although Mitchell had signed the request for each one.

"Bullshit," Nixon said again.

Sullivan, Haig said, had insisted to FBI investigators that Mitchell had signed all of the requests to the FBI.

"It's another nail in John Mitchell's coffin," Nixon said.[73]

They talked for the last time that day shortly after 7:00 p.m., when Haig said he had learned what really happened with the tap logs. Sullivan had believed that Hoover would try to blackmail the president with the details of the taps. "There's an awful lot of juicy stuff in here," Haig said. "It's all wrapped up in this terrible gut fight to run the FBI." Felt, Haig said, "will be a victim in this thing."

Nixon agreed but said firing Felt alone would enable Felt to "go out and babble" about what he knew about the wiretaps. "Sullivan is against Felt, you know," Nixon said.

"Very much," Haig answered.

"Sullivan's our man," Nixon said.[74]

By the end of May 11, the embattled president had reinforced Haig's knowledge of the secret White House tapes, revealed the meeting in which he told Haldeman to use the CIA to block the FBI's investigation, and pleaded with Haig to believe him that he had not obstructed justice. For the chief of staff who already believed the president was guilty of crimes that would prematurely end his presidency, it was an arrow pointing to where Haig could find the evidence to prove Nixon's guilt. Haig's challenge was to expose that guilt without exposing his own culpability.

Haig spent Saturday, May 12, trying to learn the final details of Ruckelshaus's report on the FBI wiretaps and coordinate his story with Sullivan, so they would not also be targeted. Sullivan could hide behind Hoover, while Haig could use Kissinger as a foil.

Haig's talks with Nixon this weekend had the dual purpose of persuading the president that Vernon Walters should testify about what he was told at the White House the previous June and turning Nixon against Kissinger on the wiretaps. Haig and Buzhardt had already concluded that Haldeman and Ehrlichman were guilty of obstructing justice by meeting with Walters and Helms.

Cushman's testimony hurt the White House's ability to limit the disclosure of Walters's memos, because Cushman had also given the committees his own memos. Since Haig and Buzhardt had not stopped Cushman they could not stop the committees from getting Walters's documents, too. "So we're just going to have to take the heat, Mr. President," Haig said.

It was going to get hot, Nixon said, and what Haig told him next reinforced that impression. Haldeman, Haig quoted from one of Walters's memos, "said that the whole affair was getting embarrassing and that the president wished—it was the president's wish that Walters call on Acting FBI Director Gray and suggest to him that since the five suspects had been arrested, that this should be sufficient, that it was not advantageous to have the inquiry pushed, especially in Mexico." Early reports in the Watergate investigation had traced money that went to the Watergate burglars to a Mexican bank account, which sparked speculation that CIA operations there may have been exposed.

"Yeah, that's bad," Nixon said.

For some reason, Haig thought the details of the Walters memos would not become public. Instead, he said they could limit Walters's testimony before the Senate Armed Services Committee by having Walters build a wall around Haldeman and Ehrlichman. They also needed to contact Helms, now the U.S. ambassador to Iran, and get him to echo what they expected Walters to say.

The memo, Haig said, looks bad for everyone, but "we can survive it in very good shape."

"We can survive," Nixon repeated. "It will be very embarrassing, because it'll indicate that we tried to cover up with the CIA."

"That's all right," Haig answered.[75]

It was most definitely not all right but obstruction of justice, and Haig knew there were tapes that would prove it.

Back in Washington, Ruckelshaus's report occupied most of Haig's time. Ruckelshaus and an FBI agent came to get the tap logs from a safe in Ehrlichman's White House office, and Ruckelshaus and Haig discussed the report. Buzhardt also helped Ruckelshaus write the statement. Haig also dealt with a growing number of questions from *New York Times* reporter Seymour Hersh, whom Sullivan had given information that implicated Nixon directly in authorizing the taps and indicated that Kissinger had helped him. "Sullivan made available to me copies of the White House wiretap authorizations, which directly linked Kissinger to the requests for wiretaps on his own staff aides," Hersh wrote in his 1983 book, *The Price of Power*.[76] Hersh would not back off his story, but Haig tried hard to make Hersh do so. Hersh did not realize, however, that Haig and Sullivan were talking multiple times a day about the wiretaps, the investigation into them, and how to avoid the focus falling on them.

In California the *Los Angeles Times* broke a story that Sunday that would set up drama for the first hearings of the Senate Watergate Committee, which would start on May 17. James McCord, one of the Watergate burglars, said that John Caulfield, a former New York City police detective who went to work for the White House, had told him that Nixon would give him clemency if McCord remained silent. This offer was allegedly passed to Caulfield through John Dean. The *Los Angeles Times*' scoop was picked up by papers around the country and provided another piece in the portrait of a Nixon White House actively trying to cover its tracks in Watergate.[77]

For someone who needed to relax at Camp David, Nixon spent much of his time over the weekend on the telephone with Haig, Ziegler, or Kissinger. On that Sunday morning, Nixon sought more reassurance from Haig about their plans for Walters's impending testimony, and Haig revealed they might fail in their attempts to keep Walters's written memos private because they had already allowed Cushman's memos about the agency's help for the Plumbers to be turned over to Congress.

"Why did he [Cushman] do that?" Nixon asked Haig.

"Well, I don't know," Haig said. "Now he's on notice now, and he's not going to do pull anything like that again."

Nixon did not seem convinced.

"How can you justify giving them Cushman's and not giving them Walters's?" he asked Haig. "How do you do that, Al? What's Buzhardt say?"

"Because what Walters discussed was not just a little bit of equipment for somebody but national security matters," Haig responded.[78]

Such a tissue-thin response would not stop a Senate committee determined to get Walters's memos. Walters's testimony, which Haig repeatedly assured Nixon would help him, loomed as a disaster for the president.

Haig talked with Nixon one final time that night between 10:00 and 10:30 and inconceivably told Nixon that "I think there's a good chance [Walters's memcons] will never come up. I don't think the question will ever come up."

Haig also vouched again for Sullivan, who had denied to the FBI that he had taken the wiretap logs to stop Hoover's blackmail of Nixon. "The guy who has proved to be the true, accurate voice in this thing is Sullivan," he said. "He's just one good solid loyal American who has good law enforcement credentials."[79]

On the night of May 13, the day before he was scheduled to release his report on the FBI wiretaps, Ruckelshaus received a bizarre call from a man who identified himself as John Crewdson, the *New York Times* reporter who had broken the detailed story on the wiretaps on May 11. His main source for that story was Sullivan. The caller who claimed to be Crewdson did something that Crewdson or any serious reporter would never do: provide the identity of a confidential source. That source, "Crewdson" said, was Felt. At the end of every phone call, "Crewdson" told Ruckelshaus, Felt would tell him, "'Remember, I'm a candidate for FBI director.'"

"Why tell me this?" Ruckelshaus asked the caller.

"There's something wrong with the country right now," the caller said. "I don't know what it is, but I thought you should know what Mark Felt is doing."[80]

Ruckelshaus hung up, called FBI official Bucky Walters, and told him what had just happened.

"Cut his nuts off," Walters told Ruckelshaus about Felt.[81]

The caller could only have been Sullivan, who, as leader of the FBI's secretive Counterintelligence Program, specialized in destabilizing rivals and unsuspecting victims with false leaks and threatening calls and letters. Haig told Sullivan that both he and Nixon knew Felt was leaking to *Time* magazine. Sullivan also knew the pair also believed Felt had tipped off Crewdson, and he knew that Ruckelshaus also suspected Felt and wanted a reason to fire him.

Nixon returned to the White House in the morning of May 14, a day that would turn into one of the busiest and most eventful of his presidency. By day's end, Nixon had given Haig more authority, while the chief of staff learned about a threat to the cover-up of the military spy ring, the details of Ruckelshaus's FBI investigation, the documents Dean had stolen from the White House, and the extent to which Walters endangered Nixon with his revelations about the attempted Watergate cover-up with the CIA.

The day started with an article in the *Washington Post* by Bob Woodward and Carl Bernstein that claimed that Gray had known of allegations of interference in the Watergate investigation but did nothing because he did not want to be seen as looking for Nixon's advice. "Top FBI officials warned former acting FBI Director L. Patrick Gray III several weeks after the Watergate break-in that there appeared to be a cover-up going on and urged him to immediately alert President Nixon, according to two reliable sources," the story began. "But Gray declined to go to the President, he told the officials, because he felt it would appear as if he were seeking guidance from Mr. Nixon, the sources said. Gray's exact reasons are unclear. He could not be reached for comment yesterday." Like their May 3 story, which started the internal FBI investigation into the wiretaps, this one was mostly incorrect and seemed aimed at discrediting Gray, who had told Nixon on July 6, 1972, that some of his staff were interfering in the Watergate investigation. That was slightly more than two weeks after the June 17 break-in, not the "several weeks" cited by Woodward and Bernstein. They also had details of Ruckelshaus's investigation, which was scheduled to be announced that day. The story said that seventeen government officials and journalists had been tapped and that the wiretap files had been given to Mardian at Justice by Sullivan before Hoover fired him. The story did not mention Haig or Kissinger. It cited anonymous sources, including one from the Justice Department, possibly Sullivan, and another anonymous source. If one was Felt, whom Woodward claimed to be his secret source known as Deep Throat, there are no notes of that fact kept with the rest of Woodward's Deep Throat notes at the Harry Ransom Center at the University of Texas at Austin. The section about the wiretaps, which contained advance details of the Ruckelshaus report, was tacked on at the end of the story almost as an afterthought. Unlike the section about Gray, it was accurate and indicated that someone with knowledge of the report, most likely Haig, had told the reporters.[82]

That morning, almost as an aside, Nixon gave Haig more power, anointing him with the ability to assume many of the president's responsibilities, including attending many of the meetings usually reserved for the president.

"There are many things you do better than I do or just as well," Nixon said in another sign of Nixon detaching himself from the daily tasks of the presidency and putting Haig in Nixon's place.

Then Haig transitioned the conversation to another White House aide who was in the Senate committee's crosshairs: Alexander Butterfield, Haig's old colleague from the Pentagon.

"I got a report from the Hill that they're going to have Butterfield into this thing," Haig said. "I don't know what. It had something to do with campaign funding."

"Butterfield?" Nixon said.

"Yes," Haig continued. "He had funds for campaign polling. As best as I can tell, he used [the money] only once. He had nothing to do with campaign funding. So I think he's clean as a whistle, but they think they have something on the committee on this."

"Good God, that sort of thing right now shouldn't concern us a bit," Nixon said. "What the hell, you can't find everyone who had something to do with the campaign. Can you?"

"No, sir, you can't," Haig said.

"Well, we went as far as we're going to go with [former aide Egil] Krogh," Nixon said. Krogh had to leave the Transportation Department after he was revealed as a member of the White House Plumbers. "Now with Butterfield, if he did something that was illegitimate. Yes, he had some funding. If it had to be reported and it was some kind of technical violation, then that was that. He's not going to be fired for that now."[83]

Unlike Walters, whom Nixon knew had damaging information about an alleged cover-up, Butterfield raised no alarms. Haig's mention of the committee's interest in Butterfield served to get Nixon to allow Butterfield to testify, which would turn out to be a fatal error, because Butterfield had helped install the secret White House taping system. Butterfield, Haig, and Bob Woodward have acknowledged that it was Woodward who recommended that the Senate committee interview Butterfield. Haig's comments to Nixon about Butterfield show that Haig knew about Butterfield's knowledge of the White House tapes, which he passed on to Woodward, who then told the Senate committee to interview Butterfield.

After receiving the call from Sullivan masquerading as John Crewdson, Ruckelshaus confronted Felt on Monday morning, just hours before he was to release the wiretapping report.

Felt denied he was leaking.

"You can't deny it," Ruckelshaus said. "I just heard it from the guy you talked to."

Felt said nothing.

"I'm so mad at you I don't know what to do," Ruckelshaus told Felt. "I'm going to sleep on it and decide in the morning."[84]

Felt returned the next day and gave his resignation to Ruckelshaus, who would have fired Felt if he had not resigned.

In an early afternoon news conference, Ruckelshaus said the FBI had wiretapped thirteen government officials and four journalists between May 1969 and February 1971, and the taps were ordered "in an effort to pinpoint responsibility for leaks of highly sensitive and classified information, which, in the opinion of those charged with conducting our foreign policy, were compromising the nation's effectiveness in nego-tiations and other dealings with foreign powers." That was the closest the report came to mentioning Nixon, Kissinger, or Haig by name. Also left unsaid was who had ordered the reports or who picked the targets. When Kissinger was asked for comment after the Ruckelshaus news conference, he again lied, saying that his talks with Hoover "concerned the safeguarding of classified information and not the initiation of any particular form of investigation." Kissinger lied another time when he said he knew nothing about the Plumbers, although his former aide David Young was a Plumber who had investigated the military spy ring. Ruckelshaus said Sullivan had kept the tap logs at the FBI but gave them to Mardian in July 1971 because he believed Hoover would use them to blackmail Nixon. "Mr. Sullivan does not affirm Mr. Mardian's claim," Ruckelshaus said, although Sullivan had told Haig repeatedly that was why he took the logs from the FBI. "That would account to some extent as to why these files were moved to the White House," Ruckelshaus said about Hoover's rumored blackmail. "It certainly is a logical reason."[85]

As Haig tried to manage the Ruckelshaus report and the impending Walters testimony, he and Buzhardt faced a threat that appeared from seemingly nowhere. Donald Stewart, the former FBI agent who was now the Pentagon's chief investigator, called the White House looking for Young, his former associate from the investigation into the leaks about Nixon's behind-the-scenes actions to tilt U.S. policy in favor of Pakistan in the war between India and Pakistan, an investigation that revealed the military spy ring (see chapter 1). Young had left the White House amid the fallout from the discovery of the Plumbers, so Stewart was directed to lawyer Richard Tufaro, a young member of White House counsel Len Garment's staff. Stewart vented his numerous frustrations, primarily that he was unhappy at the Pentagon. He correctly believed Buzhardt had sabotaged his investigation of the spy ring, and he wanted a more challenging job. Tufaro, who knew nothing about Stewart or the spy ring, was alarmed, particularly after Stewart hinted that his secret work could become public. Stewart's complaints about Buzhardt also struck a chord with Tufaro, who distrusted Buzhardt, as did Garment. Tufaro had warned Garment about Buzhardt handling the Watergate defense because he remained the Pentagon's general counsel and had numerous conflicts of interest. Shortly after he spoke to Stewart, Tufaro sent Garment a memo that said, "Stewart clearly is in a position to damage the Administration because of his direct involvement in White House investigations of national security leaks." Garment told Buzhardt about the call, and Buzhardt responded by reassigning Stewart to desk duty and seizing his files at the Pentagon.[86] Stewart's call let Haig and Buzhardt know that the spy ring, the subject of numerous diatribes by Nixon over the last two and a half years, had not gone away and remained a threat.

Nixon faced another threat, this time from Dean, who had appeared in the courtroom of U.S. District Judge John J. Sirica, who oversaw the Watergate criminal cases. When Nixon fired Dean on April 30, Dean took several secret documents, which he placed in a safe deposit box in a northern Virginia bank. Nixon wanted the documents back because he was worried about the embarrassing secrets they contained. Sirica, however, ruled that the documents be copied and given to the Senate committees investigating Watergate-related activities and to the Justice Department. If Nixon wanted to see what Dean had taken, he could get them from Justice.[87]

Walters's testimony before the Senate Armed Services Committee closed out the day. Contrary to Haig's assurances to Nixon, Walters was a disaster for the White House. Although Walters had testified in a closed hearing, the committee's acting chairman, Stuart Symington, told reporters afterward that Walters said Haldeman, Ehrlichman, and Dean had tried to involve the CIA in the Watergate case. The CIA, Symington said, had no connection to the Watergate break-in. "Ehrlichman and Haldeman— particularly Haldeman—were up to their ears in this, along with Dean, in trying to involve the CIA in this whole Watergate mess," Symington said.[88]

The news set off sirens at the White House.

"We got a problem with the testimony that Walters gave," Haig told the president late that evening during a meeting with press secretary Ron Ziegler and Larry Higby, Haldeman's former deputy, in the Oval Office.

"How come?" Nixon asked.

Walters, Haig said, "twisted it in a way that was bad for Bob and John."

Nixon was crestfallen. He had counted on Walters, who had served Nixon when he was vice president and had carried out secret missions with China and North Vietnam, to protect him before the Senate. "So, what do you think that Walters did?" he asked Haig. "Walters deliberately put Haldeman's and Ehrlichman's tit in the wringer on this. That makes me sick."

Nixon worked late into the night with Haig, Ziegler, and Higby, trying to come up with a plan on how to survive the Walters revelations. "This is difficult shit," Nixon said.

Haig urged Nixon to rely more on Buzhardt, although his poor advice had already led to Cushman turning over his documents to the Senate, thereby creating a dangerous precedent, and to Walters's disastrous testimony, which would only turn out to be more damaging.

"Buzhardt's in charge," Nixon said, "and at the end of the day he can tell you, well, we had this and this pack of shit today and this pack of shit tomorrow."

"That's the best way," Haig said.[89]

Haig's and Buzhardt's insistence that Walters testify about his White House meetings in the days following the Watergate break-in had turned out exactly as Nixon had feared. While Dean was exposed as a prime character in the attempted cover-up of the White House's connections to the Watergate break-in, so were Haldeman and Ehrlichman, Nixon's closest aides. And if Haldeman and Ehrlichman had tried to cover up, what did Nixon know about the break-in? The two could not have acted alone, and if they had acted on Nixon's instructions, it meant the president had obstructed justice, an impeachable offense.

Symington, who was not content with the comments he made after Walters's testimony, released more details in a news conference on May 15. Accompanying him was his Republican colleague from South Carolina, Strom Thurmond, a hard-core Nixon loyalist and ardent conservative. Yet the two men found common cause on the implications of what Walters told the committee. "It is very clear to me that there was an attempt to unload major responsibility for the Watergate bugging and cover-up on CIA," Symington said. Dean, Haldeman, and Ehrlichman, he added, "were doing everything in the world to obstruct justice."[90] Symington, who had previously irritated Nixon by criticizing Kissinger's growing secret powers as national security advisor, again had proved to be one of Nixon's most effective interlocutors. Now he, as much as the leadership of the new Watergate committee, was exposing more of the White House's dirty laundry as the public began to turn away from the president.

Symington used his influence again after the news conference by sending his top staff, along with Senator Harry Byrd of Virginia, to meet with Pentagon and intelligence community officials to discuss the documents that Sirica had taken from Dean. They focused on an internal security plan known by the name of its author, Tom Charles Huston. A passionate conservative, Huston was twenty-nine years old in 1970 when Nixon entrusted him with creating a plan to fight against student protesters and other suspected security threats. His main ally was Sullivan, whom Hoover delegated to handle the details. Restrictions that Hoover placed on illegal break-ins by FBI agents, the so-called black-bag jobs, would have been lifted by the new plan, as would some of the limits on electronic eavesdropping. The plan never went into effect, because Hoover persuaded Attorney General John Mitchell, whom Nixon had excluded from the planning, to get Nixon to kill it. The plan's existence had grave implications for Nixon. Not only had the president condoned the creation of a special investigations team, the Plumbers, that burglarized the offices of its targets, but Nixon had also approved spying on members of his own administration and journalists. The Huston Plan was one more indication that Nixon would stop at nothing to get what he wanted.

Symington did not believe claims that exposing the Huston Plan would hurt national security. Nixon had played the national security card too often, he said, and since the plan never took effect, he risked little by exposing it. Symington asked the FBI officials to "be prepared to justify in a paragraph-by-paragraph basis just what must be protected in the national interest." Despite this threat to the president, Buzhardt and Haig did not tell him about it until a day later.[91]

With the day's mail, Haig received a mysterious letter from a doctor in Philadelphia who claimed that his office had been burglarized the previous year and that files on his patient, Senator Thomas Eagleton of Missouri, were taken. Eagleton had been the vice presidential nominee for the Democrats briefly in 1972 before he had to leave the ticket because of reports that he had undergone electroshock treatments years earlier. The Eagleton affair damaged whatever chance the campaign of Democratic nominee George McGovern had of beating Nixon. This letter was a secret to Haig and Buzhardt, but it would not remain one much longer.[92]

Haig also fought a losing battle with Seymour Hersh, who was finishing a story that would place Nixon at the center of the FBI's wiretaps. Hersh, as he would write ten years later, had received copies of the letters approving the wiretaps from Sullivan. Those letters implicated Nixon. Haig, who was trying to limit his exposure as well as Kissinger's, told Hersh, "Do you believe Kissinger, whose family members died in the Holocaust, would have approved such Nazi tactics?"[93] Hersh was not deterred.

Sullivan remained Nixon's hope to shift attention from his administration's wiretaps to those of his two predecessors, Lyndon Johnson and John Kennedy. Haig, who talked to Sullivan several times a day, told Nixon that Sullivan would defend Nixon publicly, which never happened. Instead, the May 16 *New York Times* featured Hersh's story, which said that Nixon "personally authorized" the wiretaps on journalists and government officials. For all of Haig's protestations with Hersh, the article did not expose him or Kissinger as much as it could have. Perhaps Sullivan, Hersh's source, steered Hersh away from Haig, although Haig's involvement was evident. Some of the quotes from Hersh's anonymous sources read much like Haig's comments to Nixon as they worked to minimize the damage from the wiretap revelations. "Hell, yes, I was aware that it was going on," one source, most likely Haig, told Hersh. "To have done less would have been the highest order of irresponsibility."[94]

The news from Symington's press conference the previous day was bannered across the front page of the morning's *Washington Post*: "CIA Resisted Lengthy Cover-Up Attempt by White House, Hill Account Reveals." Only someone totally ignorant of the growing Watergate controversy could have missed the story and its implications. "The Central

Intelligence Agency resisted an extraordinary series of pressures by top White House aides to assist in a cover-up of the Watergate scandal over an eight-month period beginning in June 1972, Sen. Stuart Symington (D-Mo.) revealed yesterday," the story said. Nixon's closest aides tried to enlist the CIA to help them stop an FBI investigation into the Watergate break-in. Most people thought it unlikely that Haldeman, Ehrlichman, and Dean acted on their own initiative. If they had acted at the president's request, which is what Walters said he believed, then Nixon had obstructed justice.[95] That could eventually mean impeachment or possible criminal charges from the special prosecutor whom Attorney General Elliot Richardson was expected to appoint at any time.

Symington and the Senate Armed Services Committee met again with defense and intelligence officials about the Dean documents. The most sensitive was a forty-three-page "special report" that detailed the Huston Plan.[96] After Nixon rescinded his approval of the plan, a demoralized Huston lashed out, asking Haldeman who was in charge—Nixon or Hoover? Sullivan then asked each agency—the FBI, CIA, National Security Agency and Defense Intelligence Agency—to return the copies of the plan it possessed. Still, some elements of the plan were implemented, including the formation of the Intelligence Evaluation Committee, led by Dean, which was intended to coordinate all intelligence issues within the White House. Thus Dean had access to the Huston Plan, whether it formally went into effect or not, and this plan was now in the hands of the president's enemies.

Buzhardt had learned of these developments from his associates at the Pentagon and told Nixon on the afternoon of May 16.

"Don't it seem like we always have problems?" Nixon asked Buzhardt in the Oval Office.

"It has nothing to do with Watergate," Buzhardt said. "Let's start with that. Nothing to do with Watergate unless somebody draws an inference of connection. What it is basically, Mr. President, is your interagency intelligence group plan."

Some of the language in the copy of the Huston Plan kept by Dean was "quite inflammatory," Buzhardt said.

"Everything he [Huston] wrote was inflammatory," Nixon said.

"So, it's very unfortunate," Buzhardt said. "I think it presents a serious problem."[97]

As they had just days earlier with the FBI wiretaps, Haig and Nixon turned again to Sullivan, this time to confirm that the Huston Plan never took effect. Nixon hoped to mitigate the damage caused by the plan's exposure by proving it never went past the planning stages.

Buzhardt proposed an idea, which Haig quickly adopted, that Nixon confront the issue head-on. Over the next six days, this idea would grow and again put Nixon in the position of trying to explain himself to an increasingly skeptical public.

"I think, frankly, that this will be used by the [Senate Watergate] committee really to supersede the whole Watergate thing," Buzhardt said.

"Yeah," Nixon responded.

"It puts a new light on the fight," Buzhardt said.

"Yeah," Nixon said again.

"I would suggest it be handled in a much different fashion," Buzhardt said. "I think you can't let this dribble out."

Nixon agreed, and Buzhardt continued. "It's my own belief that you have to make your case for doing it. Think of the environment that it was done in. You have to lay it on the record, and there are a number of ways you could do it with something approaching a state paper, perhaps with a summary by you, say that with the leadership or otherwise. I think you should be accompanied at this point by a relaxation to the maximum extent of executive privilege, because you can't have the plan and then have anything that appears to cover up. I think we should work up into the maximum extent possible, the best darn approach."

"Yes, sir," Nixon said. "I hear you."

Buzhardt presented Nixon with a very stark view of the future. The president had little chance of preventing Walters's memoranda from becoming public. Nixon could not stop a court order. He had to strike back while making his best case, regardless of the potential dangers, which included impeachment.

Confronting the issue directly, Buzhardt said, could "precipitate action by the House [meaning impeachment]. If so, you should make your case in the strongest possible terms. Give everybody the ammunition you can to help you, and then let's go fight it. Just take them on and fight this thing head-on. Actually, it gives us a better case, because the issue can now turn on the threat to national security during this period. The document is a good one. It lays out the threat very well."[98]

Buzhardt was making a remarkable request of Nixon, whose entire administration had been built on secrecy, to admit to parts of the Watergate cover-up and to the creation of a secret security plan that resembled that of a police state.

By the end of the night, the eve of the start of the Senate Watergate hearings, an embittered, disillusioned Nixon felt surrounded by his enemies.

"We have to realize they're not after Bob or John or Henry or Haig or Ziegler," Nixon told Haig and Buzhardt. "They're after the president. Shit. That's what it's all about. You know that. They want to destroy us."

Buzhardt had at least some good news. He had confirmed through Sullivan that the Huston Plan never went into action.

"It was within two days of it being issued, to the best of their recollection," Buzhardt said.

"Jesus Christ," Nixon said, laughing.

"Sullivan thinks he has notes that will give us the precise times. But the whole thing was suspended immediately."

Nixon felt a brief flurry of encouragement. "Let's get it nailed down," he said. "Let's knock the shit out of this one. Knock the ball right out of the park."[99]

At the FBI, Mark Felt's resignation meant he would leave the bureau in June. His resignation would take on more significance after June 2005, when Felt, unable to speak for himself because of severe dementia, claimed through his children and family lawyer, John O'Connor, to have been Deep Throat, Bob Woodward's secret source. In the book *All the President's Men*, with Carl Bernstein, Woodward wrote that he and Deep Throat had a dramatic meeting on the night of May 16 in an underground parking garage at the Marriott Hotel near the Key Bridge, which connects Arlington County, Virginia, to the Georgetown neighborhood of Washington DC. Woodward described an agitated Deep Throat telling him about the damaging revelations from inside the White House. After the meeting, Woodward rushed home and called Bernstein, who joined him at his apartment. An alarmed Woodward turned on his stereo to a Rachmaninoff piano concerto and cranked up the volume in case government spies were listening. "Deep Throat says that electronic surveillance is going on and we had better watch it," Woodward typed on a piece of paper. Bernstein wrote on a piece of paper, "Who is doing it?" "C-I-A," Woodward mouthed.

"Bernstein was disbelieving," the two wrote in the book. He should have been, because much of what Woodward would type, and which both reporters would give to *Post* editors the next day, was either untrue, old news, information that Felt would not have known, or piped directly to Woodward from Haig. No evidence exists that the CIA spied on reporters or anyone connected with Watergate, and there is no proof that the dramatic garage meeting ever happened. Woodward was the only person who claimed to have been there; there were no third-party witnesses; Deep Throat purportedly told Woodward information that Felt never had and/or that was not included in FBI files.

Much of what Woodward allegedly learned that night could have come only from Haig, if the meeting happened the way Woodward claimed it did. According to Woodward, the source told him that Republican senator Howard Baker was secretly working for the White House, which was not true, and that many of the Watergate-related activities were aimed at making money, also not true. Woodward also claimed that Deep Throat told him that John Caulfield, a Nixon aide, had told Watergate burglar James McCord that he would receive presidential clemency if he remained quiet, a fact the *Los Angeles Times* had published three days earlier and that had been picked up in the *Washington Post*. As proof of the White House's machinations, the source told Woodward that CIA official Vernon Walters said the White House wanted to use the CIA to block the FBI's Watergate investigation, a claim that was no great revelation, because it had been bannered across the front page of that day's *Post*.

The new information was that the White House was deeply concerned about the documents Dean had taken from the White House. Those details were part of the multiple discussions that Haig, Nixon, and Buzhardt had had during the previous days. Deep Throat also reportedly said there were talks about domestic intelligence, a direct reference to the Huston Plan, which was also the focus of the worried conversations in the Oval Office, conversations Felt could not have known about. Instead, such details were what Haig and Sullivan had discussed all week.

Finally, Woodward wrote that there was an "unreal atmosphere" in the White House, "realizing it is curtains on one hand and on the other trying to laugh it off and go on with business. President has had fits of 'dangerous' depression."[100] Once again, only Haig, not Felt, would have been privy to such information. By May 16 he had spent almost two weeks as Nixon's latest confidant, listening calmly as the president expressed doubts about his ability to stay in office and openly mentioning the possibility of resignation. Haig's firsthand witnessing of Nixon's depression, most of it captured by the White House taping system, is the most logical source of this admission to Woodward.

Since the publication of *All the President's Men* in 1974, Woodward and Bernstein have insisted on the unerring accuracy of Deep Throat's information and his reticence about being exposed as a source. The details Deep Throat allegedly provided in the parking garage on May 16 belie Woodward and Bernstein's reputation for accuracy. Some of what Deep Throat told Woodward was incorrect, such as Howard Baker's blind allegiance to Nixon and that White House officials were trying to make money off Watergate. Some information would turn out to be accurate, such as Nixon's dangerous depression. Other bits of information were things that a casual reader of the *Post* would know, such as Walters's testimony about White House cover-up attempts.

Nevertheless, Woodward and Bernstein took this pastiche of factoids to the Georgetown home of *Post* editor Ben Bradlee in the middle of the night and breathlessly told him that they were all in danger. In reality, there were no threats to anyone, as the taped meetings of Nixon and his staff would prove. These tapes show a desperate president, his administration beset by mounting threats from inside and out, trying to regain his footing. Nixon lashed out often, but his threats meant little. No one, especially Woodward's source, who spent half his days in the Oval Office, had anything to fear other than the discovery of earlier scandals.

The contents of Woodward's late-night parking garage rendezvous reveal the source of the information to be a combination of people, particularly Haig and Buzhardt, and not Felt. Given his distaste for Felt and alliance with Sullivan, it is highly unlikely that Haig would have used Felt as his conduit to pass information to Woodward. In fact, the events of this week show that Haig was far more likely to use Woodward as a messenger to others. After all, Woodward told his *Post* colleague Len Downie that Haig spoke with Woodward often and promptly and personally returned his calls to the White House.[101] Also, why would Felt have contacted Woodward for a secret garage meeting the night after his FBI career was terminated to pass along a hash of gossip and old news when Felt preferred to give such information to Sandy Smith at *Time* magazine? He would not.

For the White House, the first day of the Senate Watergate hearings started with a Woodward and Bernstein story bannered across the front of the May 17 *Washington Post*: "Vast GOP Undercover Operation Originated in 1969."[102] It was, as Ron Ziegler noted to Nixon that morning, a set-up story that established a range of White House–related espionage and dirty tricks activity since Nixon took office in 1969.[103] Just like the duo's May 3 story on the alleged "vigilante squads" of former CIA and FBI agents spying for the White House, this article contained several questionable assertions and also conflated the White House Plumbers with other activities. It also bore the unmistakable fingerprints of Alexander Haig.

The story reported that Ehrlichman had the confidential health records of Senator Thomas Eagleton. Haig and Buzhardt told Nixon on May 17 that Haig had received a letter from a doctor two days earlier in which he stated that his office was burglarized and Eagleton's records were stolen.[104] This revelation then materialized in the *Post*. The story also mentioned that the White House "has promulgated 'national security' guidelines for use in the Watergate investigation that are designed at least in part to prevent testimony about the undercover operations by those with knowledge of them." Haig, Buzhardt, and Nixon had developed these guidelines to prevent Walters's testimony, the release of Walters's memcons, and any testimony about the military spy ring. Again, that information showed up in the *Post*, courtesy of Haig.

Woodward's work as Haig's messenger continued in May. In *All the President's Men*, he and Bernstein wrote that Woodward went to Capitol Hill around the time the Senate hearings started on May 17 to tell his friend Scott Armstrong, now a member of the Watergate committee staff, how he and his colleagues needed to interview Alexander Butterfield, Haig's old friend from the Pentagon and the aide who helped install Nixon's taping system.[105] Nixon had told Haig about the tapes on May 8 and again on May 11, emphasizing each time how the tapes would prove who was telling the truth and who was not.

Butterfield's potential testimony, which would reveal the taping system, aligned with another critical piece of information Haig learned on May 17. He and Nixon left the White House for Nixon's hideaway office in room 180 of the Old Executive Office Building. The president had taken to disappearing from the West Wing more frequently, and shortly after 4:00 p.m., Nixon told Haig about something that would soon create a situation in which both the president and vice president faced crises that would force them from office. A federal grand jury in Baltimore was investigating bribery and tax evasion allegations about the Baltimore County executive, Dale Anderson, who had succeeded Vice President Spiro Agnew in the job after Agnew became governor of Maryland. The investigation did not stop with Anderson. Soon witnesses told investigators they had bribed Agnew, too, including giving him envelopes of cash in his vice presidential office. Agnew learned the initial details in April and told Haldeman on April 10. Since then, Nixon had shared the details he knew about the investigation with a few others, in particular, Ehrlichman, William Rogers (Nixon's secretary of state but also a former attorney general), and Henry Kissinger.

Agnew, Nixon told Haig, wanted Haldeman "to call Glenn Beall's brother and have him cool the grand jury investigation here because it might embarrass him, Agnew," Nixon told Haig. Glenn Beall was the Republican senator from Maryland, and his brother, George, was the U.S. attorney handling the Baltimore grand jury. "If I had done that when I was vice president, Ike would have fired my ass," Nixon continued. "Agnew can't play this holier-than-thou attitude.

"Just say you wanted him to know the president is trying like hell to keep this from getting out," Nixon said of Agnew's request. "You can't tell what will come out."[106]

Nixon wanted Haig to call Agnew and work out the details.

So by May 17, as Haig realized the extent of Nixon's problems, he had already learned from the president himself that Agnew was taking bribes and desperately wanted Nixon to make Agnew's problems disappear. There are multiple signs that Haig knew at least a month earlier, shortly after Agnew told Haldeman about the grand jury investigation. Agnew, Haldeman wrote, "called me over and said he had a real problem, because Jerome Wolff, who used to work for him back in Maryland, was about to be called by the United States Attorney who was busting open campaign contribution cases and kickbacks to contractors." Agnew "feels it would sound bad." The vice president wanted Haldeman to reach out to Senator Beall "to straighten it out." When Haldeman refused, Agnew said he would probably contact Charles Colson, one of Nixon's most ruthless aides, who had just left the White House and started a new law firm.[107]

Haldeman and Ehrlichman told Nixon about Agnew's request on the morning of April 14 while they were surveying the deteriorating political landscape. They discussed whether former attorney general John Mitchell, who was Nixon's 1972 campaign manager, had ordered the Watergate break-in. Then Ehrlichman dumped another problem on Nixon's lap.

Agnew and his associates met often in the Maryland governor's office to discuss potential contracts and who was giving them campaign contributions, Ehrlichman said. Wolff participated in those meetings "and wrote those comments down," Ehrlichman told Nixon. When Wolff fell under the scrutiny of the Baltimore grand jury, he ran with the notes to his lawyer, who then went to George White, Agnew's longtime associate and attorney. Agnew realized that he, too, would soon be under scrutiny. He called Haldeman.

"Thank God I was never elected governor," Nixon said before ruminating on the corruption cases that had ensnared multiple governors around the country, such as Otto Kerner of Illinois, who was being tried in 1973 on federal corruption charges.

What does Agnew want us to do? Nixon asked.

Haldeman speculated that the White House's support of Senator J. Glenn Beall's 1970 campaign with $200,000 passed through a special political fund would make him tell George Beall to back off. "We can't quash the case," Nixon said. They should ask Colson to contact [Agnew attorney George] White to see what they could do. "I can't imagine Glenn Beall's brother hitting the vice president," Nixon said. Still, he continued, "[Agnew's] just got to ride that through."[108]

At 11:31 a.m. Haldeman and Ehrlichman walked out of the office, and Haig and Henry Kissinger walked in. There is no indication that Haldeman and Ehrlichman told the other two about Agnew. However, between April 14 and May 17, Nixon discussed Agnew's fate with multiple aides, including Kissinger. "Agnew's got a problem, as I told you, on this," Nixon told Kissinger and Rogers on May 11. "The poor son of a bitch has a grand jury working on him."[109] Any of them could have told Haig, who could have learned about it from Colson, with whom Haig had a long and close relationship. When Haldeman and Ehrlichman resigned on April 30, Colson, along with Haldeman, pushed the hardest for Haig to become the new White House chief of staff.[110]

None of this proves that Colson told Haig of Agnew's legal problems in mid-April 1973 or that Haig told Woodward, who then told his fellow reporter Richard Cohen. But the evidence is more plausible than what Cohen and Woodward have written. In his 1974 book about the Agnew case, *A Heartbeat Away*, Cohen wrote that Woodward told him in April 1973 that Deep Throat told him that "FBI files contained apparently unverified allegations that Agnew had accepted a bribe while vice president." The grand jury, Cohen wrote, "was heading Agnew's way and the Vice President was in fact its target. This seemingly preposterous information

was received in April, nearly a month before the prosecutors acknowledged getting the first veiled hint that Agnew had taken kickbacks and
nearly two months before they learned anything specific."[111] However,
publicly available FBI files on Agnew reveal nothing about the bribery
investigation from before August 1973, when the news about Agnew's
problems exploded in public view.[112] It was only then that the FBI was
asked for help providing polygraphs. Agnew's problems came from an
IRS investigation. By August, Mark Felt no longer worked at the FBI.
Again, Haig knew more about Agnew's problems than most people, and
he had been supplying Woodward with information.

Meanwhile, the first Senate Watergate Committee hearing on May 17
was a low-key affair that opened with its chairman, Democratic senator
Sam Ervin of North Carolina, spelling out his expectations. "If the many
allegations made to this date are true," Ervin said, "the burglars who
broke into the headquarters of the Democratic National Committee at
the Watergate were in effect breaking into the home of every citizen of
the United States."[113] At age seventy-six, Ervin seemed like an artifact of
a bygone political era, like a character in an Allen Drury novel. Nixon
and his aides thought Ervin would not wear well with the television
audience. They wildly underestimated the folksy country lawyer, whose
demeanor belied his Harvard Law School education.

"He's our biggest asset, Ervin," Buzhardt told Nixon, because Ervin ran
terrible hearings and did not let his professional counsel ask questions.[114]

Buzhardt was wrong on both counts. Chief committee counsel Sam
Dash, a former district attorney, would conduct large chunks of the
questioning, and Ervin would turn into a folk hero for how he managed
the hearings, which drew huge television audiences. Ervin and Dash's
strategy called for building up their witnesses to a crescendo throughout
the summer, each one adding to the testimony of the previous witnesses.
Just a week into his job as Nixon's Watergate counsel, Buzhardt had
already made some significant errors in judgment. His miscalculation
about Ervin was just another day at the office.

As they analyzed the hearings and tried to determine how much of the
Huston Plan would leak out, Nixon lapsed into a digression about one

of his favorite examples of betrayal, the military spy ring and the theft of thousands of documents from the White House by Yeoman Charles Radford. Nixon considered the spy ring a national security breach of a greater magnitude than the Huston Plan or the Plumbers, and it was so secret that he would not include it in any white paper that Buzhardt was writing.

"I'm sure you're aware of the India-Pakistan story," Nixon said.

"I wrote the report on that, Mr. President," Buzhardt said of the report he wrote that covered up Haig's sharing with the Joint Chiefs information that Nixon had wanted to keep secret.

"About the yeoman?" Nixon asked.

"Yes, sir, the yeoman, the admiral, the [taking of Kissinger's files from his briefcase]," Buzhardt said. "Mr. President, not too many people know about that, and I'm very afraid it's going to come out."

"If it comes out, you know who it's going to hurt," Nixon said.

"It's going to kill the chairman [of the Joint Chiefs of Staff, Adm. Thomas Moorer]. I'm aware of it," Buzhardt answered.

Nixon fulminated about Radford, that "goddamn yeoman. . . . He knew too much," adding that they had to let him go.

"We had circumstantial evidence," Buzhardt said. "That's all we had. . . . People were concerned, and they started the investigation with the wrong people over there [at the Pentagon]."

"Oh," Nixon said, surprised.

"As soon as [Defense Secretary] Mel [Laird] found out about it, he told me to take it away from them, because he was afraid of it leaking, and then said, 'Give me a full report' so he'd know what happened," Buzhardt said.

"Is that so?" Nixon said. "Mel knows?"

Nixon had spent the first four years of his presidency specifically bypassing Laird, the defense secretary, as he put together much of Nixon's national security policy. He always underestimated Laird's ability to learn about and conceal information Nixon wanted to hide from him.

"Mel knows the whole story, absolutely," Buzhardt said. "Top to bottom."

Nixon called the spy ring a major national security threat, but prosecuting those involved "would have accomplished nothing, except it would have embarrassed Moorer, the military-industrial complex, and maybe would have embarrassed Jack Anderson," the columnist whose stories with leaks from the NSC led to the uncovering of the spy ring.

"I'm not even sure it would have embarrassed Jack Anderson," Buzhardt said.[115]

Meanwhile, in the Senate Armed Services Committee hearing room, Vernon Walters was testifying again about the attempted White House cover-up of the Watergate investigation. The testimony that Haig and Buzhardt had assured Nixon would actually hurt Dean continued to damage the president's claims that he had nothing to do with any cover-up. Walters said that L. Patrick Gray had told Walters he had recommended that those involved in the Watergate cover-up needed to be fired and that Gray was willing to resign if that did not happen. Walters's latest claims were contained in a series of affidavits he had given to the committee and its acting chairman, Stuart Symington, while Walters testified in a closed session with Richard Helms, the former CIA director who was now the ambassador to Iran. After the hearing, Symington said that Walters and Helms told the committee that they did not know if Nixon knew about the attempts to block the FBI investigation, "but it's hard for me to visualize that the President knew nothing about this."

Walters put the blame on Bob Haldeman for raising the possibility of blocking the FBI investigation. "As I recall it, Mr. Haldeman said that the Watergate incident was causing trouble and was being exploited by the opposition."[116]

This testimony, along with a story that revealed new details about the FBI wiretaps in that morning's New York Times, gave more momentum to Haig and Buzhardt's call for the white paper. The Times' latest story by Hersh implicated Kissinger directly in the selection of targets for the wiretaps started in May 1969, saying that he "personally provided the Federal Bureau of Investigation with the names of a number of his aides on the National Security Council whom he wanted wiretapped." Hersh's source was impeccable: Sullivan, whose claims were damning. The wiretaps proved nothing, he told Hersh, except that some NSC officials were not personally loyal to Kissinger: "There wasn't one member of the [National Security Council] staff who was disloyal to the country. But they were disloyal to Kissinger, and they were giving him real problems." Some of the liberals Kissinger had hired, Sullivan said, "began to disagree with him and they weren't with him. Actually, they were disloyal—not to the country, but to him. Henry didn't mind disagreement in the family, but what he didn't like was these fellows arguing and losing and then going outside to leak things."[117]

Haig had two goals on May 18: talking with Agnew about his future and learning exactly what Dean had taken from the White House and whether he, Nixon, and Buzhardt could keep it secret. They could not. Stuart Symington already had the documents, and he had no desire to maintain secrecy; Symington had already rushed to spill the details of Walters's secret testimony about the White House cover-up attempts. Haig knew the damage done to the president this week had been severe. Nixon knew it, too. He had spent much of the two previous days alternating between raging about the enemies who were treating him unfairly and contemplating resignation.

"Shit," Nixon said. "If I were to resign, I would admit the whole goddamn thing. If I resign because they've made my job too hard, everybody will say the son of a bitch is guilty. I'm not going to do that, damnit."

"That would be impossible," Haig said.

"I've got to fight it out," Nixon said.

"Of course you're going to fight it out," Haig replied.[118]

Around this time there occurred another fateful meeting. Rear Adm. Robert Welander met for lunch with his former subordinate on the USS *Fox* and at the Pentagon, Lt. Bob Woodward, who told him that the story of the military spy ring might soon become public. What could Welander say about it? "[Woodward] said the issue was going to come up again and everything else and did I have anything further to say," Welander said. No, Welander said. He had been sworn to secrecy when he had been forced from the Joint Chiefs' liaison office and sent to a destroyer command in the Atlantic. Now, back at the Pentagon, he wanted to avoid the problems that forced him into exile.[119]

Woodward's meeting with Welander came just days after Pentagon investigator Donald Stewart had called the White House and mentioned his dissatisfaction at the Pentagon and his suspicions that Buzhardt had killed Stewart's investigation for political reasons. The options for Woodward's sources were limited: either Haig, Buzhardt, Len Garment, or Richard Tufaro, the White House lawyer who first spoke to Stewart. However, only Haig had a relationship with Woodward.

But Woodward did nothing with this great scoop; instead, he sat on it for months. Welander said Woodward that did not tell him his source, but when it was suggested to him in a 1987 interview that Woodward was not honest, Welander said, "I'm glad other people think so, too."[120] Publishing such a bombshell during the tumultuous days of May would have exploded the White House. The military leadership would have been implicated in the theft and leaking of White House secrets, which could have jeopardized Nixon's upcoming summit with Soviet leader Leonid Brezhnev. And if those involved were honest about their actions, then Haig's role in the spy ring would have been revealed, a betrayal that would have forced him out of the White House, ended his career, and perhaps led to prison. Woodward put keeping Haig's secret ahead of informing his readers.

After two weeks of deliberations, tentative feelers to potential candidates and rejections, attorney general designate Elliot Richardson selected a special prosecutor for Watergate. It was Archibald Cox, a solicitor general for John Kennedy, a Harvard Law School dean, and a venerable Yankee Democrat. Cox had been Richardson's mentor at Harvard, and the two shared an easy familiarity. Of all the possible choices, Haig and Nixon thought they could work with Cox.

"I see he got a humdinger," Haig said to Nixon about Richardson's choice.

"Who'd he get?" Nixon asked.

"A fellow named Cox that used to be solicitor general for Kennedy," Haig said.

He is well respected, Nixon said. "I don't think he's too bad. Did he take him?"

Not yet, Haig said, but the word is out, and it will be difficult for Cox to decline or for the Senate not to confirm Richardson.

"Cox is not a mean man," Nixon said. "He's partisan, but not that mean."

"That's right," Haig said. "That's the description I got. He's not a zealot."[121]

In less than two weeks, Nixon, Haig, and the small defense team would reverse gear and zealously attack Cox as a vicious partisan out to get Nixon. Their initial optimism faded as they realized Cox and his prosecutors had a wide mission and were taking every opportunity to dig into areas the president and his chief of staff preferred to avoid.

Although Nixon had agreed to release the white paper detailing the national security issues that led him to create the White House Plumbers, wiretap his staff and journalists, and try to block parts of the Watergate investigation, he still could not make a clean breast of everything. He complained about the treatment he was receiving from the press and his political enemies. Haldeman, who still talked with the president frequently, advised against giving up too much.

"My resigning didn't clear my name," Haldeman told Nixon on the afternoon of May 18. "My resigning proved to everybody in the world except the few people that believe in me that I'm guilty."

"The same as John [Ehrlichman]," Nixon said.

"And your resigning will prove it conclusively," Haldeman said. "It will prove that you're guilty, and that I'm guilty, and that everybody else here is guilty."

So, Nixon said, I need to fight.

"Because you aren't guilty," Haldeman said.

"I know I'm not," Nixon answered.

Haldeman's resignation, he told the president, "doesn't shake the world; your resigning does."[122]

As he fought, Nixon refused to reveal the military spy ring, because he could not let the world know how his cult of secrecy sowed the distrust that military leaders had toward him.

Nixon fretted as Haig and Buzhardt drafted the white paper. They also consulted the White House tapes so they could buttress their claims with enough facts to be convincing. As he worked closely with Haig, Garment said that it was obvious Haig was consulting something: "It was Buzhardt, myself, I think [speechwriter] Ray [Price] was involved and [Patrick] Buchanan and pieces would be—and Haig, and pieces would be drafted and taken into Nixon in the old Executive Office Building office for him to pass on it. From time to time Haig came back with detail that did not seem to be top of the head memory."[123] Nixon's schedule and the tapes show just how much he leaned on Haig and Buzhardt: Nixon spoke with Haig three times on May 20 as Nixon tried to relax at Camp David and then another thirteen times, including a trip together on the presidential yacht, *Sequoia*, on May 21, the day before the paper's release.[124]

Haig cared less about Watergate and more about the so-called national security events that led up to it, because "we've got to build a climate, the situation, what we were faced with," Haig told the president.[125]

Nixon's mood reflected the stress he endured each day. Not only were the Watergate hearings churning out a daily dose of bad press as witnesses recounted attempts to cover up the Watergate break-in or to spy on rival politicians, but leaks about non-Watergate missteps came at a rapid clip. Nixon also had to contend with the strains of running the government. His war policies faced growing congressional opposition; both houses of Congress were cutting money for the wars in Southeast Asia and trying to limit his war-fighting powers. A national energy crisis loomed on the horizon as gasoline prices had started to rise, which also threatened to spark another surge in inflation. His Republican allies feared the drag Nixon posed for their electoral futures and sought reassurance. These pressures would have taxed the most resilient politician, let alone one immersed in an existential crisis that would end in disgrace and exile.

Haig tried to calm Nixon even as he coaxed the president into authorizing a document that would implicate him in covering up the White House's connections to the Watergate break-in, approving the Huston Plan, and wiretapping his own staff and reporters. No one would accept Nixon's claims of national security reasons to justify himself. Haig, with Buzhardt's canny assistance, was maneuvering the president into signing his own death warrant.

The testimony of Watergate burglar James McCord on May 21 fueled the interest of Senator Lowell Weicker, the tall and voluble Connecticut Republican, to investigate the FBI's Internal Security Division, which had aided McCord and the Nixon campaign in identifying possible threats to the 1972 Republican National Convention. Weicker suspected more, however, such as a White House–directed crackdown on civil liberties and peaceful protests. He sought out Sullivan, hoping he would reveal what his division had done. Sullivan started as a willing participant, eager to cast his rivals in a negative light, but he soon proved skittish and evasive as the questioning turned toward him. Sullivan had much to hide, as his division handled some of the most politically sensitive and explosive issues of the previous twenty years, including an extensive infiltration of the U.S. Communist Party called Solo. Through Solo, the code name for the Chicago-based brothers Morris and Jack Childs, the FBI learned that Stanley Levison, an influential aide to civil rights leader Martin Luther King Jr., had ties to the Communist Party. Sullivan himself wrote King a threatening anonymous letter in 1964 in which he promised to ruin his life. Sullivan badly wanted to keep such actions secret. He could not afford an investigation that pried them into the open and also exposed Haig.

Before Nixon could release his white paper, Tom Huston appeared late on the afternoon of Monday, May 21, before the Senate Armed Services Committee and Stuart Symington. Huston had left the White House in disgust in the summer of 1971, angered by the president's failure to implement the plan that bore Huston's name. What Nixon attempted to explain away as the result of cataclysmic domestic security threats seemed more sinister under the lights of the Armed Services Committee hearing room. Huston's plan, much of which still remains secret almost fifty years later, was breathtaking in scope. It would have allowed the FBI to resume surreptitious break-ins of the homes and businesses of suspects without a warrant. The National Security Agency was granted more power to eavesdrop on the calls of people in the United States, a violation of its charter. The CIA had already violated its charter with Operation Chaos, a campaign to target student antiwar protesters, and would have been granted similar powers with the Huston Plan. Nixon feared its implications, whether it took effect or not, because while he wanted the power, he did not want the American people to know about it. When they did, the immediate reaction justified Nixon's fears. "There didn't seem to be any limitation to the amount of burglary," Symington said after the hearing. "This is the most fantastic document I've ever read."[126] Senators already distrusted Nixon's national security arguments; Henry Jackson of Washington had called Nixon on those arguments a week earlier as intelligence officials tried to keep the plan secret. Now Symington had released many of the plan's details, and while Huston's work came two years before the failed Watergate break-in, his plan and Nixon's desire for it easily fell under the banner of the Watergate scandal.

It was the fourth time in a week that Symington had exposed a key White House secret to the public. His hearing on May 14 led Vernon Walters to acknowledge the meetings at the White House in which Bob Haldeman and John Ehrlichman had tried, on Nixon's orders, to get the CIA to block the FBI's Watergate investigation. Symington then conducted a news conference the following day to amplify what Walters had testified to in a closed hearing. On May 17 his panel questioned Walters again, who provided even more details about the White House's attempted obstruction. And now he had Huston before his panel explaining the intent of his plan.

As the Pentagon's chief lawyer, Buzhardt could have stopped the release of the documents to Symington. "These documents were turned over to the committee by the Defense Department without consultation with the FBI or to our knowledge National Security Agency or CIA," an FBI memo shows.[127] Buzhardt knew which documents Dean had removed from the White House two days before Buzhardt told Nixon about their contents. During the same conversation he and Haig pushed Nixon to reveal his support of the Huston Plan and the reasons why he supported covering up the White House involvement in Watergate.

The document that press secretary Ron Ziegler and Garment released on the afternoon of May 22 was presented as Nixon's final version of the truth. It had three main goals: "To set forth the facts about my own relationship to the Watergate matter," to deal with some of the topics that "are currently being discussed in Senate testimony and elsewhere," and "to draw the distinctions between national security operations and the Watergate case." In this remarkable document, Nixon acknowledged using his Watergate cover-up to protect his earlier cover-ups, and while he hoped national security considerations would explain away most of his actions, Nixon had opened himself to more questions about whether he obstructed justice. Nixon admitted that his first-term policy successes— opening relations with China, creating détente with the Soviet Union, and ending the Vietnam War—depended on obsessive secrecy and that "leaks of secret information about any one could endanger all."

On the question of the FBI wiretaps, Nixon took full responsibility, although he privately blamed Henry Kissinger for pleading for them in order to stop leaks. "I authorized this program," the white paper stated. "Each individual task was undertaken in accordance with procedures legal *at the time* and in accord with long-standing precedent." Nixon's anodyne acceptance of responsibility for the wiretaps raised more questions and obscured what had actually happened. Kissinger, as Nixon and Haig knew, provided much of the impetus for the early taps, and he and Haig actively selected the targets. Haig particularly wanted to tap the phones of Col. Robert Pursley, the military aide to Defense Secretary Melvin Laird. Nixon also knew the White House used the national security wiretaps for political purposes, such as when the White House was lobbying Congress to approve a planned antiballistic missile system.

As for the Huston Plan, details of which started to spill forth in that morning's *Washington Post* after Symington's hearing with Huston, Nixon emphasized that it had not taken effect. "It was this unused plan and related documents that John Dean removed from the White House and placed in a safe deposit box," Nixon wrote in the white paper. While the plan never officially got started, it spawned another unit, the Intelligence Evaluation Committee, which was meant to coordinate intelligence on radical groups generated by all agencies. Dean was the point man for that committee, hence his possession of the documents. Also, Nixon wanted the Huston Plan to work. He backed down only because he feared antagonizing J. Edgar Hoover at the FBI, who, while a diminished force in the administration, remained powerful enough for Nixon to fear crossing him.

Nixon's incomplete explanation of the creation of the Plumbers ignored the goriest details. "This was a small group at the White House whose principal purpose was to stop security leaks and to investigate other sensitive security matters," Nixon said. Nixon created the unit not because he wanted a complete investigation of Daniel Ellsberg and the leaking of the Pentagon Papers but because he wanted to destroy Ellsberg and hide whatever documents existed about Nixon's use of an intermediary in late October 1968 to persuade the South Vietnamese government to skip a meeting at the Paris Peace Talks to end the Vietnam War. Nixon told the truth about having no knowledge of the break-in at Ellsberg's psychiatrist's office, but he created and fostered the culture that led to it, which he acknowledged. "However, because of the emphasis I put on the crucial importance of protecting the national security, I can understand how highly motivated individuals could have felt justified in engaging in specific activities that I would have disapproved had they been brought to my attention," he wrote. Some things, Nixon said, remained too sensitive to reveal. These vital national security issues, he insisted, would have to remain secret.[128]

Perhaps the greatest single issue Nixon was hiding—the existence of the military spy ring—was not mentioned at all in the white paper. That would remain a secret.

If Nixon hoped the white paper would quell the demand for more information from him and other officials, public reaction quickly stripped away those illusions. Garment and Ziegler were immediately beset by questions from the White House press corps about specific details in the white paper and whether Nixon would conduct another news conference.

"President Nixon's lengthy statement on the Watergate scandals reveals more of the truth than he or any of his senior associates had previously been willing to put on the record," the New York Times editorialized. "The involvement of the President and his White House aides in the tangled events that led to these assorted crimes and conspiracies and the subsequent attempt to cover them up is much more extensive than had previously been acknowledged. Although the President's latest statement discloses more of the truth, only the statements of other principals can show whether the whole truth has yet been revealed," the *Times* concluded. "Mr. Nixon has reiterated several specific denials about the extent of his knowledge of and therefore his culpability for various misdeeds. Those denials have to stand the test of time. Meanwhile, it is abundantly clear that an inflated and erroneous conception of 'national security' led to criminal behavior which has brought the office of the President into grave disrepute."[129]

Haig and Buzhardt not only talked Nixon into releasing the white paper, which, despite its numerous falsehoods, also admitted to covering up the Watergate break-in, wiretapping his staff and reporters, and creating the Plumbers, but also persuaded him to renounce claiming executive privilege to limit the testimony of his current and former staff. That meant leads generated by his admissions in the white paper could be followed by Senate and special prosecutor investigators with few limits. Haig and Buzhardt persuaded Nixon to admit potential crimes and then to limit his tools for defending himself. As Nixon himself wrote, "Thus I set more traps that would be sprung by the tapes months later."[130]

Nixon and Haig tried to absorb the fallout. Nixon told Haig that he had to weaken the first draft of the white Paper he received: "I ordered that they use any means necessary, including illegal means, to accomplish this goal. The president of the United States can never admit that."

Haig also shared a piece of good news. He had talked to William Ruckelshaus at the FBI, who told Haig that Felt, whom they suspected of leaking details of the FBI wiretaps, had been fired.

"He [Ruckelshaus] is fine," Haig said. "He's giving this guy notice."

"Felt?" Nixon asked.

"Yeah, he'll be leaving in two weeks," Haig said. "He's fired."

"Why?" Nixon asked.

"Because he just—he didn't tell him why," Haig said.

"Is that right?" Nixon said.

"He did the right thing," Haig said. "This son of a bitch. He's the source of an awful lot of the heat that developed two weeks ago."

Now Felt was gone, and the president and Haig enjoyed his demise, not realizing that their supposed ally, Sullivan, was the person causing their problems.[131]

The Senate confirmed Elliot Richardson as attorney general on May 24 by a vote of 82–3. He immediately appointed Cox as the special counsel for Watergate and what would become a growing portfolio of other potential cases. Nixon and Haig almost immediately started to view Cox as an enemy. After hosting a grand dinner at the White House for the recently freed prisoners of war from North Vietnam, Nixon retired to the White House and called Haig. Tired, his voice slurred, Nixon at turns celebrated the dinner and lamented his future prospects.

"Coming right down to it, Al, when you look at it, you know, all this crap we're taking, and the Congress being Democratic and the Republicans being weak and all the rest, wouldn't it really be better for the country, you know, to just check out?" Nixon asked.

Haig just laughed.

"No, no, seriously, I mean that, because I—you see, I'm not at my best," Nixon said. "I've got to be at my best, and that means fighting this damn battle, fighting it all out. And I can't fight the damn battle, you know, with people running in with their little tidbits and their rumors and all that crap, and did the president, you know, make a deal, you know, to pay off this one and that and the other thing. Huh?"

Haig tried to reassure Nixon, telling him the POW dinner was a huge success and that the white paper had helped the stock market to rise the previous day. The Watergate committee hearings, Haig continued, were not going well and "proved that these bastards don't even know what they're talking about." He praised Nixon's speech and said the White House had turned a corner.

Nixon still feared Richardson, whom he would watch being sworn in the next afternoon.

"See, Richardson's in the spot where, as you know, he's going to have to prove that he's the white knight and all that bull, and so he's going to try to—he and Archie Cox will try to try the president, you know, well, and all that crap. How do you handle that?"

"I don't think those people are going to—well, Richardson, what does he gain by that?" Haig answered. "He's going to have to keep that guy under control, that Cox. But Cox, he's not much."

"You don't think so?" Nixon asked.

"No. No. I've checked on him," Haig said. "He's not an effective guy. In fact, I'm not sure those things will ever even come to trial. . . . He'll have these cases, these portfolios, so screwed up nobody'll be able to be brought to court."

Haig had to buck up Nixon's emotions at this moment, but he also displayed a seriously flawed view of Cox's effectiveness. Within days, the White House would be complaining about the ruthless Cox and how he was pushing beyond what they considered his charter. Nixon sensed the sharks circling his life raft, but Haig acted as if the fins poking above the waves were from dolphins. "Hell, they've dug up all they can dig," he said, but Nixon knew better.

"No, they've got more," he said, adding that John Dean would try to save himself with his upcoming testimony.

Again Haig dispensed more bad advice.

"Well, I think he said most of what he had to say," Haig said. "I really do believe that, sir. And it doesn't make any difference what they have. The power of the office is in there. The power of your accomplishments in the past and ahead arc going to swamp any of these other difficulties."[132]

Nixon attended Richardson's swearing in at the White House the following afternoon after he and Richardson met for about twenty minutes in the Oval Office. Richardson praised Nixon for saying he would not use executive privilege to prevent his staff members from testifying. Nixon cautioned him, however, that he would still use executive privilege to protect presidential documents. The two reminisced about how Nixon campaigned for Richardson when he was a candidate in Massachusetts in the 1960s, when Nixon was just a former vice president working for a New York law firm. Their attention turned to the Plumbers, who, both men recognized, made some incredibly stupid decisions as they tried to stop leaks from the White House. "They did lead us to controlling a lot of leaks," Nixon said. If they did not, then the SALT arms talks would not have worked or the opening to China. "I didn't inform Mel Laird," the defense secretary, Nixon said, which Nixon did not realize was why Laird was spying on the White House. "The Russians would have been up the wall.... It's become a heroic act to destroy a policy you're against."[133]

With that, Nixon ushered Richardson into the White House for his swearing in. Cox had taken his oath a few hours earlier in a ceremony surrounded by members of the Kennedy family, including Nixon nemesis Edward Kennedy, the senator from Massachusetts and brother of the slain president. The twin oaths put the problems for Nixon in a different realm. He now had a dedicated prosecutor with free rein to look into all aspects of the Watergate case and any other potential wrongdoing that caught his eye or the eyes of his aggressive staff. Investigators who had felt frustrated by what they had considered White House interference in their investigation had a new outlet, and they intended to take advantage of it. Richardson's challenge was that after being appointed to his third cabinet post by the president, some people considered him a Nixon stooge. Richardson demonstrated his independence by giving Cox the leeway to explore whatever leads he wanted. Nixon and Haig now worried they faced a runaway prosecutor.

Nixon's Watergate problems were spilling into other parts of his presidency. On May 31 the Senate voted 63–19 to cut off funding pay for the bombing of rebels in Cambodia on behalf of the besieged government. It was the exposure of Nixon's secret bombing campaign in Cambodia in May 1969 that led him, Kissinger, and Haig to seek wiretaps on government officials they suspected of leaking. Now a war-weary Congress wanted to end the bombing ordered by an administration whose credibility diminished every day.

Few presidents had weathered a month as calamitous as May 1973 was for Nixon. He started the month alone and without his top two aides, Bob Haldeman and John Ehrlichman, on whom he had relied constantly. In Alexander Haig, Nixon thought, he had found someone to replace Haldeman as his sounding board and enforcer. By month's end, Haig was firmly in control and ready to add some allies to the White House staff to further lock in his influence.

3   June 1973

Nixon weathered May with his presidency intact, but the wounds from the month would be fatal. He just did not know it yet. But Alexander Haig did. Enlisted to save Nixon, Haig only exacerbated the president's problems. Either alone or with Fred Buzhardt's help, Haig allowed the damaging testimony by Vernon Walters that exposed the White House's attempt to use the CIA to block the FBI's Watergate investigation. He let Robert Cushman, Walters's predecessor at the CIA, give up records that showed how the CIA helped the Plumbers harass Daniel Ellsberg. Those records broke Nixon's ability to claim executive privilege with the white paper.

After reshuffling the cabinet in May, Haig consolidated his hold on the White House by bringing in new White House aides: former defense secretary Melvin Laird took the role once filled by John Ehrlichman, and Bryce Harlow, a skilled advisor and Capitol Hill player from the Eisenhower administration and first Nixon term, returned as a bridge between the White House and Congress. Laird, a sixteen-year House veteran, and Harlow knew Congress and Republican Party politics as well as anyone in Washington. They could gauge the shifting moods among the GOP caucus and sense what political capital remained for Nixon, whose landslide reelection the previous November appeared as only a distant memory.

Recruiting Laird reunited Haig and Buzhardt with their fellow conspirator in the military spy ring cover-up. Laird and Haig butted heads multiple times during Nixon's first term, often over troop levels in Vietnam and the Vietnamization program, which replaced U.S. troops with South Vietnamese soldiers, but they agreed that the military needed to know more about Nixon's secret maneuvering. Haig maintained one channel with the Joint Chiefs of Staff, for which Nixon would have fired him if he knew about it, and Laird knew it. When the spy ring was first uncovered in December 1971, Laird commissioned Buzhardt's report for the Pentagon to cover up for Haig and himself. Laird eagerly agreed to ship Yeoman Charles Radford, the young aide who stole White House documents for the Chiefs, far from Washington. For his final year as defense secretary, Laird had the best of both worlds. He had eliminated the Chiefs' liaison office at the National Security Council, which he knew the White House used to bypass him, protected his clients in the uniformed military, and scored a favor from Haig.

Nixon, Haig, Laird, and Harlow met for an hour and thirty-five minutes in the Birch Lodge at Camp David to determine the terms of their joining the White House staff. Harlow had a long and respected pedigree. He had worked on Capitol Hill for two House Democrats and then joined the White House staff of President Dwight Eisenhower, writing speeches and working as his chief lobbyist to Congress. After Eisenhower left office, Harlow became the chief lobbyist for the Procter & Gamble Corporation, the giant consumer products company, and then jumped back to the White House after Nixon's election in 1968 to run congressional relations again, leaving in 1970. Now Nixon had the difficult task of coaxing Harlow back from Procter & Gamble again to join a White House reeling from scandal. Selling Harlow on returning was more difficult than selling Laird, who was more interested in keeping his own secrets.

Laird's wife never trusted Nixon, and she feared her husband would sink deeper into an ever-thickening morass, so Laird asked Nixon directly: "Mr. President, did you have anything to do with the break-in or the cover-up?"

"Absolutely not," Nixon said.[1]

This account, from Laird's memoirs, is hard to believe. Laird worked for Nixon for four years as defense secretary. He did some of Nixon's campaign dirty work in 1968, floating rumors that President Lyndon Johnson had agreed to some kind of nefarious deal with North Vietnam to stop the bombing there. In fact, it was Nixon who was engaged in the campaign trickery, working with a go-between, staunch anticommunist Anna Chennault, to tell the South Vietnamese government not to go to Paris for peace talks with the North Vietnamese before the 1968 election because Nixon would give them a better deal than the desperate Johnson. Nixon would spend his entire presidency covering up the "Chennault affair" with Laird's help.

The attempts to lure Laird and Harlow to the White House staff came as Democratic senators began to attack Haig's dual status as chief of staff and four-star army general. Haig's alleged temporary appointment was a sham; Nixon and Haig had already decided he would stay through the second term. Now Democratic senators Stuart Symington of Missouri and William Proxmire of Wisconsin wanted the Pentagon to say how long Haig would remain on active duty.[2] Symington had bedeviled Nixon since almost the moment the president took office, taking issue with the secret use of the CIA in Southeast Asia, criticizing Kissinger's role leading a secret government inside the White House, and exposing the White House's attempt to use the CIA to block the FBI's Watergate investigation. In a four-and-a-half-page letter to Deputy Defense Secretary William Clements, Symington implied that Haig's appointment violated the law and asked sixteen questions about the appointment and how long it could last before Haig would have to leave the army. Proxmire, one of the Senate's biggest mavericks, had also called for Haig to resign either the chief of staff job or his army post.

On June 3 Nixon was hit by two bombshell stories in the *New York Times* and the *Washington Post* that detailed how John Dean had met with Nixon forty times between January and April to discuss the Watergate cover-up. More dangerously for Nixon, the *Times* reported that its source "also suggested that Mr. Dean may have tape recorded some of his White House conversations.... 'Everybody taped everybody else then,' the source said. 'Dean did it himself.'"[3] Both Nixon and Haig knew Nixon held the real tape recordings of those meetings.

Nixon wrote in his memoirs that the *Post* story filled him with dread as he read about Dean's claim that they had discussed hush money for the Watergate burglars in March 1973. "I felt discouraged, drained and pressured," Nixon wrote. "I asked Haig whether I should resign." Haig said no and urged Nixon to listen to the tapes.[4]

Nixon spoke with Ron Ziegler, his press secretary, that morning to determine their next moves. They shared a renewed but misplaced sense of optimism, and Nixon displayed a complete ignorance of what was happening with his new chief of staff.

"I didn't talk to Al very long, because we had other problems, but he seemed to think you made considerable progress on your meetings and plans and so forth," Nixon told Ziegler, adding that Haig said he thought Laird would join the staff. "Well, Al's a real operator," Nixon continued. "You know, when you think of sacrifices, Al's making the biggest one. He's going to have to resign from the army."

"Yes," Ziegler said, "I talked to him about that last night. He said, 'Ron, I've always done all my life what I thought was the right thing to do. I'm not going to back off from that now.' I had a nice talk with him last night, and he's a fine man."

"By God, there's so much character in that man, it's unbelievable," Nixon said.

Ziegler agreed.

"Unbelievable," Nixon said. "Well, I called him later last night. Um, I just don't know many people who would do that."

"He's a very selfless man," Ziegler said.

"He's a four-star general living in that beautiful free house and all those servants and everything and good God almighty. It's really something," Nixon said.

"Well, he's made it very clear, like a lot of people around here, he's going to do what he can to help the president," Ziegler said.[5]

Later that day, Nixon called Haig and asked what they could do to counter Dean, with whom Nixon had spent hours plotting the Watergate cover-up during March. Haig downplayed the reports, saying that most Americans did not care about Watergate: "They're not reading it." Polls, however, showed Nixon's support dropping quickly, and his credibility was eroding.

Dean's allegations of a Watergate cover-up were no surprise, Nixon said. "We have not denied I was aware of a cover-up. The point is I was investigating the son of a bitch [Dean] to find out what he's up to."[6]

Nixon's problem, as the tapes from March showed, is that while Dean had participated in the cover-up, so had Nixon. They had spent most of the eight days between March 13 and 21 determining how to craft a written "Dean report" that would absolve the White House of any involvement in the cover-up. At one point on March 16, Dean assured Nixon on the telephone that "we will win."[7] It was a far cry from Dean's claim in recent interviews that he came to Nixon, aggrieved about what he had learned about the cover-up, to let the president know about "a cancer on the presidency." The cancer was not the cover-up itself, in which Nixon and Dean were fully immersed, but the blackmail attempts coming from the Watergate burglars.

Haig said Americans were sick of Watergate and that he disagreed with Buzhardt, Ziegler, and Len Garment, who wanted to take "a big offensive."

"I'm glad you're keeping morale," Nixon said. "I don't know how you do it."

If the latest report had come out on May 10, when the White House was absorbing constant body blows of bad news, "it would have knocked us over," Nixon said.[8]

Nevertheless, Nixon had to know what he and Dean had discussed. He remembered the multiple meetings with his counsel that started at the end of February, but the specifics remained cloudy. The stories in the *Times* and *Post* in which Dean claimed to have met with Nixon up to forty times during that period nettled the president, who knew he had only one way to determine who was telling the truth: the White House taping system.

In his memoirs, Haig characterized the morning of June 4 as one of desperation for Nixon.

"Al, this Dean testimony is fatal to me," Haig wrote that the president told him.

"Mr. President," Haig said he asked Nixon, "I must know in order to serve you. Is Dean telling the truth?"

"No, Al. He's lying. But the damage is done. The question is, Should I resign, put an end to things, save the country the agony of what's coming?" Haig wrote.[9]

Haig's account is gripping, self-serving, and, based on the tapes and Nixon's logs, most likely inaccurate. The Monday after the Dean revelations was June 4. The White House tapes indicate Nixon and Haig met that morning for about twenty minutes and discussed possible staff moves as well as the Dean allegations. Haig wrote that he went home after the conversation in which Nixon mentioned resigning, something he had done repeatedly in the previous weeks, and then returned the next day, which would have been June 5, and told Nixon he had the means to determine the truth. "A few days earlier, Nixon had told me in an offhand way that he had the means to tape-record conversations in the Oval Office and over the telephone," Haig wrote. He also told Nixon he could consult whatever tapes existed to determine if Nixon or Dean was telling the truth.[10] As the White House tapes indicate, Nixon told Haig about the taping system in great detail on May 8 and May 11. Once again Haig conflated details about Nixon and the tapes to hide what Haig knew about the tapes and when.

Nixon and aide Steve Bull walked to the room in the Old Executive Office Building that held the tapes. There Nixon quizzed Bull incessantly about the details of the taping system and the tapes themselves. At one point, Nixon asked why a certain conversation he thought had been recorded had not been. Bull told the president he was not sure and that there could have been a mechanical problem with the tape recorder. Nixon also impressed on Bull the need for secrecy about the taping system. "Nobody should know," Nixon said.[11]

Nixon played one tape and then called Haig on the phone. They discussed the FBI wiretaps of government officials and journalists, which remained a sore subject for both men. Haig said he was looking into two possible candidates for director of the FBI, the job temporarily held by William Ruckelshaus.

"[Attorney General Elliot] Richardson wants very much to get Ruckelshaus over there as deputy attorney general," Haig reported. "I don't think so. He's not a good team—"

"He's not our man," Nixon said of Ruckelshaus, who had already held three key positions in the administration.

"Yeah," Haig said. "It's not a good team."[12]

The concerns about Archibald Cox, the new Watergate special prosecutor, had increased each day as Cox added lawyers to his team, asked for more documents, and said he would push his investigation into areas perilously close to Haig's weak points. Richardson had appointed Cox, so that made him immediately suspect, and that suspicion now apparently had started to cling to Ruckelshaus. Haig and Nixon would learn in October just how dangerous a team Richardson and Ruckelshaus would turn out to be.

Haig again told Nixon that Watergate would blow over. "Hell, if this had been three weeks ago you'd be in—our phones would be buzzing every minute."

Nixon was tapped out by listening to almost nine hours of tapes.

"This is hard work," he told Haig, who agreed. "But I've got to do it. Got to do it. And it's best for me to do it, too."

"Only you," Haig said. "Only you."

After listening to more tapes, Nixon called Haig to express relief. "The whole damn meetings are a fraud," Nixon said. "I didn't realize it, but it was a damn fraud. Yeah. [Nixon's staff] didn't find it in the files, but I've listened to stuff, and you know, looking back I can see where [Dean] may have been involved. I wasn't involved."

Then Nixon asked Haig about Laird, whom Nixon was excited to have back in the fold because he considered him a savvy political operative and occasional pain in the ass. "Right. Right. Al, you've done a great job, believe me," Nixon said. "Getting Mel to [unclear]. You'll get a hell of a load off me if you get Mel, Bryce [Harlow]—the three of you will be— you'll run the shop. You're the chief of staff."[13]

As Nixon spent most of the day listening to tapes, Richardson gave his first news conference as attorney general. Richardson answered questions carefully because he was gradually learning the details of the various cases tied to Watergate and wanted to avoid drawing fire from the White House. Still, Richardson could not ignore the obvious problems with Nixon's claims about national security, which "even as put forward by the people who were directly involved, is not convincing." He said Cox had the authority to investigate the Plumbers, a delegation of power that directly threatened Haig, who had asked for the Plumbers to investigate the first reports of leaks to Jack Anderson during the India-Pakistan war. That investigation, in coordination with Pentagon gumshoe Donald Stewart, uncovered the military spy ring. A criminal investigation could uncover Haig and Laird, who continued to hide his multiple operations spying on the White House.[14]

James McCord's testimony in May fueled an interest by Senator Lowell Weicker, a Connecticut Republican, in investigating the activities of the FBI's Internal Security Division, which had aided McCord and the Nixon campaign in identifying possible threats to the 1972 Republican National Convention. Weicker suspected more, however, such as a White House–directed crackdown on civil liberties and peaceful protests. He started talking with William Sullivan to see if the White House had abused the powers of the FBI.[15] Sullivan, eager to damage his rivals, was at first willing but then backed away. Sullivan had much to hide.

By June, Nixon and Haig knew they had a problem with Vice President Spiro Agnew that would not go away. In his memoirs, Haig claimed he first heard about Agnew's legal problems in the second week of June, just a week after Nixon listened to his tapes with Dean. Richardson came to

Haig's office and told him that "Vice President Agnew's name had come up in an investigation of kickbacks connected to public construction projects in Baltimore."[16]

Richardson said the federal prosecutors in Baltimore were taking the case seriously. Once again, Haig's account covered up what he already knew. Haig said he immediately feared that Congress would impeach Nixon and Agnew, which would make Carl Albert, the Democratic Speaker of the House from Oklahoma, president. "I called Fred Buzhardt and told him what Richardson had just told me and what I feared," Haig wrote. Haig had to "decouple" the two problems, so he rushed to tell Nixon. "The President received the news with remarkable composure," Haig wrote, not realizing that Nixon had known about Agnew's problems since April 10, when the vice president told Bob Haldeman about the investigation. "I did not learn these details until years afterward," Haig wrote.[17] However, the White House tapes show that Nixon told Haig about Agnew on May 17, and an examination of Nixon's tapes and logs shows that Haig did not go to the Oval Office after talking with Richardson to brief the president about Agnew.[18] Instead, Nixon, Agnew, and Haig met on June 14, and Agnew shared his fears about his legal future and begged for a greater role in the administration. They also plotted their plans to defend Agnew and worried about Agnew's ties with Charles Colson, the former Nixon aide who had become Agnew's attorney.

"Well, I'd tell him that he's doing a great job," Haig told Nixon before Agnew walked into the Oval Office. But when it came to specifics, such as Agnew playing a greater role in economic policy, there just would not be room for him.

Nixon and Agnew traded small talk for a few minutes before Agnew said that one of his former assistants when he was Baltimore County executive in the 1960s, William Fornoff, had just pleaded guilty to bribery. "And now, he is—has made a deal," Agnew said. "He's singing about everybody he ever gave anything to and—"

"Oh God," Nixon said.

"I'm going to be indicted, it looks like," Agnew said.

"For what?" Nixon asked.

Agnew explained the campaign contributions and the transactional nature of construction projects in Maryland. Nixon interrupted, saying that if grand juries wanted to indict someone in that world, they could indict any governor, such as Nelson Rockefeller in New York.

"Well, there are some income tax things, something of that sort," Agnew said.

"Oh, boy," Nixon said.

"It's just murder," Agnew continued. "But that's what's going on, and I think we ought to brace ourselves, 'cause this is going to get worse."

"I want your only contact on the matter of this to be with Al, and there's only one other person you should know about that we are going to bring, and we're going to announce it today," Nixon said. "You probably can guess who it is. Bryce [Harlow]. Do you trust him?"

"Absolutely," Agnew said.

"All right," Nixon said. "And Bryce, I wanted to give—he makes some real smooth plays. What do you think, Al? You think that's good?"

"Yes," Haig said.

Nixon asked Agnew what "the hell we can do."

"I don't know," Agnew said, adding that some of the people implicated in the investigation had asked him to intervene. "What do you want me to do, obstruct justice?" Agnew said he told them. He was afraid he would never be able to wash off the stink of the investigation. Eventually, someone, Agnew continued, would surface and say, "He gave me a kickback of some kind. Came over here and handed me $50,000."

Just as Nixon feared the arrest of the Watergate burglars would uncover his other secrets, Agnew feared the investigation led by U.S. Attorney George Beall would reveal Agnew's acceptance of bribes and tax evasion. That could also inflict harm on Beall's brother, J. Glenn, the Republican senator from Maryland, who had received donations from a secret Nixon fund in 1970 to get elected.

"Glenn Beall's the only way to influence this," Agnew said.

"Well, Glenn Beall better take a real deep   we helped him bury that one in '70," Nixon said, "with [Chuck] Colson," Nixon's hard-nosed political aide whose law firm now represented Agnew.

Agnew said they had to get Glenn Beall to persuade his brother to end his investigation before it reached the vice president. Complicating the issue, Agnew continued, was that some of George Beall's top prosecutors were Democrats and therefore out to get Agnew.

"See, now, frankly, if all of our enemies were in here investigating us, that's the—" Nixon said.

"Some of them right here in our own bureaucracy," Haig added.

Nixon tried to reassure Agnew.

"You forget you mentioned it to us, and let Al and me work on it," Nixon said.

Agnew, not Haig, raised the issue of double impeachment.

"They're trying to get both of us at the same time and get Carl Albert to be president," Agnew said.

"Oh God," Haig said.

"That's what it really is," Agnew said.

Nixon deftly turned the conversation from Agnew's political problems to the role he could play in the administration. Apart from speaking tours during which he would attack the news media, Agnew's role in the first term revolved around stoking the conservative base that Nixon might have alienated with his foreign policy moves with China and the Soviet Union. Now with Agnew in political jeopardy and the reelection campaign behind them, Agnew had little to do. Nixon had reduced him to begging.

"Isn't there some foreign policy assignment that's important I could do?" Agnew asked.

"Yes," Nixon said. "Yes, there could be. I don't want one, though, that looks like it's froth."[19]

Agnew got neither a bigger role in the administration nor assurance that Nixon could make his political problem go away. The vice president of the United States, a man a heartbeat away from the world's most powerful job, had been reduced to a case that was assigned to two staff aides, Haig and Harlow.

Haig remained silent during most of the meeting because he knew that everything Agnew was telling Nixon was going on tape, including how the vice president wanted the president to use his power to obstruct justice.

On June 18 Nixon welcomed Soviet leader Leonid Brezhnev to Washington for their second face-to-face summit. Despite the cloud of Watergate, they accomplished much, reaching deals on agricultural sales to continued nuclear arms limits. Nixon relished this part of the job, which played to his strengths and helped him escape his political problems, even if for just a few days.

Nixon took a break from the summitry with Brezhnev for an Oval Office meeting with Haig and Laird. Before Laird arrived, the president and Haig again reviewed Agnew's growing problems, which he had shared liberally with Haig, who told Nixon that Agnew is "very nervous about this Maryland thing."

"We need that like a hole in the head," Nixon said.

Haig said he wanted to reach out to George Beall, but without leaving a trace. He hoped Laird, the White House's best advocate with Congress, would talk to Beall's brother and ask him to make sure he had his aggressive assistant U.S. attorneys, many of them Democrats, under control.

"I think you better talk to Mel," Nixon said.

"I'll talk to him," Haig answered.

After some back and forth, Nixon reconsidered. "Is Mel or Harlow the best to do this?"

"Harlow is in St. Croix," Haig said.

Nixon suggested that congressional relations chief William Timmons should make the contact with Senator Beall instead of Laird. "He's more discreet," Nixon said.

Then, as he had throughout the day, Haig gave Nixon more false hope about Dean's impending testimony, saying that the revelations that Dean had used campaign money to help pay for his wedding in the fall of 1972 would destroy Dean's credibility. "It just finishes Dean as a threat," Haig said in another classic misreading of the situation.[20]

Nixon and Brezhnev ended their summit with meetings in San Clemente, where Nixon remained after Brezhnev departed. It was there that Nixon and Haig monitored the much-anticipated appearance of Dean before the Watergate committee.

On June 25 Dean, remade from a blond playboy into a mild-mannered young lawyer, sat before the Senate Watergate Committee to give the testimony that Nixon had feared because he knew just how much Dean knew about the cover-up. Some of the earlier leaks had helped force Nixon to release the May 22 white paper in which the president acknowledged trying to hide White House connections to Watergate. Earlier in June, leaks about Dean's impending testimony forced Nixon to spend an entire day listening to tapes of his meetings with Dean. Nixon felt the tapes showed he was telling the truth, but he still worried about his exposure to impeachment.

Dean started slowly by reading a lengthy prepared statement that consumed the first day of testimony. He recounted incident by incident from the moment he arrived at the White House, and with each step, there seemed to be plenty of blame to go around. Dean tried to downplay some of his claims, saying he was naming fellow Nixon aides only because he had to. "Some of these people I will be referring to are friends, some are men I greatly admire and respect, and particularly with reference to the President of the United States," he said. "I would like to say this. It is my honest belief that while the President was involved that he did not realize or appreciate at any time the implications of his involvement, and I think that when the facts come out that the President is forgiven."[21]

Dean's first day of testimony touched on the decisions made by John Mitchell, the former attorney general who ran Nixon's reelection campaign, and their desire for political intelligence for the 1972 race. Dean also distanced himself from the Huston Plan, the aborted attempt to unshackle the domestic intelligence apparatus. "I was instructed by Haldeman to see what I could do to get the plan implemented," Dean said of a 1970 order from Nixon's chief of staff. "I thought the plan was totally uncalled for and unjustified." Instead, Dean said, he agreed to work on an intelligence evaluation committee that would coordinate information gathered across the intelligence community. After that, the administration, he said, could remove the restraints on some intelligence-gathering practices that were called for in the Huston Plan.[22] However, Dean was a far more active participant in the intelligence world than he portrayed during the Watergate hearings. CIA records show that Dean was one of two main recipients, along with Henry Kissinger, at the White House of intelligence collected by the agency's controversial CHAOS program, which monitored antiwar and student groups.[23]

Dean also told of the White House's deliberations after the Watergate break-in and how the White House wanted to help shape the Republican staff of the Senate Watergate committee, right down to selecting the general counsel. Although Dean was an avid consumer of political intelligence developed by the reelection campaign and the in-house White House investigators, he professed shock at some of the plans developed by G. Gordon Liddy, the campaign's counsel. "I did not fully understand everything Mr. Liddy was recommending at the time because some of the concepts were mind-boggling and the charters were in code names," Dean said.[24]

After the Watergate burglars were arrested and tied back to the Nixon campaign and the White House, Dean said he followed orders to facilitate the cover-up and did not start anything on his own initiative. John Ehrlichman, he said, told Dean to go to Vernon Walters, the number 2 official at the CIA, to get the agency's help in paying off the burglars. "I also recall Ehrlichman saying something to the effect that General Walters seems to have forgotten how he got where he is today," Dean said.[25]

As for his most telling moment in the cover-up, Dean said he told Nixon on March 21 that "there was a cancer growing on the Presidency and that if the cancer was not removed that the President himself would be killed by it. I also told him that it was important that this cancer be removed immediately because it was growing more deadly every day. I then gave him what I told him would be a broad overview of the situation and I would come back and fill in the details and answer any questions he might have about the matter."[26] In Dean's retelling, he felt the pangs of conscience about the growing nature of the Watergate cover-up and felt compelled to tell Nixon. Dean used the phrase "cancer on the presidency," the same phrase that appeared in his early May interview with *Newsweek* magazine and that grabbed the most attention in May. The context in the actual conversation, which would not be seen for months, was different. Nixon and Dean met with Haldeman, not alone, and Dean's warning to Nixon was not one of aggrieved conscience but one of concern that the cover-up would not hold.

"In other words, you, [what is] your judgment as to where it stands and where we go now[?]" Nixon asked Dean on March 21.

"I think, I think that, uh, there's no doubt about the seriousness of the problem we're, we've got. We have a cancer—within, close to the presidency, that's growing. It's growing daily. It's compounding, it grows geometrically now because it compounds itself. Uh, that'll be clear as I explain, you know, some of the details, uh, of why it is, and it basically is because first, we're being blackmailed, second, uh, people are going to start perjuring themselves very quickly that have not had to perjure themselves to protect other people and the like."[27]

Such differences were why Nixon felt reassured when he listened to the Dean tapes on June 4. Nixon knew Dean wanted to save himself at Nixon's expense and believed the tapes would prove Nixon was telling the truth. "I did not watch the hearings, but the reports I read filled me with frustration and anger," Nixon wrote in his memoirs. "Dean, I felt, was re-creating history in the image of his own defense."[28]

About five weeks after his first outreach to the White House, which led Fred Buzhardt to get him prosecuted for extortion, Pentagon investigator Donald Stewart contacted the White House again on June 25. This time, he wrote a letter to William Baroody, a member of the White House staff and close aide to Laird. Stewart sought Baroody's "guidance and assistance" in getting out of the Pentagon and another job somewhere else. He would not reveal anything that had a national security interest, Stewart wrote, although he felt no limits on talking about the Ellsberg and Jack Anderson cases because he did not believe Buzhardt's "interest in the Ellsberg or Anderson case was for security interest but rather totally for political considerations. . . . I knew professionally he [Buzhardt] was running the [Ellsberg] case for politics and not security." As for the Anderson-Radford case, the details spoke for themselves, since everyone involved was still working and not being punished. "As you can see, the foregoing is enough to upset an honest investigator and I just want to get the hell out of DoD."[29]

Just as he had with his telephone call in May to Richard Tufaro, Stewart had miscalculated. Baroody was no ordinary White House staffer but a longtime aide and friend of Laird, having joined the Wisconsin Republican's staff on the House Appropriations Committee in 1961 and then followed Laird to the Pentagon in 1969. Baroody was more than an aide; he was a Laird loyalist and the most likely person in the White House to sound the alarm on the threat Stewart caused.

Dean's testimony stretched into a second day, and he finally concluded reading his statement. Weicker, who had started pulling a thread of investigation that led to the police state tactics used by the White House, focused on those topics when he questioned Dean. If allowed to go unchecked, Weicker could have stumbled on details of the FBI wiretaps and other programs that would have implicated Haig.

Weicker voiced an even greater threat to Haig, although no one other than Haig and perhaps Sullivan realized it at the time.

"Mr. Chairman. I think one point that I would like to make clear here is that I have had a rather lengthy discussion with Mr. Sullivan on the subject matter which is being discussed here now," Weicker said. "I know that it would not be fair for me to state what the substance of that conversation was, I would much prefer to have it with Mr. Sullivan and I would hope when we are through with this particular witness we will give Mr. Sullivan the opportunity to explain his particular role in this matter."[30]

Before the final day of testimony, Haig, Buzhardt, and Garment made a half-hearted attempt to reel in Dean and challenge some of the inconsistencies in his testimony. In what was called the "Golden Boy" memo, they collected a series of details in which Dean presented false or misleading information to the committee.

The White House gave the information not to Howard Baker, the committee's top Republican, or his staff but to Senator Daniel K. Inouye, a Democrat from Hawaii and a World War II hero. Inouye read the details of the memo to Dean on June 27, and Dean danced around the discrepancies between his earlier interviews and his testimony. While Dean was shaken by some of the questions, they had little impact, and many of the memo's details focused just as much on the alleged illegal activities of John Mitchell, Nixon's former attorney general and campaign manager. Under questioning by Senator Edward Gurney, a Florida Republican and Nixon's biggest defender on the committee, Dean said the idea to have the CIA block the FBI's Watergate investigation was Mitchell's idea.

"Mitchell brought it up to you and then you brought it up to Haldeman and Ehrlichman, is that right?" Gurney asked.

"That is correct, yes," Dean said.[31]

It was not correct. Mitchell's logs would later show that he never spoke to Dean during the time in which Dean said they had the conversation that led to the fateful "smoking gun" conversation between Nixon and Haldeman on June 23, 1972.[32]

But, as Nixon soon realized, the facts did not matter. "I worried about the wrong problem," Nixon wrote in his memoirs. "I went off on a tangent, concentrating all our attention and resources on trying to refute Dean by pointing out his exaggerations, distortions, discrepancies. But even as we geared up to do this, the real issue had already changed. It no longer made any difference that not all of Dean's testimony was accurate. It only mattered if any of his testimony was accurate. And Dean's account of the crucial March 21 meeting was more accurate than my own had been. I did not see it then, but in the end it would make less difference that I was not as involved as Dean had alleged than that I was not as uninvolved as I had claimed."[33]

While Haig and Buzhardt had struck out in challenging Dean's testimony, on June 28 they focused on attacking Stewart. Buzhardt and Garment thought Stewart was trying to blackmail the White House into giving him another job, even making him FBI director. Garment said he was swayed by Haig and Buzhardt, who told Garment something along the lines of Stewart being a "troublemaker and we should do something."[34] Buzhardt, Garment said, "believed it would be calamitous for the country to have [the spy ring] come out. Haig also felt this way. . . . I accepted that the disclosure of Moorer-Radford would be hurtful." Buzhardt called Elliot Richardson on June 28 to talk about prosecuting

Stewart, and Garment sent Richardson an "eyes only" letter the next day. He included the memo Tufaro wrote in May and Stewart's letter from a few days earlier to Baroody. "Stewart," Garment wrote, "is using the threat of disclosure" to leverage a high-level job. Richardson, Garment concluded, needed to investigate the issue to determine if Stewart should be prosecuted.[35]

Buzhardt had other business in the last week of June. He went to Laird's home one evening near the end of the month to visit his old friend and boss at the Pentagon, and they went into Laird's basement.

"I've misled you, Mel," Laird said that Buzhardt told him. "The president was involved in the cover-up."

"How do you know?" Laird asked.

"I've listened to some of the tapes," Buzhardt said, "and he was in the cover-up right up to his eyeballs from the beginning."[36]

That was a stunning disclosure from the president's own attorney, one that violated attorney-client privilege and showed that the bond between Buzhardt and Laird outweighed that between Buzhardt and the president. It also indicated that Buzhardt knew about the June 23, 1972, taped conversation between Nixon and Bob Haldeman. Only Haig, who knew about the taping system and had listened to Haldeman and Nixon discuss the June 23 meeting, could have guided Buzhardt to that tape.

"I shouldn't be telling you this, because I am counsel for President Nixon," Laird said Buzhardt told him. "I was your counsel for four years over in Defense, and I've always tried to protect you. I've gone over all the tapes, and he's guilty."

Buzhardt's admission meant that he, too, was obstructing justice, because he had evidence of Nixon's guilt, as did Haig. What Laird did next would further unravel Nixon's defense. "I felt that I had to tell Bryce [Harlow]," Laird said.

So by the end of June, four of Nixon's main defenders, all of whom joined the White House after May 3, knew he was guilty. Haig, Buzhardt, Laird, and Harlow had to argue Nixon's innocence before Republican members of Congress and the media. They would all claim ignorance about the truth as they served their own interests and while ostensibly claiming to protect the president.

Laird said he confronted Nixon the next day as they walked back to the Oval Office after an early evening meeting in Nixon's hideaway office in the Executive Office Building.

"That's when I confronted Nixon," said Laird. "I can remember it as if it were yesterday. I told him that I had been advised that he had not leveled with me on his involvement in the Watergate cover-up, and it was hard for me to stay and work there. I said at the time, 'I would have come here probably anyway, if you'd have told me the truth. I was here to help because my friends on the Hill wanted me to be here to help. But having not been told the truth, it's very hard to help somebody. I just can't stay.'"

"Well, I hope you don't leave," Nixon said.[37]

Such a dramatic conversation would have alerted Nixon of the depth of his political problems. But if it happened, it was not in the last week of June or the first week of July. Nixon was in San Clemente from June 23 until July 9. His schedule for June indicates no meetings with Laird at the Old Executive Office Building, and no recordings exist of any such meetings.[38] Instead, it is more likely that Buzhardt knew about Nixon's guilt far earlier than he told Laird, his old friend, and that Laird took the job anyway because he had priorities that went beyond Nixon. Laird knew from the four years of the first term that Nixon routinely excluded him from information and that the uniformed military distrusted the president. Laird could cover up the multiple ways that he and the military spied on Nixon better from inside the White House than from anywhere else.

4   July 1973

About ninety million Americans watched some or all of John Dean's Senate testimony, which riveted the nation and rattled the White House. Still, Dean had not proved that Nixon had obstructed justice by abetting the cover-up or that he knew anything about the Watergate break-in. Each day, more Americans believed Nixon knew more than he admitted, but such feelings could not impeach him or make him quit, regardless of the president's private musings in the White House.

Nixon spent the first nine days of the month at his home in San Clemente, California, which on July 3 became the focus of more unwanted scrutiny. The *Los Angeles Times* reported that morning that Watergate Special Prosecutor Archibald Cox had started an initial inquiry into the $1.5 million that Nixon had paid for the home and the source of his money.[1] Cox and his staff wanted to know if any of that money had come from unions, corporations, or Republican campaign donors. Ever since Elliot Richardson named Cox, Nixon had suspected Cox's motives, believing the former Harvard Law School dean was out to get him for purely partisan reasons and wanted to remove him with the help of a cadre of dedicated and highly partisan prosecutors. Haig fed Nixon's paranoia, perhaps because he also suspected Cox wanted to take his investigation toward Haig.

Nixon told Haig to call Richardson back in Washington to share Nixon's dissatisfaction. At the same time, George Beall's team of prosecutors had driven from Baltimore to Washington to tell Richardson about the deepening investigation into Vice President Spiro Agnew. Haig had known since May that Agnew was in jeopardy as the grand jury into bribery and kickbacks into Maryland government contracting gained momentum. Agnew himself told Nixon and Haig in June that he feared a possible indictment, and Agnew had confessed his fears for his future to Haig since then. That afternoon, Richardson performed a delicate dance as he sat in his conference room with Beall and his prosecutors and then darted into his private office to talk to Haig, who kept demanding answers after talking to Nixon. Shortly after 1:00 p.m. Eastern Time, Haig again called Richardson, and Nixon got on the line, telling the attorney general he wanted a clear-cut and immediate public denial from Cox that any investigation into the San Clemente purchase was going on. Cox would give Nixon that denial, but the pressure from the president had so unnerved Richardson that he pondered quitting that day.[2]

While the countdown to Agnew's eventual demise continued, the Senate committee closed in on two fronts that threatened Haig and Nixon: the existence of the White House taping system and the internal security plans of the White House, which also included the FBI wiretaps that Haig enabled. On July 5 Larry Higby, a deputy to Bob Haldeman and then Haig, met with committee staffers to describe the workings of the White House staff, particularly as they related to Haldeman. Along with Nixon, Haldeman, and Alexander Butterfield, Higby was one of four people in the White House who knew about the taping system, because he had passed Haldeman's order to Butterfield to have it installed. Weeks earlier, Higby had asked Haldeman what he should do if the committee asked him about the tapes. Haldeman told Higby to claim executive privilege and say no more. During his July 5 interview, Higby felt the questions were heading to the taping system, but they eventually shifted direction, and he avoided having to say anything. Soon, Higby knew, someone who knew about the tapes would be asked a direct question.[3]

The next day, Higby told Haig about the meeting and asked what he should do if he was asked about the tapes in another interview. "I told him, 'Al, they're eventually going to get to the taping system,'" Higby said. Haig said the committee already knew about recordings made with Nixon's Dictabelt machine, but Higby said the committee seemed on the verge of discovering the entire taping system, which Higby then described to Haig in greater detail. Haig, Higby said, seemed astonished. "'I'll get back to you.' And I said, 'Fine. I've got to have guidance before I go up there.'" Higby had not been told yet that he would definitely be called to testify, but he believed it likely that he would be called.[4]

Higby expected Haig to also tell him to claim executive privilege. Instead, Haig told Higby the next day, July 7, to tell the truth, which Higby interpreted as meaning he should tell the committee about the tapes. That surprised Higby, but he thought Haig was just acting on Nixon's orders.[5]

Nixon was pushing back against Senator Sam Ervin and his committee. On July 7 he told the senator that he would neither appear before the committee nor give it any documents.[6] He did not know that soon enough he would be in a bigger fight over the fate of something far more damaging than any documents. In a misguided attempt to discredit Dean or somehow sabotage the White House's own case, Buzhardt, with Haig's approval, was sending documents to the committee's minority staff that would eventually boomerang back against Nixon.[7]

Senator Lowell Weicker, the maverick Connecticut Republican on the Watergate committee, was pushing ahead with his investigation into the various intelligence activities within the White House, starting with the Intelligence Evaluation Committee—the residue of the stillborn Huston Plan—and the FBI wiretaps. He or his staff had spoken with William Sullivan, the former FBI associate director, in May and June about the wiretaps and potential abuses of the FBI's Intelligence Division and the Justice Department's Internal Security Division, which had been under the direction of Robert Mardian, who later became the lawyer for the Nixon reelection committee. After his first attempts at obtaining information from the FBI and Cox's office were rebuffed as too broad, Weicker kept trying.

He and Sullivan met again on July 9 in Washington.

Weicker said he wanted to narrow the request to "those areas where there might be a request that was not correct."

Sullivan knew Weicker wanted him to testify before the committee, which he did not want to do. Under oath, unanticipated questions could arise and generate unexpected, embarrassing, or incriminating answers. Angry senators with an ax to grind could take their frustrations out on the witnesses, sparking a confrontation that could alter lives and careers. Although he was at the end of his career, Sullivan still harbored a desire to return to the FBI, which would not be helped by testifying before an open committee.

Sullivan hinted that he could lead Weicker to records that showed requests for illegal surveillance from the White House. Weicker wanted to know more about the FBI wiretaps, so he, Sullivan, and an aide went off to talk alone.

Why did the records of the wiretaps leave the FBI? Weicker asked.

"Mardian said there was a presidential request that the taps be brought in—then the request that the summaries of the taps be collected," Sullivan said. "[Mardian] wanted them all together in one bundle."[8]

Sullivan was maintaining the lie that he had told FBI investigators back in May, that he had nothing to do with Mardian's request to hand over the tap logs. In fact, it was Sullivan who created Mardian's request by telling him in July 1971 that he feared that FBI director J. Edgar Hoover, fearful that Nixon would try to fire him, would use the existence of the taps to blackmail Nixon into keeping him. Mardian then told Attorney General John Mitchell, who told Nixon, who ordered Mardian to fly to San Clemente and meet with him. Upon his return, Mardian asked Sullivan for the logs.

All of the details of the wiretaps were kept in Sullivan's office, away from the central files, Sullivan said. Hoover knew the taps were trouble and wanted to keep his distance. "I had seen nothing like it in thirty years at the FBI," Sullivan said.

On July 12 Sullivan was interviewed by Watergate committee investigator Scott Armstrong, a high school friend of *Post* reporter Bob Woodward. Once again, Sullivan was asked about the FBI wiretaps, and he repeated the lie that he had nothing to do with Mardian's request for tap logs. However, Mardian did not know the wiretaps existed until Sullivan told him.[9]

Haig and Buzhardt's continued cover-up of Haig's aid to the military spy ring hit a snag on July 2, when Henry Petersen, chief of the Justice Department's Criminal Division, told Attorney General Elliot Richardson there was no reason to prosecute Pentagon investigator Donald Stewart for blackmail. "We do not believe that the materials furnished by you and Mr. Garment warrant a criminal investigation of Stewart," and he added that it "is not at all clear" that Stewart had made a "threat" to disclose classified information, Petersen wrote. Richardson did not care. He wrote a note on Petersen's memo asking if Stewart could be charged with extortion or blackmail. That note landed on the desk of Carl Belcher, the head of the General Crimes Division at Justice. Stewart remained oblivious to all these machinations; he had not heard back from William Baroody after his June 25 letter, and no one had told him that his pleas had somehow been turned into evidence of alleged blackmail.[10]

On July 11 Mitchell, Nixon's former law partner and first attorney general, gave the Senate Watergate committee a glimpse of what he thought was happening inside the White House. When Senator Daniel Inouye of Hawaii asked Mitchell what the White House would do if the committee subpoenaed the papers that John Dean had stolen from the White House, Mitchell said, "Well, I am afraid you are going to have to ask Mr. Buzhardt that; he seems to be making most of the decisions over there."[11]

The following day, July 12, would upend Nixon's presidency. He awoke around 5:00 a.m., wracked by a sharp pain in his chest. The previous weeks had worn down his health and resistance to infection. At 5:45 a.m. he called Maj. Gen. Walter Tkach, his physician, who led several examinations in which one doctor thought Nixon had an intestinal infection, while another diagnosed pneumonia.[12]

Nixon pushed ahead much of the day, meeting with doctors in the morning and then with Henry Kissinger and the West German foreign minister. He then spoke with Senator Ervin and said he would not give the committee presidential files. Ervin had written Nixon on July 7 warning about a possible constitutional confrontation. Nixon thought Ervin was grandstanding, mostly because Ervin leaked the letter to the press before he sent it. While he declined to give up the documents, Nixon agreed to meet with Ervin one-on-one later to hash out the details.[13]

By the end of the day, Nixon was exhausted. Tkach had concluded the president had viral pneumonia. Nixon told Haig he needed to check into the hospital and "sit on my ass for a week." Although sick, Nixon remained combative. "Okay, fine, they want the papers," Nixon said about the committee's request. "They aren't going to get the papers."

Haig told Nixon that Richard Moore, a White House aide who had been in the office with Nixon and Dean during some of their March meetings on the cover-up, had been a devastating witness before the Watergate panel.

"He got up there and read a statement that was just—that was the best thing ever," Haig said. "He just killed Dean. Absolutely crucified him."[14]

During his statement, Moore contradicted Dean's testimony two weeks earlier about what Nixon knew during that week in March. "Indeed, Mr. Dean's own account that he and I agreed on the importance of persuading the President to make a prompt disclosure of all that the President had just learned is hardly compatible with a belief on Mr. Dean's part that the President himself had known the critical facts all along," Moore said at the end of his opening statement. "In one of my talks with the President, the President said he had kept asking himself whether there had been any sign or clue which should have led him to discover the true facts earlier. I told him that I wished that I had been more skeptical and inquisitive so that I could have served the Presidency better."[15]

Moore "clobbered" Dean and discredited him, Haig said.[16]

Dean's credibility remained a huge obstacle for Nixon's opponents. In the weeks running up to Dean's testimony, his leaks to sympathetic reporters created a blizzard of stories that carried Dean's claims about Nixon and the cover-up. The *Newsweek* interview in early May that first mentioned the "cancer on the presidency" had focused attention on Dean's claims of Nixon's alleged role in the cover-up. Dean repeated that phrase during his widely watched testimony, and most viewers in the Senate or on television believed him over Nixon. But his testimony was not conclusive enough to spur impeachment. Soon Nixon's enemies would get that chance, courtesy of Haig.

But first, Nixon, Haig, Ron Ziegler, and Tkach needed to explain where Nixon was going and why.

"In any event, if it is just a virus, my inclination is to go," Nixon said. "I don't know, thinking of the PR aspects, Ron, people don't go to a hospital for a virus. They stay at home, don't they?"

"Yes, they do, sir," Tkach said. "They go to the hospital for a virus."

"Really?" Nixon asked.

"Yes, sir," Tkach replied.

"Particularly a president," Ziegler said.

"What do you think, Al?" Nixon asked, his dependence on Haig at its highest level.

"Well, I think the description on it—it has to be—there can't be any question about that in terms of the description," Haig said. "And that we have to settle before the president goes."

"Yeah, that," Ziegler said.

"Sounds like a hospital situation," Haig said.

"It has got to be one that the people are convinced that he ought to go to the hospital," Nixon said.

"Right, sir," Tkach said.

"And you have got to say—quite frankly, we have to get the diagnosis before we think of this—even talk," Ziegler said. "But let's say it is diagnosed as—hopefully it will be—as a virus. The president does feel bad. He feels weak. He has a high fever. 'This afternoon the president was diagnosed by his physician to have a high-grade virus, and he's running a high fever. As a result . . . the president obviously feels tired,' which he does. 'The doctors suggest that he check into Bethesda Naval Hospital today.'"

Tired and despondent, Nixon leaned on Haig, who had isolated most of the staff from the president, with the possible exception of Ziegler. "This will really accomplish what the bastards want, Al," he said. "They've killed me. Get rid of the old son of a bitch—people don't want him anyway. We've heard that. The only time the press room will ever be happy is when they write my obituary—only time."[17]

At 9:15 p.m. Nixon checked into the hospital, hoping to feel better but still determined to maintain the appearance of a president working hard at his job.[18]

The next morning, during the hearing, Moore resumed describing what he, Nixon, and Dean did in March to explain away what the White House had known about the Watergate break-in and cover-up. Moore damaged Dean's credibility, although the committee remained focused on confirming what Dean said he told Nixon about the cover-up. Fred Buzhardt had given the committee the key to unlock that mystery.

Moore's testimony stretched into the early afternoon of July 13. Fred Thompson, the committee's minority counsel, had been provided an account of one of Moore's conversations with Dean and Nixon in March, and Terry Lenzner, a tenacious committee investigator, asked Moore about the apparently verbatim account of the conversation. Was it accurate?

Moore and his attorney, Herbert Miller, were confused. They knew nothing about the document from which Lenzner was reading, nor did they know its origin.

Thompson eventually interrupted to say that Buzhardt had told him the memo's substance over the telephone. Thompson did not remember the exact date he received the information, he said, but "I took longhand notes. That same day, I dictated from those notes the summary which has been referred to." He then gave the document to Sam Dash, the committee's chief counsel, and the staff. "Now, perhaps the preciseness of those conversations and so forth can be disputed to a certain extent, but I believe it has been verified that the substance of what is in that document is accurate. Obviously, there is room for some slip-up in the nature of the way the thing was transmitted. We did not discuss at that time how it would be used or whether or not it would be made part of the record or whether or not it would be the official White House position. And that is the way it transpired and that resulted in the document we are referring to."

"Mr. Thompson," Dash said, "I could add this. On the receipt of it, I did make contact with Mr. Garment and Mr. Buzhardt so that if we were going to use it—they saw your reconstruction of the notes. They did come down to my office and read your notes and stated that although it was not a verbatim statement of the telephone call, it was generally accurate."[19]

At the same time Moore was being presented with an account of a conversation captured by the White House recording system, the aide responsible for installing that system was meeting for the first time with committee staffers. Alexander Butterfield had been a deputy to Chief of Staff Bob Haldeman in Nixon's first term and sat just outside the Oval Office. He saw Nixon multiple times a day, and on one day in April 1972, Haldeman asked Butterfield if he could hide $350,000 in cash that was part of a political fund that Haldeman controlled. Butterfield took the money to a friend's safe-deposit box in a bank in northern Virginia. That money became the focus of some of the early reporting on Watergate by *Washington Post* reporters Bob Woodward and Carl Bernstein. After his first term, Nixon appointed Butterfield, a former air force colonel, as director of the Federal Aviation Administration. In April 1973 Butterfield, his conscience troubled, went to federal prosecutors Earl Silbert and Seymour Glanzer to tell them about Haldeman's odd request about the $350,000 and what Butterfield did with it.[20] Butterfield also briefly testified before the grand jury looking into Watergate. Shortly after that, in early May, Butterfield called his friend at the White House, attorney Len Garment, and told him that he had testified before the grand jury. That, Butterfield thought, was that, until he got a call from investigators for the Watergate committee.

Woodward has written extensively about how he urged the Senate committee to interview Butterfield. In *All the President's Men*, his 1974 book with Bernstein, Woodward said he first told the committee about Butterfield on May 17, the day after he had a fateful meeting with his secret source, Deep Throat, who Woodward said had told him that Butterfield was in charge of "internal security."[21] FBI files, however, contain no information about Butterfield as the head of internal security and barely any mentions of him at all. In *The Last of the President's Men*, his 2015 book about Butterfield, Woodward made the claim again that he urged the committee to interview Butterfield.[22]

Committee staff members, starting with Dash and including investigators James Hamilton and Scott Armstrong, acknowledged that Woodward recommended an interview of Butterfield but said they were planning to interview him and the other "satellites" around Haldeman.[23]

Regardless of why Butterfield was there, he was nervous about the interview. He did not know exactly what the investigators wanted, but given the heat Haldeman had taken over the $350,000 and myriad other problems, Butterfield knew he risked trouble. At 2:15 p.m. he met with Armstrong, Gene Boyce, and Don Sanders, an investigator for the Republican committee members, and answered their questions calmly, detailing the inner workings of Nixon's office—who sat where and who did what. He told them about the $350,000 stuffed into a briefcase and what he told the grand jury. After a couple of hours, Sanders remembered the document Buzhardt had dictated over the telephone to Thompson about Nixon's contacts with Dean, which was the same document committee members were asking Moore about while the investigators were interviewing Butterfield. The memo surprised Butterfield, because he thought it looked too complete to have come from memory and that Buzhardt may have prepared it by consulting the tapes. He knew Haig knew about the taping system, because he had told him about it weeks earlier. Butterfield volunteered nothing, though, and no one asked him a direct question about the taping system.[24]

Sanders came back again to the Buzhardt memo, asking whether anyone could have had such a detailed account of the meetings. Butterfield said nothing. Then Sanders mentioned Dean's testimony in June, when Dean said: "The President almost from the outset began asking me a number of leading questions, which was somewhat unlike his normal conversational relationships I had had with him, which made me think that the conversation was being taped and that a record was being made to protect himself."[25] Sanders asked if Dean had any reason to believe he was being taped. Butterfield, who, like many Americans, had watched the earlier hearings, knew he had information that could determine who was telling the truth and who was not. He decided to come clean. Yes, he told Sanders, Nixon had a series of recording devices in the Oval Office, the Cabinet Room, the Old Executive Building, and Camp David. His telephone calls were wired, too. If Nixon said anything in the places where he did the majority of his business, it was recorded for posterity.[26] Now the committee investigators knew how to find the truth after they were pushed in a certain direction by evidence provided by Buzhardt, the president's own attorney. Buzhardt's document attempting to discredit Dean gave Sanders the opening to get Butterfield to make such a remarkable admission. Once the committee and special prosecutor Archibald Cox knew about the tapes, he would want copies of his own. Nixon was doomed from that moment.

After the interview with Butterfield, the three aides dispersed quickly. Armstrong and Boyce raced to Dash. Sanders found Thompson at a local hotel bar having a drink with a reporter. They all wanted Butterfield to testify as soon as possible. Dash talked to Ervin, and they agreed Butterfield had to testify. They prepared a subpoena.[27]

No one told Nixon.

The president, despite his hospitalization, kept a fairly busy schedule, as he met with Haig in the morning and his physicians, Kissinger, and family members throughout the day. He met with Haig in person twice that Friday, including between 6:00 and 6:19 p.m., after Butterfield had revealed the taping system to investigators.[28] Dash said Thompson had called Buzhardt Friday evening, which means Buzhardt told Haig, who said nothing to Nixon, thereby depriving him of the chance to claim executive privilege.[29]

By Saturday morning, the committee leaders—Ervin and Republican Howard Baker—knew they had to squeeze in Butterfield. But

Butterfield was flying that day to New Hampshire to open an airport terminal and was then leaving the following Tuesday for the Soviet Union on FAA business. That left Monday open for Butterfield to appear. Sometime that Saturday morning, a committee aide called Woodward and told him the news. "We interviewed Butterfield," an unnamed committee aide told Woodward. "He told the whole story." What story? Woodward asked. "Nixon bugged himself," the aide said. Woodward quickly called Bernstein, and they suspected a White House trick. They did not report in *All the President's Men* that they contacted anyone at the White House about their discovery, but given Woodward's long connection to Haig, it seems unlikely Woodward did not call him. Their deliberations, however, did not include telling any of their editors, who remained ignorant of this revelation. Woodward called Ben Bradlee, the *Post* editor, at home at 9:30 p.m. He told Bradlee about Butterfield's interview, and Bradlee told him it was a "B-plus" story. "See what more you can find out, but I wouldn't bust one on it," Bradlee said.[30]

In *All the President's Men*, Woodward left a tantalizing piece of evidence that revealed how he could have known to suggest that the committee interview Butterfield. "All Saturday night, the subject gnawed at Woodward," he and Bernstein wrote. "Butterfield had said that even Kissinger and Ehrlichman were unaware of the taping system. . . . Kissinger doesn't know, Woodward reflected, and he thought, Kissinger probably knows almost everything, and he wouldn't like the idea of secret taping systems plucking his sober words and advice out of the air—whether for posterity or some grand jury."[31] Butterfield mentioned Kissinger neither in his interview with the committee nor in his testimony. Only two people knew how the tapes could embarrass Kissinger: Richard Nixon and Alexander Haig. It was in the context of Nixon's desire to keep Kissinger from lying about the FBI wiretaps that Nixon told Haig about the taping system on May 8 and May 11.

"I spent hours with him in this office," Nixon told Haig about Kissinger on May 11. "That's what will kill him with these goddamn tapes, if I ever put them out, which I trust to God will never have to see the day of light, light of day. If he ever writes a self-serving thing, they're going to get out. Understand?"

"It can't be otherwise," Haig said.[32]

Woodward made his first approach to the Watergate committee about Butterfield shortly after Nixon told Haig about the taping system, and they discussed how to use the tapes as leverage over Kissinger. Not even Butterfield knew that. Woodward's source had to be Haig, who claimed in his memoirs that Woodward recommended the Butterfield interview "on instinct rather than hard information."[33]

Butterfield flew to New Hampshire Saturday morning, dedicated an airport facility, and then flew home, the dread of testifying welling up inside him. On the flight home, he wrote down some remarks for his anticipated testimony, notes that ended up in the Watergate committee files. Despite the overwhelming importance of the taping system, Butterfield's notes do not mention the tapes at all. Instead, he fixated on the $350,000 in cash he hid for Haldeman in April 1972. It was that money that Butterfield had testified about before the grand jury.

"Will you resign?" Butterfield wrote in his notes. "That one question I will answer. There is no reason for me to resign. My record is similar to that of General Haig. Throughout my entire government service I have been as honest and straightforward as he, conducted myself in an equally exemplary manner, and lived day in and day out by a standard of ethics, integrity and personal honor every bit as high. The President knows this. He knows of my military service and record, and of my long and close association with General Haig."[34]

Butterfield had multiple telephone messages when he returned home Saturday afternoon. He called Armstrong, who told him to be prepared to testify Monday. That gave him little time to prepare for his Soviet Union trip the next day, Butterfield thought, and he did not want to testify. Desperate to find a way out of this deepening predicament, he called Baker at home. "I said, 'I need to talk to you,'" Butterfield said in 2008. "I just wanted to talk to someone, you know, on that committee. So he said, 'OK, come over tomorrow morning,' meaning Sunday morning at 10:00. So I had my driver take me over there and I met with him. I went through this whole damn story, but all about the tapes and everything, everything. And he said, 'Well, that's what I heard last night.' I mean he had heard it before. And I said, 'You mean you knew all of this? You let me go on?' He said, 'Yeah.' And I said, 'Well now, I'm concerned about being held up. I can't be held up in a way. I'm leading this delegation and it's important. I don't want to get involved in the Watergate thing. I'm not involved anyway. I'm quite peripheral here.' And he said, 'Oh, I don't think you'll have to testify.' And he said, 'I'll see to it that—I'll do what I can.'"[35]

Baker had no intention of letting Butterfield off the hook, and Dash said Baker told Butterfield to call the White House.[36] Butterfield also realized he could not count on Baker alone. He called Len Garment at the White House, was told Garment was out of town, and left a message. Meanwhile, word about the impending Butterfield testimony had reached Haig and Buzhardt. Contrary to Dash's claim that Thompson spoke to Buzhardt on Friday, Thompson wrote that he talked to Buzhardt at the White House on Sunday and told him Butterfield would testify. Buzhardt pretended to be skeptical. "Well, I think that is significant, if it is true," Buzhardt told Thompson. "We'll get on it tomorrow."[37]

Steve Bull, one of the few aides who also knew about the taping system, was called Sunday afternoon by Armstrong, who told him to be ready to testify. Bull assumed it was about the taping system and called Buzhardt. "No, they couldn't know about that," Buzhardt told Bull.[38]

When Garment landed at National Airport following a trip to Florida, he had a message waiting for him that told him to go immediately to the White House, where he found Haig and Buzhardt. By 5:00 p.m. the three men knew Butterfield would tell the committee about the tapes.[39]

Still, no one told Nixon.

That was not for lack of opportunities. Nixon's calendar shows that the ailing president met or spoke with Haig twice that Sunday between 1:10 p.m. and 2:11 p.m. Haig maintained that he did not know that Butterfield would reveal the tapes until after the fact, a claim that is clearly not true. Haig and Buzhardt could have recommended that Nixon claim executive privilege for Butterfield and stopped his testimony. They did not, so Butterfield's rushed trip to the committee room continued.[40]

On Monday morning, Nixon said Haig told him about Butterfield's interview and impending testimony. "I was shocked by this news," Nixon wrote in his memoirs. "As impossible as it must seem now, I had believed that the existence of the White House taping system would never be revealed. I thought that at least executive privilege would have been raised by any staff member before verifying its existence."[41]

Haig maintained he did not tell Nixon about Butterfield's testimony before it happened, but given Haig's lies about when he learned about the taping system, Nixon's version is more convincing. Nixon's calendar shows that he spoke with Haig three times before Butterfield's afternoon testimony and four times afterward.[42]

For his part, Butterfield tried to dodge his date with destiny. Committee aide Jim Hamilton tracked him down in a barbershop and told him that he needed to appear on Capitol Hill or Ervin would order federal marshals to drag him in.[43] Butterfield first called Joseph Califano, his and Haig's former boss at the Pentagon, for help. Califano said he could not help him and told him to call Garment, who told Butterfield he could not represent him because Garment was the president's lawyer. Butterfield called Califano back; Califano then recommended that Butterfield testify without an attorney in order to make a better impression.[44] By 2:00 p.m. he had been ushered into the hearing room and placed at the table facing the seven committee members.

Thompson, leading the questioning, wasted no time. "Mr. Butterfield, are you aware of the installation of any listening devices in the Oval Office of the President?" he asked.

"I was aware of listening devices; yes, sir," Butterfield answered.[45]

Butterfield described where the recorders were, which rooms and telephones were tapped, and other details, but by then most viewers had stopped paying attention. The details meant little once Butterfield revealed that Nixon had recorded himself. There now existed the means to prove who was telling the truth: Nixon, Dean, or any of the other witnesses who told the committee what had happened inside the walls of the Oval Office. Before Butterfield left the hearing room, Buzhardt confirmed the existence of the taping system with a letter, which Ervin read out loud: "Dear Mr. Chairman: This letter is to confirm the fact stated to your Committee today by Mr. Alexander Butterfield that the President's meetings and conversations in the White House have been recorded since the Spring of 1971. I am advised that this system, which is still in use, is similar to that employed by the last Administration, which discontinued from 1969 until the Spring of 1971. A more detailed statement concerning these procedures will be furnished to the Committee shortly. Sincerely, signed, Fred Buzhardt."[46] For someone just learning about the tapes, that letter came rather quickly, a sign that Butterfield's appearance was no accident and his testimony no surprise.

In his memoirs Haig assessed the damage that he had brought about: Nixon's "guilt or innocence had ceased to matter, because no President could survive the verbatim publication of his most intimate conversations, any more than a family could expect its reputation to be the same if everything discussed in the privacy of the home, where special assumptions based on trust and deep acquaintance apply, were to be published in the local newspaper."[47]

Before the end of the day on July 16, Nixon had already dictated a letter to Treasury Secretary George Shultz declaring executive privilege for Secret Service agent Al Wong, whose team oversaw the taping system.[48] That accomplished little, since Butterfield's testimony, followed by an almost simultaneous confirmation by Buzhardt, told the committee and special prosecutor everything they needed to know. But it showed what Nixon would have done if he had known that Butterfield was going to testify about the tapes. Haig had told Nixon on May 14 that the committee was interested in talking to Butterfield, but he framed that interest only in the $350,000 that Haldeman had given Butterfield to hide for him in April 1972. If Nixon had known the committee's interest extended to the taping system, there is no doubt he would have declared executive privilege for Butterfield.

Across the Potomac River, as the drama unfolded in the Senate hearing room with Butterfield, an aggrieved Donald Stewart wrote another memo to his superior at the Pentagon, Martin Hoffmann, complaining about the political pressures that had killed his investigation into the military spy ring. Stewart had no idea that the object of his dissatisfaction, Buzhardt, had been trying to get him prosecuted by the Justice Department for blackmail and extortion, but career prosecutors there had rebuffed the attempt as misguided and unsupported by the evidence.[49] Stewart seethed at his post in the Pentagon; Buzhardt, with the help of then defense secretary Melvin Laird and Haig, shot down Stewart's initial investigation into the spy ring. Stewart suspected there was more to it and that Buzhardt was covering up for his superiors.

The morning headlines on July 17 blared out the news about Butterfield's revelation the previous afternoon. "Nixon Wired His Phone, Offices to Record All Conversations; Senators Will Seek the Tapes" was the headline on the front page of the *New York Times*.[50] Other major papers did the same. The Watergate committee was not done. Called to the committee on July 17, Wong presented Ervin with the letter claiming executive privilege, and he was excused from the hearing.[51] The day was all about damage control for the White House. Haig, Buzhardt, and Garment drove to Bethesda to meet with Nixon in the hospital. They were divided about what to do with the tapes. Buzhardt advised Nixon to destroy them before the committee or Archibald Cox issued subpoenas for them. After the subpoenas, he argued, it would be too late. Destroying the tapes then would mean obstruction of justice, a criminal and possibly impeachable offense. Garment said Nixon had to preserve the tapes.[52] In another conversation, so did Bob Haldeman, calling them essential to Nixon's defense. Haig tried to split the difference, saying that destroying the tapes would be considered a sign of guilt but that preserving them meant that Nixon's opponents would eventually get them and use them against him. The president remained undecided but hoped, as he had told Haig two months earlier, that the tapes would catch his accusers, such as John Dean, in lies of their own.

Haig did not advocate destroying the tapes outright. Instead, he hoped others would do the job for him. When Haig brought Vice President Spiro Agnew to visit Nixon, Agnew urged Nixon to burn the tapes in a bonfire on the White House lawn.[53] Nixon told Agnew he did not know what the tapes had recorded and had forgotten that the tapes were running most of the time, but he was not going to destroy them.[54]

Haig started July 18 by ordering the removal of the taping system. He placed the tapes themselves under the control of Maj. Gen. John Bennett, his deputy. "I did not discuss these actions with the President beforehand," Haig wrote later, "and he never questioned them afterward."[55] Haig also wrote that he met with Nixon at 8:00 that morning, a meeting that never happened, according to Nixon's own calendars.[56] In one of the meetings they did have that day, Nixon reportedly told Haig that Butterfield may have done them a favor by disclosing the tapes, because Nixon believed the tapes would exonerate him.

"He had a way of gazing away into the middle distance as if distracted by a thought when hearing advice he did not want to hear," Haig wrote. "That happened now. He lowered his voice. 'Al, we know that Dean lied and the tapes proved that. We don't know what other lies may be told by people who are trying to save themselves. Who knows what Ehrlichman might say, or even Bob Haldeman. The tapes are my best insurance against perjury. I can't destroy them.'"[57]

By allowing Butterfield to testify, Haig set off a legal battle that would last until the end of Nixon's presidency. The disclosure of the existence of the tapes undoubtedly hastened that end, and the battle started July 18 with a letter from Cox seeking the tapes of eight White House conversations.[58] Cox's formal request put the tapes firmly in the category of potential evidence collected in an ongoing criminal investigation, so destroying them would mean the potential obstruction of justice charges. Charles Alan Wright, a University of Texas law professor advising Nixon, wrote back for Nixon, saying the White House would not comply because only the president could decide if the tapes were in the public interest.[59] On July 19 Nixon wrote in his diary that he should have destroyed the tapes after April 30, when Haldeman and Ehrlichman quit and Nixon fired Dean.[60] That day, Ron Ziegler told the press that Nixon would not turn over the tapes.

As the tapes battle heated up, a cryptic paragraph appeared in a July

20 story in the *New York Times*. "Sources on Capitol Hill said that Melvin R. Laird, one of Mr. Nixon's counselors, had informed Republican Congressional leaders that he believes pertinent sections of the tapes should be released and that he was arguing that position within the Administration," the story said. "But, by Mr. Laird's own admission, the President has not been willing to take his advice on Watergate matters."[61]

As Laird admitted years later, he knew by this time that the tapes proved Nixon's guilt. If he was arguing for their release, even if in limited form, he knew what that disclosure would do to the president.

On July 21 Nixon wrote another note: "If I had discussed illegal action, I would not have taped. If I had discussed illegal action and had taped I would have destroyed the tapes once the investigation began."[62] Nixon's challenge, for which he did not realize he could not rely on Haig and Buzhardt for help, was how he could use the tapes to his advantage without losing control of them to the committee or to Cox. On July 23 Cox officially subpoenaed the eight tapes, declaring in a news conference that they were essential to determining the guilt or innocence of those under investigation.[63] Haig called Attorney General Elliot Richardson to complain that Cox was out of control. Not only was he asking for tapes, but he threatened to push the investigation beyond Watergate, particularly to issues tied to Haig. Richardson would later tell the House Judiciary Committee that Haig said the "boss" was very "uptight" about Cox's questions. "If we have to have a confrontation, we will have it," Haig said, adding that Nixon wanted "a tight line drawn with no further mistakes." "If Cox does not agree, we will get rid of Cox," Haig said.[64]

Nixon responded on July 25 to Cox's subpoena in a letter to District Judge John J. Sirica, in whose court the Watergate investigation had been since the break-in thirteen months earlier. "I have concluded, however, that it would be inconsistent with the public interest and with the Constitutional position of the Presidency to make available recordings of meetings and telephone conversations in which I was a participant and I must respectfully decline to do so," Nixon wrote in the letter, which was read in court on July 26.[65] That, Sirica said, amounted to a dare. "In short, the president asserted that he would turn over to the grand jury only what he wanted to turn over and that the courts had no power to compel him to turn over anything else," the judge wrote later.[66] Sirica turned the issue over to the grand jury investigating Watergate, and the grand jury voted to seek the tapes. Sirica signed a show cause order that day, directing Nixon's team to appear in court on August 7 to show why the tapes should not be introduced as evidence before the grand jury. The tapes, Sirica said, would help determine if Dean or Nixon was telling the truth.

On July 22 *Parade* magazine, a Sunday newspaper supplement, published a story by columnist Jack Anderson in which he bragged about his recent stories exposing wrongdoing by the Nixon administration. Included was a brief mention of the Pentagon's efforts to find officials who had leaked information to Anderson in December 1971 that eventually uncovered the network that was feeding White House secrets to Adm. Thomas Moorer, the chairman of the Joint Chiefs of Staff. The failed leak hunt, Anderson wrote, involved hauling suspects to room 3E933 of the Pentagon for interrogations. "They concluded mistakenly that the source was located on Henry Kissinger's staff," Anderson wrote of the investigators. "Innocent staff members were yanked from behind their desks and dragged to polygraph machines, although it was the White House, not my sources, doing the lying about Pakistan. Eventually an entire section of Kissinger's staff was scattered around the world, and Adm. Robert Welander who headed it was exiled to the Atlantic fleet."[67] Most readers did not notice the reference, but Donald Stewart did. The Pentagon investigator had conducted some of his interviews into the military spy ring in room 3E933, and, already seething about his inability to get a new job, Stewart was outraged at Anderson's casual reference to where Stewart did his work. Stewart considered Anderson a traitor for his columns that exposed military secrets, and he also blamed Buzhardt for scuttling his investigation. Stewart did not know that Buzhardt was trying to get the Justice Department to prosecute Stewart for extortion and blackmail.

Coincidentally, Donald Sanders of Howard Baker's Watergate committee staff also read Anderson's article. A former colleague of Stewart at the

FBI, he recognized the room number where Stewart had grilled suspects at the Pentagon. He told two of his colleagues on the Republican committee staff, Fred Thompson and Howard Liebengood, and then called Stewart at the Pentagon on July 24. Within hours, Stewart was on Capitol Hill talking with Sanders and Liebengood. Baker, their boss, had long suspected that the growing Watergate scandal was about more than a simple office burglary. The May 22 white paper had hinted darkly at national security secrets so damaging that no one could mention them without causing great harm. Baker wanted to know more. Stewart did not disappoint.

Stewart told them that the Indian-Pakistan affair about which Anderson wrote had far greater dimensions than anyone imagined and that his investigation was killed for political reasons. Stewart said rear admirals Rembrandt Robinson and Robert Welander had used the NSC liaison office to squirrel away White House secrets, such as planned troop levels for the Vietnam War, and sent the information back to the Pentagon. They felt compelled to spy on the White House because of Nixon's secrecy. They used Yeoman Charles Radford, who was detailed to the National Security Council, to steal documents for Robinson, Welander, and eventually Moorer. Stewart told the investigators that he had forced Radford to confess to supplying documents to his bosses, but Radford denied leaking secret documents to Jack Anderson.[68]

But Stewart only knew part of the story. Buzhardt had called Stewart back from a Florida vacation at Buzhardt's request in early January 1972 to interrogate Welander, not knowing that John Ehrlichman and White House Plumber David Young had already questioned him and that Welander had implicated Haig in helping the spy ring. Soon after Stewart's interview of Welander, Buzhardt provided a report to then defense secretary Laird that presented Haig, Moorer, and the military brass as victims of Radford's perfidy. Stewart knew nothing of that report or the investigation conducted at the White House by Young, which included the first interview of Welander. The investigation into the leaks to Anderson and the spy ring had mysteriously stopped. Stewart, who saw the entire affair as an assault on the president, had always suspected that Buzhardt killed the investigation to cover up an embarrassing political scandal.[69]

At the White House, Haig and Buzhardt remained focused on the wiretaps and the potential exposure of the spy ring. On July 23 Haig called Richardson to complain about a questionnaire that Cox's office sent to all government employees with a potential connection to wiretapping. Haig warned Richardson that Nixon wanted "a tight line drawn with no further mistakes."[70] Buzhardt also realized that Ehrlichman was scheduled to testify that week. Ehrlichman had overall authority over the White House special investigations unit, the Plumbers, which had investigated the spy ring and the Pentagon Papers leak. Some of the men who broke into the office of Dr. Lewis Fielding, the psychiatrist who treated Pentagon Papers leaker Daniel Ellsberg, were later caught trying to break into the Democratic National Committee headquarters at the Watergate office complex. Part of Ehrlichman's developing legal defense involved using his duties overseeing the Plumbers to explain that he was acting on Nixon's orders. He particularly emphasized that role in relation to the spy ring, which Buzhardt and Haig could not afford to have Ehrlichman use in his defense. On July 23 Buzhardt wrote a letter to John Wilson, Ehrlichman's attorney, claiming executive privilege over any mention of the spy ring. "As you know the President said in his Statement on May 22, 1973: 'Executive privilege will not be invoked as to any testimony concerning possible criminal conduct or discussions of possible criminal conduct in matters presently under investigation, including the Watergate affair and the alleged coverup,'" Buzhardt wrote. "This is the total extent to which the President waived executive privilege. The 1971 investigation about which you inquired was in no way related to the Watergate affair, the alleged coverup, or to any Presidential election. This matter does involve most sensitive national security matters, the public disclosure of which would cause damage to the national security. Accordingly, if your clients, Mr. John F. Ehrlichman or Mr. Haldeman, are interrogated about this particular investigation, the President has requested that you inform the committee that your clients have been instructed by the President to decline to give testimony concerning this particular investigation, and that the President, in so instructing your clients, is doing so pursuant to the constitutional doctrine of separation of powers."[71] That meant Ehrlichman could not explain why he did what he did. It also stopped a line of questioning that would expose the roles of Haig, Buzhardt, and Laird in stealing White House secrets and then covering it up.

Buzhardt's move, done with Haig's approval, frustrated Baker. He had avidly prepared for Ehrlichman's scheduled testimony on July 26. Not only did Baker want to provide Nixon with a possible explanation for what he had done before, during, and after Watergate, but Baker also wanted to know more about the apparent threats to national security. Ehrlichman took his seat at the witness table facing the committee's seven senators, and Baker jumped into the details of Nixon's May 22 white paper and any other situations about which Ehrlichman was familiar. "What I do want to know is the breadth and range of your information as to that event or other security problems that may have had some bearing on the contentions of the President in his May 22 statement," Baker said.

Ehrlichman mentioned the 1971 friendship treaty between India and the Soviet Union and a CIA document that had appeared in the *New York Times*.

"What other examples?" Baker wanted to know.

"That is as far as I can go because that is all in the public domain and I am under an express injunction from Mr. Buzhardt that executive privilege has been invoked as to the other matters," Ehrlichman responded, raising the Buzhardt letter for the first time.

Baker kept pressing and got Ehrlichman to acknowledge the issue concerned the December 1971 war between India and Pakistan. Like a good lawyer, Baker knew the answers to the questions he was asking, and Ehrlichman most likely realized it, too. But Buzhardt's letter prevented Ehrlichman from answering without violating the claim of executive privilege.

"This is a terribly important matter because on the one hand, you have an allegation by the President that national security matters accounted for part of his conduct subsequent to Watergate," Baker said. "On the other hand, we have examples of wiretapping, of the Ellsberg break-in and other things, and very frankly, I am not sure you have entirely convinced all of the committee that these are matters of extraordinary national importance that they fit the description that the President makes in his statement of May 22."[72]

Nixon's May 22 white paper, which Haig and Buzhardt had forced on him, was coming back to haunt him. In it Nixon had claimed he could not release some information because it was too secret and exposing it would endanger national security. And there *were* deep secrets of tremendous gravity. The military spy ring exposed a huge rift between the president and the military, and it also involved top military leaders leaking vital secrets to derail a presidential order—the movement of an aircraft carrier task force to the Bay of Bengal. But while the white paper contained Nixon's confession of some parts of the cover-up, it also contained tantalizing hints of other matters, such as the spy ring, the details of which Baker wanted Ehrlichman to confirm.

"I want to put a specific question to you," Baker said. "Whether or not any of these functions had to do with anything related to, say, the Indo-Pakistani war."

Ehrlichman evaded, but only because Buzhardt's letter prevented him from doing so.

"What I am asking you is, is it that important or am I playing games?" Baker asked.

"In my opinion it is that important, Senator," Ehrlichman answered.[73]

Ehrlichman had stonewalled the committee enough on the issue that Baker let it drop. His time had expired, and none of the other senators followed suit. But Baker had pried enough information from the reluctant Ehrlichman to pique the curiosity of those in the room, particularly two reporters, Jim Squires of the *Chicago Tribune* and Dan Thomasson of the Scripps-Howard newspapers. They wanted to know more about the Plumbers investigation, which had surfaced in the dialogue between Baker and John Wilson, Ehrlichman's attorney. Their editors allowed them to work together to see what new details they could find in what they started off knowing was an investigation tied to the India-Pakistan war, ensuring that this would not be the last the White House would hear of it. What neither Squires nor Thomasson knew was that Bob

Woodward of the *Washington Post* already knew about the military spy ring and was sitting on the story.

The following day, Ervin and Baker met secretly with Buzhardt and Garment from the White House to discuss Ehrlichman's testimony and whether the committee would investigate the India-Pakistan crisis and the military spy ring. Buzhardt and Garment argued that the issue was not germane to Watergate and too potentially explosive to be disclosed. Ervin reluctantly agreed, but Baker said little, because he wanted to investigate more on his own. The White House men also smeared Stewart by claiming he had tried to blackmail the president, although they knew the Justice Department had already rejected that claim as groundless. The senators' decision gave Buzhardt and Haig a brief reprieve; they did not know then that Squires and Thomasson were pursuing the story.[74]

Baker took one more shot. Stewart had told Sanders and Liebengood that he had worked with White House aide David Young on the spy ring investigation. Shortly after the meeting with Buzhardt and Garment, Baker met with Young, who declined to say anything. "This is the one thing that the president told me not to discuss at all, and I won't," Young said in the off-the-record meeting.[75] At this point, any investigation by a member of the Senate Watergate committee into the spy ring came to an end. Haig and Buzhardt had dodged a bullet, although just for a few months.

While Buzhardt and Garment were fighting off the potential Senate investigation into the spy ring, the federal prosecutors from Baltimore handling the investigation into Spiro Agnew returned to Washington for another briefing with Richardson. The case against Agnew continued to get stronger, U.S. Attorney George Beall told Richardson, and the probability that Agnew would be charged was close to 100 percent. Richardson then told Haig he needed to see Nixon. Haig told him that Agnew had already talked to him and Nixon and claimed his complete innocence. But Haig already knew the depth of Agnew's trouble. He told Richardson they would arrange a time for him to meet with Nixon soon, and Richardson left for Cape Cod for the weekend.[76]

Haig had maneuvered Butterfield to reveal the taping system, which sealed Nixon's fate. With Buzhardt's help, he had planted the idea with the committee that Nixon may have taped himself, which led to Butterfield being asked about the taping system, which he confirmed. Again, with Buzhardt's help, Haig blocked Ehrlichman from talking about the spy ring, which continued Haig's cover-up. By the end of July, Haig's position was secure, while Nixon's unraveled with each moment.

5   August 1973

Nixon had regained his physical strength by the beginning of August despite the deluge of bad news flowing from Watergate. Alexander Butterfield's revelation about the White House tapes had started a legal battle between the president, Archibald Cox, and the Senate committee. Nixon claimed executive privilege, as he refused to turn the tapes over to the committee, but his decision not to destroy the tapes also made it inevitable that they would eventually become public.

Lost in the furor that ensued after the disclosure of the tapes were witnesses who came ever closer to pinning Nixon with obstruction of justice. Bob Haldeman said on July 31 that Nixon had directed him to tell CIA officials Richard Helms and Vernon Walters to tell the FBI that the Watergate investigation might threaten the bureau's operations in Mexico, which Haldeman knew was a lie. On August 2 Helms said essentially the same thing, although he pulled back from claiming any specific wrongdoing.

By August 1 the federal prosecutors in Baltimore had finished their work against Vice President Spiro Agnew to the point where U.S. Attorney George Beall had written a letter to Judah Best, Agnew's attorney, informing him that Agnew was under investigation for bribery, conspiracy, and extortion.[1] Agnew had predicted this in June when he told Nixon and Haig he would be indicted, and it was now just a matter of time before the letter became public and the countdown toward Agnew's departure began.

Agnew "felt frustrated and helpless" when he received the letter, fearing that he was unfairly in the crosshairs of Beall's ambitious Democratic career prosecutors, who wanted to claim the biggest trophy they would ever get in their prosecutorial careers: the head of a sitting vice president. They wanted copies of Agnew's financial records and taxes. "They wanted to wreck my life," Agnew wrote. "All of a sudden my enemies found in their hands a weapon to get rid of me."[2]

Foremost among those enemies was Haig, whom Agnew called "the de facto president for all other matters while Richard Nixon struggled desperately to escape the entangling web of Watergate." Haig was making it impossible for Agnew to get a fair hearing from the prosecutors or help from Congress, which, Agnew believed, "made the administration's commitment to my departure from the vice presidency irreversible."[3]

Attorney General Elliot Richardson had been begging Haig for days to arrange a meeting with Nixon, but Haig put him off until Agnew had received the letter and learned just how bad his options were.[4]

Haig, Buzhardt, and Richardson had less luck persuading the Justice Department to prosecute Pentagon investigator Donald Stewart for allegedly blackmailing the White House to give him a job in exchange for his silence about the military spy ring. As Henry Petersen, the Justice Department's criminal chief, had done in July, Justice official Alfred Hantman wrote a memo to his boss, Carl Belcher, calling any attempted prosecution of Stewart "foolishness." Stewart's initial conversation with White House lawyer Richard Tufaro in May was "low-key" and not a shakedown attempt. "It certainly strains credulity," Hantman wrote, "to believe that if a former FBI agent, such as Stewart, intended to 'commit or attempt an act of extortion,' he would reduce such intention to physical proof in the form of a writing," Hantman wrote. Stewart was merely looking for help landing a new job, not trying to blackmail the White House into giving him one.[5] Belcher sent Hantman's recommendation immediately to Henry Petersen, who would soon become immersed in the Agnew case, and then on to Richardson.[6]

During the summer, Richardson had told Melvin Laird about the evidence against Agnew. Laird already knew from his meetings with Nixon and Haig in June that Agnew faced serious difficulties, but Richardson told him that two witnesses said they had paid Agnew kickbacks for state contracts he helped deliver to their companies when he was the Baltimore County executive in the 1960s. They also settled previous debts by delivering cash to Agnew while he was vice president.[7] Laird told Richardson to keep pushing the case hard, regardless of Agnew's position. On August 4 Laird flew on an air force plane to Groton, Connecticut, the site of the navy's submarine facility, to dedicate a new submarine. Along for the ride was Gerald Ford, the House minority leader from Michigan. The two old friends from the House and fellow midwesterners—Laird had pushed Ford for two House leadership posts—talked about Nixon, Watergate, and Agnew.

"You think things are bad now," Laird told Ford, according to an interview Laird gave to his biographer, Dale Van Atta. "They're going to get worse."

"Tell me about it," Ford pressed him.

Agnew was in serious trouble, Laird said, so Ford should be careful about siding with him and should be "prepared for some major changes."[8]

If Laird is to be believed here, and given his previous shadings of the truth, one should be careful about that, then Ford knew two months before Nixon selected him as Nixon's second vice president that Agnew was guilty. If Ford knew that, courtesy of Laird, then Ford had plenty of chances within the House Republican Conference to diminish enthusiasm for supporting Agnew. In his memoirs, *A Time to Heal*, Ford repeated Laird's story with the exception of the final sentence, in which Laird told

Ford that Agnew was in serious trouble.[9] Laird's biography, however, was published after Ford's death in 2006.

On August 5 Richardson called Buzhardt and Garment to his home in McLean, Virginia, to show them the evidence against Agnew, who believed it was the first time "the White House lawyers had learned any details of the case," but Haig had already told Buzhardt the details weeks earlier.[10] Agnew still hoped the White House lawyers might interfere with Richardson and Justice to either slow or drop the case against him, but Haig had completely different ideas. He had taken Agnew's suggestion in June of a double impeachment as gospel, and he and Buzhardt believed that Agnew had to go. They embraced the case against Agnew and moved it forward. After they talked to the Justice team, Buzhardt and Garment prepared a memorandum for Nixon the next day that said Agnew had to quit.

Richardson had his long-awaited meeting with Nixon on Monday, August 6. He arrived in the Oval Office to show Nixon and Haig Beall's letter detailing the case against the vice president. "Not wishing to breach the confidentiality between the President and the chief lawyer of his administration, I stayed away, but an optimistic Nixon told me afterward that the meeting ended with the usual admonitions and assurances that nothing about the case must leak," Haig wrote.[11] That is, again, a lie. Haig already knew what Richardson would tell Nixon, and Nixon's calendar shows Haig was in the meeting for its entirety.

That evening, the *Wall Street Journal*, followed quickly by the *Washington Post*, had the details of the letter to Agnew. Haig's lies about his presence at the Nixon meeting with Richardson, along with Haig's desire to remove Agnew, make him the most likely suspects for the leaks.

Jerry Landauer, one of the *Journal*'s best investigative reporters, had the story first and then was matched by Richard Cohen at the *Post*. Cohen wrote that Bob Woodward had passed along the initial tips about Agnew. The August tips, Cohen and coauthor Jules Witcover wrote in their book about Agnew's resignation, reached Landauer "from a source inside Agnew's office."[12] Landauer, who died in 1981, never specified his source, but he had an unlikely connection—Woodward, whom he had met years earlier on another story.

Although they worked for different newspapers, Woodward considered Landauer his mentor. Their relationship started in 1970, when Woodward was a navy lieutenant working for Adm. Thomas Moorer, the chief of naval operations and soon to be the chairman of the Joint Chiefs of Staff. The navy was then trying to expand its artillery practice range on the small Puerto Rican island of Culebra. A small group of islanders protested and hired Covington & Burling, a powerhouse Washington law firm, to represent them. Young associate Richard Copaken handled the case. As he wrote in his 2008 book, *Target Culebra*, Copaken sought Landauer's help to publicize the navy's misdeeds.[13] One of their best sources, Copaken wrote, was Woodward. "I knew Jerry ranked high in Bob's pantheon of heroes," Copaken wrote. They met for dinner at the Two Continents Restaurant in the Hotel Washington across the street from the Treasury Department, and Landauer advised Woodward on how to get a good job in journalism. Woodward told Copaken and Landauer how the navy worked with the CIA through the "special intelligence group," or OP-92. Often, Woodward said, the navy and CIA worked together in Puerto Rico without telling "the civilian heads of the Navy." Afterward, they went to Woodward's apartment, where the navy officer looked through his handwritten journals "to see if there were more he could share with us." Woodward's final tidbit of information concerned how the navy feared a possible communist takeover of Puerto Rico similar to that in Cuba and that Culebra could provide "a redoubt" similar to the role the Guantánamo Bay naval base played in Cuba.[14]

Woodward, therefore, was already a source for Landauer, while Woodward and Haig also had a long-standing relationship. It is not a great leap to believe Haig used Woodward as the conduit to Landauer and Cohen, because Haig was already feeding Woodward information. A May 17, 1973, story by Woodward and Bernstein contained information that could only have come from Haig. A doctor for Senator Thomas Eagleton of Missouri, who was briefly the Democratic vice presidential nominee in 1972, had written Haig on May 15 that his office had been burglarized and his files stolen. Also that month, Woodward met with his former commander from the navy, Rear Adm. Robert Welander, who had collaborated with

Haig in the military spy ring. Pentagon investigator Donald Stewart had contacted the White House on May 14 and intimated that he might go public about it. Haig knew about the call almost immediately, and within days Woodward had asked Welander to meet him for lunch and told him the issue was bubbling up and about to go public. Woodward then sat on the story for more than seven months. Haig also learned about the White House taping system on May 8, and days later Woodward told the Senate Watergate committee staffers that they needed to interview Butterfield. By August 1973 Haig and Woodward often shared secrets Haig wanted to hide or publicize, depending on his needs. Each time, Woodward cooperated.

Agnew had dreaded the Beall letter, and he knew that when Richardson met with Nixon and Haig he faced a serious and potentially career-ending crisis. A bare-knuckled fighter who had succeeded as a Republican in Democrat-dominated Maryland, Agnew's political antennae had few equals. He knew bribery and tax evasion charges would destroy his hopes of running for president in 1976. He had realized this from the moment he learned of the grand jury, which was why he wanted Nixon to stop Beall. Now, as the type for the next day's edition of the *Wall Street Journal* and *Post* was being set, Agnew needed the help and protection of the damaged and beleaguered president he served.

Haig blocked his way.

After he met with Richardson in the morning of August 6, Nixon spent the rest of the day dodging Agnew. Nixon and Haig left the White House for Camp David at 1:22 p.m., Nixon's schedule shows, and arrived there at 2:35. They met for another fifteen minutes between 3:15 and 3:30 and then went swimming at 4:55 for an hour. They had dinner between 6:55 and 7:27, when Haig flew back to the White House.[15] Meanwhile, Richardson met with Agnew at Nixon's request and told him his future looked dire. Angered, Agnew hoped he would have a chance to fly the helicopter back to Camp David, but Nixon had different plans.

That evening, Agnew was joined by Haig and Bryce Harlow, Nixon's Capitol Hill liaison and someone Agnew trusted. These two men, who guarded virtually all access to Nixon and his inner circle, reinforced

Richardson's message. Agnew needed to resign. "They said the President had been 'floored by the news' of the charges against me and had flown to Camp David to consider this blow against the very survival of his administration," Agnew wrote in his memoirs. From Nixon to Richardson to Haig, they all considered Agnew's indictment "inevitable." Haig said Nixon wanted Agnew to resign immediately. "I was seething with rage, frustration, and despair," Agnew wrote. "I could not imagine that they could think I would resign without even talking to the President and having at least a chance to defend myself."[16]

Nixon then called Haig at 10:35 p.m. to see if Agnew had agreed to resign.[17]

Agnew had no intention of resigning but believed he had limited options. He hoped to see Nixon and persuade him of his innocence, believing that it was Richardson, not Haig, who was leaking the damaging information about the case. Even if Nixon wanted to do something, his political capital dwindled each day. On the morning of Tuesday, August 7, the stories Agnew dreaded appeared in the *Journal* and *Post*. Agnew could no longer hope to contain the crisis in private. His problems and Nixon's deepening Watergate quagmire had become one, as the entire administration looked like a sinkhole of lies and corruption. A president desperate to save himself and his legacy could ill afford a vice president trapped in a bribery scandal. Nixon had little doubt of Agnew's guilt and had believed the worst from the beginning. Governors, he believed, were inherently corrupt. Only after Agnew's skeleton had been dragged out of the closet for the world to see, his political fortunes ruined, did Haig allow him to meet with Nixon. Haig prepared Nixon carefully. They ended the previous evening with a thirty-minute call after Haig and Harlow told Agnew to quit, and they started August 7 with another twenty-one-minute call. Nixon then spent time with Press Secretary Ron Ziegler, who gave him an appraisal of the morning's grim headlines, which all looked ominous for Agnew. After Nixon flew back to the White House, he and Haig met three more times before seeing Agnew. Haig also had three minutes alone with Nixon before Agnew entered the office at 4:04 p.m.[18]

While Haig had pushed Agnew to resign, Nixon said nothing about it during his meeting with the vice president. Haig told Nixon the night before that "Agnew was wavering between fighting and resigning."[19] When Nixon finally met Agnew that afternoon in the hideaway office in the Old Executive Office Building, the president said nothing about resigning. A desperate Agnew, an embattled Nixon, and a cool Haig spoke for an hour and forty-four minutes, in which Agnew told Nixon that the charges against him were untrue, the accusers were lying about Agnew to save themselves, and "there was still no proof the money went into my pocket."[20] Agnew vented about the unfairness of the federal prosecutors, the Democrats and liberals who were out to get the partisan vice president. Nixon had heard it before. Agnew had made the same argument in April when Nixon first learned of the bribery and tax investigation, and he had made it again with Nixon and Haig in June after Nixon had assigned Haig to watch the Agnew case.

"All they've got is the testimony of a few men who have done business together for years," Agnew said. "They were caught in a tax evasion problem and they saw a hell of a good way to extricate themselves from it by dragging me in."[21] Agnew repeated his earlier belief that the guilty plea by William Fornoff, a Baltimore County official, in June had started a chain reaction in which anyone tied to the case started to make deals to save themselves. "I don't think I'm getting a fair shake out of Richardson," Agnew said. "I want an independent review of the case."[22]

Nixon threw Agnew a bone and said he would assign Henry Petersen, the head of the Justice Department's Criminal Division, to investigate the case apart from Richardson. That did not soothe Agnew either; he believed Petersen had been roughed up by the press and Democrats for not prosecuting the Watergate case hard enough and would seek to atone by making an example out of Agnew.

If he had to depend on Haig, Agnew knew he was finished.

"Alexander Haig saw himself as in control of everything that happened," Agnew said in a 1987 interview. "And Nixon was so distraught, and upset and concerned that [Haig] was just running things. I mean that was obvious to everybody around, that Haig was, was sort of in control."[23]

Agnew, as he promised Nixon, held a news conference on August 8 in which he robustly defended himself against the accusations of bribery and corruption. He attacked the prosecutors and the leaks coming from the Justice Department.

"I have nothing to hide," Agnew said three times as he stood before two hundred reporters in the fourth-floor auditorium in the Old Executive Office Building. Nixon, Agnew said, gave him his full support. "It really isn't that important what a President says," Agnew said. "I'm not spending my time looking around to see who's supporting me."[24]

In a response to a question about when he told Nixon about his problems, Agnew was vague and made a slip that also exposed Haig's role in managing the problem before it went public. Agnew said he had told Haig about the problem "months" ago and that he assumed Haig had told Nixon. Agnew had actually told then chief of staff Bob Haldeman on April 10, and Haldeman told Nixon. Haig learned about Agnew's exposure to the corruption investigation on May 17 at the latest, and Nixon had made Haig responsible for handling it. Contrary to Haig's and Nixon's wishes, the news conference showed that Agnew would not leave quietly. The fight he promised would embroil the White House in another protracted scandal.

Haig and Buzhardt visited Nixon shortly after Agnew's news conference. The vice president may have experienced a temporary endorphin rush from vigorously defending his honor, but he had made such blanket declarations of innocence that he would soon be exposed as a liar. The evidence against Agnew, Buzhardt said, was so strong that "his denials simply won't hold up. I can't understand how he can make such flat denials in light of the facts that are bound to come out."[25]

Haig had been prepared by William Ruckelshaus, Richardson's deputy at Justice, that Nixon would need to talk to Richardson again about the growing evidence against Agnew. As the keeper of the Agnew account for Nixon, Haig knew the evidence would continue to get worse. With the exposure of Agnew's legal problems, anyone involved in the Maryland investigation with potential evidence against the vice president now had a target for their claims.

"There was never the slightest doubt that Agnew would have to go," Haig wrote. "Nixon thought that Agnew had inflicted mortal damage on himself." Nixon told Haig to call John Connally, the former Texas governor and treasury secretary, to be on hold in case the president needed him, and Haig did. Connally said he would be ready. Haig talked to Richardson and then again to Nixon, who said Agnew's combative news conference indicated he would not resign, even though resigning and then fighting to prove his innocence were the most graceful options. "We want to keep him away from the constitutional route [impeachment]," Haig wrote that Nixon told him. "We'll just say that's out of the question."[26]

That, Haig claimed, was the "first reference Nixon had made in my presence to the possibility of impeachment. But what he said made it obvious that he shared my apprehensions about a possible double impeachment and its consequences to American institutions and American democracy."[27] At best, this is an incorrect memory. Agnew had first raised the prospect of double impeachment with Nixon and Haig in June, as the vice president feared the Democrats in Congress were plotting to remove Nixon and Haig and make House Speaker Carl Albert the president. "Oh God," Haig had said then in a combination of shock and disbelief.[28]

Not only did Haig have to contend with Agnew, but he had to tell Secretary of State William Rogers that he needed to leave so Nixon could replace him with Henry Kissinger, Rogers's longtime antagonist. Rogers, Haig wrote, told him that Kissinger's Senate confirmation hearings would be difficult. "(As indeed they were, owing mainly to the fact that the 1969 FBI wiretaps, of which Rogers had no knowledge, were leaked from the Department of Justice and became an issue.)"[29] Haig again bent the truth. The FBI wiretaps and Kissinger's role in them had become public knowledge three months earlier in the FBI investigation ordered by Ruckelshaus when he was the bureau's acting director. Leaks to the *New York Times* by William Sullivan, Haig's longtime FBI ally, highlighted Kissinger's involvement. Kissinger's attempts to minimize his exposure to the wiretaps in May led Nixon to tell Haig about the White House taping system as a way to embarrass Kissinger.

Since July, Nixon's intermittent Senate nemesis, Democrat Stuart Symington of Missouri, had been conducting hearings of the Senate Armed Services Committee into the secret bombing campaign of then neutral Cambodia that Nixon had authorized in March 1969. The report in the *New York Times* of that bombing on May 9, 1969, had launched the series of FBI wiretaps. Four years earlier, during the deliberations leading up to the bombing, Laird and Rogers had opposed keeping the raids secret, realizing that they would eventually be revealed and that the secrecy would cause more troubles than it would solve. On August 9 the committee unveiled a memo that showed that Laird and military leaders had approved creating false logs showing that the B-52 bombers flying the raids had dropped their payloads in South Vietnam, not Cambodia.[30] The memo contradicted Laird's earlier claims that he knew nothing about the fake reports. It also put added strain on Laird, Haig, and Kissinger, who had lied about the secret bombing to the public. Kissinger and Haig then authorized the wiretaps and picked their targets as they launched a search mission to find who told the *Times* about the bombing.

Symington's hearings would continue to cause problems for the White House. The following day, August 10, Admiral Moorer, the chairman of the Joint Chiefs of Staff, acknowledged that troops who carried out one of the first military operations of Nixon's presidency, Operation Dewey Canyon, had ventured into Laos, one of South Vietnam's neutral neighbors. "This was the first and only time where United States ground combat forces went into Laos," Moorer told the committee.[31] That, too, was a lie. U.S. troops had ventured into Laos in 1970 as part of the ill-fated Operation Tailwind.[32]

In the week following Agnew's August 8 news conference, Nixon spent most of his time at Camp David huddled with speechwriters Ray Price and Patrick Buchanan to write another address about the need to move on from Watergate, which Congress and Watergate prosecutor Archibald Cox showed no interest in doing. Cox sent the White House a detailed note on August 13 specifying the tapes and documents he wanted as evidence in his continuing investigation, further angering Nixon.[33] One influential Democrat, Representative John Moss of California, wanted Cox to investigate Haig's hiring as chief of staff while he remained a four-star army general.[34] The reports from Camp David were grim. Nixon, associates said, veered from seeming healthy and calm to wallowing in despair. Some doubted if the speech would help. "I think he could pull out of it," one associate told the *New York Times*. "But I wonder if this is the way to do it. It could be tragic."[35]

On August 15 Haig told Nixon that Richardson said Henry Petersen's review of the Agnew case had yielded the same grim result for the vice president as Richardson had presented nine days earlier.[36]

Seemingly rested by his time at Camp David, Nixon spoke on television with a renewed fervor that night, as if he thought he could will himself out of the Watergate morass and back to the presidency he had planned on having during his final four years in office. "The time has come to turn Watergate over to the courts, where the questions of guilt or innocence belong," Nixon said. "The time has come for the rest of us to get on with the urgent business of our nation. I recognize that this statement does not answer many of the questions and contentions raised during the Watergate hearings. It has not been my intention to attempt any such comprehensive and detailed response. Neither do I believe I could enter upon an endless course of explaining and rebutting a complex of point-by-point claims and charges ... and still be able to carry out my duties."

Nixon said that he had not used the CIA to block the FBI investigation of the Watergate break-in (a lie that he appeared to repeat reflexively every time the issue arose), that no one on his staff had offered any of the Watergate defendants clemency, that he had not authorized the burglary of Daniel Ellsberg's psychiatrist, and that he depended on John Dean when he said no White House staff members were implicated in Watergate. "I had no prior knowledge of the Watergate operation," the president said. "I neither took part in nor knew about any of the subsequent cover-up activities, I neither authorized nor encouraged subordinates to engage in illegal or improper campaign tactics. That was—and is—the simple truth.

"In all the millions of words of testimony, there is not the slightest suggestion that I had any knowledge of the planning for the Watergate break-in. As for the cover-up, my statement has been challenged by only one of the thirty five witnesses who appeared—a witness who offered no evidence beyond his own impressions, and whose testimony has been contradicted by every other witness in position to know the facts."[37]

As was often the case with Nixon, some of what he said was true, and some was a whopping lie. He did not know about the Watergate break-in in advance and thought it was a ridiculous idea when he first learned the burglars had been arrested. Nixon definitely took part in the cover-up when he told Haldeman that he and John Ehrlichman needed to meet with CIA leaders to get them to tell the FBI to back off the Watergate investigation because it might stumble into CIA operations in Mexico. Nixon, Haldeman, and Haig all knew that looked and sounded like obstruction of justice, and the proof for it was contained on the tapes held in the White House. Dean, the witness to whom Nixon referred in his comments, may not have told the complete truth in his Senate testimony, but a strong plurality of Americans believed him, and little Nixon said on August 15 changed that.

On August 18 Don Sanders, the aide for the minority staff of the Watergate committee, had a four-hour meeting with former FBI official William Sullivan in Boston's Logan Airport. Sanders wanted to pursue more of the details that Senator Lowell Weicker and other members of the committee staff had learned from Sullivan in their previous meetings. The wily former intelligence chief spun through several of the points he had made during his earlier interviews but focused primarily on what he had told Dean in the previous winter about the FBI wiretaps. He also dished out rumors from the 1960 and 1964 presidential campaigns and told about the bureau's tracking of Anna Chennault, a Chinese American activist for Nixon who had helped him sabotage the Johnson administration's attempts to get the South Vietnamese government to the 1968 Paris peace talks. Sullivan had leaked details of the wiretaps to the *New York Times*, and he also leaked to reporters all over Washington. Sanders asked him about an August 15 report by Scripps-Howard reporter Dan Thomasson that cited a five-page Sullivan memo about FBI activities in previous elections. Sullivan said he had not spoken with Thomasson or Jim Squires of the *Chicago Tribune*, who were investigating the unknown national security issues that Ehrlichman could not tell the Watergate committee in July.[38]

By August 20 Agnew knew that despite Nixon's claims, Agnew had few friends in the White House. Laird had told his fellow Republicans in the House to avoid making confident defenses of Agnew because he was guilty. Laird also knew by this time, courtesy of Buzhardt, that Nixon was guilty, too, and that Nixon would inevitably be forced from office. If that happened, Agnew could not succeed him. Laird, Agnew wrote, "closed down any chance of my getting a sympathetic hearing, even poisoning the minds of many Republicans. As their actions had shown, General Haig, Laird, and their allies on the Nixon staff wanted me out in a hurry, even though they could not persuade the President to make me resign. It is logical to conclude that they permitted officials to leak all they pleased without fear of censure. Their campaign amounted to a White House staff war against the Vice President."[39]

Agnew issued a statement on August 21 accusing Justice Department officials of leaking damaging information to sabotage him and demanded in a news conference that Richardson investigate.[40] Agnew really knew, however, that Haig was the culprit. Richardson provided a convenient foil; Agnew could lash out at what he considered unfair behavior without targeting the president himself or his top aide.

On August 22 Cox and the White House lawyers met in Judge John Sirica's court to argue over Cox's tape request. "Happily ours is a system of government in which no man is above the law," Cox said. There was "strong evidence to believe that the integrity of the executive office has been corrupted, although the extent of the rot is not yet clear."[41] Haig said this argument worked because of the strong public perception of Nixon's guilt. Whatever the claims were in court, Haig and Buzhardt knew they were bogus, since they had set the court fight over the tapes in motion when they engineered Alexander Butterfield's revelation in the first place.

Rogers resigned as secretary of state on August 22, and Nixon immediately nominated Kissinger, who would remain national security advisor, to replace Rogers. While that ended the tensions between Rogers and Kissinger, it also forced Kissinger to face confirmation hearings before the Senate for the first time. As national security advisor, Kissinger had avoided testifying under oath because it was a White House staff job protected by executive privilege. Now Kissinger would no longer have that protection, meaning that everything he had done in the previous four and a half years was fair game for curious members of the Foreign Relations Committee. That included the FBI wiretaps that he had sought on members of his own NSC staff.

Nixon now said that Haig, after slightly more than three months as chief of staff, "had become bogged down in Watergate." So vast were the tentacles of the scandal that Haig had little choice, even if he had been protecting Nixon's best interests and not his own. "Al Haig, I am sure, would be the first to acknowledge that he ran a very protective White House," Nixon wrote in his memoirs. "It probably would have surprised the press corps to hear the assessments from Cabinet and staff that beneath Haig's far more affable and accessible exterior he was in many ways a more rigid administrator than Bob Haldeman.... To prevent it, he drew more and more authority and responsibility to himself."[42]

Nixon had given Haig that power, which Haig magnified by turning Nixon into a virtual prisoner in the White House and limiting his access to the rest of the staff. Meanwhile, Haig kept pressing Agnew to resign.

During a late-month trip to San Clemente, Nixon said he would fire anyone in the Justice Department who leaked information about Agnew. Nixon kept playing the good cop to Haig's bad one, lying to reporters that his confidence in Agnew's integrity "has not been shaken and in fact has been strengthened by his courageous conduct and his ability, even though he's controversial at times as I am, over the past four-and-a-half years. And so I am confident in the integrity of the Vice-President and particularly in the performance of the duties that he has had as Vice-President, and as a candidate for Vice-President." Nixon called speculation about Agnew resigning irresponsible, although he had delegated Haig to make that happen. "The Vice-President has not been indicted," Nixon said. "Charges have been thrown out by innuendo and otherwise which he has denied to me personally and which he has denied publicly. And the talk about resignation even now ... would be inappropriate."[43]

Nixon had to get Agnew out before he could fire Cox. He told Haig to warn Richardson on August 23 that Nixon was "talking about moving against Cox." Any thoughts Cox may have had about challenging Nixon's "abuse of power," Haig told the attorney general, were unacceptable, and "regardless of the price the president is not going to tolerate it."[44]

In less than a year, Nixon's abuse of power, including the wiretaps Haig and Kissinger abetted, would make up the article of impeachment against Nixon that would receive the most votes in the House Judiciary Committee.

Sirica ruled on August 29 that Nixon had to turn over the subpoenaed tapes. The White House immediately announced an appeal, claiming the order was "clearly erroneous and beyond the power of the judicial branch in that it purports to subject the President of the United States to compulsory process for acts performed in his official capacity."[45] In essence, they argued, Nixon was above the law in this regard, which by this time had been proven to be a losing argument in the courts. Nixon had no palatable options, since he knew the tapes showed he was guilty. He still did not realize, however, that Haig and Buzhardt, his main defenders, knew of that guilt, too, and were steadily undermining him.

Nixon was angry that Richardson had agreed to appoint a special prosecutor as a condition for his Senate confirmation, and he thought Richardson compounded that mistake by picking Cox, Nixon's philosophical and geographical opposite, as the prosecutor. That was no one's fault but Nixon's. When Richard Kleindienst resigned as attorney general in April because of the problems Nixon created, Nixon could have picked anyone to succeed him. Instead, he picked Richardson and boxed him into a corner.

By the end of August Haig had let Agnew's problems spill into the open and then tried to get Agnew to quit. He also leaned on Richardson to get Cox to back off and presided over the White House's attempts to keep the tapes out of the prosecutor's hands after Haig had helped expose the tapes' existence in the first place. As the summer ended, Haig was pushing the president deeper into two crises that would speed Nixon's eventual departure: Agnew's resignation, which would lead to the appointment of a more desirable vice president who could succeed Nixon, and the firing of Cox, which would trigger the demands for Nixon's impeachment. Nixon saw none of it coming.

6 September 1973

Tensions between American presidents and their vice presidents are natural. Franklin Roosevelt had three vice presidents; his first, John Garner, contemplated challenging Roosevelt for the 1940 Democratic nomination. Nixon himself felt ignored by Dwight Eisenhower in the 1950s. But nothing in previous administrations matched the pitched battle that began in September between the president's top aide, Alexander Haig, and the sitting vice president, Spiro Agnew. Haig had not made Agnew's problems go away; instead, Agnew faced a choice between resignation or conviction and prison. Haig, helped by Fred Buzhardt and Melvin Laird, kept up the leaks to undermine Agnew while also bullying the vice president into resigning and isolating Nixon from the political damage. Agnew already suspected Haig ran the White House. Nothing in the following month would persuade him otherwise.

Nixon and Haig remained focused on the Agnew problem for all of September, but the fate of the vice president was just one of Nixon's challenges. Energy prices had risen steadily all summer because of high demand and the manipulation of the oil market by the newly powerful Organization of the Petroleum Exporting Countries. Rising oil prices pushed inflation higher; controls the administration had started to put into effect in June had not worked. In South America, Chile, where Nixon had tried to stop the democratic election of Marxist Salvador Allende as president in 1970, was melting down after three years of economic sanctions and U.S. interference. By the end of September, Allende would be dead and a military junta in power. The tenuous peace in Vietnam accomplished after four years of secret negotiations by Henry Kissinger threatened to blow apart, as fighting there had never really stopped. Such challenges would bedevil the most secure president. For Nixon, they added more strain to an already overloaded fuse box.

Nixon flew to Washington from San Clemente and arrived early in the morning of September 1 to give Agnew the meeting he had requested days earlier. The meeting started at 10:40 a.m. and lasted for two hours.[1] "The strains were beginning to show" in Agnew, Nixon wrote. "I could see that he was no longer as sure as he had been in our first meeting that the charges against him were not provable in court; now he reflected on the fact that no court anywhere near Washington or Maryland could possibly treat him fairly."[2] Agnew knew Haig and Buzhardt were behind the unfair treatment from the White House. Leaks, Agnew said, were destroying his civil rights, something for which he blamed the Justice Department. Just as often, however, these leaks came from the White House, where Laird was spreading negative information about Agnew with his friends on Capitol Hill.

Even with all of the other news, Agnew dominated Nixon's news conference on September 5. The president would not disclose what he had discussed with Agnew during his September 1 meeting and made a hedged defense of Agnew's integrity "during the period that he has served as a vice president, during which I have known him."[3] Haig, meanwhile, was continuing to consult with Attorney General Elliot Richardson and with Agnew, who kept complaining that Justice and the White House were not sharing information.

"This is the most bizarre thing I've ever seen," Agnew told Haig. "All we have is what we see in the newspapers. Why can't we be leveled with?"[4]

Buzhardt, Haig told Agnew, was meeting with Richardson again that afternoon and would know more. "All I know is we got kicked in the ass," Agnew said.[5]

Once again, this memory from Haig seems incongruous. Agnew did not mention it in his memoirs, although he catalogued virtually every utterance he had with Haig. By September 5 Agnew knew Haig was out to get him because Haig continued to force Agnew to resign. Agnew did not seem to understand the problems he had caused, Nixon told Haig on September 6. "Nixon wanted Buzhardt to read the handwriting on the wall to the vice president," Haig wrote. "I want Agnew to know, without Buzhardt telling him that I know, what a very strong case there is, so that my rather limited support will be understood."[6]

It bothered Nixon that Agnew had never told him that he would step aside if Nixon wanted him to, as Nixon had told Eisenhower during the height of the 1952 presidential campaign. Then, dogged by press accounts of how he spent a secret fund of money donated by political supporters, Nixon told Eisenhower he would quit the presidential ticket if Ike wanted him to.[7]

Agnew said he was fighting for his life, Haig said.

Maybe so, Nixon said, but Agnew never said, "I want to do what's best for the country."[8]

That was because Agnew, like the president he served, viewed what was best for him as what was best for the country. Agnew believed he represented a constituency of harder-edge conservatives who felt consistently shortchanged by the man they thought represented them—Nixon. Meanwhile, Nixon viewed himself as the leader who had reversed America's decline and who had scored a series of foreign policy successes—ending the Vietnam War, opening relations with China, and reaching nuclear arms deals with the Soviet Union—of which other presidents could only dream. Nixon still feared that Agnew had enough influence with conservatives to undermine Nixon's chances of surviving Watergate. He wanted Haig and Buzhardt to make Agnew realize how bad the prosecution's case in Baltimore looked for him.

Haig and Buzhardt went to Richardson on September 8 to recommend that if he did present the Justice Department's case to a federal grand jury, then he should do it without angering Agnew and his supporters.[9] They did not, and most likely could not, say how to bring a case against a sitting vice president without attracting attention. Richardson said he wanted to make Agnew quit and prevent him from taking the case to the House of Representatives, where Agnew presumed he had enough support to stop an impeachment move.

On September 10 Haig and Buzhardt met with Agnew and his lawyers again, and again the message was the same: resign.[10]

Buzhardt laid out the legal case against Agnew as dispassionately as possible. He told the vice president about his former associates and employees who had testified against him, how they talked about giving Agnew envelopes of cash in the vice president's office, and of a culture of kickbacks and corruption that went back to Agnew's tenure as Baltimore County executive. "I was to be a living demonstration that the President spurned cover-ups, let the chips fall where they might—this was the whole idea behind the White House move to make me quit," Agnew recounted. Then Haig said Agnew had to quit now. Judah Best, Agnew's attorney, interceded, telling Haig that Agnew did not deserve to hear such a conversation. Agnew then left the office so that Best, Haig, and Buzhardt could continue the conversation without him.[11]

Agnew still would not resign, but he let Best crack the door open to resignation. On September 11 Buzhardt told Richardson that Agnew's lawyers were ready to start talking.[12]

A day later, Haig and Buzhardt went back to Agnew's office at 6:05 p.m. to try again. Haig said Nixon had ordered Richardson and Henry Petersen to review the facts in the case again. "The president wants to do what's right," Haig said.[13] Buzhardt followed with a recitation of what Richardson had told them. Agnew's longtime friend, I. H. "Bud" Hammerman, had testified that he had collected payoffs from eight state contractors and then given half of the money to Agnew while keeping 25 percent for himself and giving the other 25 percent to Jerry Wolff, another longtime Agnew associate and the Maryland roads commissioner. Agnew was not satisfied and wanted confirmation from the Justice Department itself. He told Haig and Buzhardt he would keep fighting.

"Richardson thinks it's a strong case," Haig said. "It's a hell of a situation. If we go along with the move to the House, Elliot will move concurrently and ask Speaker [Carl] Albert to hold it up. Albert will want to wait."

How do you know that? Agnew asked.

Nixon had checked with members of Congress. "You won't be supported," Haig said. "The President has lost his ability to exercise any power. The House action will take six months. There will be a clamor for a trial."[14]

In the Senate, the issue of the FBI wiretaps had arisen in Kissinger's confirmation hearings to be secretary of state. He denied any serious involvement in the taps, including the selection of the targets. On September 10 Richardson came to his rescue, telling the Foreign Relations Committee that he could not release the FBI's May report on the taps. "It has been Justice Department policy that this kind of material should not be disclosed unless an overruling public interest makes it essential," Richardson said. Such a comment and the way Justice dribbled out access to the report to two senators—Democrat John Sparkman of Alabama and Republican Clifford Case of New Jersey—showed how Justice wanted to keep the details from the rest of the committee. Richardson, who had spent much of the summer helping Haig try to persecute Pentagon investigator Donald Stewart, was helping Kissinger cover up the wiretaps. Laird and Bryce Harlow were Nixon's two best sources of information about the mood on Capitol Hill, where Laird had sabotaged Agnew's support among House Republicans.[15]

Agnew finally realized his options had all but disappeared. Best told him that they should at least listen to what the Justice Department and White House had to say. Their one condition was that Agnew not be prosecuted and not do jail time.[16]

While Haig continually pressured Agnew to resign, he had also succeeded in conning the vice president into believing that the momentum came from Richardson, with whom Agnew had an animosity that dated back to the early days of the first term. Agnew believed Richardson harbored designs on the 1976 Republican nomination for president, a race that would be markedly easier without an incumbent vice president as an opponent. Best, Agnew's attorney, went to see Richardson and Petersen on September 13. The two Justice officials seemed skeptical that they could negotiate Agnew's resignation. But Buzhardt had already orchestrated everything. Agnew mistakenly believed that Nixon had agreed to push Agnew out of office to make Richardson feel better when Nixon fired Watergate special prosecutor Archibald Cox. "So again I was treated like a pawn in the game—the game of Watergate cover-up," Agnew wrote in his memoirs.[17]

Agnew still had his defenders. Senator Barry Goldwater of Arizona, the staunch conservative who lost the 1964 presidential race to Lyndon Johnson, visited Agnew at his home. He told Agnew not to lose heart and that Laird had been on Capitol Hill "trying to cut [Agnew's] legs off." It was another example of how Laird worked with Haig and Buzhardt, Laird's close friend, to protect their interests. In this case, eliminating Agnew in order to get a more politically acceptable vice president served them all. "Hang in there and fight it," Goldwater told Agnew. "They're just trying to ride you out. Go to the House, but don't tell the White House—just go on your own." Goldwater then called Harlow and complained about Agnew's treatment.[18]

At the same time, Richardson told U.S. Attorney George Beall to present evidence to the federal grand jury in Baltimore when it resumed work in two weeks. Haig told Nixon that Justice had given a plea bargain agreement to Agnew's lawyers, and Buzhardt believed the agreement language would push Agnew to reach a final deal. "If that doesn't satisfy him, I may have to play tough," Nixon told Haig.[19]

Whether Haig believed him is another matter. Throughout the Agnew crisis, from the time Nixon first heard about the grand jury investigation in April to the end game in the fall, Nixon let Haig do his dirty work for him. Not once in his meetings with Agnew did Nixon tell his two-time running mate that he had to leave office, that he lacked confidence in him, or that he considered him a crook. Nixon believed all those things, yet he delegated the duty of being "tough" to his chief of staff, the same man who believed Agnew had to go so Nixon could be forced out.

On September 14, spooked by Goldwater's call, Buzhardt and Harlow flew to meet the senator in Phoenix, where they showed Goldwater the evidence against Agnew. Goldwater said he did not "give a damn if Agnew was as guilty as John Dillinger." He would not support the White House's attempts to deny Agnew his right to defend himself in court. Goldwater knew Nixon did not like Agnew much, so he felt little guilt about telling Agnew to protect himself by going to the House.[20]

Goldwater's opposition notwithstanding, the momentum against Agnew continued to build. Richardson and his team conducted a seven-hour meeting on September 15, after which they concluded they could let Agnew resign in exchange for a no-contest plea to tax evasion.[21]

As Agnew twisted in the wind, Archibald Cox started three days of meetings with Buzhardt on September 17 to find a compromise on getting some of the tapes. The battle in the courts ground on, and while the tide seemed to be in Cox's favor, there was no guarantee that he would prevail in the end or that Nixon would honor whatever the court decided. Buzhardt could not simply hand over the tapes as long as Nixon opposed giving them up. So Buzhardt had to grind away gradually, creating obstacles to Cox while he and Haig sought other ways to undermine Nixon. Somewhere in the discussions, Cox made the unfortunate mistake of suggesting that a third party might be able to verify transcripts of the tapes. That suggestion, author J. Anthony Lukas wrote, "would soon come back to haunt him."[22]

After Richardson's help on September 10, Kissinger returned to a closed session of the Foreign Relations Committee a week later to testify more about the wiretaps. As he had since the issue first arose earlier in the year, he lied, this time under oath. "First, I never recommended the practice of wiretapping," he told the panel. "I was aware of it, and I went along with it to the extent of supplying names of the people who had had access to the sensitive documents in question. Despite some newspaper reports, I never recommended it, urged it or took it anywhere."[23]

Nixon, Haig, and the few others in the White House familiar with the wiretaps knew that was a lie. Kissinger's denials about the wiretaps so angered Nixon that he told Haig about the existence of the White House taping system to expose Kissinger. But he now needed Kissinger confirmed as secretary of state. Nixon remained quiet, as did Haig, and they hoped the issue would go away. It did, but not for long.

By September 18 leaks about Agnew's resignation had started to appear in the press, and the White House did little to stop the speculation that Agnew was on the outs. Gerald Warren, Nixon's deputy press secretary, said the president stood by his September 5 assertion that he believed in Agnew's integrity as vice president. Still, Agnew's supporters believed the damage was done. "This is calculated by the White House to keep the Agnew story alive," said Victor Gold, Agnew's former press secretary. "I blame the staff at the highest level, by which I mean Melvin Laird and General Haig."[24]

In response, Haig and Laird lied and told the *Post* they had nothing to do with trying to get Agnew to resign.[25]

Agnew's lawyers met with Richardson, Henry Petersen, and George Beall at the Justice Department on September 19 to begin negotiations in earnest. Richardson, Agnew wrote, shared his concern that Nixon might end up leaving office before Agnew.[26] Nixon's sudden admission to Bethesda Naval Hospital in July for viral pneumonia spooked Richardson, who wondered if Nixon had more serious health problems. Maybe the stress had caused Nixon to have a stroke. "There could be speculation about the pressures on the vice president to resign," Agnew wrote that Richardson told him. "Indeed so! And who would know more about those pressures than he, himself—unless it might be General Haig?" Agnew also met again that day with Haig, who again pushed Agnew to resign. He told Agnew that prosecutors in Baltimore would try to have the grand jury indict Agnew and make their case public. Immediately after that, Haig said, Nixon would call on Agnew to resign. Agnew continued to wonder just how much of what he heard from Haig came from Nixon and "how much was dictated by Haig."[27]

Nixon left the White House on September 19 to spend the night at the Bethesda, Maryland, home of his daughter Julie and her husband, David Eisenhower, the grandson of the former president. He returned the following morning and huddled or spoke with Haig five times before he met with Agnew in his hideaway office in the Old Executive Office Building. During their eighty-two-minute meeting, Agnew told Nixon he had not violated the public trust, and Nixon said he believed him. Richardson, Agnew said, was being completely vindictive and was out to get him, but he would resign if Richardson pledged not to prosecute him for a felony. "The President must have realized that a long, drawn-out trial not only would be ruinous for me, it would also be disastrous for him," Agnew wrote. "His overpowering desire was to save himself in his struggle for survival against the Watergate special prosecutors who were relentlessly closing in on him."[28]

Nixon called Haig as soon as Agnew left, and the two met for almost an hour before they walked to the Oval Office, where they talked for another half hour.[29] Haig then brought in Buzhardt, and together they called Richardson. They told the attorney general he could not force Agnew into a trial, and Richardson pushed back. He would not agree to let Agnew simply plead no contest to federal tax evasion charges and resign without admitting he had done anything wrong. After all, why would Agnew resign if he had done nothing wrong? There had to be an admission, and without one, Richardson would not agree to drop charges in exchange for a guilty plea. Haig and Buzhardt pushed back even harder; Agnew had to go, and the sooner the better. Richardson could not stand in the way. But Richardson would not budge.[30]

Richardson called Buzhardt on the morning of September 21 to say that he had not changed his mind about the need for Agnew to admit guilt, and to his surprise, Haig called him back and said Nixon had reconsidered and decided he would rather force Agnew to acknowledge guilt than have Richardson resign in protest, particularly as the White House continued to negotiate with Cox about the fate of the White House tapes.[31] Buzhardt told Nixon at 3:45 p.m. that there seemed to be a breakthrough with Agnew.[32]

Starting on Saturday, September 22, Richardson spent the weekend talking with Haig and Buzhardt about the shape of a deal with Agnew. Also that Saturday, Nixon welcomed Kissinger to the White House for his swearing in as secretary of state, an event that attracted celebrants who reflected Kissinger's wide swath of friends and supporters: New York governor Nelson Rockefeller, actor Kirk Douglas, members of the National Security Council staff, and two members of the Joint Chiefs of Staff. Kissinger had withstood the scrutiny of his involvement in the FBI wiretaps with Haig, a relief to both men, but the Senate did not look that hard. By the time they voted 78–7 to confirm him on September 21, most senators saw Kissinger as the island of stability in the roiling seas of the Nixon administration.

The deal with Agnew started to blow up even as Richardson tried to negotiate Agnew's plea and resignation. The *Washington Post* reported accurately, through leaks, that Agnew was negotiating for a resignation. Henry Petersen told CBS *News*, "We've got the evidence" against Agnew. "We've got it cold."[33] By Sunday, September 23, Agnew was no longer willing to plead no contest and quit: he wanted to fight. "If we have to go to war," Agnew told Judah Best, "we will blow a lot of people out of the water."[34]

Agnew scheduled a meeting with Nixon for the morning of September 25. Before the president saw Agnew, Nixon huddled with Haig and Richardson for ninety minutes and then with Petersen for another twenty-seven minutes.[35] Richardson and Petersen had met with Nixon before Agnew got there. Richardson told Nixon he would take the case to the grand jury in Baltimore that day. They thoroughly prepared Nixon for another session with the increasingly bitter Agnew. Nixon's aides had worked with him long enough to know how much he hated confrontation, even with his subordinates, like Agnew. They were right to be worried. Agnew told Nixon he never received any money while vice president—which Nixon had to know was a lie after meeting with Richardson and Petersen—and that the charges being pushed by Richardson were just another attempt to ruin him politically. He would only resign if granted complete immunity from prosecution.

"Then, for a moment, his manner changed, and in a sad and gentle voice he asked for my assurance that I would not turn my back on him if he were out of office," Nixon wrote.[36] Agnew told Nixon he would take his chances with an impeachment investigation by the House of Representatives, where the elected officials who would judge him had a more nuanced view of campaign contributions and relations with donors than the members of any federal grand jury in Baltimore. Although he said he wanted Agnew to resign and was frustrated with his refusal to do so, Nixon told Agnew he had to wait until later in the afternoon to announce his plans to go to the House, because Nixon wanted to make sure Agnew did not spark any sudden moves by federal prosecutors in Baltimore.[37]

Agnew reached out to House Speaker Carl Albert that afternoon with his plan to have the House of Representatives begin a full impeachment inquiry. Richardson had already talked to Albert and told the Oklahoma Democrat that Agnew would be indicted. Haig wrote that Albert wanted to get rid of Agnew so he could become president once Agnew and Nixon were gone.[38] That is sheer fantasy concocted by Haig for his memoirs to justify his pushing Agnew out. There is no evidence that Albert, an unassuming man of sixty-five, ever coveted the White House. He believed that as a Democrat he had no claim on the office that had been won twice by Nixon, a Republican. Albert said that if anything had happened to Nixon and Albert somehow became president, he would appoint a Republican vice president and then resign.[39] Plus, as Haig also wrote, Nixon had no plans to let the office of vice president stay open long enough for Albert to fill the breach.[40] Nixon asked Haig to call John Connally and prepare him for a call to be nominated as vice president when Agnew resigned.

Albert quickly rejected Agnew's impeachment gambit on September 26. Agnew now faced the grand jury in Baltimore, and his legal team moved on September 28 to block the grand jury, claiming that the saturation news coverage of his case meant he could not get an impartial jury. Agnew also had another plan. On September 29 he traveled to Los Angeles, where he played golf with his friend Frank Sinatra and gave a belligerent speech before a convention of Republican women in which he pledged not to resign even if indicted. The Justice Department, Agnew said, was trying to frame him through a series of "malicious leaks" and perjured testimony.[41] The supportive crowd roared, and Agnew felt emboldened. The speech, he wrote, "touched off a wave of anger and fear inside the White House."[42] This reaction prompted Haig to call Nixon at Camp David, where the president was trying to determine what to do about the tapes that Cox had subpoenaed.[43]

Agnew also feared Haig was behind leaks that claimed Agnew had a four-stage plan to attack the prosecution against him, starting first with Petersen, then moving to Beall, then to Richardson, and finally to the president. Agnew believed this plan gave Haig the justification he needed to tell Nixon they had to give Agnew an offer he could not refuse, after which Agnew would resign. By this point, it was hard to determine who wanted Agnew to resign more, Nixon or Haig. While Haig had his reasons to get rid of Agnew, because his resignation would make it easier to remove Nixon, the president had also tired of the drama surrounding the vice president he had reluctantly picked in the first place.

In Camp David, Nixon's secretary, Rose Mary Woods, had started to transcribe the tapes that Cox had subpoenaed, even as the White House fought turning the tapes over. They ran into a problem on September 30, when they went to look for the tapes of conversations from June 20, 1972, involving aides Bob Haldeman and John Ehrlichman. They could not find one of the tapes, and Steve Bull called Haig for guidance. Haig talked to Buzhardt, who told him that only the conversation with Ehrlichman was included in the subpoena.[44]

By the end of September, Haig had cleared the hurdle of Kissinger's confirmation hearings without damaging disclosures about the FBI wiretaps. Kissinger had perjured himself, but he had lied before and gotten away with it. He seemed to have done that again. Agnew was finally getting the message and was close to resigning, which would let Nixon fire Cox and close the special prosecutor's office. Haig's plans were aligning, but problems he could not see were building beyond the horizon.

7 October 1973

Spiro Agnew's endgame seemed virtually complete by October 1. Fred Buzhardt had shuttled between the Justice Department and Agnew to force him to resign in exchange for not going to trial, although Elliot Richardson and his Baltimore prosecutors knew they had the evidence to convict Agnew. Few in the White House, particularly Nixon and Haig, wanted a protracted criminal trial. They just wanted Agnew gone, Nixon because every day Agnew remained in the news it reinforced the public impression of sleaze, and Haig because as long as Agnew remained Nixon could not appoint a vice president who could eventually replace him.

As the turmoil around Agnew swirled, a life-and-death crisis developed in the Middle East. Egypt, which had been stung with the rest of the Arab world by Israel's stunning victory in the 1967 Six-Day War, had amassed troops along the Suez Canal to attack the Israeli-occupied Sinai Peninsula. A preoccupied White House failed to focus on the movements until it was too late.[1]

On October 1 Rose Mary Woods, Nixon's longtime secretary, came into his Old Executive Office Building office to say she had mistakenly erased part of a tape from June 20, 1972, that she had been transcribing. Nixon called Haig, who called Buzhardt, who said the tape was not covered by the subpoena. "Buzhardt confirmed this, so the peculiar incident did not seem to present any problem," Nixon wrote. Haig and Buzhardt already knew Nixon had obstructed justice, so the new erasure gave them ammunition to use against the president later. After their brief meeting on the tape, Nixon and Haig took the presidential limousine for a long drive around Washington so they could talk about what to do about Agnew, who still had not quit.[2]

On October 2 Agnew's new press secretary said Agnew planned another aggressive speech on October 4, which enraged Haig. He already feared Agnew would keep escalating tensions with the West Wing, so he called Art Sohmer, Agnew's chief of staff, and said Nixon wanted no more Los Angeles–style speeches. Agnew could forget a deal if he kept attacking Justice or any other part of the administration, Haig told Sohmer. Agnew had no idea that Haig was bluffing. The White House could not afford a protracted trial and political fight.[3] Meanwhile, Nixon kept sending conflicting messages, such as his statement on October 3 that Agnew's decision to remain in office was an "altogether proper one."[4]

Haig did not agree. Either with Nixon's imprimatur or on his own, Haig met on October 4 with Gen. Michael Dunn, Agnew's military aide, who wrote Agnew a memo that spelled out Haig's dire warning. Haig, Dunn wrote, "knows of every phone call made by" Agnew. Haig implied that he knew all of Agnew's attempts to save himself, but there was no way out. If Agnew resigned, he would not be prosecuted, Dunn wrote, which was the same message Agnew had been told for the last week. "Haig's threat made me realize, with a sickening shock, that I had finally lost the last slim thread of hope that the president would help me in my fight," Agnew wrote. "On the contrary, he had turned against me and become my mortal enemy. Haig insinuated that if I went against the President's wishes and refused to resign, there would be no more help from the White House to prevent a jail sentence and no assistance with the IRS finances, placing my staff, or the other carrots Buzhardt had dangled."[5] Haig disputed Agnew's description in his memoirs, but it was clear something was said.[6] Agnew had little will to fight left.

Agnew's surprise at Haig's tough message is hard to square with the White House Agnew described. "The American people should know that in the last hectic year or more of his residence in the White House, Richard Nixon did not actually administer all the powers of the presidency." Haig, Agnew realized, "was the de facto president." Despite his delusional protestations of innocence in the face of mounting evidence, Agnew realized that "Haig had the power of the bureaucracy at his command, and the Washington insiders knew he was standing there behind Nixon, pulling the strings. Haig had direct connections with the CIA and the FBI and every other agency. . . . His power extended into any agency he chose. The very survival of the Nixon presidency was threatened."[7]

When Agnew's memoirs were published, few paid heed to his complaints about Haig. Agnew's insights were discounted as the complaints of a corrupt and discredited politician, but he had correctly assessed who had the power in the Nixon White House: "I am also convinced that Haig desired not only to move me out, but in due course, after someone else had been brought into the vice-presidency, to move Mr. Nixon out, too. I really think that by this time, Al Haig already knew enough about the discrepancies in the tapes—and the truth about Nixon's involvement in the Watergate cover-up—to be convinced that eventually the President himself must go. And Haig did not want me in the line of succession."[8]

Twelve years later, Haig's memoirs acknowledged Agnew's suspicions.[9] Haig knew Nixon would not survive his second term and that the corrupt Agnew would not survive either. Haig also made the same claim to reporters Bob Woodward and Carl Bernstein in a September 1974 interview that was only made public in 2011, after Haig, Agnew, and Nixon had died.[10] Melvin Laird also knew Nixon was guilty, because Buzhardt told him. Agnew correctly assessed the situation.

Shortly after Haig met with Dunn, he left with Nixon for Key Biscayne, where on October 6 they learned that Egyptian and Syrian forces had launched a surprise attack on Israeli positions in the Sinai Peninsula and the Golan Heights, which Israel had also claimed in 1967. U.S. intelligence detected some movements by the Egyptians and Syrians, but nothing that indicated an attack of such magnitude.[11] In Florida, isolated by Haig, Nixon was a bystander, while Kissinger, in New York, met constantly with foreign officials. He desperately but unsuccessfully worked the phones to stave off the fighting. He and Haig, not Nixon, controlled the American response. The president, stressed out and drinking too much, marginalized himself.

Haig shaded the truth in his memoirs. "It has been stated elsewhere that Nixon, who was in Key Biscayne on Yom Kippur, did not learn of the attacks until hours after they had taken place," Haig wrote. "That is not true. Within minutes after hostilities began, I was informed by the White House situation room, and I informed the President, that the Arab offensive was under way. It was then about 6 a.m. He decided within the hour to return to Washington to take personal command of the crisis."[12]

In fact, Nixon remained in Florida all day and did not return to Washington until 10:00 p.m. on October 7.[13] Kissinger wanted Nixon to stay on the sidelines, and Haig kept him there.

Haig and Kissinger spoke at 10:35 a.m. on October 6.

"I wanted to bring you up to date on where we stand and to tell you my strategy," Kissinger said. "You may have to calm some people down."

"Good," Haig responded. "I am sitting with the president."

Egypt started the fighting, Kissinger said, and the United States needed to determine if the Soviets had advance notice and then to go to the United Nations Security Council to get a joint resolution for a cease-fire. As Kissinger spelled out his plan, Haig listened, giving one-word responses when Kissinger paused for breath.

"The President is seriously considering going back to Washington," Haig said.

"I think that is a grave mistake," Kissinger responded. "There is nothing we can do right now. You should wait to see how it develops. Wait until at least this afternoon. So far not even a Security Council meeting has been called."

"He agrees with that," Haig said. "His problem is that if it is an all-out war for him to be sitting down here in this climate would be very, very bad."

Kissinger said they needed to wait for the Soviets' response and remain calm. Nixon should stay in Florida.

"You will make sure that the President is comfortable with this strategy," Kissinger said. "I think it is our only possible course and it has to be seen in the general context of his ability to act and of what follows afterwards."[14]

Not only was Nixon not flying back to Washington to confront the crisis, he was relying on Haig to talk to the main crisis manager for the United States—Kissinger, who spoke with Haig two hours later.

"I wanted to tell you the President feels he definitely has to come back to Washington," Haig said.

"I think you are making a terrible mistake," Kissinger said.

"We are not going to announce it and we will not go back until 7 tonight," Haig said.

"I would urge you to keep any Walter Mitty tendencies under control," Kissinger said, referring to the fictional character who lived in a fantasy world.

"That is not the problem," Haig said. "He has a situation with Agnew which prohibits his staying down here. On top of that he knows if he is sitting here in the sun and there is a war going on he is in for terrible criticism."

Nixon, Kissinger said, could not just slip into Washington unnoticed.

"That is true but he feels very strongly that he is just not going to sit down here," Haig said.

"What does he think is going on?" Kissinger asked.

"He thinks nothing is going on," Haig said.[15]

At the same time, Haig and Kissinger debated about what to do with Nixon, Haig and Buzhardt were finishing the details for Agnew's resignation. The Justice Department had presented them with a memo that said the vice president could be indicted without being impeached first, although the president could not. That gave Haig a hammer to use against Agnew if he remained intransigent. They called Agnew's lawyer,

Judah Best, who flew to Key Biscayne and arrived after midnight. He and Buzhardt negotiated the details until about 4:00 a.m.[16]

On the morning of October 7, Attorney General Elliot Richardson met with his team and said the outbreak of the war made it even more important that Agnew resign. Worried about Nixon's health, Richardson worried that if something happened to Nixon, Agnew would succeed him.[17] In Florida, Haig told reporters that Agnew could resign as early as the next day.[18]

Kissinger updated Haig at 9:35 a.m. So far, Kissinger said, they had no word from the Soviets. He suggested that Ron Ziegler announce that the United States would go to the Security Council with or without the Soviets. No one, Kissinger said, really wanted a Security Council session, particularly the Israelis, who wanted to settle the issue on the battlefield.

"What we don't need now is a war council meeting and getting ourselves into the middle of it," Kissinger said. "To the American people it is a local war. Let them beat them up for a day or two and that will quiet them down."

Haig said Nixon would return that day, which Kissinger opposed again.

"What is he going to do?" Kissinger asked.

"It is conceivable we will have an announcement about the Vice President," Haig said. "That is the first thing."

"That is a slightly different problem," Kissinger said.

"You bet it is and what I am telling you is the two are going to be linked together," Haig said. "He cannot be sitting down here in the sun with what is going on in the VP thing. It is not firm yet but we will know very shortly."

"If that other thing is happening then I can see a reason for coming back from the point of view of diplomacy," Kissinger said. "I would keep his return for later. Supposing the Soviets get tough and if he then returns that would be a good move. If he returns early it looks like an hysterical move. I am giving you my honest opinion. If the Soviets took a position of having kicked us in the teeth that would be a signal that things are getting serious. We will not have heard by 3. We probably won't know until the first thing in the morning."

"Alright," Haig said. "I will try to hold this thing down here."

"I would hold him until the first thing in the morning," Kissinger said.

Kissinger said the principals had included Nixon in the morning telephone calls, as if including the president of the United States in these vital calls was doing Nixon a favor.

"But don't you agree, speaking personally?" Kissinger asked.

"I know, except I know about the other problem," Haig said, meaning Agnew.

"You are a better judge of that," Kissinger said. "The problem I am handling in my judgment is if we played this as a crisis—say nothing, act tough, without stirring up the atmosphere."

Haig said he would check with Nixon.[19]

Kissinger feared that any overreaction by Nixon would send the wrong message to the Soviets, and with Nixon in Florida, Kissinger also enjoyed a free hand. At 1:10 p.m. he called Haig again to ask Nixon to stay in Florida unless he had a compelling reason to return. Nixon needed to stay calm, Kissinger said. Haig said he had settled Nixon down. Kissinger said he wanted to include Nixon in a way that would help the country.[20]

In a normal administration, the president would make those decisions, not a cabinet secretary, even one with Kissinger's influence. Nixon knew enough to realize it looked bad if he stayed in Florida while the crises with Agnew and the war went on. Yet Kissinger and Haig isolated the president. Their reasons would become more apparent in the coming days, as they believed they could not let Nixon exercise the power he had earned by winning two elections as president.

Throughout it all, Nixon remained a bystander. He finally returned to Washington that night.

The next morning, Agnew's attorney, Judah Best, called the vice president in New York to tell him about the deal for his resignation. Agnew told Best to remind Haig and Buzhardt that Agnew would not agree if it was not stipulated that Agnew would not do any time in prison. "I was deathly afraid of a double cross," Agnew said.[21]

Agnew's attorneys met with Richardson on October 9 to lock in the deal. Agnew would not go to prison. "It is my recommendation that there be no term of imprisonment," Richardson told U.S. District Judge Walter Hoffman, who oversaw the Agnew case. That afternoon, Agnew went into the Oval Office to see Nixon, who looked haggard and drawn and seemed genuinely sorry. That was an act. Nixon mostly felt relieved.[22]

Agnew walked into Hoffman's court on October 10 and stunned the crowd by pleading *nolo contendere*—no contest—to tax evasion. He then resigned as vice president. In exchange for not pushing a criminal trial against Agnew, Richardson gave Haig what he wanted almost from the moment he learned about Agnew's legal troubles. By quitting, Agnew allowed Nixon to appoint a new vice president acceptable to Democrats and Republicans. That person also had to be considered a viable president, since the pressure to force Nixon from office would not stop.

Anyone close to Nixon knew he wanted to name John Connally—the former Democratic governor of Texas and a former treasury secretary—as vice president. However, members of both parties distrusted him. Democrats resented his recent switch to the Republican Party, while Republicans never considered Connally one of their own. Haig said Nixon asked him not to help him pick a vice president, because Nixon wanted to consider Haig as a potential nominee. Nixon, Haig said, sent various lists of candidates to Republicans all around the country. Meanwhile, Melvin Laird polled his former colleagues on the Hill, although Laird had his favorite candidate, House Minority Leader Gerald Ford of Michigan. A former college football star at the University of Michigan, Ford was a genial midwestern conservative acceptable to his fellow Republicans and to most Democrats.

As the White House focused on Agnew, an odd story by Bob Woodward and Carl Bernstein appeared in the October 10 *Washington Post*. Nixon, they reported, had approved more wiretaps than the seventeen conducted by the FBI on government officials and journalists between 1969 and 1971. The FBI tapped two more unnamed targets in late 1971 and early 1972, the story said. However, they did not report what Woodward already knew: one tap was on Yeoman Charles Radford, the chief suspect in the military spy ring. Instead, the story implied that Nixon was lying about the number of wiretaps and exaggerating national security threats. Nixon had ordered the FBI to monitor Radford to see if he leaked any classified information after Nixon had ordered him transferred away from Washington. The taps on Radford and an associate of his followed stricter guidelines than those ordered in 1969, and they stopped after the Supreme Court ruled that all wiretaps required a judge's approval.[23]

The Woodward and Bernstein piece came as reporters Jim Squires of the *Chicago Tribune* and Dan Thomasson of Scripps-Howard were closing in on the mysterious "national security" topics that John Ehrlichman was forbidden to mention while testifying before the Senate Watergate committee in July. The main topic, as Senators Howard Baker and Sam Ervin already knew, was the spy ring. Woodward already knew about the spy ring, too; he had asked his former commander, Rear Adm. Robert Welander, about it in May. The October 10 story in the *Post* appeared more as a bit of work for Haig by Woodward instead of a story that broke news. Woodward was withholding news that he alone knew, not informing his readers.

With Agnew gone, Buzhardt pitched an idea aimed at breaking the deadlock on the White House tapes with special prosecutor Archibald Cox. Instead of turning over the subpoenaed tapes to Cox, Buzhardt suggested, why not have Senator John Stennis of Mississippi, a Democrat and former judge, review summaries of the tapes and verify their accuracy for Cox and the federal court?[24] Buzhardt and Stennis knew each other well from the years Buzhardt spent as an aide to South Carolina senator Strom Thurmond on the Senate Armed Services Committee. In May Buzhardt had suggested using Stennis to help stifle the Watergate committee investigation, calling Stennis the "undertaker" of the Senate because he could bury a political controversy by stacking a committee hearing with friendly witnesses to create the illusion of a fair investigation. Stennis, however, was seventy-three and hard of hearing, and he had spent most of the year in the hospital after being shot during a January robbery attempt outside his Washington home. Buzhardt's proposal came just days after Stennis returned to the Senate. Haig agreed, while

Nixon was hopeful this could prevent the disclosure of his guilt in the cover-up. Sam Ervin did not take the offer seriously, saying it was meant to precipitate a crisis that would get Cox fired.[25]

On October 11 Nixon told Haig to call Connally and tell him that congressional opposition made it impossible to nominate him to be vice president. Haig said he told Connally that Nixon's decision would actually help him, because "we are probably going to fire Cox within a week or ten days. There is a good chance that if your name goes forward Saturday that you will be held up in any event. There could be a merger of impeachment [of both the president and vice president]. That is the great danger."[26] That made no sense, since Agnew's resignation meant there was no vice president to impeach. For Connally to be impeached with Nixon, he would first have to be confirmed, which Haig had just told Connally was unlikely. Connally said he thought he could survive a confirmation battle and even win over a prominent Democrat such as Edward Kennedy, whose brother, President John Kennedy, was killed by the same bullet that wounded Connally in Dallas on November 22, 1963.[27] According to Nixon, Connally acknowledged he had little chance of confirmation. Haig also wrote that Connally said he would support Nixon if he wanted to name Gerald Ford.[28]

Haig then called Ford to say Nixon would appoint him as vice president. He noted that Ford became the fourth person to know Nixon's plans after Connally, Nixon, and Haig himself. Nixon and Haig planned to make the announcement the following day.[29]

Haig and Buzhardt then told Nixon about the Stennis compromise. Nixon's calendar shows he met with Haig and Buzhardt for close to an hour at 1:35 p.m. and then with Haig, Buzhardt, and Ron Ziegler for slightly more than thirty minutes starting at 2:51 p.m.[30] Nixon told his two aides, Haig wrote, that "the first order of business is to fire Cox." The president wanted Elliot Richardson to know that Nixon planned to fire Cox but keep Richardson as attorney general. If Richardson felt he needed to resign, Nixon could live with that. He just wanted to fire Cox.[31]

Haig's handling of the Cox firing would soon become one of the greatest debacles of his tenure as Nixon's chief of staff. His version of the events also does not match those of Richardson and the other participants. Either Haig willfully led Nixon, Richardson, and Cox into a politically destructive move that would play out in nine days, or he was just stunningly incompetent. Now that Agnew had resigned, the end game for Cox was in motion; its resolution would leave Nixon even more crippled.

On Capitol Hill, Senator Lowell Weicker continued his quest to have the Watergate committee subpoena former FBI official William Sullivan as a witness. He knew Sullivan had more information about Nixon's use of FBI wiretaps to track suspected leakers. Sullivan had spent much of 1973 dodging responsibility for his part in the wiretap saga. He alternately teased Weicker and committee staffers with tantalizing hints of wrongdoing, only to reverse direction and claim ignorance. In June he complained to Weicker that John Dean had lied in his testimony about Sullivan and the wiretaps, and he gave contradictory and misleading signals to committee investigators in July, August, and October. Sullivan's interests in not testifying converged with Haig's; if Sullivan testified under oath, the very real chance existed that he could spill damaging information about Haig at a time when criminal charges from the wiretap program remained possible.

Cox angered the White House again when he announced that Egil Krogh, the leader of the White House Plumbers, had been indicted for perjury in the case of the September 1971 burglary of the office of Dr. Lewis Fielding, Daniel Ellsberg's psychiatrist. Krogh lied to cover up that break-in as well as other aspects of the Plumbers' work. If Krogh went to trial, he would use evidence from the Plumbers' work in his defense, including the spy ring investigation.

Nixon had more than picking a vice president and the tapes to handle on October 11. The war in the Middle East had taken a serious toll on the Israelis, who told Kissinger they had lost at least five hundred tanks in the fighting. The Soviets had kept up their supplies to Egypt and Syria, while U.S. aid to Israel remained stalled.[32]

By day's end Nixon must have felt overwhelmed. He flew to Camp David shortly after 5:30 p.m. and talked to Kissinger from 6:19 to 6:32 p.m. He spoke with Haig twice, from 7:30 to 7:40 p.m. and from 7:54 to 7:58 p.m. Haig called again at 8:08 p.m. but was not connected to Nixon, most likely because Nixon was passed out drunk.[33] Around that time, Maj. Gen. Brent Scowcroft, Kissinger's deputy at the NSC, called Kissinger to inform him that British prime minister Edward Heath wanted to talk to Nixon. Kissinger told Scowcroft no, because the last time Kissinger had spoken to Nixon that day—for thirteen minutes after 6:00 p.m.— Nixon was "loaded."[34]

At 8:28 a.m. on October 12 Haig called Richardson and summoned him to the White House for a meeting. The mission to fire Cox was heating up. Richardson called Cox and expressed surprise that Cox had indicted Krogh, which Richardson considered a national security case they needed to avoid. Cox said he thought it was just a simple case of perjury. Regardless, Richardson said, there existed a strong possibility that they both could get fired. Richardson had insulated Cox from the frequent pressure Richardson received from Haig and Buzhardt. The attorney general knew from his meeting with Haig in the morning that Nixon wanted a reason to fire Cox; Richardson did not want to give Nixon one so easily.[35]

Nixon returned to the White House in the morning and told Haig he would pick Ford as vice president. They called Connally and told him he had lost out to Ford. They arranged for a celebration at the White House after the official announcement of Ford's appointment. "Haig gave an order that we should have a grand celebration," White House aide Steve Bull said. "Dave Gergen and I said no, this wasn't a time for a celebration. It was a tragedy. A vice president had just resigned, and we'll get hammered in the press for appearing to celebrate. We were overruled, and the next day, we were hammered in the press for it. Haig called us into the Roosevelt Room, where he said that we should never leak information if a decision goes against what we want. I told him that wasn't true."[36] Betty Beale, the *Washington Star* columnist, called Nixon to task for what Haig had ordered. "What other President tossed a joyous party in the East Room to announce a new Vice-President even while the pictures of the former Vice-President were being removed from the walls of the West Wing?" Beale wrote.[37]

The president, never the most publicly devout politician, held a prayer service at the White House on the morning of Sunday, October 14. Among the invitees was Stennis, whom Nixon called into the Oval Office to ask him if he would agree to the compromise Buzhardt had concocted.[38] Stennis said he would consider it depending on what Cox and Senators Ervin and Baker said. Stennis had kept many secrets for Nixon before and was willing to help Nixon again, but he wanted cover from his two Senate colleagues.[39]

With Stennis's tentative agreement, Haig and Buzhardt increased the pressure on Richardson to fire Cox. On October 15 they told Richardson that Nixon would prepare his own tape transcripts and then fire Cox. They did not, however, tell him about the Stennis compromise. Haig only did that after the meeting, when he called Richardson back and mentioned it for the first time.[40] He also did not tell Richardson that Stennis had signed on to the compromise. Richardson was being pushed into firing his law school mentor, Cox, at the behest of Nixon, the target of Cox's investigation. Nixon did not realize, however, that Haig was telling him one thing and Richardson another.[41]

Haig called Richardson and added more conditions, saying Cox could keep his job if he agreed not to ask for more documents or tapes than the ones that Stennis would verify. Agreeing to such terms would have closed off potential avenues of investigation to Cox, making him dependent on the whims of Stennis, Buzhardt's ally, to determine any future investigation. No serious prosecutor, Haig and Buzhardt had to realize, would accept such a deal. Richardson only reluctantly considered it to avoid firing Cox. But Richardson did not agree to the new conditions. He said he would have to call Haig back.[42]

Haig and Buzhardt then went to Capitol Hill to see Stennis, who threw a kink into their plans. Stennis said his hearing would not let him listen to all of the tapes, which he did not realize were of a sporadic quality that would challenge even the most perfect hearing. Ever helpful, Buzhardt told Stennis he would listen to some of the tapes for him, thereby eliminating the ostensible neutrality that made the Stennis compromise even remotely plausible.[43]

All sides were hurtling toward a crisis. Richardson called Haig at 3:20 p.m. and agreed to the Stennis compromise but not to limit Cox's ability to get any new documents or tapes. Haig said nothing about the second point, which Richardson assumed was agreement. They met at 4:00 p.m., when, as Richardson later told the Senate, he told Haig that he would resign before firing Cox. They did not need to provoke a confrontation with Cox, Richardson said, and a fair compromise would combine the Stennis proposal with Cox's future ability to ask for more materials. Haig, however, told Nixon that Richardson had agreed to everything: firing Cox, the Stennis compromise, and the limits on Cox seeking additional materials. He did not, however, tell Nixon that Richardson would not back Nixon if he tried to fire Cox. So Haig misled Nixon into believing that Richardson agreed with his plan.

Richardson told Cox about the Stennis compromise in a 6:00 p.m. meeting. Cox was not enthusiastic.

Richardson agreed to everything, Haig wrote. "I think Cox should go along with it," Richardson said in Haig's account, which differs from those of the other participants.[44] Haig had his own reasons to fire Cox, which he did not share with Nixon, and he had already placed Nixon in no-win positions before, particularly with the revelation of the White House tapes and Vernon Walters's memcons from June 1972. Given Haig's established credibility problems, his version is hard to believe.

Meanwhile, the *New York Daily News* published a story on October 14 that exposed some of William Sullivan's machinations with Weicker and the Watergate committee. Sullivan, the *Daily News* reported, had conferred multiple times with Weicker and had provided evidence against Robert Mardian, the former head of the Justice Department's Internal Security Division and later the counsel to the Nixon 1972 campaign. "The Sullivan interviews, undertaken over the past several weeks by committee member Sen. Lowell P. Weicker (R-Conn.), reportedly have elicited a number of 'solid leads' from the onetime FBI official," the *Daily*

News reported.[45] The *Daily News* story was impeccably sourced; one of Weicker's top aides, Richard McGowan, had spent years on the *Daily News* staff before joining Weicker. McGowan also doubted Sullivan's honesty. "Bill Sullivan is a viper," McGowan wrote in a memo to Weicker.[46] The *Daily News* story also connected Sullivan as a source of Bob Woodward, especially for one of the Deep Throat interviews. Details of the *Daily News* story, primarily the accusations against Mardian, matched what Deep Throat told Woodward during their meeting in a bar in Prince George's County, Maryland, on March 5.[47]

Sullivan reacted on October 16 by writing Weicker to say he did not want to testify before the committee.[48] He also wrote the *Daily News* to deny he had talked to Weicker, despite the evidence to the contrary, and he also wrote Weicker to complain that investigators had badgered him all year.[49]

On October 17 Richardson detailed his understanding of the proposed deal with Cox in a memo to Buzhardt. Cox and the White House would negotiate any future requests by Cox for new documents. Buzhardt objected, so Richardson said he would delay anything regarding new tapes and documents.[50] A decision that day by Judge John Sirica that the Senate Watergate committee lacked the standing to seek the tapes meant Cox faced the White House alone, an awkward position, since Cox technically worked for the president.[51] Cox made his situation worse the next day, October 18, when he told Richardson he could not agree to the Stennis proposal, calling it problematic for one person to review the tapes. Nor would he limit future requests for information, because that would unfairly hamstring the investigation.[52]

Most, if not all, of the misunderstanding between Richardson and Nixon could have been avoided if the two had spoken directly. But they could not. Cox, the investigator of Watergate-related crimes, worked for Richardson, who had to preserve the investigation's independence, which would disappear if Richardson and Nixon talked directly. That placed more authority in the hands of Haig, who by now had demonstrated he did not have Nixon's best interests at heart.

Richardson took Cox's written rejection of the Stennis compromise to the White House, where he met with Haig, Buzhardt, Len Garment, and Charles Alan Wright, the University of Texas legal scholar advising Nixon on Watergate. Haig said Cox's rejection meant he should be fired. Richardson presciently argued that the public would blame Nixon, not Cox, if Nixon carried out his threat. Told about the meeting, Nixon erupted. "No more tapes, no more documents, nothing more!" he told Haig.[53]

"More than ever," Nixon wrote, "I wanted Cox fired."[54]

Richardson knew he and Cox were doomed. He went home on the night of October 18 and wrote a letter that explained why he had to resign.[55]

Cox's work triggered another decision that aggravated Haig. Egil Krogh, indicted by Cox for perjury, pleaded not guilty on October 18, which signaled a potentially difficult trial that could damage Haig's spy ring cover-up.

Whatever Haig thought he had accomplished unraveled on October 19 and 20. Richardson opened the morning by showing his staff the letter about resigning if Nixon fired Cox. Richardson's aides agreed with his plan, so Richardson had his secretary type it into a memo.[56] Richardson then called Haig, who said Wright and Cox were still talking. Richardson said he wanted to see Nixon if those negotiations broke down. Meanwhile, Wright sent Cox a letter that confirmed the details of their conversation from the night before. Cox said he could not agree to limit his requests because he had promised the Senate when he was confirmed in May that he would take the investigations wherever they led. He would not violate his word, Cox told Wright.[57]

Haig kept selling Richardson on the Stennis proposal. Richardson might have agreed, but he then saw the letters between Cox and Wright and realized the White House still wanted to handcuff Cox's future requests, which Richardson thought he had already resolved in Cox's favor. Someone, either Haig or Nixon, was not dealing in good faith. Richardson would not agree to limit Cox's requests or fire him, but he kept talking to Buzhardt, Garment, and Wright.[58] Meanwhile, Haig had told Nixon exactly the opposite—Richardson would fire Cox and not resign. Nixon also wrote that Haig told him it was Richardson's idea to put "parameters" around Cox to keep him from being fired.[59] Haig then kept trying to sell Richardson on the Stennis plan, although he omitted key details, such as that Senators Ervin and Baker did not know the scope of the compromise. Haig had not told Ervin and Baker they would only get summaries of tapes, not verbatim transcripts. Haig also said that Nixon needed maximum flexibility to deal with the Middle East crisis, a bogus plea to anyone who knew how much Kissinger and Haig had pushed Nixon to the sidelines. Nevertheless, Ervin and Baker agreed to pitch the compromise to the other committee members.[60]

After all that, Haig then told Richardson the truth, claiming he had tried to budge an uncompromising Nixon. Upset, Richardson felt used and lied to. He knew Cox would not agree to Haig's terms, that Cox would get fired, and that Richardson himself would have to resign. Meanwhile, Nixon said Haig told him that Richardson had only displayed mild dissatisfaction about the limits on Cox but would stay on the job.[61] Richardson called Cox and read him Nixon's letter about the tapes. Cox predictably disagreed.

Also that afternoon, White House Deputy Press Secretary Gerald Warren announced that Nixon was sending Kissinger to Moscow to negotiate a Middle East peace deal with the Soviets. Kissinger resisted the attempt to link his mission with the impending Stennis announcement, telling Haig that afternoon that it was a "cheap stunt" and "poor tactics" that would "look as if [Nixon] is using foreign policy to cover up a domestic thing. I will not link foreign policy with Watergate. You will regret it for the rest of your life." Haig backed down.[62]

Haig ordered the release of a White House statement about the Stennis compromise at 8:00 p.m., after the evening news broadcasts and close to the deadlines for the morning newspapers. Nixon, the release said, would end the tape controversy. Cox had rejected a compromise backed by Ervin and Baker, the statement said, and there would be no more requests for tapes and documents. It was all a lie based on Haig's deception of Nixon, who mistakenly believed he had Richardson's agreement.[63]

Richardson returned to his home in McLean, Virginia, where he received a call from Bryce Harlow. Richardson surprised Harlow by saying he had never been treated as shabbily as he had in the last few days.[64] Harlow reported back to Haig, who called Richardson. The attorney general, who had spent the last week being whipsawed by Haig and Buzhardt, told Haig he had just poured himself a drink and that they could talk about it later, a comment Haig used to smear Richardson as a drunk.[65] Haig wrote that Richardson's speech was slurred and that he would not fire Cox and would resign if he was forced to.[66] Despite that, there is no indication that Haig presented that information forcefully to Nixon, although Haig closed out Nixon's evening with a fifteen-minute call at around 11:00.[67]

Richardson started Saturday, October 20, with a letter to Nixon that said he would try to persuade Cox to agree to the Stennis compromise but would not limit future requests for tapes and documents. Haig saw that as Richardson refusing to carry out a presidential order. Cox followed with a 1:00 p.m. news conference at the National Press Club in which he declared he would not agree to the Stennis plan or any other limits. Haig called it a "bravura performance" in which Cox labeled the Stennis compromise a "Nixonian design" to mislead the American people.[68] Cox did not realize at the time that the plan was actually hatched by Haig and Buzhardt and abetted by their Senate ally, Stennis.

Cox's statement outraged Nixon. Len Garment called Richardson from Haig's office to say they had watched the news conference. Nixon was too busy dealing with the Middle East, Garment said; he asked Richardson if he would fire Cox and then resign if he felt he needed to. No, Richardson told Garment, he would not fire Cox. Haig then called Richardson, who repeated what he had told Garment.[69]

Richardson went to the White House at 4:30 p.m. to meet an angry Nixon, who fumed about Richardson's insubordination. He asked Richardson to wait to resign until the end of the Middle East crisis. Richardson declined. The man whom Nixon had appointed to run three cabinet agencies—Health, Education, and Welfare; Defense; and Justice—thanked Nixon for giving him so many great opportunities. He then resigned and went to Justice to tell his staff. Haig called Justice and asked for William Ruckelshaus, Richardson's deputy.[70] A few months earlier, Haig had questioned the idea of Ruckelshaus joining Richardson there because Haig doubted Ruckelshaus's loyalty to the White House. Now, as acting attorney general, Ruckelshaus validated Haig's earlier concerns. Haig again invoked the Middle East crisis when he told Ruckelshaus he needed to fire Cox. If the crisis was so dire, Ruckelshaus responded, then why not wait a week to fire Cox? Your commander in chief has given you an order, Haig said, so you must follow it. Ruckelshaus resigned instead and handed the telephone to Robert Bork, the solicitor general and third-ranking official at Justice.[71] Now the acting attorney general, Bork agreed to fire Cox, reasoning that Nixon would go down the chain of command at Justice to find someone willing to fire Cox. Haig dispatched a limousine to pick up Bork and drive him to the White House. Inside the limo were Buzhardt and Garment, dispatched by Haig to make sure Bork did not change his mind. Bork met with Nixon from 5:59 to 6:08 p.m., and he agreed to fire Cox. The president then went to the White House residence to watch a movie.[72]

The first bulletins about the firings started to move shortly before 7:00 p.m. All the major television networks broke into their regular programming to break the news. Press Secretary Ron Ziegler stepped into a seething White House briefing room shortly after 8:00 p.m. to announce the firings. Foreign elements, the prepared White House statement said, may be prepared to use Watergate to do things they would not ordinarily do.[73] Few in the press corps believed the official explanation. They considered Cox an honorable prosecutor and Richardson and Ruckelshaus two of the most credible administration officials. Before the night was out, the event was being called the Saturday Night Massacre, and the calls for impeaching Nixon gained intensity.

Haig planned not only to fire Cox but to shut down the entire special prosecutor's office. Shortly after the firing, Haig ordered the police to close and seal the offices. Cox's staff converged on the scene as the news spread, but the police stopped them from taking anything, including their personal items.[74]

In his memoirs, Haig expressed remorse for plunging Nixon into such a crisis. "I could not help but be aware that what happened must also have shaken Nixon's confidence in me," he wrote. Nixon just wanted to fire Cox and be done with it, Haig claimed, but Haig had led Nixon to pursue the Stennis compromise. "Urging him to do otherwise was the greatest mistake I made as Nixon's chief of staff," Haig continued. "From the emotional point of view, facing the results of my advice was the low point of my time in that job."[75] Haig blamed Richardson's staff for spinning the events to make Haig look bad, but it was no distortion—it was reality. Haig not only pushed Nixon into the crisis but also consistently lied to Nixon and Richardson, telling the president that the attorney general had agreed to fire Cox when he clearly had no intention of doing so. Haig's machinations had succeeded in getting rid of a nemesis, Cox, but had the collateral effect of further weakening the president he was meant to protect.

In Moscow, Kissinger on October 21 bridled at a memo Nixon had sent him the previous day. "I now consider permanent Middle East settlement to be the most important final goal to which we must devote ourselves," Nixon wrote. "U.S. political considerations will have absolutely no, repeat no, influence whatever on our decisions in this regard. I want you to know that I am prepared to pressure the Israelis to the extent required, regardless of the domestic political consequences."[76] Kissinger shot an angry telegram to his deputy, Scowcroft, saying he "was shocked by the tone of the instructions, the poor judgment in the context of the Brezhnev letter and the failure to let me know in advance that a press statement be issued. Did you, as I asked, take these matters up with Haig before the final decisions were made?" Following Nixon's wishes, Kissinger fumed, would "totally wreck what little bargaining leverage I still have." Nixon's tone was "unacceptable," he continued. "Please show this message to Haig."[77]

Despite Nixon's interference, Kissinger and Leonid Brezhnev managed to work out a draft of a Middle East cease-fire. Kissinger immediately flew to Tel Aviv to show the cease-fire to the Israelis. Scowcroft messaged Kissinger later to try to excuse away Nixon's comments. "You must understand that the President was demonstrating his leadership in the crisis," Scowcroft wrote. "All the actions which took place were designed to illustrate that he was personally in charge." The Cox crisis that Haig had exacerbated had exploded and "is now dominating the news and activities here," Scowcroft continued. "Initial media reaction has appeared quite negative."[78] By marginalizing Nixon earlier, Haig and Kissinger had created the leadership vacuum that Nixon was now desperately trying to fill. If Kissinger had had his way, Nixon might never have left Key Biscayne.

House Speaker Carl Albert and other House leaders asked the House Judiciary Committee on October 22 to consider impeachment motions. That environment, Haig wrote Kissinger, was "of major national crisis which has resulted from the firing of Cox and the resulting resignation of Richardson and Ruckelshaus. Because the situation is at a stage of white heat, the ramifications of the accomplishments in Moscow have been somewhat eclipsed and their true significance underplayed." Kissinger, Haig said, had to brief the press and a bipartisan congressional delegation and promote the historic nature of the cease-fire. "In this one instance, it is most important that some effort be made to refocus national attention on the critical events in the Middle East and to emphasize above all the crucial role of the Presidential leadership," Haig concluded.[79]

Kissinger had already lost patience with Nixon. The president's lengthy absences, his excessive drinking, and his preoccupation with Watergate irritated the secretary of state, who believed he was single-handedly running U.S. policy on the Middle East. He considered Nixon a liability, a nonfunctional president, and the manifestations of this feeling would emerge more forcefully in the next week.

On Monday, October 22, as the damage wreaked by the Saturday Night Massacre had become clear to everyone, Woodward called Haig to tell him that he and Bernstein were writing a story that would say Richardson believed Nixon had tried to block Cox's investigation. Not so, Haig told Woodward. Their conversation, according to Woodward's notes, now stored at the Harry Ransom Center at the University of Texas at Austin, was on "deep background," meaning Woodward could use the information for guidance but not attribute anything, even anonymously, to Haig. It was the same type of reporter-source relationship Woodward claimed in *All the President's Men* to have had with Deep Throat. Haig told Woodward that it was "totally untrue" that he tried to get Richardson "to limit the Cox probe" and that such claims were "scurrilous and typical in today's sick atmosphere."[80] That, as was later shown by Haig's own memoirs, was not true. Haig had repeatedly tried to stymie Cox as well as sway Richardson.

In an October 23 *Washington Post* article, Woodward and Bernstein quoted one anonymous source as saying that "Richardson was so concerned about the Mideast crisis . . . that he discussed the possibility of submitting his resignation confidentially and not announcing it until the Mideast crisis had been settled." That, too, was incorrect. It was Nixon who had asked Richardson to delay resigning until after the crisis was solved; Richardson declined and resigned anyway. Haig's deep background guidance for Woodward was that Richardson had asked Haig about the Middle East and said, "Elliot Richardson is interested in the Mid-East and always has been."[81]

Most significantly, however, is that these notes, which are cited here for the first time, show the ongoing reporter-source relationship between Haig and Woodward. It was not the first time the two men had talked, as Haig said during the conversation when he told Woodward that he knew that "you and your colleague will be fair as you have in the past."[82] It again exposes the lie Haig told in his memoirs that he did not know Woodward until after Nixon resigned.[83] Woodward could reach Haig when he needed to, and the president's chief of staff felt comfortable enough in their relationship to share his side of events and realize he would be treated fairly, which was not something most people on the inside of Nixon's White House believed about the press at that time. Haig's comments also indicated that he had spoken to Woodward previously for stories written by him and Bernstein, another sign of their ongoing relationship.

Haig badly needed to get Ford confirmed, and as the confirmation hearings approached, he received reports from the FBI as its agents conducted the background checks on Ford. One day in late October, he called Ford's office to relay information to the nominee, and Benton Becker, an attorney Ford recruited to help with the hearings, heard Ford's end of the conversation. "And it is very obvious to me that Al Haig was getting reports from the Bureau on the background checks that the Bureau was making on the nominee, which background checks and reports were going to be given to the committee chairman only, and not to the nominee," Becker said.

Becker walked around Ford's desk and motioned to him that he wanted the phone. Ford gave it to him, and Becker listened as Haig continued talking as if Ford was still on the line.

"General, general, general," Becker said. Haig finally realized Ford was no longer on the phone. "Let me give you my name. My name is Benton Becker, and I'm representing him before the House and the Senate, and before we're finished before these committees, I can tell, I guarantee you, he will be asked and re-asked the question, did the White House feed in any information about the FBI reports—the White House prepare him improperly—because the members were not getting the reports, just the committee chairman?"

"When that question is asked, General, the answer is going to be a truthful answer, and the answer is no," Becker continued. "We don't need or want you to do this anymore. He's in good hands, he will be confirmed well and it will be fine."

There was about eight to ten seconds of silence, before Haig said, "May I have your name one more time, please?"[84]

That was Becker's first encounter with Haig. Ford was indeed asked the question multiple times during the hearings.

By October 23 more than twenty bills calling for Nixon's impeachment had been introduced in the House since Nixon fired Cox. Albert urged Congress to confirm Ford as vice president as soon as possible, which mattered because the Twenty-Fifth Amendment required both the House and the Senate to approve the nomination. In dueling news conferences, Richardson and Haig offered their versions of what led to the Saturday Night Massacre. "There had been issues drawn earlier in the week in which I had made clear that if certain actions were taken I would be forced to resign," Richardson said.[85] Haig, accompanied by Ziegler and Charles Alan Wright, said the White House position had been "subject to a great deal of misunderstanding, a great deal of mis-information over the past weekend."[86] That message found few takers. Three days after the firing, public opinion had crystallized: Nixon fired Cox because of Nixon's continued cover-up of Watergate.

Wright also appeared in Judge John Sirica's court that day with a stunning announcement: Nixon would turn over the tapes that Cox had been fired trying to get. The president changed his mind because he now believed that a continued fight jeopardized Ford's confirmation chances and because of "a need to relieve the domestic crisis in order to reduce the temptation the Soviets would feel to take advantage of our internal turmoil by exploiting the international crisis in the Middle East."[87] Nixon knew firing Cox would start a controversy, but he did not know just how bad it would be. "To the extent that I had not been aware of this situation, my actions were the result of serious miscalculation," Nixon wrote.[88] Nixon miscalculated because Haig had so isolated him that he heard mostly only from Haig and Ziegler; others had difficulty breaking through that wall.

Events in the Middle East finally took precedence over Watergate on October 24, but not in the way anyone desired. What transpired was a series of events unparalleled in U.S. history during the nuclear age. A checked-out Nixon, who had spent the night of October 23 at Camp David, was reduced to being a footnote in the most momentous deci-sions of the day.

Egyptian and Israeli forces had violated the cease-fire Kissinger had negotiated with the Soviets. Brezhnev wrote Nixon to urge the United States to curb the Israelis. Kissinger told a meeting of the Washington Special Actions Group, a small group of high-ranking national security officials, that U.S. pressure on the Israelis had stopped the gunfire between the warring parties. Haig, Kissinger said, had called the Israeli ambassador, and "Israel knows they cannot survive without us. They know they would have lost this war except for us. They were on their knees on October 13 and they couldn't have recovered." Reflecting on what he had engineered on his own, Kissinger called it "the best-run crisis we have ever had."[89] Such optimism would not last.

Brezhnev sent another note to Nixon that called for joint U.S.-Soviet action to stop the continued cease-fire violations. By this point, the Israelis had reversed the Arabs' early gains and were moving on both Cairo and Damascus. The United States had gained a diplomatic advantage with both sides during the crisis, which Nixon did not want to cede to the Soviets. Brezhnev's message hinted that if the United States did not agree, the Soviet Union would go it alone, perhaps by sending combat troops to the region, a notion that alarmed the White House.[90] Everyone believed they had to do something, but the accounts by Nixon, Haig, and Kissinger all obscured how Nixon remained a bystander. Nixon claimed he was sufficiently alarmed by the threat of unilateral Soviet intervention that he ordered a special meeting at the White House. "Words were not making our point—we needed action, even the shock of a military alert," Nixon wrote.[91] Nothing on the record, however, shows that Nixon or his top staff had contemplated an alert at that point. Haig claimed Nixon called the situation the most dangerous since the Cuban Missile Crisis. "We've got to act," Haig wrote that Nixon told him. In Haig's telling, Nixon told him to lead the meeting of the Washington Special Actions Group without him. "As usual, he preferred to let others set the options while he made his decision in solitude."[92]

However, the record shows that Haig and Kissinger, who spoke on the telephone at 9:50 p.m., worked on their own without waking Nixon. "I just had a letter from Brezhnev asking us to send forces in together or he would send them in alone," Kissinger said.

"I was afraid of that," Haig responded.

"I think we have to go to the mat on this one," Kissinger said.

Haig said he did not believe the Soviets would commit troops at the end of the war, while Kissinger said they could still send in paratroopers. The Israelis should agree to back up, Kissinger said.

"We didn't expect the Israelis to take that sort of thing," Haig said. "Do the Israelis know? I mean, have you brought them along?"

"I have kept them informed," Kissinger said. "Should I wake up the president?"

"No," Haig answered.[93]

Haig and Kissinger spoke again at 10:20 p.m. "I don't think they would have taken on a functioning president," Kissinger said, again reflecting his contempt for the incapacitated president. "Don't forget this is what the Soviets are playing on. They find a cripple facing impeachment and why shouldn't they go in there?"

"If they do and start fighting, that is a serious thing," Haig said, adding that he suspected the Soviets were already "on the ground all over the place."[94]

Haig asked Kissinger to have a meeting at the White House and then spoke to Nixon, although there is no independent record of what they discussed for eighteen minutes, including if Nixon ordered Haig to call a military alert.[95] There is, however, no proof that Nixon knew anything about an alert before it happened.

At 10:30 p.m. Haig, Kissinger, Defense Secretary James Schlesinger, CIA director William Colby, Adm. Thomas Moorer, the chairman of the Joint Chiefs of Staff, and Jonathan Howe, a navy commander and a member of the NSC staff, gathered in the White House situation room. Moorer took notes that reflected the unique and impromptu meeting. Early on, the participants agreed they needed to respond vigorously to Brezhnev's letter. Kissinger said Israel's violation of the cease-fire triggered the Soviet move. "Today, they only made one proposal to us and this proposal escalated the dialogue to a threat," he said. "The overall strategy of the Soviets now appears to be one of throwing détente on the table since we have no functional president, in their eyes, and consequently, we must prevent them from getting away with this."[96]

Haig, Moorer noted, "seemed to be convinced that the Soviets were going to move at daylight—which was just a few hours away." The Soviets, Haig continued, realized they were losing influence in the Middle East and were trying to capitalize on the uncertainty caused by the Saturday

Night Massacre, which also "has served to weaken the president. Haig said the Soviets only invited Kissinger to Moscow when they realized their client, Egypt, was losing." Moorer said the facts showed that Israel, not Egypt, had violated the cease-fire and that "the Soviets were correct in saying that the Israelis had violated the ceasefire." Schlesinger also mentioned the possibility of the Soviets moving into Egypt, and Kissinger again mentioned how they were taking advantage of Nixon's weakened condition. On Friday, before the firing of Cox and the resignations of Richardson and Ruckelshaus, conditions were stable. After that, however, Nixon was faltering and open to exploitation, Kissinger said. Moorer doubted the Soviets could move troops as quickly as Haig and Kissinger surmised, but Kissinger was having none of it. "The overall strategy of the Soviets now appears to be one of throwing détente on the table since we have no functional President, in their eyes, and, consequently, we must prevent them from getting away with this," Moorer recorded Kissinger saying.[97]

The U.S. response, completed at 3:30 a.m. on October 25 after five hours, was extraordinary. The nuclear alert level for U.S. forces was raised to DEFCON III, the third-highest level, although the top two levels—I and II—had never been declared. U.S. aircraft carriers in the Mediterranean Sea were sent closer to Egypt and Israel, and forces in Asia and Europe were alerted. Haig and Kissinger essentially acted on their own and without Nixon's input. While Nixon, Haig, and Kissinger claimed later that Nixon was intimately involved in the decision, the facts show otherwise.[98]

Haig and Kissinger told Nixon about the alert at 8:00 a.m. on October 25. They all pretended that Nixon had made the decision. Kissinger later met with a skeptical press corps to explain the reasons behind the alert, which most analysts considered extreme.[99] Rather than make Nixon look strong, the alert made him seem desperate enough to change the topic from Watergate to push the country close to a nuclear confrontation with the Soviet Union.

Nixon believed his own hype enough to conduct a rare news conference at 7:00 p.m. on October 26. He described a world that only he could see, one in which he firmly guided the nation through unrivaled crises. "The tougher it gets, the cooler I get," Nixon said. "I should point out that even in this week when many thought that the President was shell shocked, unable to act, the President acted decisively in the interests of peace and the interest of the country," he said in an account of events that ignored how his aides declared a nuclear alert while Nixon slept. He claimed that his personal relationship with Brezhnev helped solve the Middle East crisis, gliding over the nuclear alert declared just more than a day earlier. "It's because he and I know each other, and it's because we have this personal contact that notes exchanged in that way result in a settlement rather than a confrontation," Nixon said.

He also defended firing Cox and made news by announcing that he authorized Acting Attorney General Robert Bork to appoint a new special prosecutor who would have the independence needed to do the job properly and cooperation from the White House. Nixon may have felt better after the thirty-nine minutes of questioning by reporters at the news conference, but Kissinger and Haig did not.[100]

"The crazy bastard really made a mess with the Russians," Kissinger said in a call to Haig that started at 7:55 p.m., just fifteen minutes after the end of the news conference.

"What?" Haig asked.

"Didn't you listen to his press statement?" Kissinger asked. "First we had information of movements of Soviet forces. That is a lie. Second, this was the worst crisis since the Cuban Missile Crisis. True, but why rub their faces in it? Third, Brezhnev and I exchanged brutal messages. That has never been acknowledged before. Four, Brezhnev respects me because I was the man who bombed Vietnam on May 8 and mined the harbors on May 18."

"I don't think that's a third of the problem," Haig said. "He just let it fly. He got all he had about the Middle East from you. I assumed you had cleared that. I was surprised."

Kissinger compared Nixon's news conference with a recent one in which Kissinger said there was no serious confrontation with the Russians.

"How about the rest of it?" Haig asked. "Disaster."

"Yes, a disaster of something that is already a disaster," Kissinger responded.[101]

The two colleagues, often rivals but often bound by their ridicule of Nixon, decided that Haig needed to call Anatoly Dobrynin, the Soviet ambassador to the United States, and reassure him of the administration's intentions. Kissinger, in his 2003 book about the crisis, skipped this telephone call completely.[102]

Haig spoke with Dobrynin at 8:04 p.m. "I just came back from the President and I told him that his remarks tonight were I thought over-drawn and would be interpreted improperly," Haig said. "And I wanted you to know that he did not in any way have the intention of drawing the situation as sharply as he did." Nixon, Haig continued, "is quite upset about it because he did not intend it to be that way."[103] Haig invented Nixon's alleged feelings, because Nixon's schedule includes no record of Haig and Nixon speaking between the end of the news conference and Haig's conversation with Dobrynin. Nixon's records show he tried unsuccessfully to call Haig at 7:51 p.m. They did not speak until Haig and Nixon met at 8:16 p.m. for more than one hour.[104]

Dobrynin objected to the military alert, saying no one gave him a heads-up before it was declared, which emphasized the alert's ad hoc status. The unnecessary alert, Dobrynin said, damaged the progress made during Kissinger's recent visit.[105]

Kissinger and Haig continued to lose patience with Nixon and the hard-liners in the Defense Department who distrusted the Israelis. "I do not think we can survive with these fellows in there at Defense—they are crazy," Kissinger said in an early afternoon call on October 27 during which he and Haig also dealt with the continuing blowback from Nixon's news conference the previous evening. "Schlesinger wants to check on whether the Israelis are lying—will you please help me with him?" Kissinger asked. "I will do my best," Haig said.[106]

During an October 24 news conference, Bork reinforced Nixon's claim that he would appoint a new special prosecutor and said he wanted

someone who would have "a mandate no less free than Archibald Cox."
He could not tolerate being forced to pick someone beholden to the
White House.[107] That, however, was not Bork's decision alone to make. The
real selection fell to Haig, who would not repeat Richardson's mistake
with Cox. This time, Haig determined, the prosecutor would know the
difference between the real crimes related to Watergate and the national
security issues, primarily the FBI wiretaps and the Pentagon spy ring,
which threatened Haig.

For advice, Haig turned to his old friend from Lyndon Johnson's Pentagon: Morris Leibman, the lead partner in a Chicago law firm and an
ardent anticommunist liberal active in national security issues. In modern
terms, Leibman would be called a neoconservative, a term that did not
exist in the 1960s and 1970s. Starting in the 1950s, Leibman represented
two brothers from Chicago, Morris and Jack Childs, who had infiltrated
the U.S. Communist Party and who were informing on the party to the
FBI and William Sullivan, Haig's longtime friend who ran the bureau's
anticommunist network. "It has been one of the greatest experiences of
my life working these past years with Bill Sullivan," an effusive Leibman
wrote J. Edgar Hoover in 1961.[108] Information acquired by the Childs
brothers, known inside the bureau as Project Solo, informed the FBI that
Stanley Levison, one of the close advisors to civil rights leader Martin
Luther King Jr., was affiliated with communists.[109] That inspired Sullivan to write an anonymous letter to King urging him to kill himself.[110]
With conservative foundation executive Frank Barnett, Leibman started
a variety of anticommunist groups, such as the Institute for American
Strategy, that worked with FBI and CIA officials to trumpet the dangers
of international communism.[111]

Leibman chaired the American Bar Association's Standing Committee on Education against Communism, which put him in close contact
with longtime Haig ally Fritz Kraemer in the army.[112] Kraemer had recommended Haig for his first job at the NSC, while Sullivan set up the
FBI wiretaps with Haig's help. In 1964 Johnson named Leibman to his
informal group of sixteen "wise men" to advise him on military policy,
a panel that included former secretary of state Dean Acheson and Gen.

Omar Bradley, a former chairman of the Joint Chiefs and army five-star general.[113] In collaboration with Sullivan, Leibman arranged for Hoover to write an article about the Ku Klux Klan for the ABA's monthly journal, an article that was actually written by members of Sullivan's staff.[114] On December 5, 1969, Leibman was among members of the prowar Tell It to Hanoi committee, which met with Nixon in the White House to promote the idea of setting a deadline with North Vietnam for peace talks.[115] After the deadline, the group wanted an all-out push to win the war on the battlefield, a position that Nixon had long abandoned, although group members did not know that. When Kraemer celebrated his sixty-fifth birthday on July 3, 1973, Leibman, Barnett, and Sullivan, along with Vernon Walters from the CIA, were among the small band of friends who presented him with a crusader's sword made by the Wilkinson Sword Company as a gift.[116]

Leibman advised Haig to talk to Texas attorney Leon Jaworski, lead partner in a Houston law firm and a former ABA president.[117] Jaworski had investigated major cases for Johnson and cooperated with the Warren Commission, which was investigating the Kennedy assassination, while working for the Texas attorney general. Although Jaworski was a Democrat, he understood the need to protect national security. It was no accident that Haig, who had multiple national security secrets to hide, sought help from Leibman and no surprise that Leibman recommended Jaworski.

Jaworski's impeccable Establishment credentials belied his rough upbringing. The son of Polish immigrants, he grew up speaking German at home in Waco, Texas, where he went to local Baylor University at fifteen. He spent one year as a Baylor undergraduate and then entered the university's law school, from which he graduated at nineteen. Jaworski then became the youngest lawyer in Texas history. His practice grew steadily and took him to Houston. After Pearl Harbor, the thirty-five-year-old Jaworski was too old to volunteer for combat, so he joined the Judge Advocate General's Corps and became a colonel. After the war's end, he joined the prosecution corps for postwar war crimes trials.[118]

Jaworski was not surprised when Haig called him on October 30. Haig had enough regard for Jaworski's skills to know he was among the few people with the gravitas and experience to handle the chore of being the new special prosecutor. Richardson has also put out feelers to Jaworski about the job in May. Jaworski had also received a call from a close friend, who said that Haig would call him. Haig wrote in his memoirs that he had asked John Connally to make the call to Jaworski, which neither Connally nor Jaworski confirmed.[119] "I can tell you that I had a call before that—although I will not disclose who it came from—that I could expect a call from Haig," Jaworski said. "I have never disclosed who that call came from."

But Fulbright & Jaworski was one of the nation's biggest law firms. If he stayed absent for too long, Jaworski would have to cash out, a step that could cost him millions of dollars in partnership payouts and taxes. Haig sold Jaworski hard.

"I very much need to talk with you about a matter that is of great importance to this country," Haig told Jaworski. "In fact, I know of nothing that is as important to the country right now than what I'm about to say to you. We want you to serve as a special prosecutor to take Archibald Cox's place."

"Well, General Haig, are you aware that I looked at this matter once and didn't see that I could accept it under the circumstances that exist?" Jaworski said.

"What are you having reference to?" Haig asked.

"Because I just wasn't assured of the independence," Jaworski said. "On top of it, now Cox has been fired which looks, to me, as though there is no independence!"

"Now wait just a minute!" Haig said. "We can give you the independence that you want."

"Well," Jaworski chuckled, "you know, everything to date has been in the opposite direction."[120]

As Haig tried to persuade Jaworski, Buzhardt went to Judge John Sirica's court on October 31 and told him privately that two of the conversations subpoenaed by Cox and scheduled to be turned over by Nixon had never been recorded. One was a June 20, 1972, telephone call with

John Mitchell, and the second was the April 15, 1973, meeting between Nixon and John Dean, which Dean had emphasized in his testimony in June. Sirica ordered Buzhardt to go into open court and tell everyone.[121] Buzhardt claimed the tapes never existed, because the taping system, while thorough, was not perfect. However, the existence of the April 15 tape was in dispute. Also, Secret Service records of the tapes Nixon checked out on June 4 when he listened to all of the Dean tapes showed that the April 15 tape was included in that mix. Buzhardt's latest revelation devastated Nixon's already weak credibility. "People felt that I was toying with their patience and insulting their intelligence," Nixon wrote later.[122]

Despite his reservations, Jaworski agreed to fly to Washington the following day, October 31. Haig dispatched a government plane to Ellington Air Force Base near Houston and a White House car and driver to meet Jaworski at Andrews Air Force Base and take him to the White House.

At the White House, Haig told Jaworski he was putting "the patriotic monkey" on his back to get him to take the job.[123] Haig went into the Oval Office to talk to Nixon, emerged, and then a procession of remaining White House aides and cabinet officials—Melvin Laird, Bryce Harlow, Len Garment, Robert Bork, and William Saxbe, the Ohio senator and attorney general designate—all came to lobby Jaworski to take the job.

"There is no question—this—this was said to me by Bork; it was said to me by Haig in the presence of others who were sitting there," Jaworski said. "I met with all of these people. They were all trying to persuade me to take it, and I met with all of them before I made my decision. They were all trying to say to me: Well, look, not only is this much needed; but you can have all the assurance—every assurance that you want. And all of them put in their oar to try to get me to accept it. And it was clearly stated to me that the calls had come—had gone to many people all over the country and that as a result of these calls, they had decided to talk to me."[124]

Thus reassured, Jaworski agreed to take the job.

After meeting with Jaworski, Haig went to Capitol Hill to lobby nervous Republicans about Nixon's innocence. He told them the tapes were "exculpatory," particularly the tape of the March 21 meeting between Nixon and Dean, who then told the president about the "cancer on the presidency."[125] That tape, Haig told Republican leaders, was when Nixon first learned of the cover-up. But Haig knew then that he was telling the Republican members a lie. He had talked to Nixon on June 4, as the president listened to the Dean tapes, which showed that Nixon and Dean worked for more than a week in March to come up with a better story for the cover-up. The March 21 tape mainly recorded Dean's worries about the blackmail attempts by the Watergate burglars, which were getting larger and more insistent. Haig and Buzhardt talked every day, and Buzhardt had long concluded that Nixon was guilty. Haig also realized early on that Nixon would end up leaving office before the end of his term. Haig's assurances of Nixon's innocence guaranteed that when Republicans learned the truth, they would react angrily and push for Nixon's resignation or impeachment, which is exactly what would happen nine months later.

Haig may have won over Jaworski, perhaps with Leibman's help, but he still faced problems connected to the military spy ring. Egil Krogh, the embattled former head of the Plumbers, filed a motion on October 31 seeking a range of White House documents he called vital to his defense. Among those documents were

> certain tape recordings of conversations in which one of the participants was the President of the United States, to wit:
>
> b) meetings of the President with John Ehrlichman and/or David Young in December, 1971, and January through February, 1972, in which the work of the Special Investigations Unit was discussed, the India-Pakistan leaks were discussed, and/or instructions were given on the necessity for absolute secrecy regarding the activities of the Special Investigations Unit.[126]

Before he was fired, Cox wanted some of these documents for his investigation. A *Time* magazine story that appeared in the final days of October reported that Cox wanted details on the Plumbers and the FBI wiretaps for his continuing investigation.[127] Now Krogh was weighing in on the same issues.

Krogh's motion went to the heart of the investigation into the military spy ring that Nixon called off and that Haig, Buzhardt, and Laird had derailed at the Pentagon. If the motion were granted, then the messy details of the military's chronic lack of faith in Nixon and Haig's betrayal of Nixon's secrets could spill out into open court, much as the Plumbers' existence was revealed during the Daniel Ellsberg trial the previous spring. Krogh's motion had to be stopped.

8 November 1973

Nixon careened into November with the revelations that two of the nine tapes sought by the special prosecutor's office were either missing or had never existed. Judge John Sirica had forced Fred Buzhardt to acknowledge the missing tapes in open court on October 31, and the fallout from that revelation blanketed the administration like ash falling from an exploding star. "What is inconceivable is that the President and his advisers could wait until the last minute, just before the scheduled delivery of the tapes to Judge Sirica, to announce to the public, to the grand jury and to the court that this vital evidence did not, in fact, exist—and never had," the *Washington Post* editorialized, summing up the wholesale frustration felt at the White House's delay and obfuscation.[1] That Buzhardt, Haig's hand-picked Watergate counsel, botched the handling of the tapes makes more sense, given his collaboration with Haig in setting up the revelation of the tapes' existence in the first place and his knowledge that Nixon, his client, was guilty.

The missing tapes nagged at Nixon, who believed he had a reasonable explanation for why they did not exist. He scribbled these notes on the top of a briefing paper on November 1:

There were no missing tapes.

There were never any.

The conversations in question were not taped.

Why couldn't we get that across to people?[2]

Instead of Archibald Cox, the White House had a new special prosecutor to handle, one who Haig hoped would be more understanding of Haig's particular concerns. Leon Jaworski's hiring was announced on November 1, complete with the assurances to the public that he would have the independence denied Cox. The White House officials who persuaded him to take the job—Haig, Buzhardt, Melvin Laird, and Bryce Harlow—already knew Nixon was guilty and would not finish his term. Hiring Jaworski and letting him go after Nixon would guarantee that the president would be either impeached or convicted of a crime. For Haig, Jaworski's arrival was a relief; some accounts described Haig as "exultant." Haig knew Jaworski would avoid the sticky "national security" areas that posed a problem for him while he stayed with Nixon, who decamped to Key Biscayne shortly after the Jaworski announcement, followed closely by speculation about when he would resign and who would persuade him to do it.

Nixon's escape to Florida provided no relief. Some Republicans said on November 2 that Nixon should testify before the Senate Watergate committee. Prominent columnists James Reston of the *New York Times* and Joseph Alsop said Nixon needed to consider resigning.[3] Reston and Alsop personified the core of Establishment Washington thinking, and while Nixon resented the Establishment, he craved its approval. Those opinions also gave cover to timid members of Congress who needed signals of shifting winds to move. So insistent were the calls that Gerald Warren, Nixon's deputy press secretary, felt compelled to insist that Nixon would not resign.[4]

In Washington, White House aide Steve Bull testified in Sirica's court that Nixon had listened to tapes on June 4 and that there existed a "tape of tapes" from that session.[5] The recorders logged Haig's meeting with Nixon that day, making it clear that Haig knew about Nixon's taping at least by then. Other tapes showed that Nixon told Haig about the taping system on May 8, less than a week after Haig became chief of staff.

Nixon's approval rating from the Gallup poll hit 27 percent in the survey released November 3, a day on which *New Yorker* political writer Elizabeth Drew wrote, "The thought seems to have spread that the President must leave office."[6] Buzhardt and Len Garment apparently agreed. They flew to Florida to meet with Nixon and persuade him to resign. Bob Woodward and Carl Bernstein wrote in *The Final Days*, for which Haig and Buzhardt were major sources, that Buzhardt and Garment wanted to get Nixon to quit, while Nixon, who did not meet with them, wrote that the duo wanted to quit themselves.[7] Either way, Haig blocked Buzhardt and Garment's access to the president, instead shuttling between them to give messages and try to shape some kind of response to the mounting crisis.

The missing April 15 tape of the meeting between John Dean and Nixon particularly vexed Sirica and the White House. Bull said he had checked it out when he got the tapes for Nixon on June 4. Its existence and then apparent disappearance reinforced the growing belief that Nixon was hiding or destroying evidence. Buzhardt and Garment believed Nixon could have also dictated his thoughts after the meeting into his Dictabelt recorder. After searching everywhere in the White House where such a recording might be kept, they concluded it did not exist. "I had put Buzhardt in an untenable position," Nixon wrote. Nixon had first raised the possibility that a Dictabelt recording, not a reel-to-reel tape, existed of the April 15 meeting. He had Buzhardt write a letter to Cox in June to that effect. "Len Garment felt the public revelation of this latest blunder would throw us into a fatal spin," Nixon wrote, adding that Buzhardt and Garment were so discouraged that they wanted to quit. "We were always in a completely reactive situation, and there seemed to be no prospect for changing that pattern no matter what we did," Nixon wrote.[8]

Haig told Nixon about his meeting with Buzhardt and Garment, and the president sensed the two lawyers wanted out. "I could not blame them."[9]

Haig also told Nixon that no one in Key Biscayne or Washington could find the Dictabelt. The president, Haig said, responded with an incredible suggestion: "You know, Al," he said, "as far as the Dictabelt is concerned, all we have to do is create another one."[10]

"Nixon's words shocked me," Haig wrote, "in the literal sense that I felt something like the tingle of an electrical current along my scalp.... 'Mr. President, that cannot be done,'" Haig said he told Nixon. "It would be wrong; it would be illegal; it would be totally unacceptable. It's just impossible."[11]

Nixon let the idea drop, and Haig rushed to tell Buzhardt and Garment, who both threatened to resign. Haig told them to reconsider. If they resigned, then the world would want to know why, and if they told the truth about why, then Nixon would be impeached, Gerald Ford would not be confirmed as vice president, and Carl Albert would rise to the White House from his position as House Speaker. Once again, Haig fell back on the "Albert as president" canard, knowing full well that Albert had no designs on the White House. In fact, Albert had urged a speedy confirmation of Ford as vice president so he could be in place to succeed Nixon if and when he resigned or was impeached.[12]

"Doubt is not proof," Haig wrote that he told Buzhardt and Garment. "Whatever this man is, whatever he's done, whatever office he holds, he has the right to due process. If you won't defend him, knowing more about the case than anybody else, who will?" Buzhardt and Garment went home.[13]

The truth was that Haig continuously undermined Nixon's defense. He picked Buzhardt as the president's Watergate defender, and then Buzhardt told his allies, especially Laird, that Nixon was guilty, which eroded Nixon's support from within. Haig recommended against using executive privilege to stop Vernon Walters from testifying in May, and then Walters told the Senate that key members of Nixon's staff had urged him to get the FBI to back off the Watergate investigation. Haig knew about the White House taping system and that Alexander Butterfield would tell the Senate about it but did nothing to alert Nixon or stop the testimony. He pushed Spiro Agnew out of the vice presidency to find a more politically palatable successor to Nixon when he inevitably left office. Haig's claims that he warned Buzhardt and Garment not to quit, when they had actually gone to Florida to get *Nixon* to resign, ring hollow.

If those calling for Nixon to resign knew what he had suggested to Haig about the Dictabelt, the cries would have surged. On November 5 someone on the White House staff, most likely Haig or Buzhardt, contacted Woodward at the *Post*. Some of the White House tapes have been intentionally erased, the source told Woodward. In *All the President's Men*, Woodward and Bernstein wrote that the source of that information was Deep Throat, whom Woodward later said was former FBI official Mark Felt.[14] That, like much of the Deep Throat mythology, cannot be true. By November Felt had been gone from the FBI for five months. Only five people at the White House knew about the June 20, 1972, tape from which Rose Mary Woods had mistakenly erased five minutes. They were Woods, Steve Bull, Haig's aide John Bennett, Haig, and Buzhardt. None trusted Felt to tell him about the tapes, and if Felt had known, he would have gone directly to Sirica instead of telling Woodward. The tip sent Woodward and Bernstein scrambling for confirmation.

Jaworski also threw a curveball at Haig and Buzhardt on November 5. The pair thought Jaworski would back them up on national security issues, but the new prosecutor signed a brief from his staff opposing the White House claim of national security for the records that Egil Krogh wanted to use in his defense. Included in Krogh's October 31 defense motion was a call for materials related to the White House Plumbers' investigation of the India-Pakistan crisis of December 1971, which also involved the discovery of the military spy ring operating inside the NSC and assisted by Haig. National security, the prosecution team wrote, was too often used as a "talisman" to scare away legitimate inquiries. There was no need to allow that to happen with Krogh, the prosecution wrote.[15]

The furor over the tapes continued on November 6. Bull testified in Sirica's court about the White House staff's often casual handling of the tapes. Woods took some with her, as did Bennett. Bob Haldeman checked out some for his use after he resigned the previous April.[16] Bull's testimony shredded the White House's claim that it kept the tapes closely held, and he also helped heighten the suspicion that the Nixon had somehow destroyed the two missing tapes to protect himself. Not only were Sirica, the prosecution, the press, and the public unwilling to give Nixon the benefit of the doubt, when it came to the president, there was no doubt at all: more and more Americans simply assumed he was guilty. Each new disclosure turned up the pressure for him to go. Nixon, the *New York Times* reported, was increasingly isolated and relied almost exclusively on Haig and Ron Ziegler for support.[17]

On November 7 Nixon went on television to introduce energy-saving measures to cope with the oil embargo placed on the United States by Arab nations during the war with Israel. He called for the relaxation of some environmental standards, a lower speed limit to save gas, and lower thermostat settings at home as winter neared. The embattled president said he would not resign. Nixon looked defeated, an impression heightened by Congress's move that day to override Nixon's veto of the War Powers Act, which limited the president's ability to commit troops to conflicts without congressional approval. The act was a direct reaction to the disclosures through the year about Nixon's authorization of the secret bombing of Cambodia and secret missions by U.S. troops into Laos, two neutral countries in the Vietnam War. Ziegler said in the White House press briefing that the president would provide answers to the new questions about the tapes and that Nixon was not seeing a psychiatrist or taking tranquilizers as the pressures on him mounted.[18]

That day in Sirica's court, Bennett compounded the impression that something was wrong with the White House tapes. Woods, Bennett said, complained to him the previous day that one of the conversations she was trying to transcribe "seemed to trail off in mid-conversation." Haig, Bennett testified, told him Woods was transcribing the tapes for Nixon, although Bennett added that Woods might be summarizing the tapes instead of making verbatim transcripts. Sirica, whose zeal to push the Watergate investigation had angered the White House for more than a year, announced in court that he wanted electronics experts to analyze the tapes and tell the court "the reasons that might exist for the non-existence of these conversations." This phase, he said, "may well be the most important and conclusive part of these hearings."[19]

If Woods told Bennett about problems with the tapes on November 6, then Bennett told Haig and Buzhardt. Woods had already told Nixon that she had mistakenly erased part of a June 20, 1972, tape on October 1. Who knew about the issues with the tapes would become more important the next day, November 8.

That morning's *Post* contained a story about Bennett's testimony paired with a Woodward and Bernstein story that had been sparked by the tip three days earlier about problems with the tapes. "According to White House sources questioned over the past three days, there is serious concern among the president's aides and advisers that the latest problems regarding the tapes will further strain the credibility of the White House," the duo wrote. "Of five sources who confirmed that defects have been found in the tapes, one said the problems are 'of a suspicious nature.' According to this source, some conversation on some of the tapes appears to have been erased or obliterated by the injection—inadvertent or otherwise—of background noise." They also included a knowing quote from a White House aide: "This town is in such a state that everybody will say, 'They're doctoring the tapes.'"[20]

Into the already heightening suspicion that Nixon was destroying evidence and obstructing justice dropped this nuclear bomb. It followed Buzhardt and Garment's unsuccessful trip to Florida to get Nixon to resign and Nixon's suggestion to make a fake Dictabelt recording. Woodward and Bernstein wrote that the White House officials were interviewed over the last three days, which would put the first tip to Woodward and Bernstein on November 5, within hours after Buzhardt and Garment returned to Washington. Nixon and Haig arrived back in Washington on the evening of November 5. That put Haig in Washington in time for him to tell Woodward about the tapes.

Someone was doctoring the tapes. It just was not the person—Nixon—or for the reasons that many people suspected.

Woods testified before Sirica on November 8. Samuel J. Powers, the new White House attorney hired to handle the tapes case, questioned her about the alleged gap in the tapes.

"Are you satisfied there is no gap in the tapes?" Powers asked.

"Perfectly satisfied," Woods said in an answer that would eventually boomerang back on her and Nixon in unforeseen ways.[21]

Her questioner, Powers, was also a member of the Morris Leibman stable of attorneys. He had recommended Powers, a Miami attorney, to Haig.[22] Powers also worked closely with Leibman on American Bar Association issues, including anticommunism; they were both members of the ABA's Standing Committee on Education against Communism.[23] Not only did Leibman recommend Jaworski to Haig, he was helping pick the president's defense. It would not end there.

In a telegram to Kissinger, who was in Jordan, Haig summed up the darkening mood in the White House. "Due to overriding necessity to reinforce confidence here, the President feels strongly that there should be no, repeat, no announcement of any easing of oil restrictions from your party if you are also able to add this feather to your cap," Haig wrote. "He hopes that progress made in this area could be announced by him from the White House after your return. . . . I promise you early notice on any new jolts," Haig continued. "As of now the problem I anticipated is under control but I will keep you advised in [a] timely manner."[24]

The danger increased again on November 12, when Nixon sent a statement to Sirica that the April 15 Dictabelt never existed. "My personal diary file consists of notes of conversations and dictation belts of recollections, and I believed in June that I had dictated my recollections of April 15, 1973, of conversations which occurred that day." He had not, said Nixon, who closed with a sentence that captured his magical thinking: "It is my hope that these steps will clear up this aspect of the Watergate matter once and for all."[25]

On November 13 Haig summoned Jaworski to the White House in the late afternoon to meet with him and Buzhardt. They gathered in the White House Map Room to discuss urgent business with the new prosecutor, and they dived right in, according to Jaworski's handwritten notes. The demands from Egil Krogh's lawyer in the October 31 court filing were "trouble" that risked exposing a sensitive national security case, Haig and Buzhardt told Jaworski.[26] That case, the two continued, involved a "yeoman used as secretary by Haig" and "tremendously sensitive conversations and agreements with heads of state," copies of which were sent to the chairman of the Joint Chiefs of Staff. Haig and Buzhardt described the spy ring operation that Haig abetted with the help of navy yeoman Charles Radford, who was caught in December 1971 and shipped to a base in Oregon. They also told Jaworski of the January 10, 1972, report prepared by Buzhardt at Laird's request that whitewashed Haig's involvement and sealed off the matter for good from the White House. Both Haig and Buzhardt knew that a more detailed White House investigation conducted by David Young, one of the Plumbers, existed, but that report cut too close to Haig. By steering Jaworski to a limited and fraudulent investigative report that buried the issue for the Pentagon, they obstructed justice.[27] Perhaps Jaworski did not care, given his coziness with the national security establishment, but by accepting Haig and Buzhardt's guidance, he protected Haig. The following day, Jaworski told U.S. District Judge Gerhard Gesell, who oversaw the Krogh case, that the White House, with Nixon's approval, would grant him access to some of the tapes and documents that Krogh sought. Those materials, Jaworski told Gesell, would allow him to look for "any information of an exculpatory nature or relevant to punishment."[28]

The November 13 meeting was the first of what would become many between Haig and Jaworski. They usually met in the Map Room, where Haig handed Jaworski documents intended to prove that the White House was acting in good faith. In the meantime, Buzhardt would drag his feet on requests from other prosecutors and Congress, creating the outward impression of a White House pushing back hard against the thundering hordes of Watergate zealots. The reality was that Haig gave Jaworski virtually everything he wanted. "So they would meet in the Map Room, and Haig would move close to Leon, stare at him intensely with his blue eyes, and warn Leon about the dangers to the nation that Watergate posed," an aide to Haig told author Seymour Hersh. "The aide says, with obvious admiration, 'Haig understood the play,'" but given the Leibman seal of approval and Jaworski's willingness to take the job, Jaworski understood the play as well.[29]

Buzhardt and Sam Powers sat down November 14 to listen to the tape from June 20, 1972, between Nixon and Bob Haldeman that Rose Mary Woods had accidentally erased in October. Powers said Buzhardt warned him they would encounter a four-to-five-minute gap. But as they listened to the tape with headphones and a stopwatch sitting on the table next to them, the gap kept going until it reached eighteen and a half minutes long. An astonished Powers had expected a much shorter gap, but now, in the presence of Buzhardt, he realized Nixon had a more serious problem. Buzhardt and Powers went to see Haig. "When we notified Al Haig that evening, the President, as I understood it, was entertaining some senators, some of the leadership of the Senate," Powers said later in an interview. "In the East Room of the White House. And Haig didn't want to interrupt him."[30] Nixon reassured the fourteen Republican senators gathered that they had seen the last of the bad news to emerge from the White House about Watergate.

Nixon met for breakfast with Republican House members on November 15, still ignorant of the mysterious erasure. Haig still had not told Nixon, despite the warning from Buzhardt and Powers the evening before. Nixon told the House members they were turning the corner on Watergate. Then Nixon, still in the dark about the erasure, spoke to a convention of Realtors at the Washington Hilton and said he did not violate the law. Haig did not want to rattle Nixon before the Realtors speech, although he had information that would have influenced what Nixon told them. Haig waited until 4:00 p.m. to tell Nixon about the tape gap and another bombshell: the tape was also on the list of tapes subpoenaed by the special prosecutor. A gap of more than eighteen minutes on a tape that was not covered by subpoena meant little, but on a subpoenaed tape that gap meant the destruction of evidence, whether intentional or not.

The missed signals between Haig, Buzhardt, and the other attorneys working on Nixon's defense reflected Haig's tight control. Only he could talk to Nixon alone. Even friends of Nixon, such as Illinois judge John Sullivan, who was brought in to help in November, left shortly after arriving, realizing they had nothing to do.[31] Cecil Emerson of Dallas, a Nixon defense attorney, said Buzhardt controlled the access to Nixon and the tapes, and Buzhardt did nothing without Haig's knowledge and approval. An unnamed White House aide confirmed Emerson's impression, saying, "Any assessment that Buzhardt controls access to the tapes and what is on them is absolutely correct and it is one that causes some concern to members" of the legal team.[32] Nixon lacked a strong defense when he needed it most, but his chief of staff had no interest in giving him one.

After the first weekend of the month, when Nixon weathered a barrage of bad news tied to the missing tapes and the calls for resignation from his top lawyers, he resolved to turn things around by rallying Republicans on Capitol Hill and taking his case to friendly audiences around the country. The press called it Operation Candor. On November 16 Nixon traveled to Orlando for an address to the American Society of Newspaper Editors and a question-and-answer period. He told the audience that the missing tape from June 20, 1972, was a record of a call to John Mitchell, his friend, former attorney general, and campaign manager, to cheer him up three days after the Watergate burglars were captured. On the issue of taping meetings in the Oval Office, Nixon said his predecessors, John Kennedy and Lyndon Johnson, also taped their calls and meetings. Nixon said he created the Plumbers to stop the national security leaks that had bedeviled his administration. One, he said, was so serious that Senators Sam Ervin and Howard Baker of the Watergate committee agreed "it should not be disclosed." That was the spy ring, which Buzhardt and Garment had persuaded the senators to leave alone in July. As for the two missing tapes, Nixon said, "[The fact that they were not there was a] very great disappointment . . . and I just wish we had had a better system. I frankly wish we hadn't had a system at all. Then I wouldn't have to answer this question."[33]

Nixon moved on to Macon, Georgia, where he said in a news conference that the American people needed to have faith in the president's integrity and to know whether he was a crook or not. "Well, I am not a crook," he said, adding another line to the growing Nixonian lexicon. "From then on, variations of the line 'I am not a crook' were used as an almost constant source of criticism and ridicule," he wrote.[34] In Memphis on November 20 Nixon said he did not think there would be any more bad revelations to come, but he did not know then that none of the eighteen-and-a-half-minute gap on the tape could be recovered. Shortly after the Memphis appearance, Haig checked with Buzhardt, who told him he could not reproduce the buzzing sound on the tape gap. In fact, Buzhardt said the sound was such that it did not appear the gap could be accidental. Someone had erased the tape on purpose.[35]

Haig told Nixon about the gap on the flight back to Washington. The president would suffer another devastating blow to his credibility. "The headline in papers all across the country the next morning was my assertion that there would be no more Watergate bombshells," Nixon wrote.[36] Later that morning, November 21, Buzhardt met in Sirica's chambers and described the tape gap, how a shrill buzz blocked out more than eighteen minutes of conversation between Nixon and Bob Haldeman from June 20. Buzhardt tried to persuade Sirica to keep this latest revelation private, arguing that its disclosure would be devastating. Jaworski countered by saying they had to disclose the longer gap immediately. Sirica sided with Jaworski, and minutes later, Buzhardt told a stunned crowd in the courtroom about the missing eighteen minutes of conversation on the tape.[37]

Sirica said he wanted to take control of the tapes. "This is just another instance that convinces the court that it has to take some steps, not because the court doesn't believe the White House or the President [but because] the court is interested in seeing that nothing else happens," he said.[38]

Just how the eighteen minutes disappeared from the tape has stumped experts for the last forty years. Only a handful of White House officials and staff members had access to the tapes: Nixon, Haig, Buzhardt, John Bennett, Steve Bull, and Rose Mary Woods. Of those, only Haig and Buzhardt had the motive to erase part of the tape to further discredit Nixon. They had engineered Alexander Butterfield's revelation of the taping system in July, shared the news of Nixon's guilt with Melvin

Laird and Bryce Harlow, blown the handling of Archibald Cox's firing, and argued that Nixon needed to resign. Buzhardt also used the tapes the most and was the most adept at handling the Uher tape recorder the staff used to listen to the tapes and make the transcripts. Buzhardt also had a convenient witness when he first discovered the length of the gap—Samuel Powers, the attorney picked with the help of Haig's old friend and advisor, Morris Leibman. Finally, Buzhardt knew the tape was not relevant. While Nixon and Haldeman discussed Watergate in that June 20 conversation, they did not do so in great detail. The damaging conversation, as Haig and Buzhardt had known since the previous May, came on June 23, when Nixon authorized Haldeman to tell the CIA's leaders to tell the FBI director to slow down the investigation into the Watergate break-in. That tape, the true smoking gun, still existed intact and remained for future discovery.

But Buzhardt said none of that to Sirica, the president, or anyone else. He professed ignorance and confusion about the cause of the gap. Woods testified that she had caused the gap accidentally while transcribing the tapes for Nixon. Few people inside the court believed her, assuming she was taking a bullet for her longtime boss. Haig also testified, claiming that a "sinister force" had erased the tape. Haig was right, but he failed to say the name of that force—Buzhardt.

Nixon and Haig knew the latest disclosure crippled the White House. "If Nixon felt any special sense of foreboding over this development, he did not show it," Haig wrote.

> But of course he knew, as we all did, that the revelation that a vital segment in one of his tapes had mysteriously been erased, coming on the heels of the announcement that two other key tapes had never existed and a critically important Dictabelt had been lost, would be the straw that broke the back of public opinion.
>
> And so it was. Another media story lighted up the skies over Washington. Accusations flew; suspicions festered; the mood of the Establishment darkened. And as a practical matter, the burden of proof on the questions of the guilt or innocence of the President of the

United States for crimes still to be discovered or named had shifted. He was now faced with the necessity of establishing his innocence, a process known by the legal profession to be so far beyond human ingenuity that the Founding Fathers had abolished it from American practice in the Bill of Rights.[39]

Haig knew that innocence could never be proved. And within days, Nixon's eventual replacement, Gerald Ford, would be confirmed by Congress as the new vice president, replacing the unacceptable Spiro Agnew, whom Haig had forced to resign the previous month. The Senate on November 27 confirmed Ford by a 92–3 vote. The House, where Ford had served for a quarter century, was next, and it was virtually guaranteed to replicate the same lopsided vote.

As the month closed on November 30, Haig received an unexpected break when Krogh, whose requests for documents about the Plumbers' investigation of the military spy ring threatened to expose Haig, pleaded guilty to perjury. That prevented embarrassing details about the Plumbers from surfacing in court.

Also on November 30 Laird announced he would leave the White House staff early the following year. While Laird did not say so publicly, he had accomplished what he needed to do when he joined the staff in June: preserve the cover-up of the military spy ring with Haig and Buzhardt, push out Agnew, and promote the nomination of his longtime friend and ally Ford as vice president. Ford, Laird said, would take over the domestic policy duties, although presumably with more access to the president than Laird had.

While Laird had managed to keep a lid on the spy ring, it still remained a threat to those who had participated in it and covered it up. As Laird announced his departure from the White House, Donald Sanders, the Watergate committee staffer who got Butterfield to reveal the existence of the White House tapes, met with his old friend from the FBI, Donald Stewart, the chief investigator at the Pentagon who discovered the spy ring. While the Watergate committee leadership had agreed not to investigate the spy ring, Sanders's boss, Senator Howard Baker, believed it was a key to much of what motivated the secrecy in the Nixon White House. He was not letting go. Stewart wrote Sanders a memo the next day to summarize their meeting and highlighted how Buzhardt covered up the Defense Department's exposure in the leak of the Pentagon Papers in 1971.[40]

Nixon started November reeling from the news that two of the tapes subpoenaed by the Watergate special prosecutor did not exist. Two of his main defenders, Buzhardt and Garment, believed he had to resign. By month's end, Buzhardt had revealed the destruction of another tape, knowing that the real evidence of Nixon's still remained available for discovery. Nixon still believed he could weather the fight, but his chief defenders knew better.

FIG. 1. A tired Richard Nixon. By the summer of 1974, President Richard Nixon was on the verge of losing his grip on the presidency, but he did not know his chief of staff, Alexander Haig, already knew Nixon was guilty of obstruction of justice. Courtesy National Archives and Records Administration.

FIG. 2. Vernon Walters served Richard Nixon for years, but when Nixon's men tried to get Walters and the CIA to block the FBI's investigation of the Watergate break-in, Walters wrote a series of detailed memos and gave them to Alexander Haig. Those memos provided the impetus to learn that Nixon had authorized obstruction of justice. Courtesy National Archives and Records Administration.

FIG. 3. Admiral Thomas Moorer, the chairman of the Joint Chiefs of Staff, was frustrated by Nixon's refusal to share information with the military. He authorized the creation of a spy ring operating the National Security Council that would steal documents and bring them back to the Pentagon. Haig went to great lengths to hide his cooperation with the spy ring. Courtesy National Archives and Records Administration.

FIG. 4. Former Defense Secretary Melvin Laird, left, joined the White House as a special aide to Nixon, center, in June 1973. Laird cooperated with Haig, right, in covering up the spy ring, and he also knew Nixon was guilty more than a year before the rest of the country. Courtesy National Archives and Records Administration.

FIG. 5. Admiral Elmo Zumwalt, second from right, said Nixon ranted and rambled during this December 22, 1973, breakfast meeting with Nixon, Haig, Defense Secretary James Schlesinger, and the rest of the Joint Chiefs at the White House. Courtesy National Archives and Records Administration.

FIG. 6. Henry Kissinger, Nixon, Gerald Ford, and Haig talked in the Oval Office shortly after Ford was nominated to be Nixon's second vice president in October 1973. At the time, Kissinger and Haig were keeping Nixon in the dark about details of the Arab-Israeli War. Courtesy National Archives and Records Administration.

FIG. 7. Melvin Laird, left, considered J. Fred Buzhardt, who was both the general counsel for the Pentagon and Nixon's chief Watergate lawyer, one of his closest friends in Washington. Buzhardt told Laird that the Watergate tapes showed Nixon was guilty before the world even knew the tapes existed. Courtesy National Archives and Records Administration.

FIG. 8. Alexander Butterfield, seated at his White House desk, suspected Haig of creating a fake memo to frame Butterfield about wiretaps that were placed by the FBI on government officials and journalists. Butterfield did not know about the wiretaps. Courtesy National Archives and Records Administration.

FIG. 9. Nixon assigned Haig to take care of Vice President Spiro Agnew's problems with the U.S. attorney in Baltimore's investigation of bribery, which had ensnared Agnew. Haig responded by forcing Agnew out of office so he could be replaced by someone more politically appealing. Courtesy National Archives and Records Administration.

FIG. 10. Instead of turning over transcripts of the contested White House tapes to special prosecutor Leon Jaworski, Nixon took a gamble by releasing transcripts his staff prepared to the public. His rough language and conspiratorial obsessions shocked many readers who did not expect this from a president. Courtesy National Archives and Records Administration.

9 December 1973

In November Nixon had tried valiantly to rebuild what remained of his image and public standing. Although often ridiculed, Operation Candor made some progress; Nixon's approval ratings perked up slightly. They could not match what Haig had done—either intentionally or by accident—to sabotage Nixon, starting with the revelation in the *Post* about intentional gaps in the White House tapes and then the revelation of the eighteen-and-a-half-minute gap on a tape that had been subpoenaed by the special prosecutor. Now Nixon stood accused of intentionally destroying evidence in a desperate attempt to save himself. December would provide no respite. Hearings into the tapes continued, and the president's erratic behavior drew increasingly concerned reactions. As Gerald Ford's confirmation as vice president neared, more people inside and outside the White House wondered how much longer Nixon would remain president.

A December 4 *New York Times* article highlighted the concerns about Nixon's health, citing reports that his July bout with viral pneumonia was worse than acknowledged and that the president lacked energy. It raised anonymous speculation that once Ford was confirmed, Nixon could enact the Twenty-Fifth Amendment and step aside temporarily. "Some of the greater signs of stress have been seen, not in the President himself, but in his staff," the *Times* reported. "Mr. Haig, J. Fred Buzhardt, Nixon's Watergate counsel, and others have appeared extraordinarily fatigued from time to time."[1]

In October Haig and Buzhardt concocted the ill-fated plan to have Mississippi senator John Stennis authenticate summaries of the White House tapes for Judge John Sirica and the special prosecutor, then Archibald Cox. The wrangling over the Stennis compromise became part of the pretext to fire Cox and eventually replace him with the more cooperative Leon Jaworski. On December 5 in an interview with Bob Woodward and Carl Bernstein of the *Washington Post*, Stennis demolished many of the White House's claims about the Stennis compromise. Stennis told the *Post* that he "had no idea" the White House wanted him to authenticate transcripts to be given to the court instead of the tapes themselves. "I was to deliver two copies, one for the White House and one for the Senate Watergate committee," Stennis said. "There was never any mention about the court. I wouldn't have done it if there was. No, no, no, I was once a judge and the courts can ask for what they want."[2] Stennis's refutation of the White House's version of the deal did not blow back on the architects of the compromise—Haig and Buzhardt—but on Nixon, who had merely acquiesced to what his aides gave him. And Senator Sam Ervin, one of the intended recipients of the Stennis summaries, piled on, saying that he too had been misled by the White House. Once again, as the move toward impeachment gained momentum, Haig had weakened the president's credibility.

Also on December 5 Haig began testifying in Sirica's court about the tape gap. Nixon, Haig said, was "very, very disturbed" about the gap, which Haig did not tell him about until after he spoke to a group of Realtors on November 15, a day after Buzhardt told Haig about the problem. "I felt the situation was sufficiently worrisome I should let him complete his speech," Haig said about the delay in informing the president.[3] Haig maintained that neither he, Buzhardt, nor Nixon knew the June 20, 1973, tape was subject to the subpoena. If so, however, why was Rose Mary Woods, Nixon's secretary, bothering to transcribe it in the first place? Haig told the court that Buzhardt told him the gap on the tape was longer than the five minutes they expected—eighteen minutes and fifteen seconds, to be exact—and that it was covered by the subpoena. "I said, 'This is a pretty late date to be telling me something like that,'" Haig said he told Buzhardt.[4] Haig's claim about the tape gap is hard to believe. It made no sense for Woods to waste time transcribing tapes not included in the subpoena, and Haig controlled the flow of information inside the Nixon White House. He and Buzhardt dominated the White House response to Cox, and he and Buzhardt engineered the plan that led to Cox's firing. Haig knew about the original erasure by Woods and is the logical suspect for leaking concerns about problems with the tapes to Woodward, his old associate from the National Security Council. Then, once Haig learned from Buzhardt and Sam Powers that the tape erasure was much longer than expected, he waited almost an entire day before telling Nixon and let the president give a high-profile speech without accurate information.

Haig continued his testimony on December 6. He inadvertently tipped his hand under questioning by Len Garment, admitting that Nixon had told him about the taping system in late May. He later said under cross-examination by prosecution lawyer Richard Ben-Veniste that he had learned that "some recordings of some conversations existed." Mostly, however, Haig continued to blame Woods for the entire eighteen-minute gap. Haig testified that Woods would be wrong about how much tape she erased, because he knew women who thought they had talked for only five minutes when they had actually talked for an hour. Sirica asked Haig if the tape could have been erased intentionally.

"Yes," Haig answered. "There's been discussion of what I've referred to as devil theories."

Sirica then asked Haig who the "sinister source" was Haig suspected of erasing the tape.

Haig did not mention any suspects, although he said the court had to narrow its focus to those who had access to the tapes—Woods and Steve Bull.[5]

Haig knew that answer was not true. Buzhardt had constant access to the tapes, and the erasure had grown from the time Woods discovered it on October 1 to November 14, when Buzhardt allegedly stumbled on the eighteen-minute, fifteen-second version with Powers. Buzhardt knew how to work the tape recorder better than anyone in Nixon's inner circle, and Haig and Buzhardt had the motive and opportunity to lengthen the erasure and then sandbag Nixon by not telling him about it. When Haig was asked why the White House did not reveal the longer gap until November 21, when Sirica forced Buzhardt to disclose it in open court, Haig said: "We had just had two nonrecordings, which was fairly traumatic from our perspective, and it was important we not have a repeat of that kind of thing, which led to perceptions by the American people which I don't think were justified by the facts."[6]

Impeachment loomed as a greater possibility as Gerald Ford moved even closer to being confirmed as vice president. The House debated on his nomination and voted on December 6. Senator Jacob Javits, a liberal New York Republican who had voted to confirm Ford in the Senate, said Ford's imminent confirmation brought Nixon's resignation into play, another indication of how badly Republicans viewed the extent of the damage Nixon's continued presence in the White House was having on their political fortunes. The House voted overwhelmingly to approve Ford, who was sworn in that evening.[7] Haig sat next to Pat Nixon in the House gallery to watch Ford become the first person sworn in as vice president under the Twenty-Fifth Amendment. It was a moment Haig had waited for since he learned of the bribery investigation that made Spiro Agnew politically radioactive. Nixon's replacement was now in place. "The atmosphere on Capitol Hill revealed more about the political realities of the day than perhaps had been intended," Haig wrote. "Ford was treated throughout the ceremony and afterward as a President in waiting, especially by Republicans, and there can be little question that Richard Nixon's presidency was over, in their minds, from the moment his successor took the oath. By then, the left wing of his own party, and much of the center, had effectively given up hope that he could be saved."[8]

Many others shared that same feeling. Tom Wicker, a *New York Times* columnist, identified a growing consensus within Congress. The morning after Ford was sworn in, Wicker wrote that Ford's presence now opened a chance for Nixon to depart gracefully. "Another possibility flowing from it is that Mr. Nixon might now seek to arrange something like an 'Agnew deal' with the new vice president," Wicker wrote. "He could arrange to step down, that is, in return for certain assurances from President-to-be Ford that indictments or other legal action would not be pursued in the case of a private citizen named Richard Nixon."[9]

Nixon rushed to assure Ford he had no intention of quitting. During his first news conference on December 7, Ford said, "I can assure you the president has no intention whatsoever of resigning. I heard him say it before and he reiterated it today. I don't think he should resign. I see no evidence whatsoever that would justify a favorable vote in the House of Representatives on impeachment."[10]

Ford, however, had been tipped off in August by Laird that Agnew was guilty. It is not a stretch to believe that Laird, Ford's old friend and booster in the House, had shared what he knew about Nixon as well. But since Nixon had no intention of leaving office, it would have been politically suicidal for the newly installed Ford to say anything to challenge Nixon's future. But Ford knew better, and he knew his options. Now settling in as vice president, Ford had to maneuver through an obstacle course that required protecting Nixon politically while also preserving his own credibility. Much of the public and many of his colleagues underestimated Ford, but few people rise as high as he did without mastering the system. Ford, after all, had maneuvered to get on the Warren Commission, which was investigating the assassination of President John F. Kennedy.[11] He also ousted two incumbent members of the Republican House leadership in the 1960s, including minority leader Charlie Halleck in 1965.[12] Ford's allies in Congress worried that Ford did not distance himself enough from Nixon, but the new vice president knew what he was doing.

Although Egil Krogh pleaded guilty on November 30, which eliminated the problem of a trial that would expose details of the Plumbers operation damaging to Haig, the Plumbers issue still threatened him. On December 10 reporter Seymour Hersh of the *New York Times* had a story that detailed many of the Plumbers' activities, particularly their investigation of Pentagon Papers leaker Daniel Ellsberg and the rivalry between Krogh and David Young, the former NSC aide to Kissinger who helped Krogh run the special investigations unit.[13] It was that tension that contributed to John Ehrlichman's disbelief of Young's suspicions of Haig's involvement in December 1971 with the spy ring, because Krogh was close to Ehrlichman, while Young was identified with Kissinger. By this time, prosecutors had given Young immunity, so he would also not be tried. Hersh showed how the decision to break into the office of Dr. Lewis Fielding, Ellsberg's psychiatrist, was made and the links between the Plumbers and Ehrlichman, Nixon's close aide who supervised them. Every time a White House aide close to the Plumbers could avoid a trial, the better it was for Haig. Ellsberg's trial in the spring showed how trials often took on lives of their own, spinning off new evidence and causing untold collateral damage. Ellsberg's trial exposed the existence of both the Plumbers and the FBI wiretaps on seventeen government officials and journalists. A Krogh trial, especially if the defendant was allowed to use evidence about the investigation into the leaks during the India-Pakistan war, would have shown how the Plumbers knew Haig helped the spy ring steal secrets from the White House and then reveal those secrets to columnist Jack Anderson. Not only did Haig pass information to the military that Nixon did not want it to have, but then he, Laird, Buzhardt, and Adm. Thomas Moorer covered up what they had done with a whitewashed Pentagon investigation.

Haig's negotiations with Jaworski walked a similar tightrope. While Jaworski complained that Buzhardt withheld information that Jaworski considered essential to the case against Nixon and his top aides, Haig was funneling tapes and other documents to Jaworski. Claiming to act in the name of the president, Haig requested help in mid-December from the National Security Agency, a division of the Pentagon, to make duplicates of certain tapes. Defense Secretary James Schlesinger was reluctant to get his department drawn into anything having to do with

Watergate. Schlesinger consulted with Martin Hoffmann, his special assistant, about the propriety of Haig's request, and Hoffmann suggested they could honor it if they had a member of Jaworski's staff accompany them. That angered Haig, as did Schlesinger's claim that if Haig was copying the tapes to make it easier for more people to listen to them, he should have no problem letting the prosecutor's staff watch the copying. "Haig abruptly hung up; there would be no more Watergate-related calls to Schlesinger from Haig's office," Hersh wrote.[14] Many of Jaworski's staff were suspicious of his frequent meetings with Haig, but they did not know how much Haig was doing to help their case. Haig could not afford the exposure that Schlesinger's proposal would have generated.

Signs of Nixon's slippage, real or contrived, continued. On December 13 he met alone in the White House with Anatoly Dobrynin, the Soviet ambassador and Kissinger's longtime secret negotiating partner. They spoke for almost an hour, covering the recent developments in the Middle East and other issues. "The private conversation was unusual both in content and form in that he was extraordinarily frank about domestic questions," Dobrynin wrote in his memoirs. Nixon, Dobrynin said, was unusually candid about Israel and Kissinger, who he said "strongly indulged Israel's nationalist sentiments, for which he had to be corrected. . . . Finally he told me to give no credence to the hue and cry in the American media about his possible resignation or impeachment. He said he would stay in the White House until the end of his term, he was a persistent person, and he would be as good as his word—make no mistake about it."[15] Neither Nixon nor Haig gave Kissinger a heads-up, which enraged him. Kissinger sent his deputy, Brent Scowcroft, an angry telegram demanding to know why Nixon had met with Dobrynin and citing the dangers of having such a meeting without him. "Thus, I must insist that I be given a full report of the Dobrynin conversation with the President," Kissinger wrote. "I am flying blind without it, which at this point could have disastrous consequences for all we are trying to do here and at home to build a peace and restore foreign and domestic confidence in this administration."[16] As he had through the Middle East crisis, Kissinger resented what he considered Nixon's interference.

He did not trust the president, because he thought Nixon's grasp on reality was slipping.

So did some of Nixon's allies. The president invited Senator Barry Goldwater to dinner at the White House on the evening of December 13. Sitting with Pat Nixon, Julie and David Eisenhower, Rose Mary Woods, and other close Nixon associates, Goldwater watched in horror as Nixon spoke in "gibberish" and appeared openly drunk. "Act like a president," Goldwater told Nixon.[17] Haig called this incident "one of many stories, apocryphal and otherwise, that fed rumors of a Nixon driven to drink and clinical depression by his troubles. The truth is that Nixon maintained psychological equilibrium under conditions that would have driven a saint around the bend."[18] As with much of Haig's memoirs, that claim is simply not true. Every day Haig watched Nixon unravel, and he played on those displays to marginalize the president and maneuver for his removal.

Haig asked Nixon about his meeting with Dobrynin and reported to Kissinger on December 14. Nixon told Haig he had mostly sought continued cooperation with the Soviets on the Middle East and their help with Syria in freeing Israeli prisoners of war. That did not placate Kissinger. "I hope in the future if you are given any other hare-brained orders similar to the instructions to get Dobrynin in you will first check them with Haig to see if he can get them reversed," he wrote in a telegram to Scowcroft. "As I indicated in my note to Haig, nothing could have gone on at that meeting that could do us any good at all."[19]

Around this date, Buzhardt had learned enough from the people interviewed by Jim Squires of the *Chicago Tribune* and Dan Thomasson of Scripps-Howard to call both of them in for a meeting at the White House. The two reporters from different news organizations had joined forces the previous July after John Ehrlichman's mysterious testimony about national security issues. By the time of Buzhardt's call, the two were close to publishing, which Buzhardt most likely picked up from his sources. "Well I think he was trying to play poker with us and I think sometimes you know, we played a better game than he did, because I really believe that he thought we knew at that juncture one hell of a lot more than we did know," Thomasson said. "And he was trying to tell us something," Thomasson added, which was that Yeoman Charles Radford, the Pentagon's scapegoat for the leaks to Jack Anderson and the existence of the spy ring, had been packed up and shipped out of the Pentagon to Oregon, where "they were baby-sitting this guy."[20]

The Senate Watergate committee, which had stopped its hearings in November, kept up its pressure. On December 19 it issued an omnibus subpoena for hundreds of documents and tapes from the White House. At the top of its list, chief counsel Sam Dash noted, was the June 23, 1972, conversation between Nixon and Bob Haldeman. Dash did not know at the time that that conversation was the so-called smoking gun that proved Nixon had authorized using the CIA to block the FBI investigation into the Watergate break-in. "In the staff list this conversation was rated A and described as a conversation between the President and Haldeman on how to use the CIA to limit the FBI investigation," Dash wrote.[21] The committee did not obtain the tape transcript until the following July. Haig, however, knew when the subpoena arrived that the conversation was fatal to Nixon. He had known that since May, when he first learned of the White House taping system and that Haldeman acknowledged that Nixon had told him to tell the CIA to block the FBI.

On December 20 the House Judiciary Committee, as it geared up for the impeachment investigation, hired its chief counsel, John Doar, a Republican attorney who had led many of the Justice Department's toughest cases during the civil rights era of the 1960s. He, too, came from the list of Morris Leibman, the unofficial placement officer for Watergate-related lawyers.[22] As a longtime leader of the American Bar Association, Leibman knew most of the nation's top lawyers. He also worked closely with Haig throughout the final months of the Nixon administration as Haig and Congress picked their top investigators.[23]

By mid-December Haig had started a series of meetings with Jaworski at the White House. In the Map Room, Haig often let Jaworski listen to tapes in what the prosecutor considered a misguided attempt to show Nixon's innocence. As Haig knew, the tapes proved exactly the opposite: Nixon may not have ordered the Watergate break-in, but he knew about the cover-up. Haig told Jaworski that the March 21 tape in which Nixon and John Dean discussed the cover-up was "terrible, beyond description," but added that the White House lawyers believed it did not show criminal conduct by Nixon. Jaworski believed that the tapes showed Nixon was guilty. "I told Haig that in my judgment the president was criminally involved and told him that he'd better get the finest criminal lawyers he could find in the country to pass on this information," Jaworski said he told Haig on December 21.[24] Haig, who had known about Nixon's guilt for months, had shown the prosecutor in charge of determining Nixon's guilt information that he called terrible, beyond description, and then seemed shocked when Jaworski agreed.

Nixon eventually pulled back on Haig's disclosures. "And then the president got tremendously jittery," Jaworski said. "And then it happened that the president said nothing else would be turned over to me except that which he passed on himself because he—I think he woke up fearing that I had gotten more information that was inculpatory than he had thought was actually there."[25] Nixon's jitters made sense. He realized his chief of staff had given Jaworski evidence that would help drive him from office.

Nixon scheduled a rare Saturday morning breakfast on December 22 with the members of the Joint Chiefs of Staff; it took place in the second-floor dining room in the White House residence. Haig and Scowcroft joined the president, Defense Secretary Schlesinger and his deputy, Bill Clements, Admiral Moorer, Army Gen. Creighton Abrams, Adm. Elmo Zumwalt, Air Force Gen. George Brown, and Marine Commandant Robert Cushman to review the upcoming military budget. The unraveling that Goldwater had seen a week earlier remained, and the military leaders listened in mostly stunned silence as Nixon rambled. "The meeting went on for a long period of time and was almost totally a monologue by the president," Zumwalt said in a 1991 oral history interview that Zumwalt asked to remain classified until 2013.

> At one point Tom Moorer was able to make a short pitch for the bud-get, and at another point I was able to make a short pitch about the Navy part of the budget. I don't think any other chief said anything,

and the speech was full of such things as "we've got to stick together," "this is the last best hope," "the effete, elite, Eastern establishment is out to do us in." In a way it was rambling, and in a way it was hortatory, and in a way he would seem to come back and focus on us from time to time. When we left the office, I turned to my friend, General Abrams, and said, "Did you get the same general impression that I got?" General Abrams said, "I don't want to talk about it, I don't want to make a minute about it, and I don't want to have heard it." I never talked to any of the other chiefs about it, Abe was the only one I felt close enough to talk to.[26]

Zumwalt said he did not mention anything to Schlesinger about the meeting, but three to six weeks later, Schlesinger issued a directive that no troops would be moved on Washington without his personal approval, because Schlesinger feared an unhinged Nixon would try to use the military to stay in power.[27]

It was at this time, Zumwalt noted, with Haig as chief of staff and Kissinger as secretary of state running the government, that the United States was "as close to fascism during the last year of the Nixon era as we have ever come in this country. I hope and pray that we will never again have such a combination of factors that we have two power-seeking men and a greatly weakened president."[28]

Nixon decamped to San Clemente on December 26, fooling the press and many on his own staff by slipping into a Lincoln Continental, not his traditional limousine, and driving to Dulles International Airport in suburban Virginia for a commercial airline flight to California. He left Haig behind.[29]

Haig and Jaworski met again on December 27, when Haig said he had talked to James St. Clair, a skilled criminal trial lawyer from Boston. Once again, Haig had consulted with his consigliere, Morris Leibman, just as he had when he hired Jaworski and Samuel Powers.[30] St. Clair had handled dozens of complicated cases and had defended the army during the 1954 Senate hearings led by Wisconsin senator Joseph McCarthy during the worst of the anticommunist witch hunts of the 1950s. Len Garment had recused himself from the Watergate defense, and Nixon was apparently mad at Buzhardt for his lapses handling the erased tape. St. Clair then flew to San Clemente, where he met with Nixon for more than an hour on December 31.

"I want you to represent the office of the president exclusively," Nixon told St. Clair, stressing that the presidency, not the fate of any one man, needed to be preserved.[31] In that respect, Nixon and Haig shared the same idea. Haig's allegiances, to the extent they were ever tied to Nixon, had long skipped to the presidency and other institutions he valued.

10   January 1974

The existence of the military spy ring, which Nixon, Alexander Haig, the military, and Bob Woodward covered up for months, could remain a secret no longer. By the beginning of January, reporters Jim Squires and Dan Thomasson were on the brink of confirming the ring's existence and publishing their first stories. Their impending articles triggered a flurry of reporting by Woodward meant more for Haig's benefit than for Woodward's readers. Woodward, who had known about the spy ring since the previous May, began to contact the ring's key players, shadowing the work done by Squires and Thomasson but publishing none of it. As much as anyone, Woodward would join the spy ring cover-up that was desperately vital to his old associate and crucial source, Haig. The president, meanwhile, virtually disappeared from public view, remaining in California until January 13.

Haig's sales job with James St. Clair had succeeded. He agreed to be Nixon's defense attorney, while Fred Buzhardt became the official White

House counsel and resigned as the Pentagon's general counsel, finally eliminating the conflict of interest that had existed from the moment Buzhardt went to the White House in May. Len Garment would shift from working as part of the legal team to be an assistant to Nixon. Press accounts at the time reported that Buzhardt and Garment had angered Nixon with their botched handling of the erasure of the June 20, 1973, tape and the two other tapes that had been subpoenaed but had turned out not to exist. But Buzhardt had other priorities. The existence of the military spy ring was on the verge of blowing open. He, Haig, and Melvin Laird, in his final days at the White House, had to minimize the damage.

Although hiring St. Clair appeared to be a coup for Nixon, the new attorney had the same problems as the others who had been brought in to help the president. Buzhardt still controlled access to the tapes, and St. Clair could not meet with his client unless Haig was present. Little had changed.[1]

As the White House announced St. Clair's hiring, Haig got the shock he had feared was coming. Aldo Beckman, the White House reporter for the *Chicago Tribune*, approached him in San Clemente with a pressing question: Was Adm. Thomas Moorer involved in a spy ring that stole secrets from the White House and brought them back to the Pentagon? Haig looked stunned.

"Oh shit, I knew this was going to get out," Haig said, turning white. "Let me get back to you."

A few hours later, Haig found Beckman.

"There's not a word of truth in it," Haig said.[2]

Squires and Thomasson had the White House comment they needed and now put the final touches on the story they started to report in July.

Shortly after Beckman questioned Haig, Woodward went to work, calling Yeoman Charles Radford at his home in Oregon on January 7. Woodward told Radford that the news about the spy ring, the reason why he was rushed to Oregon from the Pentagon two years earlier, was about to break. "When I realized it was going to come out in the newspaper, I was sick to my stomach," Radford said. Woodward kept asking questions, which Radford declined to answer.[3]

Then Woodward called Donald Stewart, the Pentagon investigator and former FBI agent whose questioning had forced Radford to reveal the spying.

"What do you know about a telephone tap on Charles Edward Radford?" Woodward asked. Stewart refused to answer and referred Woodward to the Pentagon press office. Stewart likely knew nothing about the telephone tap, because the tap was authorized by John Mitchell, then the attorney general, to see if Radford was leaking classified information after he was transferred.

Woodward kept asking questions, and Stewart, while declining comment, took notes.

What did Stewart know about Radford "feeding information from the White House to the Joint Chiefs of Staff and also to them from Kissinger and General Haig?"

Stewart said he was in no position to answer. "Where did you pick up this information?" Stewart asked.

"I have sources and I can't tell you," said Woodward, who then asked, "Were you there when the Plumbers were formed?"

Stewart said he must have been, since he had worked at the Pentagon for eight years.

"Did the Plumbers get into the Radford case?" Woodward asked.

"I don't know."

Was Stewart interviewed by the Senate Armed Services Committee about Watergate or related matters?

Stewart said no.

What about the Watergate committee?

Again, Stewart said no, which was technically not true, since Stewart had met in July with Senator Howard Baker and his staff.

"What do you know about Admiral Welander?" Woodward asked. Rear Adm. Robert Welander had been Woodward's commanding officer when Woodward served on the USS Fox off the coast of Vietnam.

"Who is he?" Stewart answered. Stewart knew about Welander, since he had interviewed him in early January 1972 for Buzhardt's report, which covered up key details of the spy ring.

Were the allegations against Radford and Welander legitimate?

Stewart again declined to answer.

Why was Welander's office closed in December 1971 by the White House?

"I don't know and didn't even know he had an office there," Stewart said.[4] Kissinger had closed the office in a fit of pique shortly after learning about the spy ring and listening to the taped interview of Welander by John Ehrlichman and David Young.[5] Laird, who opposed the office's existence from the time he became secretary of defense, used the spy ring to force the White House to close the office.[6]

Stewart wrote a memo immediately after the Woodward call and reported the call to his superiors, writing that "Woodward took me totally by surprise. . . . I asked him why he bothered to call me," Stewart continued. "He indicated he just wanted to verify what he already knew."[7]

Haig's collaboration with Chicago superlawyer Morris Leibman placed another lawyer in a key spot in the impeachment fight. The Republican members of the House Judiciary Committee picked Chicago attorney Albert Jenner, another former officer of the American Bar Association and the lead partner of the huge firm Jenner & Block.[8] Jenner had formidable credentials as a member of the national security establishment and as a board member of the giant defense contractor General Dynamics, and he was also a senior counsel on the Warren Commission, which investigated the assassination of President John Kennedy. In his memoirs, Haig claimed to be suspicious of Jenner because of his family friendship with Democratic Illinois senator Adlai Stevenson III, who had predicted that Nixon would not last long in office.[9] Given Jenner's close ties to Leibman, Haig's clearinghouse for Watergate lawyers, Haig's after-the-fact concerns about Jenner's loyalties have little credibility. By January 7 Leibman had been instrumental in the selection of the chief Watergate prosecutor, Leon Jaworski; Nixon's lawyer for the fight over the tapes, Samuel Powers; the president's impeachment defense attorney, St. Clair; the chief counsel for the House Judiciary Committee's impeachment effort, John Doar; and the committee's minority counsel, Jenner.

Haig's dance with Jaworski over White House tapes and documents continued. At the beginning of January, Jaworski had asked Haig to listen to the June 4, 1973, "tape of tapes," in which Nixon, assisted by Steve Bull and Haig, listened to the tapes of his previous meetings with John Dean. Haig was willing to agree, although Buzhardt reportedly objected, according to the Woodward and Carl Bernstein account, *The Final Days*. "But Haig saw a possibility of bringing Watergate, at least the special prosecutor's investigation of it, to an end if Jaworski could be convinced that the White House had nothing to hide," Woodward and Bernstein wrote.[10] Given Buzhardt's knowledge of Nixon's guilt and his and Haig's record of false statements about virtually every point of the Nixon defense, it is hard to believe Buzhardt's objections. After all, Jaworski had already told Haig that he thought Nixon was guilty and needed to hire a criminal attorney, which was why St. Clair had joined their defense team. Haig and Buzhardt already knew of Nixon's guilt, too; that had been assured from the moment Nixon told Haig about the White House tapes and Haig listened to Bob Haldeman tell Nixon that the president had asked him to obstruct justice. When Jaworski came to the White House on January 8 to listen to the tape, the president's chief of staff had to know he was letting the Watergate prosecutor hear even more evidence damaging to Nixon's case. As with many of the tapes, the poor quality of the recording, combined with the background noise, shuffling of papers, and scribbling of notes, made it difficult for Jaworski to make much of it. He asked Buzhardt for a copy, and Buzhardt declined. He called Haig, who told Buzhardt to give a copy to Jaworski.[11] The next day, Jaworski sent Buzhardt a letter asking for twenty-five more White House tapes. Haig reported to Nixon what had happened, and the president ridiculed him for cooperating with Jaworski. No more tapes for anyone, Nixon ordered.[12]

By this time Woodward had called Welander, his former commander, about the spy ring.

"He said the story is going to break and I have to write, and what can you tell me about it?" Welander said that Woodward asked him.

Like Stewart, Welander said little and denied any wrongdoing.[13]

Woodward was correct about the story being ready to break. Squires's story appeared January 11 in the *Chicago Tribune*, while Thomasson's moved on the Scripps-Howard news wire. Woodward, who had known about the story since May, had nothing.

The treatment of the stories by the *Tribune* and the Scripps clients showed the scope of the issue. "Probers Charge Pentagon Spied on Kissinger in 1971," the *Tribune* headline blared over the top of the front page. "A still-secret White House investigation in 1971 disclosed that top-ranking military officials engaged in a spying and eavesdropping campaign against Henry Kissinger, The Tribune learned today," the lead of Squires's story said.[14] Both stories said that an unnamed "spy" had taken "top secret information" from the National Security Council and passed it to the Pentagon and to Moorer in particular. The reporters did not identify Radford and Welander; their names remained secret. They accurately reported that the military was angry at the secret moves made by Kissinger—under Nixon's orders—and the general paranoia within the Pentagon about White House policies made without the military's input. Especially interesting, since it did not come up in the White House and Pentagon investigations, is the mention of "eavesdropping" on the White House by the military. Laird had used the National Security Agency during his time as defense secretary to monitor the secret communications by Kissinger on his various missions for Nixon that the Pentagon did not know about.

The two stories landed with megaton force inside the White House. Haig and Buzhardt knew they were coming, and Woodward was running interference for them, but the stories stirred up a Washington press corps hungry for something different from the latest twist in the Watergate saga. Now Nixon's claims of national security for why he left some issues undiscussed in his May 22 white paper from the previous year started to make sense. In the *New York Times*, Seymour Hersh had the story, while Woodward and Bernstein had the *Post*'s version. Hersh led with the report conducted by David Young, one of the White House Plumbers, with Donald Stewart. It showed how the Plumbers had uncovered the spy ring "attempting to relay highly classified information on the China talks and other matters" to Pentagon officials. Some of the officers, Hersh wrote, were assigned to the National Security Council, and Young's investigation started because of the leaks to Jack Anderson. Hersh also named Welander as the officer punished for the spying. He also mentioned the stories by the *Tribune* and Scripps-Howard and attributed the spying to the White House's secrecy and habitual exclusion of the Chiefs and Laird from critical deliberations. Finally, Hersh included the White House claim that Radford, though unnamed in the story, was responsible for the espionage and the leaks, and he quoted Anderson saying Welander was not his source.[15]

The *Post*'s story, by contrast, bore the distinct fingerprints of Alexander Haig. It did not mention the stories by Squires and Thomasson, giving *Post* readers the impression that Woodward and Bernstein had broken the story on their own, which Woodward had had the opportunity to do since he first learned of the issue the previous May. Despite Woodward's head start, the story was less complete than Hersh's, and it named Radford as "the central figure in the matter." Woodward's experience working in the Pentagon and delivering secrets to the White House should have been enough for him to conclude how ridiculous that claim was. The story was also shot full of inaccuracies, starting with its claim that the investigation that uncovered the spying "was ordered by an angry Kissinger after documents on U.S. policy in the India-Pakistan war were leaked to columnist Anderson in late 1971." It was Welander who sought the investigation after discovering the leaks in Anderson's column; he told Haig about the problem, and Haig told John Ehrlichman, the ultimate overseer of the Plumbers. As Woodward and Bernstein did in their story on October 10 that first mentioned more FBI wiretaps, this account emphasized the wiretaps and said their details were sent to David Young, one of the Plumbers and the investigator most suspicious of Haig. The story also said that four unnamed sources said the "information distribution" was not spying, although that was exactly how Nixon and the investigators characterized it. Woodward and Bernstein also said that the investigation was led by Fred Buzhardt, not Young and Donald Stewart. Buzhardt only started his investigation after Melvin Laird and Haig wanted to override whatever Young and Stewart had discovered in their probe, which Nixon then called off. It was during Young and Stewart's investigation that Welander admitted to Ehrlichman that Haig routinely passed along White House secrets to the Pentagon through Welander and his predecessor, Rear Adm. Rembrandt Robinson. Kissinger was also incorrectly cited as calling for an end to verbatim notes being taken during critical national security meetings; actually, he continuously recorded his own telephone calls in order to create an accurate account of his activities. The story also said that Kissinger had long wanted to kill the Chiefs' liaison office in the NSC. It was Laird who opposed that office from the beginning, correctly viewing it as a means for Nixon to bypass him and go straight to the Chiefs, and who used the discovery of the spy ring as leverage to wrest the investigation away from the White House and give it to Buzhardt. Woodward also cleared his former skipper, Welander, saying that he now held an important job that "Pentagon officials said would not have been given to anyone suspected of unauthorized distribution of classified material."[16]

Finally and most importantly, the story did not mention that its main author, Woodward, had worked for two of the men at the heart of the investigation, Welander and Moorer, and that Woodward had delivered Pentagon documents to Haig while Woodward served in the navy. While the *Post* story delivered the impression that it revealed deep secrets about the flawed relationship between the White House and the Pentagon— complete with the frisson of Nixonian treachery on the wiretaps—it delicately diverted the focus of the spy ring from Woodward's former bosses at the Pentagon and his key source, Haig, to the hapless Chuck Radford, now exiled in Oregon.

Hersh had a follow-up story the next day, January 13, about how an unnamed investigator, Stewart, had tried to blackmail the White House into giving him another job, including consideration as FBI director.[17] This, Hersh said later, was a direct leak from Haig, who had tried to shake Hersh off the story about the FBI wiretaps the previous May.[18] "The White House told the Senate Watergate committee last summer that a Government official who participated in the investigation of the unauthorized passing of National Security Council documents to the Pentagon had, in effect, sought to 'blackmail' his way to a more important job by threatening to make the secret materials public," the story said. Haig and Buzhardt knew well that the Justice Department had already rejected their attempts to prosecute Stewart for blackmail, saying he had done nothing wrong. It was true that Buzhardt and Garment told the senators leading the Watergate committee in July that they believed Stewart was blackmailing them, but they also knew at the time that Henry Petersen, the head of Justice's Criminal Division, had called the blackmail claim bogus and refused to prosecute. The leak to Hersh was, pure and simple, an attempt to damage the credibility of one of the people who knew the most about the spy ring and limit Stewart's chances of testifying against them. Hersh regretted the story. "I had an early deadline," he said in a 1987 interview. "I remember that I had an early fucking deadline, it was a Saturday story. And I certainly didn't do Don Stewart any good in that story. There's no question I should have gone to him and gotten comment and been balanced."[19]

Woodward and Bernstein also checked in again on January 13. Their story looked at the role of the Plumbers in the spy ring investigation and whether Nixon exaggerated the national security implications of the spy ring as part of the Watergate cover-up. "Now it's all public and you can see that national security was invoked because it would scare everyone and be the best justification. . . . [Y]ou can see that no government is going to fall," they quoted one White House official saying. Buzhardt's efforts to block criminal trials of the three White House officials closest to the Plumbers were highlighted.[20] He wanted to stop John Ehrlichman, Charles Colson, and Egil Krogh from going to trial, specifically because they wanted to cite their investigation into the spy ring as part of their defense. Buzhardt's motives hewed closely to Haig's; they wanted to stop the investigation into the spy ring because it would expose Haig's involvement and the possibility that the military's top leaders leaked secrets to stop Nixon's policies.

Almost everyone connected to the spying and the leaks about U.S. policy toward India and Pakistan had a reason to cover up. While Buzhardt's

Pentagon investigation pinned the spying and leaks on Radford, a more thorough probe would expose other suspects, such as the men at the top of the military brass to whom Radford gave the stolen documents from the White House. Moorer, Welander, and Robinson all praised Radford for what he was giving them. If they had truly not asked him to steal for them, they could have told him to stop at any time or transferred him to a less sensitive post. They did not. The navy's top commanders, as well as Laird, also knew they had serious reservations about sending an aircraft carrier task force into the Bay of Bengal during the height of the India-Pakistan crisis, a powerful motive for them to leak Nixon's orders to Jack Anderson.[21] An investigation more honest than Buzhardt's could have exposed them. Nor did the administration keep the movements of the carrier task force so closely held that Kissinger and Haig could not tell the Chinese their plans during a December 10 meeting at the United Nations.[22] Laird was also using the National Security Agency to monitor Kissinger's calls, an eavesdropping operation that let Laird know much of what Nixon tried to hide from him. It was also a potential breach of the NSA's charter that would have blown back on Laird.[23] Haig faced both threats. He cooperated with the military by sharing information that Nixon wanted to hide from it, thereby violating the president's trust, and he stood liable to be exposed for that and, by extension, any of the leaked classified secrets that reached Anderson. The move toward a congressional investigation, perhaps something of the scope of the Watergate hearings, was gaining momentum.

Of the two competing newspapers, the *Times* and Hersh had the most consistently reliable reporting. Hersh was not compromised by his relationship with Haig, as was Woodward, and he was not hiding information to protect his two former commanders, as Woodward was with Moorer and Welander. Hersh followed his story about Donald Stewart, planted courtesy of Haig, with a more detailed report on January 14 that highlighted David Young's role in the spy ring investigation.[24] On January 16 he reported the anonymous claims from White House officials—no doubt Haig, Buzhardt, and maybe Laird in his final days in the West Wing—that Young's investigation was "ludicrous." None of the officials deriding

Young's accurate report had the courage to put their names behind their accusations, which were all aimed at damaging the credibility of the one legitimate investigation into the spy ring. Hersh also showed why Nixon wanted to keep the spy ring secret; "public disclosure," he wrote, "of the incident would put the 'whole military command structure on the line.'"[25]

Luckily for Haig and the rest of the plotters, their fate rested in the hands of a willing Senator John Stennis, a longtime friend to the military, Nixon, and Buzhardt. The Mississippi Democrat had recovered from the gunshot wounds that he had received the previous January and that had sidelined him for months and was now firmly back in control of the Senate Armed Services Committee, which would handle any Senate investigation into the spy ring. Buzhardt had called Stennis the "undertaker" of the Senate for his ability to bury inconvenient issues with a hearing stacked with friendly witnesses. His absence for much of 1973 had shown the White House how much it missed him, as Senator Stuart Symington, who chaired the committee in Stennis's absence, had exposed Nixon's support of the Huston Plan, the attempt to use the CIA to block the FBI investigation into Watergate and the secret bombing of Cambodia. Now, Haig and Buzhardt, on behalf of themselves and everyone else who stood to be exposed, were asking Stennis to pull out his shovel again. "I certainly want to take a look at this matter and I don't expect [the White House] to hold anything back," Stennis said about his investigation. Stennis also dodged claims that he had been briefed about the spy ring before it was revealed in the press. "Until the story broke, I didn't know a thing about it. I was not confided in in anything at all," he said.[26] Hersh also reported that the spy ring had drawn Jaworski's attention for potential inclusion in his list of cases. Jaworski knew about the spy ring because Haig and Buzhardt warned him in November not to pursue it.[27]

At times, the "investigation" into the spy ring devolved into farce. Defense Secretary James Schlesinger said through his spokesman on January 15 that he would investigate the reports, although he was skeptical of the seriousness of the accusations, because, after all, Admiral Moorer had been appointed to a second term as chairman of the Joint Chiefs of Staff after the discovery of the spying.[28] Schlesinger had no idea that

Nixon had done this on purpose, believing that he could blackmail Moorer at will into following his orders because the threat of exposure hovered over him. Jerry Friedheim, Schlesinger's spokesman, also said Schlesinger would consult with Buzhardt and Laird—two of the architects of the Pentagon cover-up—for his investigation. Michael Getler, the *Post*'s Pentagon reporter, noted in his January 16 story that the report done for Laird by Buzhardt may have differed from Young's investigation for the White House. He was correct, but neither he nor the public knew just how right he was.[29]

Jaworski continued to turn up the pressure on the White House about the missing eighteen minutes on the tape of Nixon's June 20, 1972, conversation with Bob Haldeman. He asked for the FBI to investigate the apparent erasure on January 16, and the White House agreed the next day to give the bureau the cooperation it needed. Nixon talked about the investigation into the erasure with Haig and said he wanted "to get to the bottom of the situation," said Gerald Warren, his deputy press secretary.[30] Of course he did, because Nixon had no idea how the erasure happened and knew that it was one of the many factors destroying his credibility.

Jack Anderson weighed in with a January 17 column that spelled out exactly how information passed from Radford to Moorer, who Anderson said created the spy ring out of frustration with Nixon's secrecy. Radford took the documents from the White House, Anderson wrote, and then gave them to Capt. Arthur Knoizen, Moorer's assistant, who passed them to Moorer. "Knoizen also circulated those documents to the other military chiefs," Anderson wrote. "Nothing appeared in writing to indicate the documents had been copied from Kissinger's files. But sometimes Knoizen sent a cover memo warning of the 'sensitivity' of the material." Anderson had details about the spy ring that Radford, accused by Buzhardt's report and Woodward's reporting as being the prime figure in the spying, would not know about. Radford would not have been involved with the writing of Knoizen's cover letters or how the information passed to Moorer. Nor would Radford know of how Capt. Howard Kay, another Moorer deputy, routed information to Knoizen and Moorer. Anderson said Radford did not leak secrets to him; those only came from officers more highly placed in the Pentagon.[31] The signs of what happened in the White House and Pentagon, the theft of documents Nixon wanted to hide, and the leaking of them to Anderson were there for anyone to find, whether the facts came from Donald Stewart, Radford, or Anderson's columns. Haig and Buzhardt, eager to cover their tracks, were doing their best to keep those facts from being discovered.

At the Pentagon, Don Stewart watched the unfolding cover-up of the spy ring with alarm and some amusement. "In my opinion, Buzhardt and some White House people were more concerned in protecting the military and the White House people from embarrassment than they were concerned about the National Security interests of the country," he wrote in a memo dated January 21 to Martin Hoffmann at the Pentagon. Stewart laid out how Buzhardt had covered up at the Pentagon and engineered a second interview of Welander to hide the disturbing details of what Welander had told Ehrlichman and Young at the White House. "Buzhardt and I interviewed Welander in the first week of January 1972 after I got called back from vacation," Stewart wrote. "After the interview I prepared a 14-page memo. Buzhardt only wanted the original for his file, but since I know how things get misplaced, I prepared an extra copy for our office file. It was there when my files were removed in May 1973 for integration into the Defense Investigative Service files. This, of course, was never done." Stewart also kept a copy for himself.[32]

On January 22 Kissinger had a news conference during which he lied about the spying and tried to cover for Moorer. When the spy ring was first discovered, Kissinger had wanted everyone involved prosecuted. He raged when he realized Nixon wanted to paper it over. Now, as secretary of state and in charge of the administration's national security responses, he could take a more lofty stance. "I have no reason to question the argument that has been made by Admiral Moorer, that this incident of the unauthorized transfer of papers from my office to his office reflected overzealousness on the part of subordinates and in any case gave him no information that he did not already possess," Kissinger said.[33] The issue went beyond whether Moorer obtained information from the White House through unconventional means. The issue was whether he or other top military officials knowingly leaked classified information to the press to subvert the president's orders. The leak about the *Enterprise* moving to the Bay of Bengal hurt Nixon's ability to counter India, and the leak about the tilt toward Pakistan despite the official position of neutrality in the India-Pakistan war damaged his credibility. Kissinger was still trying to minimize his connections to the Plumbers and their illegal break-ins and collaboration with the CIA on U.S. soil. An honest investigation into the spy ring put that at risk.

Not satisfied with the anonymous leaking of the bogus blackmail claim against Stewart, Haig and Buzhardt leaked his name to the *Post* and *Times*. On January 24 Woodward called Stewart and told him that he was identified as the alleged blackmailer, which Stewart denied.[34] Stewart then wrote a memo to his superiors detailing the conversation, as he had done earlier in the month when Woodward had first called him. Both papers had stories on January 25 that implicated Stewart in the alleged blackmail, which at least four officials in the Justice Department, including the head of its criminal division, had reviewed and found unwarranted. Stewart had done nothing wrong, but Haig and Buzhardt wanted to damage his credibility to make him too radioactive a witness to call before any hearings by the Senate Armed Services Committee. Haig told Hersh that he had told Stewart to "go to hell" when the White House received the blackmail claim, which was false.[35] Stewart never talked to Haig. Stewart called Hersh and got his first chance to deny on the record that he had blackmailed anyone. "I was looking for a job, no question about it," Stewart said. "But I wasn't trying to put the muscle on them. I don't have a damn thing to hide and I didn't shake anybody down." Stewart told Hersh he "would be tickled to death" to testify. Until the stories citing alleged blackmail appeared in print, Stewart had no idea what lies were being spread about him by the White House or what Justice was doing to debunk them.[36]

During the last week of January, Stennis met with Haig, Buzhardt, Kissinger, Moorer, Welander, and Schlesinger to determine the nature of and witnesses for the upcoming hearings by the Armed Services Committee. The fix to cover up the details of the spy ring was in. Conspicuously absent from those Stennis consulted were Stewart, Young, and Ehrlichman, who had investigated the leaks to Jack Anderson and the military spy ring. The men who knew the most about what happened between the Pentagon and the White House were being shut out, while those who had the most to hide were allowed to dictate the terms of the investigation. That, Laird said, was by design. "The Senate wanted to bury it and the Senate committee wanted to bury it," he said. "They didn't want to get into this."[37]

Stewart learned just how much the White House had damaged his reputation on January 29, when Hoffmann showed him the evidence of the White House's smear campaign. Hoffmann gave Stewart the memo from Henry Petersen that showed that Justice had rejected the blackmail claim on July 10, more than two weeks before Buzhardt and Garment met with Senators Ervin and Baker of the Watergate committee on July 27 and claimed that Stewart was still under investigation.[38]

Nixon, who had remained silent during the evolving spy ring crisis, had spent much of the month preparing for his January 30 State of the Union speech. Ordinarily, such an address would be a chance for a president to lay out his plans for the upcoming year and propose new legislative initiatives. This was no ordinary time or president. In the days leading up to the speech, Saudi Arabia's King Faisal lobbied Nixon to include language that supported the Arabs' claims against Israel. In exchange, Faisal would promise to lift or curtail the Arab oil embargo against the United States, which had sent gasoline prices soaring. Kissinger and Nixon worked to determine the right tone for any statement in the speech, and Kissinger continued to denigrate Nixon behind his back. "If I was the President I would tell the Arabs to shove their oil and tell the Congress we will have rationing rather than submit and you would get the embargo lifted in three days but I am not President until this GD constitutional amendment," Kissinger told Brent Scowcroft, referring to a change in the Constitution that would have to happen for a foreign-born U.S. citizen, such as Kissinger, to be eligible to run for president.[39]

The White House machinery moved ahead as if Nixon was a figurehead. He showed Kissinger a draft of the speech, which Kissinger praised.

Their brief conversation also reflected the extent to which Kissinger and Haig were shaping much of Nixon's decisions. The draft, Kissinger said, was a "great and courageous speech."

Nixon said he had "coppered down that Arab part. The coercion bit bothers me, but Al said you thought it was important. It's a shot across the bow. We gotta let them know we don't have to have them."

"You'll get more credit for having said it," Kissinger said.[40]

That evening, Nixon rode the length of Pennsylvania Avenue for what would be his final State of the Union address. Many Democrats sat on their hands, while his fellow Republicans, beleaguered and wishing he would leave, applauded in all of the traditional places. Nixon offered a variety of policy proposals that had little chance of passing in a hostile, Democrat-controlled Congress and then closed with a relatively defiant plea to move on. "One year of Watergate is enough," he said, vowing to remain in office to keep doing "the job that the people elected me to do for the people of the United States."[41]

On January 31 Stennis announced his plan for hearings into the spy ring. Kissinger and Moorer would be the sole witnesses, and anyone else would be called if necessary. Some members of Stennis's committee wanted more. Harold Hughes, a liberal Democrat from Iowa, wanted a deeper investigation, much like the one that had been conducted the previous July into the secret bombing of Cambodia while Stennis was still in the hospital.[42] Stuart Symington of Missouri had pushed that probe in Stennis's absence, and it implicated Nixon in the expansion of the Vietnam War into a neutral country and then the falsification of bombing records to show that the bombs were dropped in South Vietnam, not Cambodia. Now that he was back in charge, Stennis had no intention of letting that happen again. The undertaker had dug his hole. He just needed to put in the coffin and lay the spy ring to rest.

11 February 1974

Nixon enjoyed a smaller-than-normal bump in support from the State of the Union speech. While many members of Congress supported specific parts of his agenda, mostly because they were important to voters at home, there was little momentum for Nixon's plan as a whole. Despite his plea that one year of Watergate was enough, Nixon would not receive a reprieve from the crisis consuming his presidency. Throughout February, Alexander Haig focused on maintaining the cover-up of the spy ring while negotiating a series of conferences about the expanding global energy crisis and the peace negotiations in the Middle East. Haig had to manage both a deteriorating Nixon, who maintained delusions that he could remain a vital force in world affairs, and an increasingly antagonistic Kissinger, who believed Nixon was a spent force and a distraction.

Haig continued his secretive negotiations with Leon Jaworski. As the special prosecutor was waiting for official word from the president's new lawyer, James St. Clair, about whether the White House would release more tapes, Haig called him to the Old Executive Office Building for a meeting. He told Jaworski that the White House had determined it would no longer give any more tapes to Jaworski for "political" reasons.[1] No information exists that Nixon knew of Haig's meeting with Jaworski, and Jaworski said Haig was concerned that Jaworski not tell anyone that they had met or that Haig had reneged on his earlier commitment to supply more documents and tapes. Haig's concern could have been for show; he already had turned over enough information for Jaworski to conclude that Nixon was guilty.

In the West Wing, Nixon's top aides still had much to worry about with the evolving spy ring scandal.

"I have to testify on the JCS spying business," Kissinger told Defense Secretary James Schlesinger during a February 1 meeting. "[Senator Stuart] Symington is pushing. He wants to know why I was uncharacteristically unenergetic about finding out what was taken."

"Admiral [Rembrandt] Robinson did the same," Schlesinger said, "but he didn't take papers. He just briefed on the material. You should testify after March—after the recess. I don't know what the Laird/Buzhardt angle is, but the Buzhardt report says that it was a two-way spying operation designed to bypass Laird."[2]

Such a claim was one of several reasons why Buzhardt's report, done at Laird's request, was a cover-up. The spy ring was run by Adm. Thomas Moorer, the chairman of the Joint Chiefs of Staff, to find information the White House was hiding from the military. Buzhardt aimed his report at clearing the military and Haig of their guilt. Kissinger corrected Schlesinger. "They passed the JCS documents to us as part of official business," he said. "The President ordered it, because it was a different relationship than we have. We couldn't find out what Laird was doing. Were DoD documents taken?"

"I gather so," Schlesinger said, again showing he was misinformed by Buzhardt.

"It is a morally different position whether the JCS steals from the President or whether the President steals from the JCS," Kissinger said.

"It may come out that this was a Kissinger-military conspiracy,"

Schlesinger said. "Mel [Laird] and Fred [Buzhardt] have the fish to fry in this. Moorer is getting a bum deal."

Then Kissinger, who had disavowed any knowledge of what his former aide, David Young, had done while a member of the White House Plumbers, acknowledged what those in the administration already knew. He knew exactly what Young had done, and he had a scathing view of his former subordinate.

"I have read the Young report," Kissinger said. "It is a report of a failure trying to make himself important. It is sick."

Schlesinger, who consulted Buzhardt and Laird on the details of the spy ring, revealed just how badly the Pentagon needed to cover up for Haig, Moorer, Robinson, and Rear Adm. Robert Welander.

"Mel has a big set of documents which weave a web which he says shows the evolution of the statutory role of the secretary of Defense," Schlesinger said. "The documents don't show Moorer set it up but that he was knowledgeable. The report indicates you were getting material to which you were not entitled.

"If it weren't for the climate, we would just say that Welander was working too hard to please," Schlesinger concluded.[3]

As national security advisor to the president, Kissinger was entitled to see any Pentagon documents Nixon wanted him to see. Nixon's decision to hide information from the Pentagon created problems of trust with the military and helped spawn the leaks that caused Nixon to use the FBI to spy on his own staff. He had the right to do that, whereas claiming that Kissinger somehow benefited from an illegal scheme to steal documents from the Pentagon showed just how desperate the military was to hide its tracks.

Seymour Hersh published another story in the *New York Times* on February 3 that showed how far ahead he was on the story. The spy ring, he wrote, had started working in 1970, a year before previously believed and shortly after Moorer became chairman of the Joint Chiefs. Moorer was frustrated with being excluded from information from the White House. "During the period of Yeoman Radford's activities, the White House was involved in intensely secret negotiations with China, the

Soviet Union and North Vietnam," Hersh wrote. "Former White House aides have acknowledged that details of those talks were restricted to a very few officials in the White House." Gen. Earle Wheeler, Moorer's predecessor as Joint Chiefs chairman, told Hersh that he did not have a similar system when he led the military for six years and that he did not think that Rembrandt Robinson, the first admiral running the ring, "would dream up anything like this" on his own. Hersh leaned heavily on Young's report, which was more accurate and less tainted by conflicts of interest than the one conducted later by Buzhardt. His story captured almost all the key details, with the exception of the mysterious thinking behind the administration's refusal to punish anyone involved in the spying or the leaking of secrets to Jack Anderson. Buzhardt, unsurprisingly, called the Young report "ludicrous," and when confronted with facts that made it clear the White House and the Pentagon were lying about the extent of the spy ring, an unnamed White House official, most likely Haig, said, "I don't think there's been any injustice to the facts."[4]

Senator Harold Hughes, the liberal Democrat from Iowa who had exposed the secret bombing of Cambodia in July, wanted a deeper investigation. He thought the Cambodia probe, while it had revealed some critical details of the bombing campaign, had fizzled. "No once-over-lightly in executive session with Admiral Moorer or Kissinger is going to suffice," he said. Yeoman Radford and Young needed to testify, Hughes said, and the committee needed to read Young's report. "The stakes are very high here," Hughes said. "This involves the ability of the chief executive and his advisers to be in command of an operation and to keep to themselves whatever information they have."[5] Hughes's plea to Senator John Stennis made little impact.

Moorer advanced his testimony with a February 5 letter to Stennis in which he reversed course from his earlier statements about the documents he had obtained from the spy ring. Moorer acknowledged he had kept documents that Radford had gathered on his trips to Pakistan and Southeast Asia with Kissinger and Haig in 1971 and that he had been told in December 1971 that Radford "had not only been retaining papers in the course of his clerical duties but, also, had been actively collecting them in a clearly unauthorized manner." He and Kissinger, Moorer continued, saw each other all the time, so he did not need to have someone spy on Kissinger. Such a claim contradicted the years of complaints by the military about how Kissinger had excluded it from deliberations with the Soviet Union on arms control, a 1970 dispute over Cuba in which Kissinger sought plans from Robinson without Moorer's input, and the White House's control over military operations in Cambodia conducted outside of Moorer's authority. Those were just a few of the times when Moorer learned of White House decisions without being consulted. Moorer also wrote Stennis that he wanted to have Radford court-martialed for taking the documents from the White House but was dissuaded by "civilian leadership," which ruled that Radford should be transferred immediately. In fact, Nixon wanted to prosecute Moorer, not Radford, and had to be talked out of it by John Mitchell, the attorney general, whom Nixon directed to warn Moorer that he would be on a short leash from then on.[6]

Moorer's testimony on February 6 was a master class in dissembling. Moorer claimed he had first learned of the spying on January 5, 1972, when Buzhardt briefed him. That was a lie. Laird told Ehrlichman on December 23, 1971, that he had already talked to Moorer about the spying, and Mitchell had, too. Moorer's deception continued with his claims of a great relationship with Kissinger. The charges, Moorer told the Armed Services Committee, "sicken me as a man, concern me as a military officer, and deeply disturb me as the nation's senior uniformed official." Moorer said he told Welander to give whatever documents were stolen back to the White House, although he actually gave whatever information he did not need back to Haig personally when Haig was Kissinger's deputy. Nothing he obtained from Welander or his predecessor, Robinson, came as a surprise to him, Moorer testified, because he had already gotten the information from other sources. If the materials were so unimportant, asked Senator Thomas McIntyre of New Hampshire, why were Moorer's close aides wasting his time by delivering such meaningless information? Moorer switched course, saying that the documents were important but that he had already seen them.[7]

Kissinger followed Moorer at the witness table, and he did what he was becoming used to doing when it came to testifying about his actions during the Nixon administration: he committed perjury. Yes, he had closed the Chiefs' liaison office at the NSC after he learned about the spying, but he had only done that in a "fit of pique." It was also true that he was "enraged" when he listened to the tape of Welander's interview with Ehrlichman and Young, but he relaxed when he thought about how close his relationship was with Moorer. And yes, again, the papers that Radford stole from Kissinger's office and briefcase were "extremely sensitive" and not meant to leave the White House, but it was "absurd to argue that there was any subject of any major significance that was kept from the Joint Chiefs of Staff." Why, Kissinger continued, no one in the Chiefs ever explicitly complained during one of the scores of NSC meetings they had participated in with Kissinger.[8] The national security advisor turned secretary of state had fought enough bureaucratic wars to know that the Pentagon did not launch frontal assaults on a proposal in an open meeting; military leaders leaked to friendly reporters and members of Congress to get them to do the fighting for them. Perhaps Kissinger would have answered differently if he had known then that Laird had the NSA eavesdrop on Kissinger's communications overseas; that Laird had the air force inform him of Kissinger's secret flights to Paris; and that the navy aide assigned to him, Lt. David Halperin, was reporting back to the navy on the secret meetings for which he took notes for Kissinger. But Kissinger knew none of those details, and his priority in this hearing was to make the entire issue go away, courtesy of the friendly Stennis, who stepped outside the hearing room and gave his absolution to both Kissinger and Moorer. He did not see Moorer or Kissinger as being at "the root of any conspiracy," which was technically true, since Kissinger did not conspire with the military to steal his own documents. Still, Stennis announced, the committee would call Radford and Welander as witnesses in the next two weeks.[9] For his part, Moorer said he had recommended that Radford be court-martialed for his alleged theft and leaking of secrets, although there is no proof that he had done anything other than agree to have Radford whisked out of Washington and deposited at a navy base in Oregon, complete with his top secret security clearance.

For all the drama and absurdity of the Senate hearing, it was obscured that day by the House's 410–4 vote to authorize the House Judiciary Committee to start its impeachment investigation. Public opinion showed that a majority of Americans disapproved of Nixon's performance as president and suspected his guilt in at least some part of the Watergate affair but were still deeply skeptical of impeachment. No president had ever been removed from office; it remained a step that many Americans feared taking, despite their antipathy toward Nixon.

Radford, who had been kept away from most reporters, weighed in on February 7 with an interview on CBS radio with Mike Wallace, the tenacious interviewer and cohost of TV's 60 Minutes. Radford said that anything he did was done on the orders of Moorer, Welander, and Robinson. He described what they told him to do and why he did it and said that he looked forward to testifying about it before Stennis's committee.[10]

One potential witness for the Armed Services Committee, Pentagon investigator Donald Stewart, still had not heard from Stennis's staff, despite his obvious interest in testifying. He did, however, receive a call on the evening of February 7 from an aide to another committee, Donald Sanders of the Watergate committee's minority staff. Stewart wrote. Sanders called him at 9:30 p.m. and said he wanted to talk to Stewart with George Murphy, another Baker aide. The reluctant Stewart had already talked to them twice before and thought they had written his information in extensive memos. In a memo to Martin Hoffmann, Schlesinger's special assistant, Stewart wrote, "I advised him I did not want to become indiscriminately involved as I didn't want to prejudice or preempt any testimony I may later have to give before Senator Stennis' committee should I be called."[11] For someone so normally attuned to the Byzantine ways of Washington bureaucratic politics, Stewart could be amazingly naive. Haig and Buzhardt had so vigorously tried to discredit Stewart with their false claims of blackmail that Stewart had no chance of testifying before Stennis's committee.

After his testimony before Stennis, Kissinger flew to Panama to sign a treaty turning over control of the Panama Canal to that nation's government. There he received a telegram from Brent Scowcroft, his deputy, about the latest moves to end the Arab oil embargo, which had so rocked the U.S. economy. In it Scowcroft detailed the wrangling to keep Nixon from making a diplomatic mistake with the Saudi Arabians. The telegram reinforced Kissinger's growing disdain for Nixon and what Kissinger considered his interference in the whirlwind of global diplomacy. Haig, Scowcroft reported, had just met with Nixon, who told him he wanted to summon the Saudi ambassador into the White House Map Room and hand him a letter that said the United States had kept its commitments, and now the Saudis had to honor theirs by ending the embargo.

"I told Al that this was a bad idea, that, as he had seen from the traffic that I had shown him, the Saudis were coming along and that a move by the President himself could hardly be helpful," Scowcroft wrote. Haig told Scowcroft it was either do that or deal with John Connally, his rival for Nixon's attention and the former treasury secretary, who had met with Nixon for more than an hour that day.

"He thought this almost harmless by comparison," Scowcroft continued. "Al has asked that we prepare some talking points for the President to use in meeting with the Saudi Ambassador," Scowcroft wrote, and "I can probably stall until late afternoon, but Al says the President is quite determined to move today."[12] Nixon did meet with the Saudi ambassador that day, accompanied by Scowcroft, for almost an hour.[13]

In that meeting, the details of which Scowcroft reported back to Kissinger, Nixon made a stunning announcement: "I am the first President since Eisenhower who has no commitment to the Jewish community, and I will not be swayed." He criticized Kissinger's remarks the previous day that the continuation of the embargo by the Saudis while the United States was trying to broker a Middle East peace agreement constituted a form of "blackmail" to get the United States to force Israel into making concessions against its interests. Nixon vowed that he would remain in office for another three years and that his successor, whoever that was, would be controlled by "groups" tightly aligned with Israel.[14] It is hard to imagine that Kissinger would have allowed such a meeting to take place or those comments to be made if he had been in Washington.

The next day, February 8, Hersh acted on a hunch and flew to Denver's Stapleton airport, where he met a surprised Charles Radford, who was changing planes as he flew east from Oregon to Washington. There, Radford reinforced what he had told Mike Wallace a day earlier. "The yeoman acknowledged that he had pilfered hundreds of documents [that] were funneled to the office of Adm. Thomas H. Moorer," Hersh wrote.[15]

At 1:10 that afternoon, Stewart received a call in his office from Bob Woodward, who fired a series of questions about the hearings at him. "After five to ten minutes of sparring, the only thing of interest that developed was did I know that Radford and [Jack] Anderson had dinner together on December 12, 1971," Stewart wrote in a memo to Hoffmann. "This surprised me because this particular date had to come from the file. I commented I had no particular knowledge of this. This and the general questioning Woodward put to me makes me believe that he, too, is being provided info from the White House." Stewart was right. Woodward was getting his information directly from Haig and Buzhardt, who were trying to discredit Radford and Stewart, the two most damaging witnesses in the spy ring investigation. About two hours later, Woodward called back and asked Stewart: If Buzhardt said what he knew about the spy ring, would Admiral Moorer get court-martialed? Stewart said he didn't know what Buzhardt knew and hung up.[16]

Now in Washington, Radford met with Stennis for more than two hours on February 9. Radford was also presented with a subpoena to testify before the committee. "He was cooperative fully and I have no complaints about him," Stennis told reporters after the meeting. Radford said nothing. Stennis had asked him not to give any more interviews. "I'm sure we fully understood each other," Stennis said. "All of Radford's constitutional rights have been preserved."[17]

Stewart, who desperately wanted to testify before Stennis, instead heard on February 11 from Hoffmann that it was the Senate Watergate committee that would subpoena him to testify. Hoffmann told Stewart he would notify the Armed Services Committee of the Watergate committee's interest in him. Hoffmann said the subpoena for Stewart would be for the following day, but then later in the day the interview was moved to February 19 "because Senator Ervin desired to personally conduct the interview with me," Stewart wrote in a memo. "Mr. Hoffmann had advised also that he had communicated the fact I was subpoenaed to the Stennis Armed Services Committee and they apparently were concerned."[18]

Nixon hosted a huge dinner at the White House on February 11 for the attendees of the Washington Energy Conference, designed to find more sources of energy amid the global crisis and the Arab oil embargo. Haig and Kissinger fretted about Nixon saying something stupid and wrecking the progress they had made.

"How is it going?" Haig asked Kissinger in a 3:40 p.m. call.

"So far so good. It is going to come out alright. Nevertheless, the situation, and we should not kid ourselves is exactly as I described it and I hope he does not dribble over them too much tonight," Kissinger said.

"I don't think he will," Haig said. "I told him he can't." Haig had already outlined Nixon's dinner remarks. "He is not going to speak formally tonight. He will just draw from the remarks that were given to him and keep it informal."

The Arab oil embargo, Kissinger said, was about to be lifted not because of the letter Nixon gave the Saudi ambassador but "as a result of our threat of stopping all diplomatic efforts. . . . It proves that the only thing these guys understand is toughness," Kissinger said. "When we were sucking around them, they kicked us in the teeth."

Haig agreed.

"You will tell this to our leader," Kissinger said.

"Yes, I will be seeing him in a few minutes," Haig answered.

"Tell him to stay steady," Kissinger admonished. "Be conciliatory but not groveling but not to believe the bullshit about the great cooperation they are extending."[19]

Kissinger maintained his dismissive attitude of Nixon. On February 14, as Nixon was in Washington preparing to travel to Florida, Kissinger expressed to Haig his frustration and contempt for having to deal with a president he felt was barely functional. Kissinger wanted to bring the foreign ministers from Egypt and Saudi Arabia to Florida to meet with Nixon so they could finalize the deal. "I'll stay here and wait for them and, what's the president's schedule?" Kissinger asked.

"He's going to leave here Monday," Haig said.

"I mean, he isn't going over to Walker's Key?" Kissinger said, referring to the island in the Bahamas where Nixon's friend Robert Abplanalp had a home where Nixon often went to get drunk.[20]

Stewart went to Capitol Hill on February 19 to meet with Ervin and members of the Senate Watergate committee staff, but when he arrived, he found Senator Howard Baker instead, along with Sam Dash, the chief majority counsel, and investigators George Murphy and Don Sanders. Now Stewart could tell Baker directly about what he had discovered. Over the next two hours, Stewart told about how he was brought into the investigation, who his collaborators were, and what they had found. Radford, Stewart said, had been Anderson's source all along, "and this was a good vehicle for him to use as a cover, ostensibly to be getting this stuff for Welander, but at the same time peeling off what he wanted for Anderson." Stewart deeply believed this, despite Anderson's claims that he never received anything from Radford. Stewart also realized that neither Baker nor his staff knew much about the details of the spy ring and had not seen any of the critical documents generated by Stewart's investigation. Stewart told Baker about the report he had given to Fred Buzhardt in early 1972, and Baker asked if he could get a copy. Stewart said Buzhardt had taken the document when he ordered Stewart's files seized in May. Baker was puzzled by the continued national security claims surrounding the spy ring and the pressure on him and Ervin not to investigate.

"As a taxpayer, if I found out that the military was spying on a president of the United States, it would worry the hell out of me," Stewart responded.

"Me, too," Baker said.[21]

Radford received his chance to testify before Stennis's committee on February 20, two weeks after Moorer and Kissinger did their part to cover up what they both knew—that Moorer had commissioned a spy ring to gather intelligence from the White House. Stennis did his best to minimize Radford's importance and to challenge his credibility, while other members of the committee tried their best to pierce what they knew was an attempt to hide what had really happened. Stuart Symington said the administration's claims of national security had fallen flat when he managed to see the documents John Dean had taken with him from the White House after Nixon fired him in April 1973. Those, Symington said, did not warrant the national security claims aimed at hiding them.[22]

Despite having the military's top officer and the secretary of state aligned against him, Radford more than held his own. Robinson, his first boss at the liaison office, had high standards and drove him hard, Radford said, but he wanted to make Robinson happy. "He further stated that he worked directly for the chairman and that it was his responsibility to keep the chairman informed and that I was to help him do that," Radford said. That meant staying on the lookout for anything that would help the Pentagon better understand the decisions made in the White House. Robinson also wanted to keep his activity secret, Radford said. "One on occasion I did tell Captain Shephard that the admiral was in the west wing to see General Haig. . . . He explained that I was to act in a low key manner so as not to raise questions or cause excitement in those with whom he worked."[23]

What Radford described, although he lacked the understanding of the entire scope of the enterprise, was a military intelligence-gathering operation that touched all aspects of the White House and National Security Council. Under questioning, Radford mentioned Robinson's many visitors at his office in the Old Executive Office Building: NSC members Helmut Sonnenfeldt, one of the officials wiretapped by the FBI in 1969; Kissinger deputy John Negroponte; Sven Kraemer, the son of Haig's mentor, Fritz Kraemer; Russell Ash, an NSC official and close ally of William Sullivan, Haig's friend at the FBI; and Navy Lt. David Halperin, an acolyte of Adm. Elmo Zumwalt, the chief of naval operations, and an aide to Kissinger.[24] They all passed information through Robinson to Moorer. Zumwalt called Halperin his best source at the NSC. Moorer told the panel two weeks earlier that he knew much of the information he received from Radford, but he did not say how he knew it. He knew not because Kissinger had told him but because Moorer had a deeper, more sophisticated operation funneling White House secrets to him than he revealed.

Radford inadvertently let on that someone had already tipped the Pentagon off to Kissinger's secret China mission. Radford told the committee what Welander had asked him to look for when Radford accompanied Kissinger on the July 1971 trip from which he split off to go to China. "I was approached about going on a trip with Henry Kissinger in July 1971, and I agreed to go," Radford testified. "Admiral Welander told me that he would be interested in anything that 'I could get my hands on.' I remember something specifically, something about diplomatic dealings with China and that anything I could gather in this area would be of particular interest to him. He cautioned me to be careful and don't get caught. He said, 'Don't take any chances.'"[25]

Radford did not know why Welander had asked him to find out about the China talks. But we know why now. David Halperin had taken the notes in the secret May 7, 1971, meeting between Kissinger and Joseph Farland, the U.S. ambassador to Pakistan, in which Kissinger told him about the secret trip to Peking. Halperin then told Zumwalt, who acknowledged that in a 1991 oral history that was kept secret for twenty years.[26] Haig, who was working with the military spy ring, asked Welander if Radford could accompany Kissinger on that trip, and Welander agreed. It was through this secret network that the top leaders of the military learned that Nixon, whose career had been built on stoking the fears of a communist China, was talking secretly with the leaders of a country that so many in the Pentagon considered an imminent threat to the United States.

Welander testified the following day before a skeptical committee. Despite the allegations from his superiors, who had somehow not seen fit to prosecute Radford, the committee members had a favorable impression of the young, tall, and almost impossibly thin yeoman. Although Stennis seemed eager to wrap up the hearings and dispense with the whole matter once and for all, enough of the other members smelled something rotten in the claims by Moorer, Kissinger, and now Welander.

The rear admiral who had been shunted off to a destroyer command after Kissinger closed the liaison office blamed the entire spying affair on Radford, saying that he immediately concluded that Radford had leaked secrets to Jack Anderson after seeing in Anderson's columns details of the memos Radford had typed. Welander said that he had taken his concerns to Haig in the NSC and that Haig then tapped John Ehrlichman and the Plumbers to investigate.[27]

Welander's testimony was so at odds with Radford's that Senator Hughes concluded: "His and Admiral Welander's testimony have direct discrepancies in almost every account and they are both under oath.... In my opinion, one or other of you have perjured yourself before this committee, because you are testifying to two different things, or there is a third party involved that neither of you are aware of."[28]

Senators Thomas McIntyre of New Hampshire, Sam Nunn of Georgia, and Hughes had a difficult time following Welander, who claimed that no one had told Radford to take documents while he was traveling with either Haig or Kissinger and that the documents could have been obtained in other ways. Yet, Welander said, he still gave the documents to his superior, Moorer. Welander also acknowledged that the documents that Radford typed and delivered to Haig at the NSC had multiple copies and that it was possible that one of those copies could have been leaked to Anderson.

Senator Harry Byrd of Virginia, one of the most promilitary members of the committee, also picked up on one of the inconsistencies in Welander's testimony. "You mentioned you were not aware of Dr. Kissinger's original trip or exploratory trip to Peking?" Byrd asked.

"No, sir," Welander answered.

But Moorer testified that he *had* been told about it, Byrd said.

"He could well have been, sir," Welander answered, at a loss to explain the obvious discrepancy between what he, Moorer, and Radford testified to.[29]

Hughes pressed Welander on the security in Haig's office and the possibility that the memos could have come from there.

"The possibility remains that the question of security in General Haig's office is a question that we have not resolved yet," Hughes said.

"Yes, sir," Welander answered.

Welander also acknowledged that Radford brought documents from one trip that had details of the situation in Vietnam that were different from those Welander and Moorer had seen.

Nunn also wanted Welander to explain why Radford had come to Welander's office and asked him if he wanted to see a certain document if he had the ability to get the document through normal channels.

"Senator, I do not know," Welander said.

Throughout his testimony, Welander stuck to his claim that Radford acted on his own, that he had stolen documents without any authorization from his superiors, and that whatever Radford did steal was something Welander and Moorer could have obtained on their own. And through all of that, no one told Radford to stop."

"And again," Welander said, "I guess I should have told him not to."[30]

That Welander did not give that order and that the stolen documents kept moving from the White House to the Pentagon diminished the importance of his testimony. It did not matter, however, as Stennis remained determined to make the entire issue go away.

Radford stepped back into the witness chair after Welander testified. He remained unshakeable, despite some attempts to move him off details of his earlier testimony. Strom Thurmond, the conservative Republican from South Carolina, asked if Radford considered it "a coincidence that you had dinner with Jack Anderson the day before these leaks appeared in his column?"

"Yes sir, I do; most definitely I do," Radford said.[31]

Stennis had no further witnesses, although the panel had heard repeatedly about the roles Stewart and Young had played in the investigation in late 1971 and early 1972. Stennis's aides knew about Stewart's interview with Baker on February 19, and they knew that Stewart wanted to talk to the Armed Services Committee. Young, too, was available. He had been granted immunity in the case of the Plumbers' break-in at the office of Daniel Ellsberg's psychiatrist, so Young remained untainted by that. He, too, was ignored.

Three days after Welander and Radford testified, on February 24

Seymour Hersh had another story in the *New York Times* that answered one of the most pressing questions about the entire spy ring affair. Why did Nixon not push to prosecute Radford and his bosses in the Pentagon for stealing documents? Nixon called off the potential prosecutions because he did not want to expose the stealing to the public, especially in the middle of secret negotiations with North Vietnam to end the Vietnam War and with the Soviet Union on nuclear weapons. Hersh cited Young's investigation, which concluded that Moorer and Welander knew about the spying. He also noted Nixon's total silence about the spy revelations since they broke six weeks earlier. Hughes, perplexed by what Kissinger, Moorer, and Welander told the Armed Services Committee, told Hersh there was no reason why Radford or the others could not have been court-martialed. "If it was stopped the way Admiral Moorer says it did, I don't know why and how," Hughes wrote.[32]

On February 25 the legal fight against Nixon took several troubling turns for the president. Herbert Kalmbach, Nixon's personal attorney and chief fund-raiser, pleaded guilty to charges that he helped run an illegal fund-raising operation in the 1970 campaign and promised a better assignment for an ambassador in exchange for money. Kalmbach, Leon Jaworski told the court, had agreed to cooperate in future cases. "What added fuel to the fire from [Nixon's] standpoint was that we had gotten Herb Kalmbach to capitulate, his own counsel," Jaworski said. "And Kalmbach not only had to talk freely with us, but he gave us more and more information, because this is a part of the plea bargaining: all right, you plead guilty to a felony; you have to tell us everything that you know, now. All right, now they hear about Kalmbach folding; and this created real consternation at the White House. Then they begin an attack on my plea bargaining and try to get [Attorney General William] Saxbe to interfere."[33] Kalmbach's plea, Jaworski said later, shut off the flow of future documents from the White House. Already "jittery," Nixon stopped allowing Haig to give Jaworski more information, a decision that made sense from Nixon's view but that limited Haig's ability to assist the prosecutor in establishing a case against the president.

Haig appeared before the grand jury the same day. Although prosecutor

Richard Ben-Veniste pushed him hard on multiple fronts, Haig said he "had no knowledge of any thought or action on Nixon's part that could possibly provide grounds for criminal charges."[34] That, of course, was a lie. Haig knew that Nixon had obstructed justice, and he had known it since the previous May, when Nixon and Bob Haldeman sat in the Oval Office and recounted how Nixon told Haldeman to block the FBI investigation into Watergate.

Nixon reinforced his administration's new attitude in a news conference that evening in which he said there needed to be a criminal offense in order for the House to impeach him, which he predicted the House would not do. He vowed not to resign, and in what had to be alarming news for his fellow Republicans, he said he would not leave office even if it looked as if Republicans would suffer grievous losses that November at the polls. Nixon said he would cooperate with the House Judiciary Committee's investigation, but he couched that cooperation in such circumscribed language that it could hardly be considered cooperation at all. Any cooperation, he said, would be "in any way consistent with my constitutional responsibility to defend the office of the Presidency against any action which would weaken the office and the ability of future Presidents to carry out the great responsibilities that the President will have."[35]

12 March 1974

By March 1 President Nixon faced crises all around him. The House Judiciary Committee investigation gained momentum each day as its investigators pored over the growing trove of evidence it had gathered, often with help from Leon Jaworski's office and Judge John Sirica. In the Middle East, Henry Kissinger shuttled from capital to capital to build a peace deal between the sides in the October war while simultaneously managing the Soviet Union toward another summit meeting between Nixon and Leonid Brezhnev and renewed arms talks. Kissinger's resentment toward Nixon kept growing, and the cutting references toward the damaged president continued. By this time, Kissinger was in it for himself; his alliance with Nixon had frayed almost to the point of disintegration. The progress Kissinger had made in preventing a renewed outbreak of war and in bringing the Arab nations closer to the United States was real and possibly ensuring, and he did not want a compromised president, often absent or under the influence of alcohol or pills, meddling in his affairs and ruining what he had done.

At home, the energy crisis continued to dominate the news. High fuel prices had made the winter one of the most expensive ever. Americans endured the cold wrapped in warm clothes indoors as they kept their thermostats set to sixty-five degrees. They drove more slowly on the highways, which traded better gas mileage for longer trips than usual. None of this endeared the president to the American people, already weary of a political crisis that had stretched into a second year with little visible end.

On March 1 Nixon suffered a huge blow when seven of his closest associates—John Mitchell, H. R. Haldeman, John Ehrlichman, Charles Colson, Robert Mardian, Gordon Strachan, and Kenneth Parkinson—were indicted by the grand jury in the Watergate case for crimes including conspiracy, obstruction of justice, and perjury tied to the Watergate break-in and cover-up. Alexander Haig and Ron Ziegler gave Nixon the news shortly after a meeting about energy policy, and the president took it hard. The charges cut to the heart of the Nixon White House, particularly the president's ruling triumvirate of Mitchell, his attorney general and former law partner; Haldeman, his first chief of staff; and Ehrlichman, his onetime counsel and domestic advisor. Particular attention in the indictments was paid to the March 21, 1973, conversation between Nixon and John Dean, then Nixon's White House counsel, about the attempts to raise money to buy the continued silence of the Watergate burglars. Haldeman's perjury indictment hinged on his testimony about the conversation.[1]

Firing Archibald Cox in October had not stopped the Watergate special prosecutor's office. Jaworski had taken the staff and honed their work to a razor's edge. While Haig had managed to turn Jaworski's focus from the national security issues that most threatened him—the spy ring and the FBI wiretaps—he had also helped direct Jaworski closer to the president himself. The evidence the White House provided to Jaworski helped lead to the seven indictments issued on March 1, but it also led more closely to Nixon, whom the grand jury also wanted to indict. Confused by conflicting legal advice about their ability to indict a sitting president, the grand jurors held off issuing an indictment for obstruction of justice to Nixon. Instead, the grand jury named Nixon an unindicted coconspirator, which they kept secret and which Jaworski held in reserve to extract more concessions from the White House.[2] A secret report from the grand jury was sent to Judge John Sirica, and Vice President Gerald Ford said that report should be sent to the House Judiciary Committee, which was weighing impeachment.[3] For Haig, who already knew the details of Nixon's guilt, the events of March 1 showed again the extent of Nixon's increasing vulnerability.

While Fred Buzhardt dragged out the process of releasing documents to the court, Watergate committee, and House Judiciary Committee, Haig had leaked enough information to Jaworski through their meetings to give the prosecutors more leads in their investigation. That, in turn, spilled over to the Judiciary Committee, whose investigators were using what they received from Jaworski and company to build the impeachment case against the president. Nixon had demanded that the cooperation stop, but it never did. The president's case was eroding from within.

A curious profile about Haig appeared in the March 3 *New York Times*. It veered between accuracy and fantasy. Haig, the story reported, was a fusion of H. R. Haldeman and John Ehrlichman. That much was true, as were the sentences that described the strain on Haig, primarily his chain-smoking and long hours. But the passages that said Haig had aspired to a new openness in the White House seemed concocted from the ether; from the moment he took over as chief of staff, Haig had limited the access of other officials to the president and controlled Nixon's activities to an unprecedented degree. He had also maneuvered Nixon into a series of disastrous admissions and mistakes, from the misguided May 22 white paper that acknowledged parts of the cover-up, to the disclosure of the White House taping system, to the Saturday Night Massacre. They all combined to leave Nixon's approval rating in the Gallup poll released that day at 27 percent. "General Haig is not and cannot be his own man," the *Times* profile said. "His powers are meaningless unless the President survives." Haig, however, was doing whatever he could to make sure Nixon did *not* survive.[4]

Senator John Stennis's Armed Services Committee released on March 2 the transcripts from the testimony two weeks earlier of Yeoman Charles Radford and his onetime superior in the NSC liaison office, Rear Adm. Robert Welander. That generated reports in the *Times* by Seymour Hersh and the *Washington Post* by Michael Getler that demonstrated the competing narratives of the spy ring that the different parts of the government were trying to peddle. Hersh reported that the desire to cover up the burglary at the office of the psychiatrist of Pentagon Papers leaker Daniel Ellsberg and other activities of the White House Plumbers was behind much of the Watergate cover-up. That was based on reporting on the prosecution. However, those behind the cover-up knew little about the Ellsberg burglary at the time of the Watergate break-in. Nixon mostly feared the disclosure of the Plumbers' investigation into the spy ring. Although the revelation into the spying and the subsequent hearings by Stennis took the sting out of the national security argument, Nixon truly feared that if the U.S. rivals in Moscow and Beijing knew about the deep rifts between Nixon and the Pentagon, his ability to negotiate would be damaged, and his chances at improving the United States' power would disappear.[5] In the *Post*, Getler's story followed the same line that Defense Secretary James Schlesinger used with Henry Kissinger during their meeting in early February: Kissinger and the White House were not just the victims of spying but also the perpetrators. "It was a two-way street," a source told Getler, who noted that the Chiefs' liaison office at the NSC was authorized "but highly 'unorthodox.'" Draft versions of Pentagon documents had ended up at the White House before they were completed. As Kissinger told Schlesinger a month earlier, that was hardly spying, since the Defense Department reported directly to the president. Getler wrote that Melvin Laird was "upset" when he learned about the office, but Laird had complained to Kissinger before Nixon was even sworn in for his first term that the office would cause him problems. Kissinger ignored him until it was too late.[6]

During an early morning breakfast with Schlesinger on March 6, Kissinger gave the lie to the claims of harmony with the military that he told Stennis's committee a month earlier. He and Schlesinger had a standing weekly breakfast meeting during which Kissinger's deputy, Brent Scowcroft, took copious notes. As Watergate continued to grind on Nixon, Kissinger and Schlesinger took ever bolder steps to shape U.S. national security policy on their own, recognizing the precarious conditions facing the country as crises mounted and Nixon unraveled.

Contrary to his belief at the beginning of October, when the Egyptians and Syrians attacked Israel, Kissinger said he was "now convinced that the Soviet Union didn't know of the October war" and that the Soviets have "gotten little from détente" with the United States. He also told Schlesinger that "someone has managed to implant in the public mind that you and I are split. I think most of the leaks [on nuclear arms talks] have come out of Defense."

"I have said there are no divisions within the government," Schlesinger said.

"I don't feel we are in conflict, but it seems as if we were, the country couldn't stand it," Kissinger said. "The way this debate is going, the President is being put in a box—that while Defense is wanting to build up our defense while Kissinger wants to give things away. Then if the President makes an agreement, he is giving things up."

Schlesinger talked about the specific deals of the Strategic Arms Limitation Treaty talks with the Soviets.

"That isn't what bothers me," Kissinger said. "I think [Joint Chiefs of Staff Chairman Thomas] Moorer is playing a cynical game."[7]

That evening Nixon conducted another news conference. This time, the March 21, 1973, meeting between Nixon and Dean drew extra scrutiny, and Nixon told the reporters assembled for the forty-one-minute conference that anyone who listened to the tape could draw different conclusions about what he meant. "But I know what I meant," the nervous Nixon said, his lip quivering, "and I know, also, what I did. I meant that the whole transaction was wrong, the transaction for the purpose of keeping this whole matter covered up." Nixon said he did not know why $75,000 was paid to E. Howard Hunt, one of the leaders of the Watergate burglars, shortly after the March 21 meeting. "I have no information as to when a payment was made," Nixon said.[8]

Nixon also said he did not believe his political problems would cost the Republican Party seats in the upcoming elections, a comment that was proved wrong almost immediately, as the votes were being counted that night for a special election to fill the Cincinnati-based House district of Republican William Keating, who had resigned to become a newspaper executive. Democratic City Councilman Thomas Luken beat his Republican counterpart, Willis Gradison, a highly respected moderate, to become the first Democrat elected from the district in decades. The result reflected the drag that Nixon had on all Republican candidates and was a harbinger of a blowout to come in November. Republicans in competitive sections of the country sounded the alarm. Massachusetts Governor Francis Sargent, a liberal Republican, said the country would be better off if Vice President Gerald Ford were president.[9] He said openly what many other Republicans believed but remained too reluctant to say openly.

More cracks in Nixon's standing emerged among Republican members of the House Judiciary Committee, which was investigating whether the president should be impeached. Nixon had said a week earlier that only evidence of a serious crime would warrant impeachment, but an influential group of committee Republicans disagreed, saying that proof of conspiracy to obstruct justice, a more tepid violation, would suffice. Representative Robert McClory of Illinois, the committee's second-ranking Republican, said he did not know what was in the sealed grand jury report sent to Sirica but that conspiring to obstruct justice "would be in the category of serious offenses" that would make impeachment possible.[10]

One reason committee Republicans were open to considering evidence against a president of their own party was the work done by Albert Jenner, ostensibly the Republicans' lawyer, to counter the push by committee Democrats to impeach Nixon. Jenner, committee staffers noted, worked closely with John Doar, the majority counsel, to present evidence that pointed toward Nixon's guilt, not away from it. "He was out to do sort of an independent investigation," said Bernard Nussbaum, one of the committee lawyers.[11] "He formed the view pretty early on that the President was going to be impeached," said William Weld, one of the

Republican lawyers on the committee and later the Republican governor of Massachusetts. "I remember him saying that to me and a couple
of other people in a car in March or April and that was not yet in the
newspapers, I don't think. So he got there pretty quickly and he and
Doar spent a lot of time together."[12]

The colorfully dressed Jenner charmed most of the staff and swayed
enough Republican members that the tide turned toward impeachment.
But some of the panel's more partisan Republicans, such as Delbert
Latta of Ohio, distrusted Jenner. They began to turn to Sam Garrison, a
more partisan Republican on the legal staff, because, committee lawyer
Evan Davis said, they "thought he was not sufficiently telling the other
side of the story."[13] By then it was too late. Jenner, another pick from the
stable of Haig's legal advisor, Morris Leibman, had broken some of the
partisan barriers to impeachment.

John Ehrlichman and Charles Colson were indicted again on March 7,
this time for violating the civil rights of Dr. Lewis Fielding, Ellsberg's
psychiatrist, whose office the Plumbers broke into on September 3, 1971.
The break-in was aimed at finding information in Fielding's files the
White House could use to smear Ellsberg as mentally unstable. Also
charged were four members of the Plumbers team involved in the Fielding break-in: G. Gordon Liddy, Bernard Barker, Eugenio Martinez, and
Felipe de Diego. Egil Krogh, E. Howard Hunt, and David Young were
unindicted coconspirators, and Hunt and Young were granted immunity
so they could testify against the others. These new indictments presented
another chance for testimony that could endanger Haig by dredging up
some details about the spy ring but had become far less likely after the
denial of Krogh's bid to use records from the Plumbers' investigation
in November.

The Plumbers' role in investigating the spy ring played a big part
in the testimony of the final witness before Stennis's committee on
March 7: Buzhardt. The president's lawyer and the former Pentagon
general counsel took the committee on an elliptical journey through
the case, running senators through circuits of logic that left many of

them confused and frustrated. Buzhardt brought a copy of the report on the spy ring, and he presented it to Melvin Laird, then the defense secretary, on January 10, 1972, but he would not show it to the senators or give them copies without Laird's permission, which Laird said Stennis never sought. "It represents your personal opinion on some of the matter, which is another reason why I think that we should have to specially handle it," the always helpful Stennis said.[14] Buzhardt agreed. It was mostly a collection of observations mixed with some personal opinion. Nor, Buzhardt continued, did it contain national security information that could not be revealed. So if it was not really a report or laden with national security information, why could no one see it? Well, Buzhardt said, the report might not be completely accurate because the testimony so far by Welander and Radford had led Buzhardt to reconsider. "As these facts have developed and all, particularly the circumstantial evidence is not as strong as I thought it was in the beginning, because of the reports I heard, I have changed my mind somewhat about this," he said. If it was no longer accurate, Buzhardt said, the report could then be libelous to either Radford or Welander. Also, Buzhardt added, he had used information gathered from polygraph examinations from the witnesses, and since polygraph examinations were not admissible in court, it would be improper to release a report that contained them.[15]

Buzhardt said he told Laird that no one could be prosecuted for spying because the cases against them were too circumstantial to stick. While Welander suspected that Radford had given documents about the India-Pakistan war to columnist Jack Anderson, Buzhardt said they did not have the evidence to prove it. Also, the testimony of Welander and Radford two weeks earlier had demonstrated that multiple copies of the key documents existed, thereby expanding the number of possible leakers. The alleged case against Radford—that he knew Anderson socially and had developed a special affinity for Indians while stationed in New Delhi—was thin compared to the motives of Laird and the navy brass, who questioned sending an aircraft carrier task force into the Bay of Bengal during the height of the war. That information was not public knowledge at the time, and Buzhardt, Laird, and the navy leadership were not keen to make it so. Buzhardt also said he believed that Adm. Thomas Moorer, the chairman of the Joint Chiefs of Staff, had received information from the spying that he should not have received but that he never formally interrogated Moorer as part of his investigation.

Senators of both parties remained perplexed by the collusion between Stennis and Buzhardt to keep them from seeing the Buzhardt and Young reports. With Buzhardt at the witness table in front of them, they spoke as though he was not there and therefore unable to give them the documents they wanted. Buzhardt's Byzantine logic confounded them. He would not give the Young report to the current defense secretary, James Schlesinger, because it was a White House document, and Schlesinger was not authorized to receive it. He could not give either report to the committee, because it would not be fair to do so. Senator Barry Goldwater of Arizona, a conservative stalwart and the 1964 Republican nominee for president, jousted with Stennis and demanded answers.

"Let me say this on that, Senator, if you will yield to me: I have said I negotiated with Mr. Buzhardt here on the so-called Buzhardt report," Stennis said. "I have been negotiating with him too about the Young report, and there has been no finalization absolute on that but he is really working on it, and I think the chance is we will get the report. If you could hold that in abeyance now."

"I don't want to hold it in abeyance," Goldwater said.

"No, but I think it will help get the report," Stennis said.

"Will the senator yield?" Senator Stuart Symington said. "I have written the chairman and suggested we get that report."

"I have been trying to get it before then," Stennis said.

"Are you negotiating for the whole report?" Goldwater asked.

"Yes, that is what I asked for, Senator, the whole report," Stennis said.

"I am interested to know why we cannot see it," Goldwater said.

"He will talk to any of you," Stennis said. "I think he needs a little more time now and ask him to finalize some things on it. I am sawing wood, I can assure you of that, and not going to put it off on anybody. I want to get it and I want to get through with it."

"Would you say the chances are 50-50?" Goldwater asked.

"I think so," Stennis said. "I don't want to, I cannot speak for him, though. He has got the situation about it that he has got to cope with. He is trying, I am satisfied with that. I thank you very much for your attitude about it. It just takes time, negotiations.

"All right, gentlemen, shall we go vote?"[16]

With that, Stennis dismissed one of the Senate's leading Republicans, as well as Democrats Harold Hughes of Iowa and Symington of Missouri.

Senator Sam Nunn of Georgia, the youngest member of the committee, also sensed something wrong. Someone had lied to the committee, either Radford or Welander, and there needed to be a deeper investigation to determine the perjurer. That Welander, a high-ranking member of the navy leadership, had escaped punishment made no sense, Nunn said. "I also would like to observe if some disciplinary action is not taken against Admiral Welander, either in his career, administratively or some prosecution is not pursued, I have a very difficult time understanding how our committee or the Department of Defense or anyone else can expect the proper conduct from high-ranking officials," Nunn said.[17]

Hughes, who had suspected a whitewash, was the last to fall. He wanted to see Buzhardt's report and said he would ask Buzhardt privately. Stennis asked him to reconsider. Hughes said he would ask for a committee vote, but too many of his colleagues had left the hearing room by the time Hughes made his request, so they lacked a quorum. Stymied, Hughes let it drop, and with that, the committee's investigation petered out. No one would see Buzhardt's report or the one written by David Young with investigator Donald Stewart's help. No one would listen to Young and Ehrlichman's interview with Welander in which Welander placed Haig in the middle of the spy ring. Young, Stewart, and Ehrlichman would not be witnesses, although Hughes had asked for at least Ehrlichman to testify. Stennis, Buzhardt's "undertaker" of the Senate, had helped him bury the investigation of the spy ring and with it the chances of exposing Haig for spilling Nixon's secrets.[18]

Republicans increasingly rallied around Ford, gravitating to his office and maneuvering to get closer to him. Ford openly supported Nixon, but small cracks started to develop in that support. On March 11 Ford said at an appearance in Boston that he did not believe Nixon was involved in the Watergate break-in and cover-up, "but time will tell."[19] In the White House, aide Jerry Jones said, Haig openly disparaged the president he had isolated from the rest of the staff. "Haig made fairly continual derogatory remarks about Nixon," Jones said. "He did not have high regard for him. He crapped on him every chance he could."[20]

Jones, who had helped Haig fill the dozens of empty administration jobs that they confronted in 1973, had moved from the personnel office in early 1974 to help Haig oversee the tapes. Gen. John Bennett, who had testified about problems with the tapes in November, had resigned in disgust, Jones said, because of what he had witnessed in Haig's service.[21] Bennett died in a 1980 plane crash in Alaska.

Nixon tried to maintain a steady pace of public appearances to give the impression that he remained focused on his job. He spoke to the Veterans of Foreign Wars convention alongside Stennis at the head table. He traveled to Chicago to speak to business executives. Watergate and its growing shadow hung over the president with each step. He could not escape it or its fallout. A Harris poll in mid-March showed that 54 percent of those surveyed believed Nixon should be impeached if he did not give material to the House Judiciary Committee. William Saxbe, the acerbic new attorney general, said Nixon was just like any other citizen before the law and would get no special favors from him.[22] Judge John Sirica ruled that the Judiciary Committee could receive the material that he had received from the grand jury, meaning they would have the report that concluded that the grand jurors believed Nixon was guilty.

Compounding the gloom were reports such as one in the March 15 *Washington Post* by Bob Woodward and Carl Bernstein about how prosecutors used the March 21 tape of Nixon and John Dean to match up the final payment of hush money to the Watergate burglars. Prosecutors, the *Post* reported, had tracked the movement of Nixon campaign aides Fred LaRue and Manyon Millican on March 21, 1973, and shown how LaRue gave Millican an envelope filled with $75,000 in cash. Millican took that envelope to the suburban Maryland home of William Bittman, Hunt's lawyer. The story also reported that some of the prosecutors believed the tape itself only gave one piece of information for an indictment, while the passage of money from LaRue to Millican to Bittman on the same day of Nixon's talk with Dean gave them a critical second element to make a case. Haig and Jaworski had discussed how bad the March 21 tape was for Nixon in December, when Jaworski told Haig that Nixon needed a criminal attorney. The latest news showed that others had focused on the same problem.[23]

Arab nations lifted their embargo on sales of oil to the United States on March 19, which promised relief from the energy crisis crippling the U.S. economy. Kissinger, whose tireless negotiations around the Middle East had helped achieve this, met with Schlesinger that morning to review arms control strategies and possible moves by the Soviet Union. Kissinger said the recent diplomatic gains with the Arabs in the Middle East had closed off the Soviets. "What have the Soviets gotten from détente?" Kissinger asked. "The psychic satisfaction of reducing the chance of war and gaining equality with the U.S. Nothing else. We have defused the peace movement here. The Middle East must be painful to the Soviets."

Still, Kissinger and Schlesinger worried about Western Europe and NATO and having the right U.S. commander there to keep the Europeans in line. Each suggested a capable commander, but each one caused them more aggravation than they preferred.

Despite their successes, they saw a national security in disarray after months of scandal and years of war in Vietnam. The alliance with Europe was a mess, Kissinger said. His solution was to send Haig, his former deputy, sometime ally, and sometime rival for power, to Europe as the supreme allied commander in Europe, or SACEUR in Pentagon speak.

"How about [Adm. Elmo] Zumwalt for SACEUR?" Schlesinger asked.

"Not bad, except he is Navy," Kissinger replied. "Haig would be a good SACEUR."[24]

The only way that would happen was if Nixon decided he wanted to let Haig return to the army or if Haig was no longer chief of staff because Nixon was no longer president. Again, Kissinger's thoughts had turned to a Nixonless White House.

On March 23 the *Los Angeles Times* reported that investigators who had listened to the March 21 tape had concluded without a doubt that Nixon had conspired to obstruct justice. That tracked with the *Post* report a week earlier about that tape and reflected again on Haig's decision to give it to Jaworski. When Nixon sat down the previous June 4 to listen to his tapes with John Dean, he knew the March 21 tape posed problems for him. He said so to Haig that afternoon, and Haig agreed. Jaworski's case against Nixon gained momentum when he obtained the tape, and now that momentum was showing up in the House.[25]

Two days later, Dean testified for the prosecution in the corruption case against former attorney general John Mitchell and former commerce secretary Maurice Stans, who were accused of aiding Robert Vesco, a financier and major Nixon donor under investigation by the Justice Department. Nixon and Haig watched the case carefully. Not only did they want Mitchell and Stans, two of Nixon's closest associates, to prevail, but they wanted to gauge Dean's effectiveness as a witness. Dean was pivotal to the March 21 cover-up tape, and his testimony before the Senate Watergate committee the previous June had propelled Nixon into deeper trouble. Anything that damaged Dean's credibility as a witness would diminish his value in the impeachment fight.

The two leaders of the Judiciary Committee, Peter Rodino of New Jersey and Edward Hutchinson of Michigan, started reading documents and listening to tapes on March 27, while counsels Doar and Jenner matched the new evidence with what the panel had received earlier.

Kissinger's mood toward Nixon darkened even further by the end of his three-day visit to Moscow in late March 28. For the first time, reports said, Nixon's Watergate problems had affected talks with the Soviet Union, and some Russians joked about working with a new President Ford in the near future. Already frustrated by Nixon's detachment, Kissinger struggled to find new ways to reach a nuclear arms deal with the Soviets.

After hinting to the committee on March 11 that forty-two tapes existed to help exonerate Nixon, the White House said on March 28 that some of those tapes might not have existed in the first place. The continued back-and-forth on the tapes, all controlled by Haig and the White House attorneys, drained Nixon's credibility even further.[26]

Haig had escaped the spy ring investigation courtesy of Stennis. Now he focused on the fight over the tapes, which Nixon seemed destined to lose. Haig needed to engineer Nixon's departure without too much evidence emerging from the Judiciary Committee as it moved ahead to impeachment.

13 April 1974

By April the Nixon White House faced so many different crises from so many different angles that the beleaguered president had few places to turn for solace. Construction workers, the hard hats at the heart of Nixon's Silent Majority who had fought antiwar protesters on the streets, had turned on him. Their union leaders heartily applauded labor leader George Meany's April 1 speech calling for Nixon to resign. A congressional committee brought in to analyze claims that Nixon may have incorrectly misstated his earnings and paid less taxes than he owed reported on April 4 that he owed $400,000 in back taxes. Nixon had said he would comply with the committee's ruling, so he had to sell off assets or borrow money to pay the bill. The tax ruling compounded the impression created by Watergate, revelations of illegal campaign contributions, and the resignation of Spiro Agnew that this was an administration wracked by out-of-control sleaze not seen since the presidency of Warren Harding in the 1920s. Making matters worse, the tax report was sent to both special prosecutor Leon Jaworski and the House Judiciary Committee, giving each more ammunition to use against Nixon.[1]

Nixon's battles over the White House tapes also continued. On April 2 a new lawyer, John Chester, a litigator from Ohio and close associate of Attorney General William Saxbe, argued in the appeals court in Washington against surrendering to the Senate Watergate committee five tapes of Nixon with John Dean. The tapes at the heart of the appeals argument had already been released to prosecutors. In fact, the Nixon-Dean tape from March 21 was already causing problems for the president; leaks from Jaworski's office and Congress showed that those who had listened to the tape had concluded that Nixon was guilty. One of the judges commented that something bad had to be on the tapes if the White House wanted so badly to keep them secret. Chester's argument showed how Haig and Fred Buzhardt hid the tapes from the rest of Nixon's defense team. Chester told the court that he had not listened to the tapes himself, although other unnamed White House lawyers had. That could only be Buzhardt, because he and Haig would not allow anyone, not even chief defense counsel James St. Clair, to listen to the evidence at the heart of the case.[2]

Since February 25 the House Judiciary Committee had wanted the White House to deliver the tapes, but St. Clair and others kept delaying. Each day, a constitutional crisis loomed larger. Would the president have to provide documents that he considered classified by executive privilege to Congress? On April 4 John Doar, the chief lawyer for the committee's Democrats, wrote St. Clair and told him he had until April 9 to respond. The delays could not continue indefinitely. On April 5 Vice President Ford told a group in Colorado that Nixon could not expect to keep denying requests without consequences. Continued delays tempted impeachment by the House of Representatives, he said. Ford, who had led House Republicans until the previous December, knew the mood on Capitol Hill as well as anyone.[3]

On April 7 the first excerpts of Bob Woodward and Carl Bernstein's book about Watergate, *All the President's Men*, appeared in *Playboy* magazine. The passages included the revelation that Nixon campaign aide Hugh

Sloan had been an early and influential source for the pair's reporting on Watergate. They also introduced a secret source called Deep Throat, named after the pornographic movie popular at the time. The book described Deep Throat as a source inside the government who would only agree to talk on "deep background," meaning his or her name could not be used, and the source would only confirm what others had told the reporters. In one passage, Deep Throat said Nixon appointed L. Patrick Gray as the FBI director in February 1973 because Gray had somehow blackmailed Nixon into doing it. "In early February, Gray went to the White House and said, in effect, 'I'm taking the heat on Watergate,'" the excerpt said. "He got very angry and said he had done his job and contained the investigation judiciously, that it wasn't fair that he was being singled out to take the heat. He implied that all hell could break loose if he wasn't able to stay on the job permanently and keep the lid on."[4] Such a claim, regardless of the source, was patently false. Gray had met with Nixon and John Ehrlichman on February 16, 1973, and told Nixon he was eager to take on the FBI directorship. Gray also said that if Nixon picked someone else, the president would be accused of trying to cover up parts of the bureau's early investigation of Watergate.

The excerpts immediately set off speculation about the source's identity, a fascination that would last for another thirty-one years until former FBI official Mark Felt, then beset by dementia, claimed through his family and their attorney that he was the source.[5] Woodward verified the claim later that afternoon. But, as noted in earlier chapters here, evidence that has surfaced since 2005 shows that Felt could not be the source for all the Deep Throat revelations in *All the President's Men*. The source as written in the book is a composite character meant to cover some of Woodward's secret sources, including Haig and former FBI official William Sullivan. The first wave of excerpts showed the sources' misguiding claims, including how there was a seamless flow from the FBI wiretaps conducted on seventeen journalists between 1969 and 1971 to the White House Plumbers and the Watergate burglars. That linkage was a misdirection by Sullivan, who wanted to hide his connection to the wiretapping, which also involved Haig and Kissinger. The wiretaps were becoming a key section in the articles of impeachment being drawn against Nixon and remained a threat to those responsible for them, primarily Haig and Kissinger. While generally welcomed as a gripping tale of two reporters doggedly breaking the story of the Nixon administration's trail of secrecy and dirty tricks, *All the President's Men* also presented a false impression of who was guiding Woodward and Bernstein in their work. Their sources cared less about the truth and more about settling old scores and saving themselves. Many of Woodward and Bernstein's sources had played the two reporters, but the anti-Nixon fever ran so hot that few readers noticed or cared.

Amid the turbulence, Nixon saw enough hope that he believed he could survive. An April 8 Harris poll showed that his recent political trips to Chicago, Nashville, and Houston had lifted his approval rating by five percentage points.[6] Nixon's new optimism drove him to go to Michigan on April 10 to campaign for James Sparling, the Republican running to hold an open Republican seat. More than seven thousand people in Saginaw saw Nixon plead with them to keep the faith amid the mounting odds against them. It was not enough. Sparling lost the election a week later, and although observers thought Nixon had actually helped Sparling, he was still a drag for all Republican candidates. Republicans knew that a Nixon-led ticket in November would be crushed.

The Judiciary Committee kept pushing for more documents. Democrats and Republicans agreed that Nixon was stalling. St. Clair responded on April 9 with a letter saying that the White House needed until April 22 to be ready to comply with the panel's request. Meanwhile, Ronald Ziegler and other White House officials continued to pressure the committee to speed up its investigation, which meant the House would have to finish its impeachment investigation without the proper evidence. Not even Republicans bought it. Led by John Rhodes of Arizona, House Republicans warned the White House that their patience was running out. Edward Hutchinson, the committee's top Republican, called the White House response "offensive to the House" and hinted at a long summer of impeachment hearings and legal fights. On April 11 the committee grew tired of waiting for the White House and voted 33–3 to force Nixon to turn over forty-two tapes by April 30. "It is a little too late to make a deal," said Representative Robert Kastenmaier, a Wisconsin Democrat. "The course has been set, and it has been set by the White House. They have had forty-five days in which to reply, and an eleventh-hour offer forty-five minutes before this meeting is unacceptable."[7] By April 12 a Harris poll indicated that a plurality of Americans now favored impeachment.[8]

Nixon flew that weekend to Key Biscayne, Florida, where he and his core staff concocted a new plan: the White House would prepare its own transcripts, release them to the public, and bypass the committee. That would let Nixon eliminate the leaks from the tapes the committee already had. Buzhardt led the effort, assembling a squad of secretaries to listen to and transcribe the tapes, which he knew intimately. He then read all the transcripts and marked parts to be deleted.[9]

Buzhardt's and Haig's vise-like grip on the defense team was causing division. Cecil Emerson of Dallas, a Nixon defense attorney, told the *New York Times* in an interview published on April 16 that St. Clair did not control Nixon's defense. Instead, Emerson said, it was Fred Buzhardt who controlled the access to Nixon and the tapes, and Buzhardt did nothing without Haig's knowledge and approval. An unnamed White House aide confirmed Emerson's impression, saying, "Any assessment that Buzhardt controls access to the tapes and what is on them is absolutely correct and it is one that causes some concern to members of St. Clair's staff." St. Clair called his relationship with Buzhardt "cordial" but declined to say how much access he had to the tapes or any materials Nixon could use in his defense.[10] John Chester, who had argued some of the appellate cases for the White House on the tapes, said he never had access to the tapes, although he increasingly suspected there had to be something on at least one of them that would devastate Nixon. Haig told Chester that "if we lose on the tapes we've lost the presidency." Chester did not ask Haig how he knew what was on the tapes, and "I never said anything about it to anybody, never talked about it because I considered that simply a communication between myself and General Haig. And it was not to go any further."[11]

Saxbe, an old friend of Chester's from Ohio, thought the White House legal case was mismanaged from the start. Nixon, Saxbe said, "asked me to get him defense, and when I got him somebody, he hired St. Clair, who I thought was very ill-prepared and did a poor job." Chester, Saxbe said, won the only case for the White House, but the other attorneys "were like tramping pissants dealing with people that were just not capable of giving him a good defense, I thought."[12]

The pressure was getting to everyone, particularly Haig. On the flight back to Washington from Key Biscayne on April 16, reporters heard a military aide say that Nixon had spoken to Senate Majority Leader Mike Mansfield of Montana earlier that afternoon, a detail that had escaped Haig. Haig exploded. "What did you say?" Haig asked. "I run this White House and don't you ever forget it."[13]

Jaworski had had enough of the White House delays, which often followed times when Haig had let him listen to tapes during their Map Room meetings, so he asked Judge John Sirica to approve a subpoena for sixty-four tapes. They included conversations with John Dean, Bob Haldeman, Charles Colson, and John Ehrlichman between June 20, 1972, and June 4, 1973, the day Nixon, with Haig's help, listened to tapes of his meetings with Dean. Haig had allowed Jaworski to listen to the so-called tape of tapes, after which Jaworski asked for even more information. Jaworski wrote St. Clair that he had sought the information since January 9 and heard nothing. "I have delayed seeking a subpoena in the hope that the President would comply with our request voluntarily. Indeed, I have sought no more at this time than an assurance that the materials would be provided sufficiently in advance of trial to allow thorough preparation."[14]

Although Haig had passed some tapes to Jaworski—primarily those that led Jaworski closer to Nixon's wrongdoing—the tapes caused problems for Haig, too. The May 11, 1973, conversation in which Nixon, Haldeman, and Haig discussed Vernon Walters's memoranda about the White House's attempt to have the CIA block the FBI's Watergate investigation showed Haig that Nixon had authorized obstructing justice. You told us to do it,

Haldeman told Nixon, a claim Nixon acknowledged. Nixon had admitted he had obstructed justice in Haig's presence, which made Haig part of the cover-up, too. Instead of coming clean, Haig engineered the exposure of the White House taping system before the Senate Watergate committee to flush out the truth. Haig had to navigate the transcripts carefully by moving Jaworski toward Nixon and away from himself.

Sirica approved Jaworski's subpoena request for the sixty-four tapes, which pushed Haig, Buzhardt, and Nixon into overdrive. The discussions that started over the weekend of April 12 in Key Biscayne turned into a full-bore rush to transcribe the tapes and release the transcripts publicly before turning the tapes over to Sirica and the Judiciary Committee. On April 18 that left three fights for the tapes in play: the Judiciary Committee's request for forty-two tapes, Jaworski's for sixty-four, and the Senate Watergate committee's ongoing fight for just five. In the White House, Haig said they should give the committee summaries of the tapes, but the lawyers argued in favor of giving transcripts. Nixon took on much of the editing, tweezing his multiple bouts of profanity and anti-Semitism. Haig's account in his memoirs, particularly after the tapes had been released publicly, is laughable. "Although, inevitably, it was charged that he had also removed incriminating matter, his purpose was not to suppress the evidence, which was clearly in his favor, but to spare himself and others embarrassment," Haig wrote. "Nothing could have been more characteristic of the man; he swore little and relatively mildly, as men of his generation go, and those he was attempting to preserve from embarrassment had in many cases said far worse things about him in public than he had said about them in private."[15] The transcripts damned Nixon, and his language would scandalize his supporters, even with the deletions.

Henry Kissinger grew more frustrated with Nixon's weakness, which diminished Kissinger's status with foreign leaders. Many did not understand Watergate or how it could have unraveled Nixon. In China Zhou Enlai, Kissinger's negotiating partner during the secret July 1971 trip to Beijing, was being marginalized because, as Kissinger told James Schlesinger, he had based Chinese policy on Nixon remaining in charge.[16] Kissinger's recent trip to Moscow failed to generate anything concrete in the run-up to Nixon's visit there in June, also because the Soviets saw weakness. So, too, did the Pentagon, where military leaders had combined with Cold War Democrats like Senator Henry Jackson of Washington to demand a harder line on arms control than Nixon had pushed during his successful summits with Leonid Brezhnev in 1972 and 1973. Jackson wanted the Soviets to allow more Jews to emigrate in exchange for more progress on arms control, a linkage that annoyed Kissinger and the Russians.[17] During one of Kissinger's regular breakfasts with Schlesinger on April 23, Kissinger said the new emphasis on warhead size, the throw weight of a missile, was meaningless. Schlesinger agreed but argued that it was important from a negotiating standpoint. If the Soviets had a big warhead, then the United States needed one, too, regardless of the lack of military value.[18] The breakfast meeting foreshadowed a lengthy meeting between Kissinger, diplomats, and military leaders later that morning, in which they haggled over what kind of positions to take when Nixon traveled to the Soviet Union in June, a trip the president hoped would show him as still a vital world leader able to shape grand policy.[19] Kissinger knew that was no longer true; he considered the president who gave Kissinger power and a platform to shape history as an albatross.

On April 28 Nixon got some rare good news from a courtroom: John Mitchell and Maurice Stans, Nixon's former attorney general and commerce secretary, were acquitted of charges they had been paid off to influence the government case against financier Robert Vesco, who had embezzled more than $220 million from mutual funds he operated. The case in New York had lasted forty-eight days, as prosecution witnesses had detailed a complicated corruption case against the two men who once dominated Nixon's cabinet and reelection campaign. Mitchell ran Nixon's campaign at the time of the Watergate break-in, while Stans helped raise most of the money, including for the fund that paid for the activities of the Watergate burglars. Their acquittal showed the weakness of Nixon's main accuser, former White House counsel John Dean, who was the main prosecution witness against the two men. "The question is whom do you believe? John Mitchell or John Dean?" asked Peter Fleming,

Mitchell's defense attorney, during his closing arguments.[20] The jury believed Mitchell and Stans. Nixon hoped that if he could somehow discredit Dean with the tape transcripts he was preparing to release, he could derail the impeachment investigation and save himself from any criminal cases filed by Jaworski.

The transcripts the White House team of secretaries and clerks had prepared were ready by Friday, April 26. Buzhardt had picked through each one to minimize the damaging parts while still providing a sense of what happened in each conversation. Nixon had followed Buzhardt's trail to sand down any other rough edges he found, particularly his language and caustic characterizations of Washington personages, be they friend or foe.

Haig called Jaworski, who was in Texas, and told him they needed another Map Room meeting on Sunday afternoon, April 28. Jaworski, who arrived first, knew Nixon had until Tuesday to honor the subpoena. Jaworski thought Haig planned to tell him the White House response and then try to sell him on why it would work. "Both he and Nixon had great confidence in me, Haig said, and believed I was rendering a great service to the country—a flattering preamble to a list of 'wrongs' committed by Archibald Cox and some members of my staff," Jaworski wrote. Cox and his team had mishandled witnesses, Haig said, and the entire process was done to damage Nixon.

"That's unacceptable, Al," Jaworski said. "The approach was totally objective."

One of the prosecutors, Haig continued, had manipulated witness testimony before the grand jury.

"That's rank bunk," Jaworski said.

Haig urged Jaworski to recheck some of the testimony about what happened on March 21, 1973. He called John Dean a liar and said the tapes after March 21 would show that.

Jaworski said nothing. He believed the tapes completely supported Dean.

Nixon, Haig continued, would not turn over the tapes as required but instead give up the transcripts and make them public.

"I hope you'll study it carefully," Haig said, "and after you study it, let me have the benefit of any ideas you get. If you study it carefully, and believe it, it might solve some of your problems with the cover-up trial."

The tapes, Jaworski responded, were not just intended for the prosecution; the defendants in all of the cases would have access to them, too, and it might turn out that the tapes would acquit them. If the tapes were not made available, he said, then it was possible that some of the charges against the defendants would be dismissed.

"Well," Haig said, "that's what the defendants' lawyers want, of course," adding that some of the defendants, such as John Ehrlichman, came out well in the transcripts.

Jaworski left, realizing that Nixon hoped the transcripts would somehow satisfy the demand for the tapes. If they did not, then the president would take the issue all the way to the Supreme Court. "This would be the President's last strong effort, I felt," Jaworski wrote. "If it failed, Richard Nixon's fight to hold off impeachment would fail."[21]

Haig called a cabinet meeting for 7:30 p.m. on April 29 to announce what Nixon would say during his televised address at 9:00 p.m. The mood was grim. Instead of honoring the court order to give the tapes to the House Judiciary Committee, Haig said, Nixon was going to announce that he was releasing forty-nine volumes of transcripts of the tapes directly to the public. Nixon did not attend the meeting but prepared his speech in his office in the Old Executive Office Building. Haig was accompanied by St. Clair.

"We voluntarily turned over to the Judiciary Committee all the material given to Jaworski," Haig said. "Then they asked for 42 tapes. We asked for specificity. Three weeks later they were more specific. We answered and we said we had to review the tapes to decide how much to provide. That did not sit well, and a subpoena issued. It is due tomorrow. The President will respond with the transcripts of all relevant material comprising the President's knowledge and actions with respect to Watergate. It is in 49 volumes."

Nixon had edited the transcripts, Haig said, to remove his frequent use of bad language.

"It will be a bombshell to the American people," Haig said. "There is some tough stuff in the tapes which could not be eliminated. You will have to 'hunker down' on some of it."

To make sure no one doctored the tapes, Haig continued, Nixon would offer committee chairman Peter Rodino and Edward Hutchinson, the ranking Republican, the chance to go to the White House to listen to any tape to verify the transcripts. "This is on the subpoenaed tapes," he said. "On the voluntary documents, they can hear the part we are turning over.

"Everything pertinent to the President's knowledge and actions is here," Haig said. "There is no need for further turnovers. Material is exculpatory, troublesome, and devastating to Dean."

Haig knew this was a lie. Nixon still had the June 23, 1972, "smoking gun" tape in his possession, and he would not turn that over to anyone, certainly not voluntarily. Haig had known for almost a year that the tape showed how Nixon had authorized using the CIA to block the FBI's investigation into the Watergate break-in, a case of obstruction of justice that went to the heart of the Judiciary Committee's impeachment investigation. As for Dean, he was not the force he was when he testified before the Senate in June 1973. Polls then showed the public was split between believing him or Nixon on the key details of Dean's testimony. While Dean lied under oath or exaggerated details of his role in the Watergate cover-up, so many other things had weakened Nixon in the following ten months that debating the truth or falsity of Dean's testimony at this point was a lost cause.

Nixon's speech and the transcripts will be "persuasive to the American people," Haig said. The press will not believe it, but "any fair-minded person" would. "Read this material—I think then you will be able to stand up and be heard. If we don't make it this time, time is very short. Now is the time to turn this around."

St. Clair stepped in. Nixon had to release these transcripts, he said, because keeping them "would be getting into an even longer credibility gap, because it looked like he was hiding something." Nixon could "never prove what was enough." The only way to prove he had nothing to hide was for Nixon "to let the people know what there is and to make it public.

The transcripts will tell it like it is—it reads believably. The case will rise or fall on this presentation."

No other president had ever been this forthcoming, St. Clair said. "It is confidential—and it should also demonstrate the need for executive privilege." The transcripts show, he continued, that Nixon told the truth about what he did with the Watergate investigation and that he did not collude with Dean in the cover-up.

"We have a good case," St. Clair concluded. "The president has suffered by virtue of not turning over materials that were given to the grand juries. A fair reading of the material will exonerate the President. There will be those who will twist the material, but the weight of the material is clear."

George H. W. Bush, the chairman of the Republican National Committee, asked why they waited so long.

Nixon wanted to preserve the ability of his staff to talk confidentially with his staff. "When you read the material you will see the kind of courage it took to release these," Haig said.

"This whole thing demonstrates the personal courage of the president," Haig said, ending the meeting. "I hope we can match it in the days ahead with the flak we will get in the days ahead. The evidence, though, is conclusive. The speech is not tub-thumping. It has some humility but is strong."[22]

Nixon appeared on television less than an hour later. He sat in the Oval Office alongside a table with the transcripts stacked neatly atop it. He started by describing the Watergate break-in and how it was revealed that the burglars were connected to his reelection campaign. The FBI has investigated it thoroughly, Nixon continued, and the White House did nothing to get in its way. "These actions will at last once and for all show that what I knew and what I did with regard to the Watergate break-in were just as I have described them to you from the very beginning," Nixon said.

But they were not. Nixon still held on to the smoking gun tape, the one recording that would show that his claims of innocence were false.

"Ever since the existence of the White House taping system was first made known last summer, I have tried vigorously to guard the privacy of the tapes," Nixon continued. "I have been well aware that my effort to protect the confidentiality of presidential conversations has heightened the sense of mystery about Watergate and, in fact, has caused increased suspicions of the President. Many people assume that the tapes must incriminate the President, or that otherwise, he would not insist on their privacy.

"But the problem I confronted was this: Unless a President can protect the privacy of the advice he gets, he cannot get the advice he needs," Nixon said. Almost a year earlier, however, Nixon had been willing to burn one of his main advisors, Henry Kissinger, by releasing taped recordings that would damage Kissinger's reputation. That was when Haig first learned of the taping system.

These transcripts, Nixon said, would "provide all the additional evidence needed to get Watergate behind us and to get it behind us now. Never before in the history of the Presidency have records that are so private been made so public. In giving you these records—blemishes and all—I am placing my trust in the basic fairness of the American people."[23]

It was a bold performance, but one Haig knew was doomed to fail. While he claimed to believe the transcripts exonerated Nixon, Haig wrote, "I was aware of a struggle between my heartfelt admiration for Nixon's nearly superhuman courage in taking this hideous risk with the presidency—and his own place in history—and the rational part of my being, which told me in a most visceral way that he was finished. And indeed, by morning his long-held hope of exculpation had disappeared."[24]

Haig's explanation for the reaction to the transcripts was wholly disingenuous. As much as anyone, Haig knew why Nixon had declined to reveal the June 23, 1972, tape. Haig's wistful remembrances to the contrary ring hollow. He knew from almost the moment he returned to the White House that the president was guilty. Although Haig wrote that it would have been better to "have seen the tapes go up in smoke the previous summer," he had known since May 1973 that the tapes existed.[25] Never between then and July 16, when Alexander Butterfield told the world about the taping system, did Haig tell Nixon to destroy them.

Releasing the transcripts publicly allowed Nixon to grab some of the attention away from the stream of leaks from the Judiciary Committee and prosecutors. Americans could read for themselves about the meetings Nixon had kept secret for years.

Whatever Nixon and the rest of his team at the White House thought would happen with the transcripts did not. The transcripts covered only twenty of the sixty-four tapes that Jaworski wanted. Democrats on the Judiciary Committee thought Nixon had failed to comply with the subpoena, a feeling that gained more intensity when Buzhardt said that eleven of the forty-two conversations contained in the subpoena were not given to the committee because they were either never recorded or the recordings could not be found. Some Republicans thought they were lucky to get as many transcripts as they did and delayed criticizing the White House, while others knew Nixon's lack of disclosure would hurt him.

Nevertheless, St. Clair launched an attack on Dean as the transcripts appeared. In a fifty-page legal brief, St. Clair claimed that Dean had repeatedly perjured himself during sworn testimony before the Senate and in federal court. St. Clair cited the March 22, 1973, conversation with Nixon in which the president told Dean he wanted him to write a report of Dean's investigation of the Watergate cover-up. Dean told the Senate in June 1973 that Nixon never asked him to write anything. One White House insider said they had a rare chance to get Dean: "We've got to get him or he may get us, and now we think we really have a chance to get him."[26] As legal arguments went, it was not unreasonable; the Mitchell and Stans verdicts showed Dean's vulnerability, and the transcripts showed what were at the least serious inconsistencies with Dean's testimony.

For a few hours after the jury acquitted Mitchell and Stans, Nixon thought he had a chance. He threw the transcripts out like dice on the craps table, hoping to press whatever advantage he thought he had. It was not enough.

14 May 1974

It took a day for the details of the transcripts of the White House tapes to sink in, and the early reviews were terrible. Alexander Haig said the transcripts would give Nixon a chance to fight back and rebut the lies from his accusers, starting with John Dean. But the initial reports focused instead on Nixon's attempts to hide the details of the White House involvement in the Watergate break-in and cover-up. The March 21, 1973, tape of Nixon and Dean talking about paying off the Watergate burglars, which Leon Jaworski told Haig in December was proof of Nixon's guilt, drew particular attention. In that tape, the *New York Times* reported, "Nixon discussed over and over again paying off Mr. [E. Howard] Hunt as a viable option, and never said that silence money would be wrong. In fact, he said at one point that paying as much as $1 million 'would be worthwhile.'" The many passages marked "unintelligible," the *Times* noted, "seemed to bear on significant matters or to be in areas where the President's voice logically would have been raised."[1] In his many conversations with Dean, the transcripts showed, Nixon wanted to target his political enemies after the 1972 election was over. Dean was an imperfect witness, as demonstrated by the verdict in the case against John Mitchell and Maurice Stans, but he remained a bit player in the building case against Nixon, who the transcripts showed was a scheming, suspicious, and vindictive manipulator. The transcripts would not resurrect the president but help bury him.

That burial, however, would have to be done with the transcripts currently available. James St. Clair said on May 1 that Nixon believed he had given the Judiciary Committee and Jaworski enough information to investigate impeachment and any criminal cases adequately, and perhaps he was correct.[2] On its own, the transcript of the March 21 Dean conversation was already generating talk that Nixon was guilty. There was more. St. Clair said Nixon would invoke executive privilege and refuse to give Jaworski any more information on the seven former aides who were indicted on March 1. That meant they could not get the White House documents they considered essential to their defense, which allowed Nixon and, by extension, Haig to limit their exposure to potential criminal cases stemming from any of the information that would have been released.

Nixon's use of executive privilege reversed his earlier pledge from the previous year in which he said he would use the claim sparingly, if at all. But he had much at risk, and so did Haig. John Ehrlichman, for example, wanted to use the documents in the investigation of the military spy ring in his defense, including the tape of the interview with Rear Adm. Robert Welander. In that interview, which Haig had heard, Welander implicated Haig in the spy ring. Since Haig controlled Nixon's defense with Fred Buzhardt, he froze what could come out of the White House.

Haig had heard the footsteps of investigators coming for weeks. In April he asked Joseph Califano, his former boss in LBJ's Pentagon and his frequent advisor, to meet for a late dinner at Jean-Pierre, one of the expense account lobbyist havens on Washington's K Street. A troubled Haig told Califano that the Watergate committee had subpoenaed him to testify. At the time, the committee was investigating Nixon's income taxes and the transfer of $100,000 from reclusive billionaire Howard Hughes to Bebe Rebozo, Nixon's closest friend.

"I can't testify about Nixon or any work I am doing for him," Haig told Califano. "Shouldn't I claim executive privilege?"

"You shouldn't," Califano said, "but maybe Nixon should. It's the president's privilege."

Califano noted that President John Kennedy had done the same for Robert McNamara, his defense secretary, during a Senate hearing more than ten years earlier.[3]

On May 2 Haig went to the Senate hearing room and produced a letter from Nixon declaring executive privilege for Haig, proof that St. Clair was serious the day earlier. It was the first time a senior White House official had invoked executive privilege since Nixon released his white paper on May 22, 1973, in which he declared that "executive privilege will not be invoked as to any testimony concerning possible criminal misconduct." Senator Sam Ervin, the committee chairman, was incredulous. "Claims of executive privilege in the Haig case are totally unsupportable," Ervin said.[4] Some senators called it proof that Nixon was hiding something. Califano said senators just saw Haig as the messenger, although he had coaxed Nixon into executive privilege.

Haig's brief appearance before the committee dripped with irony. He had engineered the white paper in which Nixon said he would not claim executive privilege, and he had persuaded the president not to use it in May 1973 to stop his two deputy CIA directors from testifying before Congress. That led Robert Cushman to disclose the agency's help for the White House Plumbers and Vernon Walters to reveal how Bob Haldeman, on Nixon's order, wanted to use the CIA to block the FBI's Watergate investigation. Their testimony set much of the ensuing controversy of the following year in motion. Now, under fire himself, Haig sought the advice of the Democratic Party's lawyer and a prime Nixon antagonist, Califano, to save himself. If Haig did not have executive privilege, then the senators could have asked Haig about anything, such as the military spy ring. Senator Howard Baker of Tennessee, the panel's top Republican, already knew about that. Califano's guidance, given without Nixon's knowledge, saved Haig.

Days earlier, Haig had told the cabinet that the transcripts were Nixon's best hope for survival, but their apparent inaccuracies were drawing fire. Not only were passages suspiciously marked as unintelligible, but they did not match the transcripts of the handful of tapes the Judiciary Committee already possessed. Chairman Peter Rodino argued that the committee should have the full tapes of the conversations covered in the transcripts so its members could determine for themselves which versions were the most accurate. Rodino said John Doar, the majority counsel, would wire the hearing room for sound so members could listen to the tapes themselves. Again, the March 21 tape caused the most problems. Representative George Danielson, a California Democrat, said it seemed that Nixon approved the idea of paying off Howard Hunt.[5]

On Sunday, May 5, Vice President Gerald Ford gave an interview in which he acknowledged that the president he saw in the transcripts disappointed him and was not the Nixon he had known for twenty-five years.[6] At the White House, press secretary Ron Ziegler told reporters that people were reading too much into the March 21 tape. Few in the press room believed him; they thought the tape made Nixon look guilty.[7]

Early that afternoon, Leon Jaworski met Haig in the Map Room. The grand jury, he said, had voted 19–0 in March to name Nixon an unindicted coconspirator. The Judiciary Committee also had the secret grand jury report with the vote. That information would guide the committee as it closed in on Nixon. "I had hoped that the Judiciary Committee proceedings would be ended before this was made public," Jaworski said. "Of course, it would have to be made public eventually, at a pretrial hearing," unless the defendants pleaded guilty. Haig was stunned, Jaworski reported, although, given what he knew about Nixon's guilt, his surprise seems unlikely. "If we can find some way of reaching an accord, we won't have to divulge the matter now," Jaworski said, while the committee was still deliberating.[8]

Haig called in James St. Clair and two of Jaworski's assistants. St. Clair was at first uncertain, then concerned. Jaworski offered to cut his demand for sixty-four taped conversations to eighteen and to keep secret the news about Nixon being named an unindicted coconspirator until it absolutely had to be revealed in court. That sounded like blackmail, Haig told Jaworski. Well, Jaworski responded, there's blackmail and there's blackmail. Haig told him St. Clair did not like the proposal, while Jaworski said St. Clair just said they needed to talk to Nixon, and Haig agreed.[9]

Nixon was at Camp David. His calendar showed that he talked to St. Clair for four minutes shortly after two in the afternoon.[10] Nixon returned to the White House and began listening to the tapes again. On Sunday, May 5, at 8:02 p.m. he walked to the Old Executive Office Building hideaway, where he listened to the June 23, 1972, conversation with Bob Haldeman, the so-called smoking gun that would prove he tried to obstruct justice.[11] For almost a year, since Vernon Walters appeared with his memoranda detailing the White House attempts to use the CIA to block the FBI's Watergate investigation, Nixon knew the tape would do him in. So did Haig and Fred Buzhardt, but they never told St. Clair. Nixon's lead defense attorney was never allowed to hear any of his client's tapes. "I had indicated in all my public statements that the sole motive for calling in the CIA had been national security," Nixon wrote. "But there was no doubt now that we had been talking about political implications that morning."[12] Nixon knew that the June 23, 1972, tape shredded his claims in the May 22, 1973, white paper.

Nixon returned to the hideaway at 7:53 a.m. on May 6 and remained there until shortly after noon.[13] Haig wrote that Nixon called him into the office and told him he did not need to listen to more tapes. "We've done enough," Haig wrote that Nixon told him. "We're not going any further, not with Jaworski, not with the Judiciary Committee. We're going to protect the presidency. You tell them that." No one should listen to any more tapes, Nixon ordered. Haig needed to lock them up.

"I told him that his orders would be carried out," Haig wrote. "But as I left him, I was overwhelmed by feelings of doubt and apprehension. Something fundamental had changed. There was something bad on the tapes, and Nixon had discovered it. I was sure of this as a matter of instinct, though I had no idea what it might be."[14]

This recollection is, of course, false. Haig had known of Nixon's guilt for months.

Jaworski had hoped Nixon would accept his offer, but he realized Nixon would rather face exposure as an unindicted coconspirator than cope with whatever was on the tapes he refused to hand over. However, Jaworski mistakenly assumed that only Nixon knew about the damaging information on the tapes. Not only did Haig know about the taping system more than two months before the rest of the world, he had sat with Nixon and Haldeman as they discussed Nixon's orders to Haldeman to get the CIA to block the FBI probe. You told us to do it, Haldeman had told Nixon the previous May. Haig then did nothing to stop Walters from telling the Senate Armed Services Committee about the cover-up attempt a few days later and even told Nixon that Walters's testimony would help him. It did not. "I did not think that Haig, for all his advocacy of the President's position, would close his eyes against what he considered clear-cut proof of Nixon's criminality," Jaworski wrote.

Haig's eyes were wide open. He dribbled out the proof of Nixon's guilt while distancing himself from it and in doing so kept his secrets while releasing Nixon's.

Withholding the tapes would not save the president, Jaworski said.

"I'm not trying to save the President, Leon," Haig responded. "I'm trying to save the presidency."

That was one of the most truthful things Haig said during his fifteen months as chief of staff. For Haig, it was never about Nixon.

"You may be destroying the presidency," Jaworski said.[15]

It was obvious a week after Nixon's bold move to release the transcripts that it had backfired on him. Public sentiment was rising against the president. The multiple passages marked unintelligible made it look as if Nixon was still hiding evidence, while the deleted expletives showed Nixon's coarse nature behind closed doors. He seemed unpresidential, a diminished figure during a crisis. In the heartland, a rising chorus began calling for his resignation. In solidly Republican Omaha, Nebraska, the *World-Herald* called for him to resign. The *Chicago Tribune*'s conservative editorial page did, too.[16] Senator Hugh Scott of Pennsylvania, the

Republican leader in the Senate, said the transcripts showed "a shabby, disgusting, immoral performance by all those involved." Speculation about Nixon's imminent resignation ran wild. On May 10 Nixon and Ford met in the hideaway office, and Ford emerged again expressing confidence in the president. On May 11 Jaworski went to Judge John Sirica's court and gave him a memorandum in which he sought more tapes, which Sirica sealed because it used secret grand jury testimony.[17] Haig contributed to the fever with an interview with the Associated Press in which he said there was no reason for Nixon to resign, but he added an odd qualification that indicated the situation could change.[18] A May 12 article by Seymour Hersh in the *New York Times* reported that some of the expletives deleted in the transcripts were actually ethnic slurs. Nixon had referred to Sirica, a proud Italian American, as a wop and to Justice Department prosecutors as "Jew boys."[19]

Kissinger, meanwhile, spent May shuttling between Israel and Syria negotiating an end to the clashes that still continued after the end of the October War. Each side distrusted the other passionately. The Israeli government of Prime Minister Golda Meir teetered because the Israeli public believed it had been caught unprepared by the Egyptian and Syrian surprise attacks in October. Syrian president Hafez Assad was a ruthless military dictator who balanced atop a turbulent swirl of ethnic tensions inside his own country. Kissinger bridged these differences masterfully. He was conciliatory and understanding and then tough and uncompromising when the times demanded it. As he had for months, Kissinger continued making cutting asides about Nixon in his messages to Brent Scowcroft. On May 14 Kissinger said the Israelis' intransigence was due in part to their "assessment of presidential paralysis—the last message from the President was brushed off with disdain" by Meir. The Israelis also believed they could go directly to the Pentagon for help, so Kissinger asked Scowcroft to tell Haig to ask Defense Secretary James Schlesinger not to make any more commitments to Israel for weapons and equipment. Nixon's threat to cut off aid to Israel also frustrated Kissinger because it would "produce hysteria and maybe a military outburst."[20] Inside the White House, Haig and his small cadre of assistants knew they were barely holding together a president with a weakening grip on reality. While Kissinger received the Nobel Peace Prize for his talks with North Vietnam that had helped end the war there, his Middle East diplomacy endured much longer than the "decent interval" between the end of the Vietnam War and the inevitable collapse of South Vietnam. Kissinger's frustration with Nixon endured; Kissinger often resented the president's interference as he did the diplomatic heavy lifting needed to reach a deal.

Some savvy outsiders saw the forces inside the White House aligned against Nixon. On May 19 the persuasive John Connally called Nixon to relay a message from Jaworski. "The President has no friends in the White House," Connally told him.[21] Nixon's closest friends, such as John Mitchell, suspected correctly that Haig and Buzhardt had turned on the president.[22] Jaworski had collaborated with Haig since he took the job in November. The message Jaworski passed to Nixon through Connally reflected his sense of conditions inside the White House but also sent a warning: Nixon should come up with an exit strategy.

On May 20 Sirica upheld Jaworski's subpoena for the sixty-four conversations, meaning Nixon had to either surrender the tapes or take the case to the appeals court in Washington. Nixon appealed, and Jaworski responded by jumping past the appeals court and directly to the Supreme Court. The move held some risks. Nixon had appointed four of the court's members—Chief Justice Warren Burger and Justices Harry Blackmun, William Rehnquist, and Lewis Powell—and a fifth, Potter Stewart, was a moderate named by Republican Dwight Eisenhower. Powell was a long-time leader in the American Bar Association and an expert in national security legal issues along with Morris Leibman, Haig's legal advisor. A skillful White House argument steeped in the rights of presidential power could possibly sway enough justices. But Jaworski felt confident in his case because he knew the law: Nixon was guilty, and Haig knew it.

In the Middle East, Kissinger continued his work with Israel and Syria. Success there would end the fighting but also give Nixon a reminder for Americans of the president who ended the Vietnam War, opened relations with China, and created détente with the Soviet Union. Kissinger, however, resented Nixon's dependence and interference. A May 21 telegram from Scowcroft to Kissinger that summarized Nixon's feelings showed the tensions. "Of all your superb accomplishments since we have worked together, the Syrian/Israeli breakthrough, regardless of what comes out in the odds and ends of bargaining which still lies ahead, must be considered one of the greatest diplomatic negotiations of all time," Nixon said through Scowcroft. "I know well how hard you have worked, how discouraged you must have been at times, and I just wanted you to know how personally grateful I am for this example of diplomatic service far beyond the call of duty, which has become your trademark. I believe we should follow up this development with a trip to the Middle East at the earliest possible time. We will thereby be able to seal in concrete those new relationships which are essential if we are to be successful in building a permanent structure of peace in the area." After his deep expression of gratitude, coupled with his desperation to go to the Middle East for a triumphant tour, Nixon closed with "a personal note" that showed just how much the Watergate scandal permeated his every thought. "I thought you would be interested to know that nowhere in the transcripts or the tapes, and I had Len Garment listen to the three in question, did I ever use the terms 'Jew boy' or 'wop.' The *New York Times* following its usual practice nevertheless refuses to retract."[23]

While Jaworski fought the White House in one courtroom, John Ehrlichman fought it in another. The man to whom the White House Plumbers reported had filed a subpoena for the White House to produce his notes and files to use in his defense on perjury charges related to the break-in at the offices of Dr. Lewis Fielding, the psychiatrist for Pentagon Papers leaker Daniel Ellsberg. Ehrlichman claimed Nixon had ordered everything about the Plumbers kept secret on national security grounds, and to prove that argument he wanted to use his December 1971 interview with Rear Adm. Robert Welander, a principal in the military spy ring, to highlight the sensitivity of the issues involved in that case. Haig could not afford to have that interview reach open court, where jurors and various attorneys could interpret it in ways that would destroy Haig's career. He still depended on the president, be it Nixon or Ford, to trust him; the

Welander interview, which had been mentioned during the earlier Senate Armed Services Committee hearings, would shatter that trust. Haig had dodged a similar problem when Plumber Egil Krogh had sought similar evidence in his defense in the fall. Haig and Buzhardt lobbied Jaworski that releasing that information would damage national security. Buzhardt moved to stop Ehrlichman's subpoena through the sweeping claim of executive privilege the White House had made earlier in the month. Ehrlichman's counsel countered, arguing that Ehrlichman would not receive a fair trial without the evidence. Without the evidence, they argued, Judge Gerhard Gesell should dismiss the charges, and Gesell said he was inclined to dismiss the case if Ehrlichman was denied the evidence. Gesell had larger issues. He said on May 24 that national security was not a reason to break into an office without a warrant.[24]

The inevitable tensions between Nixon, who was desperate to remain president, and Ford, who wanted to preserve his credibility while serving for a president under investigation for impeachment, continued to rise. By the end of May Ford had said that Nixon's stonewalling of Congress would not work much longer. In a May 22 news conference, he said the White House needed to give up "any relevant material and the sooner the better."[25] Nixon, through Haig, then summoned Ford to a meeting in the White House, where they met for thirty-seven minutes shortly after noon on May 23. Haig then remained with Nixon for seventy-two minutes, a sign of how seriously Nixon had taken the meeting.[26] Ford said he had told Nixon the same thing in their meeting that he had said in public: "I indicated that there was no change in the position I had taken before, and I have shown no indication that I'm going to change again."[27] Ford's situation was untenable. Although he did not say so in public, he may have already known that Nixon was guilty; his close friend Melvin Laird, who had helped recruit Ford as vice president, had known of Nixon's guilt for almost a year. Laird had told Ford the previous August that Spiro Agnew was guilty of accepting bribes as vice president. Once Ford became Nixon's no. 2, how likely was it that Laird would not tell his close friend that the president was guilty and on the verge of losing his job? It seems plausible that Ford already knew he would become president and needed to preserve his credibility.

Just how imminent Nixon's departure would be seemed unclear on May 29, when the Judiciary Committee finished its closed-door hearings on impeachment. Democrats who wanted Nixon gone believed the evidence indicated that Nixon had committed impeachable offenses. The majority of Republicans believed otherwise. Charles Wiggins, the Orange County, California, conservative who represented the bedrock of Nixon's support, said the committee staff had not persuaded him that Nixon was guilty and that many of his colleagues agreed. Nevertheless, the committee voted 28–10 the next day to warn Nixon formally that his continued refusal to ignore its subpoenas "might constitute a ground for impeachment." The defection of eight committee Republicans showed Nixon that he could only refuse to cooperate for so long, as his own vice president and a majority of the seventeen committee Republicans wanted Nixon to provide more documents and tapes.[28]

Kissinger's toil paid off on May 30, when he announced that Israel and Syria had reached an agreement to end the fighting along the Golan Heights. Nixon exulted. Now he could travel to the Middle East in ten days and reclaim the mantle of international statesman. "It was important to move fast while the momentum was still fresh," Nixon wrote.[29]

Tempering Haig's optimism at Kissinger's news was Ehrlichman's move on May 31 to call for seven members of the White House staff, including Haig, to provide national security documents that could clear Ehrlichman of charges in the Fielding break-in.[30] Ehrlichman wanted documents into all investigations of leaks of classified information, which definitely included the spy ring and the leaks to Jack Anderson during the India-Pakistan war. That put Haig at risk; he had received the initial tip that led to the discovery of the spy ring and had been deeply involved in the Plumbers' investigation. As May closed, Haig had to stop the court from allowing the records to be released. As Haig had encouraged Nixon to claim executive privilege earlier in the month, he would go to Buzhardt to make sure the White House did so again and made it stick in court.

15 June 1974

Henry Kissinger's breakthrough in the Middle East set up a trip that Richard Nixon thought could save his presidency. His rapidly prepared itinerary would take him from Austria to Egypt, Israel, Jordan, Saudi Arabia, and Syria, allowing Nixon to bask in the adulation that evaded him at home. Nixon still believed he could beat impeachment, although his aides on Capitol Hill said his support dissipated almost daily. Alabama Republican Bill Dickinson, a House member courted by Nixon with a recent cruise on the *Sequoia*, said Nixon told him some of the tapes were too sensitive to be released, which suggested that they contained either proof of Nixon's guilt or national security matters so sensitive that the White House dared not release them.[1] Nixon already knew that the former was true; his listening session in early May showed that the June 23 tape proved that he had obstructed justice. All around him, Nixon faced threats that he had to negotiate delicately if he wanted to survive.

A new threat emerged with the publication of Bob Woodward and Carl

Bernstein's *All the President's Men*, which captured the fear and paranoia of the Nixon era and Watergate. The two reporters took readers along as they went door to door trying to coax scared White House and campaign aides to reveal the secret pools of money that paid for campaign dirty tricks, the Watergate break-in, and the resulting cover-up. As noted earlier, prominent in this account was Woodward's super source Deep Throat. Reviewers such as Doris Kearns Goodwin in the *New York Times* and Richard Whalen in the *Washington Post* injected some skepticism about the source's omniscience. "Anonymous even now—one man or possibly several—Deep Throat had access to information from the White House, the Justice Department, the FBI and the CRP," Goodwin wrote.[2] Whalen, a former Nixon advisor, wrote that if he did not have such confidence in the authors, "I would be tempted to suspect that Deep Throat is a composite character made up of several sources—he is too knowing about too many very closely held subjects in widely separated political quarters to ring quite true."[3] Both were right. At the time, however, it did not matter. Most readers wanted to believe the worst about Nixon, and Woodward and Bernstein, aided by their mystery source, gave it to them. Some members of the Judiciary Committee pored over its pages seeking guidance as they pondered Nixon's guilt or innocence.

The evidence against Nixon, much of it highly circumstantial or hearsay, continued to accumulate. On June 3 Charles Colson, the former political aide who said he would run over his mother to help Nixon, reached a deal and pleaded guilty in the Daniel Ellsberg case.[4] On June 4 the panel of electronics experts appointed by Judge John Sirica ruled that the eighteen-and-a-half-minute gap on the June 20, 1972, tape was made manually, meaning someone had erased it on purpose.[5] The blame naturally focused on Nixon, who had listened to multiple tapes and had refused to deliver more than the handful the White House had turned over to the court, prosecutor Leon Jaworski, and the House Judiciary Committee.

What few transcripts had made their way to investigators started to pose real problems for Kissinger and, by extension, Alexander Haig as they prepared to leave for the Middle East. A June 6 article in the *Post* showed that Kissinger had ordered the seventeen wiretaps on government officials and journalists that started in May 1969. The story also cited a "censored portion" of the transcript of a February 28, 1973, conversation between Nixon and John Dean that revealed Kissinger's involvement. The conversation was one of many in a four-week period in which Dean and Nixon worked on the cover-up and discussed paying hush money to the Watergate burglars.[6] The *Post* report directly contradicted Kissinger's sworn testimony before the Senate Foreign Relations Committee the previous September, when Kissinger minimized his connection to the wiretaps.

Later that afternoon, Kissinger lied in a news conference when he said he had not initiated the wiretaps and did not know about the Plumbers. He knew that his personal assistant, David Young, had left the National Security Council to join the Plumbers team and that Kissinger himself had listened to the taped interview Young and John Ehrlichman had conducted with Rear Adm. Robert Welander, one of the principals in the military spy ring. Haig suggested that the *Post* articles, coupled with a *New York Times* article that suggested that Kissinger was lying, "created in Kissinger a passion for rebuttal."[7] His news conference was a disaster, as the State Department press corps treated Kissinger like the perpetrator of a crime, not as the genius who had coaxed Israel and Syria to reach a peace deal against overwhelming odds. "That night," author J. Anthony Lukas wrote, "a reporter found Kissinger 'fuming and resentful' at a White House dinner."[8] Kissinger deeply resented Nixon's unpredictability and the constant fallout from the scandals that surrounded him. Since the start of the Arab-Israeli war in October, Kissinger had openly tried to marginalize Nixon, but he was being drawn back into the mire that had already submerged the president. All Washington felt the tremors that presaged an imminent eruption; the question was not if Kissinger would erupt but when.

Also on June 6 the secret that Jaworski had kept since the grand jury reported on March 1 came out in the *Los Angeles Times*: frustrated that it could not indict Nixon, the grand jury had named him an unindicted coconspirator.[9] Jaworski had tried to leverage that secret into persuading the White House to turn over eighteen more tapes in May, but Nixon refused. The reaction to the news was predictably bad. Nixon's growing legion of detractors considered it another sign of his guilt. James St. Clair confirmed the designation shortly after the story broke, and it immediately cast doubt on Nixon's ability to survive impeachment. If the grand jury voted 19–0 to declare Nixon an unindicted coconspirator, its members obviously believed he had done something wrong. All the information considered by the grand jury was now in the hands of the Judiciary Committee. Those committee members who had not decided their stance on impeachment could be potentially swayed to reject Nixon.

Kissinger's cover-up of his role in the FBI wiretaps unraveled further with the publication on June 9 of a Seymour Hersh story in the *New York Times* that said Kissinger's office in the National Security Council "was directly responsible" for ordering the bureau to stop the wiretaps in 1971. Haig, Hersh wrote, made the order to the FBI at Kissinger's request. The latest details, which were undoubtedly provided to Hersh by William Sullivan, Haig's ally and the former FBI official who ran the wiretaps, and by Haig himself showed that Kissinger had lied during his confirmation hearings. Then, Kissinger said he never "explicitly" dealt with the FBI on ending a wiretap and that he and Haig rarely dealt with the FBI. Although Haig was not quoted by name, an unnamed White House official told Hersh that Haig "only did what he was told to do." That same official then justified the wiretaps, as Haig had done to Hersh a year earlier for another series of stories about the wiretaps. "Those wiretaps were justified, because of extreme national security leaks. Anyone who claims otherwise is not filled in," the official, probably Haig, said. The Hersh story, quoting a "closely involved official," said that Haig had called Sullivan and said the wiretaps were no longer needed and should be shut down. "Haig always made it clear that he was a messenger," the former official said. "If Henry didn't approve of all this, he could have said so." The unnamed official was obviously Sullivan.[10] Hersh acknowledged that Sullivan was a major source for him on the wiretaps in his 1983 book, *The Price of Power*, and the quotes in the June 9, 1974, story match similar comments from Sullivan in Hersh's earlier stories.[11] The story also quoted a source saying that Haig and Lawrence Eagleburger should have been tapped if Kissinger had followed the criteria he claimed to use for picking the wiretap targets. Since Haig helped him determine the tapping targets and was in league with Sullivan, who ran the taps, it was highly unlikely that Haig would ever have been tapped.

Coming on the heels of the revelations that Kissinger had asked for the wiretaps, the story was a clear attempt by Haig, abetted by his longtime friend Sullivan, to distance himself and pin the blame on Kissinger. In his memoirs, Haig called the stories about Kissinger arrows in the back.[12] If so, Haig had put them there.

Amid the growing controversy surrounding Kissinger and the wiretaps, Nixon set off for the trip to the Middle East. Haig's nerves were fraying along with Nixon's, said Steve Bull, who was on the trip. "I can remember on the final Mideast trip we had a meeting with Haig, who said, 'If this president thinks he can run this presidency without Al Haig, he's got another think coming.' He was crazed. I thought he was unhinged."[13]

Their first stop was Salzburg, Austria, where Kissinger could not stick to the script. He decided to conduct a news conference with the traveling press corps, which he mistakenly thought would care only about the trip, not domestic matters back in Washington. Haig considered the news conference a mistake because "it would have the effect of diverting attention from the real purposes of Nixon's trip and cloaking it with a miasma of controversy that would follow us wherever we went."[14] Kissinger's news conference blew up virtually immediately. Reporters threw question upon question at Kissinger about his apparent perjury during his confirmation hearings. Kissinger tried to take evasive action, saying he had told the Foreign Relations Committee everything and that he would not say anything more about the wiretaps. "I do not believe it is possible to conduct the foreign policy of the United States under these circumstances when the character and credibility of the secretary of state is at issue," Kissinger said. "And if it is not cleared up, I will resign."[15]

While Kissinger melted down before the press, Haig slipped into Nixon's hotel suite and discovered another Nixon secret. Nixon showed Haig one of his legs, which had grown swollen and discolored from

phlebitis, a blood-clotting condition. "I saw that Nixon was in considerable pain," Haig wrote. Beyond that, however, phlebitis could turn fatal
if a blood clot broke free and flowed to his heart, causing a heart attack.
If he had known how bad Nixon's health was, Haig said, he would have
recommended calling off the trip.[16] Eleven months earlier, the last time
Nixon's health had caused him to be hospitalized, Alexander Butterfield
had revealed the White House taping system. Little wonder Nixon wanted
to avoid the hospital.

The wiretap-related problems for Kissinger and Haig were compounded
the next morning, June 12, with a story by John Crewdson in the *New
York Times* that again bore Sullivan's fingerprints. "Some of the 'original
requests' for wiretaps placed on 17 government officials and newsmen
came from Henry A. Kissinger or Gen. Alexander M. Haig Jr., according
to a summary of an inquiry last year by the Federal Bureau of Investigation," started the story, which referred to the May 1973 report ordered
by William Ruckelshaus, then the acting director of the FBI. The report,
for which Haig and Sullivan, but not Kissinger, were interviewed, said
that Kissinger was mainly responsible for picking the targets of the
wiretaps. Crewdson, citing a "source with detailed knowledge of the
wiretaps program," reported that the White House never sought to use
any technique besides wiretapping to catch suspected leakers and that
Haig would call Sullivan and say, "We want a tap on so-and-so." Sullivan never spoke to Kissinger, the story continued, and whenever Haig
called, he "made it clear that 'he was speaking for someone' in making
the wiretap requests."[17] While Crewdson's main source—it could only
have been Sullivan—attempted to carve out some maneuvering room for
Haig, he compounded Kissinger's problems. Not only did the secretary
of state face another round of hearings before the Foreign Relations
Committee, but he could be investigated by the special prosecutor's
office for obstruction of justice or worse. So Haig would be part of the
collateral damage.

Jaworski threw both men a lifeline with a June 13 announcement
that he had nothing to show that Kissinger had any criminal exposure
with the wiretaps.[18] Instead, Jaworski cared more about those who used

the wiretaps, primarily Nixon and Haldeman, to lobby Congress. Once again, Jaworski had come to Haig's rescue. If Jaworski did not go after Kissinger on the wiretaps, he would not target Haig, who had less direct exposure. Such a huge break for Haig validated his reasons for picking Jaworski to succeed Archibald Cox.

Kissinger also learned on June 13 that fifty-two senators had signed a letter declaring confidence in his performance.[19] By this time, most of Nixon's foreign policy accomplishments had been attributed to Kissinger, whose work in the Middle East after the Yom Kippur War had indeed been masterful. Senators of both parties, particularly the Democrats, considered Kissinger the one thing they liked about the Nixon administration. "He hasn't committed perjury in my opinion," said Senator John Stennis, the Mississippi Democrat and enabler of some of the White House's cover-up of the military spy ring.[20] Kissinger got the credit for the opening of relations with China, the strategic arms deal and détente with the Soviets, and the end of the Vietnam War, as if Nixon had nothing to do with anything. Although senators such as Stuart Symington and Lowell Weicker knew that Kissinger had run a secret back-channel game for years, they did not want to risk losing him. They knew Kissinger would last longer than Nixon, whose resignation or impeachment seemed imminent.

With everything that faced him—the debilitating phlebitis and the continuing implosion politically at home—Nixon managed to pull together a dazzling success in the Middle East. Almost one million Egyptians lined the streets in Alexandria and Cairo to shout Nixon's name as he paraded with Egyptian president Anwar Sadat, who had thrown off his country's dependence on the Soviet Union for an alliance with the United States. In his diary, Nixon wrote that Watergate had been put in its proper perspective and that the future looked bright. The pressure for Haig, however, remained, and his behavior became more erratic, aide Steve Bull said.

"He really did love his status," Bull said of Haig. "I remember on that trip we were in Jordan, and it wasn't long after the troops disengaged with the Israelis. We were in a motorcade from Amman to another palace, and a few vehicles got in the motorcade behind and in front of the car with the king and the president. It pushed everyone in the motorcade back, including Haig's car. When we got out of the motorcade, Haig had to walk five cars ahead to get to the president. He started saying to us that if Bob Haldeman had been here, he never would have been that far back in the motorcade. He didn't care if it had to do with the security of the president. He was just concerned about himself. He was irrationally concerned about it."[21]

On June 18, while Haig was still with Nixon in the Middle East, the Judiciary Committee started examining how Nixon's October 20 firing of Cox fueled the call by congressional Democrats for impeachment proceedings.[22] Was the Cox firing part of Nixon's furtherance of the Watergate cover-up? Many committee members knew Nixon wanted to stop part of Cox's investigation, particularly the drive to get more White House tapes. But it was Haig who had sabotaged the handling of Cox as he misled Nixon to believe that then–attorney general Elliot Richardson would follow Nixon's order to fire Cox. Richardson, however, had told Haig exactly the opposite, that he would not fire Cox. The debacle that followed pushed Nixon closer to the edge.

While Jaworski had said he would not target Kissinger on the FBI wire-taps, other investigators had made no such pledge. On June 20 another *New York Times* story laid out more discrepancies between the records and transcripts analyzed by the Judiciary Committee and Kissinger's confirmation testimony.[23] Any objective observer had to conclude that Kissinger had perjured himself. But he had also just pulled off another feat of superhuman diplomacy in the Middle East for which he and Nixon were taking a justifiable victory lap. Democrats knew that if they forced out Nixon, which seemed more likely each day, they had to leave competent people, particularly Kissinger, in charge throughout the rest of the government. Haig's challenge throughout the investigation into the wiretaps was to minimize the blast radius caused by any explosive revelations. So far, thanks to the anonymous comments in the *Times* by Sullivan, his coconspirator in the taps, Haig had been portrayed solely as the implementer of instructions from Kissinger or Nixon. If Haig needed to get Nixon involved, he knew he could maneuver the president to focus the attention on Kissinger, not Haig. After all, Nixon's anger in May 1973 that Kissinger tried to distance himself from the wiretaps led the president to tell Haig about the White House taping system, the transcripts from which were now causing Kissinger's problems. Nixon had threatened then to expose Kissinger. Haig knew the chance existed that Nixon would be willing to consider it again if he felt he had to.

Nixon returned from the Middle East on June 19 buoyed by the joyous receptions he received in each country. He capped off Kissinger's diplomacy in Tel Aviv and Damascus, and the Saudis embraced him as a brother. "My receptions in Egypt and Syria and my conversations with Sadat and Asad confirmed the tremendous potential of the new role of the United States as a force for peace in the Arab world," Nixon wrote.[24]

He had little chance to enjoy his success, as he had to plunge immediately into preparations for his third summit meeting with Soviet leader Leonid Brezhnev, which was scheduled to start on June 25. On June 20 Nixon convened a National Security Council meeting with his national security team, led by Kissinger and including Defense Secretary James Schlesinger, Adm. Thomas Moorer, CIA Director William Colby, deputy national advisor Brent Scowcroft, and Haig. Hard-liners, primarily Schlesinger and Moorer, had put détente advocates on the back foot, and they pushed for Nixon to take a harder line on arms control than Nixon knew the Soviets would accept. Kissinger's and Schlesinger's differences flared into the open, and Nixon found himself badgered by his young defense chief on the issue of how many warheads the Soviets could put on their missiles.

"Mr. Brezhnev has a very high respect for you, Mr. President," Schlesinger said. "You can be very persuasive—you have great forensic skills. I believe if you can persuade them to slow down to 85 per year versus 200 per year, you will have achieved a major breakthrough. The Chiefs have been apprehensive about [multiple independent reentry vehicle] agreements, but I believe that most of them would endorse this approach."

Moorer said the Chiefs were reluctant to extend any deal limiting warheads and that Adm. Elmo Zumwalt, the chief of naval operations, or CNO, wanted more restrictions on the Soviets and more flexibility for the United States. It was Zumwalt, unknown to Nixon, who had engineered a part of the military spy network on the White House and was a plausible suspect for leaking secrets to columnist Jack Anderson about the White House policies during the India-Pakistan war in 1971. Zumwalt viewed Kissinger's détente policies with alarm, and that concern carried over to the president.

"You mean he prefers no agreement," Nixon said.

"No, he just wants only a permanent agreement," Schlesinger responded.

"Let's put it all out on the table," Nixon said. "When he suggests something that has no chance of success that means he wants no agreement. He has now written his letter for the record and I'm sure he will go out and say it publicly. But that's OK; I will have to take responsibility for it, he won't have to."

Nixon had lost patience with Zumwalt, who was not at the meeting. He said he would only agree to something that satisfied the nation's national security interests. "But I will say that one thing that we will not accept are patently cheap shots such as what CNO has done—after the support the Navy has received from this administration, which he's aware of," Nixon said. "He knows what we have gone through. We saved the US from a diplomatic disaster by the wrong kind of end to the war in Vietnam. To come forth on paper with a position, which he knows to be unacceptable, and I'm sure he plans to go public with it. I hear a lot of this from our military—of course not from anyone in this room."[25]

The wolves were inside the door for Nixon. Haig said Schlesinger "treated the President with a mixture of condescension and thinly veiled contempt that shocked those who witnessed it."[26] Nixon called Schlesinger's statement that "with my forensic ability, I could sell the idea that he presented, was really an insult to everybody's intelligence and particularly to mine."[27]

Despite the divisions between Nixon and the Chiefs over arms control, Nixon left for his third summit with Brezhnev on June 25. A second SALT agreement seemed distant. Nixon had little leverage, and neither, it seemed, did Brezhnev. As Kissinger had predicted during his earlier conversations with Schlesinger, détente had not provided the Soviets with many tangible gains. The Middle East war had cost the Soviets their client state in Egypt, and Syria was not strong enough to make up the difference. Soviet military leaders perceived they had lost influence, and they, like their American counterparts, did not want to give up whatever advantages they thought they still had.

Meanwhile, Haig and Kissinger squabbled over the trappings of power. Each wanted the hotel room closest to Nixon, an honor Haig wrested from a piqued Kissinger. After a state dinner on June 27, Nixon pulled his two indispensable aides into the presidential limousine to avoid eavesdropping. "I suggested to Kissinger and Haig that we have a brief meeting in my car, where we could talk without being bugged," Nixon wrote. "Kissinger had seemed depressed all day. As I had guessed, the domestic harassment over the wiretaps still bothered him, as well as his realization after his talks with [Soviet foreign minister Andrei] Gromyko during the afternoon that our negotiating position had been seriously undercut by the anti-détente agitation within the administration."[28]

In Moscow and Crimea, where he and Brezhnev zipped around in one of the Soviet leader's speedboats, Nixon did his best to make something out of the third summit. Each visit with Brezhnev, Nixon knew, made the world safer. The two leaders had built a relationship in which they could communicate freely in spite of their obvious language and cultural differences. However, a politically weakened Nixon might overreach in his desperation to get a deal he could cite to save his presidency. The hard-liners, abetted by Haig, did not want to risk having Nixon give up anything more. They felt Nixon had given away too much during the first two summits; they did not want to see it happen again. Haig had helped send the military White House secrets during the heyday of the spy ring, and then he and Fred Buzhardt had helped cover it up just a few months earlier in 1974. Haig had helped make Schlesinger the defense secretary during the confusion of May 1973 and had told Nixon to make William Colby the director of the CIA. He had helped build the national security team that was causing Nixon such aggravation now, and the levers of power remained close enough to Haig that he could minimize whatever his weakened president could do.

June closed with Nixon deeply immersed in the international diplomacy he enjoyed the most. In the royal palaces of Amman and Riyadh and on the streets of Alexandria, Cairo, and even Moscow, Nixon reveled in his status as a transformational world leader. With the help of Kissinger, he had ended a war, signed a peace, and warmed by a few degrees the Cold War with the Soviet Union. In Washington, however, his political troubles only deepened. His enemies in Congress saw the accumulating evidence against him and saw their chance to get rid of him, while his allies, increasingly skeptical of his innocence, dwindled each day.

16   July 1974

President Nixon remained in the Soviet Union as July opened, desperately trying to reach another nuclear arms deal with Leonid Brezhnev. But the two sides were too dug into their positions, and the hard-liners on the U.S. side, empowered by Alexander Haig, bogged down any accommodation. The tensions created by the first Strategic Arms Limitation Treaty in 1972, signed at Nixon's apex as president, had worsened during the following two years. Military leaders such as Defense Secretary James Schlesinger and Adm. Thomas Moorer, chairman of the Joint Chiefs of Staff, had allied themselves with Nixon's domestic rivals to hold the line on more arms cuts. Nixon and Henry Kissinger tried to do more, but they failed, destroying Nixon's hope for another foreign policy triumph.

The House Judiciary Committee started its open hearings on impeachment on July 2 with Alexander Butterfield as its first witness. Butterfield drily explained how the White House staff worked, who sat where in the West Wing, and what their roles were. He described how memoranda flowed from Bob Haldeman, then the chief of staff, to other staff members. Butterfield also mentioned his long and close relationship with Haig, which started when they both worked in the Pentagon as aides to Defense Secretary Robert McNamara in the Johnson administration. Then John Doar, the committee's majority counsel, showed Butterfield a memo he had written to Jeb Magruder, then another member of the White House staff. "I ask you to look at that document and tell me whether you recognize it," Doar asked Butterfield, who said he recognized the memo.[1]

The memo, dated January 8, 1969, dealt with questions that FBI Director J. Edgar Hoover had about former Defense Secretary Clark Clifford, McNamara's successor, who was writing a magazine article aided by Morton Halperin, the former NSC aide who was the first person targeted by the FBI wiretaps in May 1969. But there was a problem with the memo. On January 8, 1969, neither Butterfield nor Magruder worked for the White House, because Lyndon Johnson remained president and the Nixon team had not started working.[2]

"Well, I am familiar with this memorandum, because it became an issue some time ago when I was talking to the staff of the Special Prosecutor," Butterfield told Doar. "But I can tell you that this is not a copy of the original. This is a copy of an altered original. It appears—I don't doubt that it is my memorandum, but a lot of the words here are words which I use, sentences are structured much as I structure them. So when I first saw this, I didn't doubt that it was mine.

"Then as I looked at it more closely, I knew for a fact in my own mind that it was not a true copy of the original, which at that time, I was supposed to be looking at the original. I was handed the original, told this was an original memo of mine, and I knew that it was not."[3]

The original memo, dated January 8, 1970, told Magruder that he "should go—first of all—to Al Haig (not to [name redacted]) and find out who participated in Henry's December 29th meeting. If he had more than one meeting on that day, you could say that it is your understanding that this particular meeting concerned Vietnam and options to our future courses of action there." Two paragraphs later, the memo said, "Al Haig can get you squared away on at least a preliminary scheme. We can build from there." "Needless to say," Butterfield concluded, "this item is every bit as sensitive as the memorandum indicates."[4]

The second memo, dated January 9, 1969, omitted the reference to Haig squaring away Magruder and had a different closing paragraph. It had been reworked to airbrush away the major reference to Haig as someone who could devise a strategy to deal with the Clifford article and the ramifications of his collaboration with Halperin, who had worked with Clifford in the Pentagon before joining Nixon's NSC. Butterfield said he had previously spoken about both versions of the memo to members of Jaworski's special prosecutor's staff, who had been given the memo by the White House. "The J. Edgar Hoover memorandum which was labeled top secret, mentioned information which had been obtained by the FBI by way of sensitive sources, or sensitive means, or something like that," Butterfield told Doar. "That evidently meant telephone taps. The reason I had been called in on that occasion to be interrogated by the Special Prosecutor's staff was because they thought I knew something about those early telephone taps which the whole world now knows about. The J. Edgar Hoover memo to me said nothing about telephone taps, but I have learned since that if I had been wiser, I would know that 'sensitive sources' means telephone taps. To me it means someone overheard someone in a restaurant or something like that. But that is what the Hoover memo was about and it did relate to something Clark Clifford was going to do. But it was about telephone taps."[5]

Butterfield realized that his old friend, Al Haig, had set him up. "The memo came from Haig," Butterfield said in a 1987 interview, "'cause he's the one, he's the one that gave it to the special prosecutor."[6]

Haig could not count solely on Jaworski's ability to cover for him on the wiretaps. In this case, he altered a government document—a form of obstruction of justice—to misdirect the prosecutors. Instead, he tried to direct them to Butterfield. By creating the fake memo and giving it to Jaworski, Haig showed just how much he still feared being dragged into a deeper investigation into the wiretaps, which were becoming part of the developing second article of impeachment for abuse of power. If, following James St. Clair's argument that impeachment was the only avenue to use against an incumbent president, Nixon was impeached and convicted of abuse of power, then as a newly private citizen he could be indicted and tried for the same crimes. And those who aided Nixon in that impeachment-worthy conduct, starting with Haig himself, could be prosecuted for those crimes, too. It was the second time Haig had given Jaworski a misleading document. The first was in November 1973, when he and Buzhardt gave him the Buzhardt report on the military spy ring.

The Judiciary Committee had bigger issues to handle than Haig, and the panel's two top lawyers, both picked with the guidance of Haig's advisor, Morris Leibman, let the issue slide. It all went into the category of more evidence of why Nixon could not be trusted. No one raised a possible tie to Haig, because he had drawn attention away from his role in the wiretaps and put it on Kissinger.

An exhausted Nixon, discouraged by not hitting a home run in the Soviet Union, returned to Key Biscayne late on July 3. Haig stayed there with him as the president spent four days watching events from afar and trying to recharge his batteries. Since June 1 Nixon had spent only ten nights in Washington. Nursing his swollen, phlebitis-ridden leg, Nixon tried to get better by taking trips on his boat and a helicopter flight to Palm Beach to Mar-a-Lago, the home of heiress Marjorie Merriweather Post and the future home of another president—Donald Trump.[7] Nixon had barely more than a month left as president, and although he said nothing about it publicly, he wavered between thinking he could survive and waiting for the end to come. "Having survived this long I am convinced that we can see it through to the end—however the end comes out," he wrote in his diary.[8] The president returned to Washington late on July 7, in time for the Supreme Court arguments the next morning by St. Clair and Jaworski in the tapes case.

Each side's arguments surrounded a simple question: Was the president above the law? Either he had to obey a legally binding subpoena to produce evidence in a criminal procedure or he did not. And if he did not, then he could essentially act with impunity. St. Clair contended that Nixon was not "above the law. Nor does he contend that he is. What he does contend is that as President the law can be applied to him in only one way, and that is by impeachment."[9] Of course, by trying to keep the tapes out of the hands of the special prosecutor and the Judiciary Committee, Nixon wanted to limit the evidence that could be used against him.

Jaworski's argument was just as simple. "This nation's constitutional form of government is in serious jeopardy if the President, any President, is to say that the Constitution means what he says it does and that there is no one, not even the Supreme Court, to tell him otherwise," Jaworski told the eight justices. William Rehnquist, a Nixon appointee who once worked in the Justice Department for John Mitchell, had recused himself. The White House, Jaworski claimed, had waived its privilege to keep the tapes when Nixon permitted the release of some aides' testimony and edited transcripts of the tapes in the major April 30 release.[10] When Haig let Jaworski listen to tapes and gave him evidence in the White House Map Room, he had blown the president's defense against releasing the tapes.

The tapes that Nixon had already turned over continued to cause him problems. On July 9 the Judiciary Committee released a 131-page list of differences between the transcripts released by the White House in late April and the transcripts created by the committee, which said it used sophisticated new technology to decipher the confusing passages of the tapes.[11] While the committee's transcripts provided no significant factual departures from what the White House provided, the new list only deepened the existing impression that Nixon was continuing his cover-up.

Nixon and company decamped from Washington on July 12 and headed to San Clemente for a two-week stay. Haig thought the weather and scenery "combined to restore Nixon to something like inner tranquility."[12] Nixon, however, described the same trip differently, writing that he learned on the flight west that John Ehrlichman had been convicted of perjury and conspiring to violate the civil rights of Pentagon Papers leaker Daniel Ellsberg's psychiatrist when he approved the White House Plumbers' break-in at his office. "I was deeply depressed by the tragic irony of this development," Nixon wrote. "Ellsberg, who had leaked top-secret developments, had gone free. Ehrlichman, who was trying to prevent such leaks, had been convicted."[13]

Nixon's description of the Ehrlichman conviction showed how little he truly understood what had happened. Ehrlichman had been denied a chance to use White House records, including his taped interview of military spy ring leader Robert Welander, to defend himself courtesy of Haig and Buzhardt, who had urged Nixon to claim executive privilege for those records. That decision was made to protect Haig, not Ehrlichman, whom Nixon browbeat to find new ways to destroy Ellsberg's reputation. Nixon did not know about the break-in at Dr. Lewis Fielding's office, but he had urged the Plumbers to break into other offices that summer of 1971. That included an order to firebomb the Brookings Institution in search of information that would implicate Nixon in the sabotage of the Paris peace talks in 1968. Ehrlichman was going to prison because Nixon had made it inevitable.

Joseph Califano's work as Haig's informal advisor and conduit to Leon Jaworski picked up added urgency on July 17. That day Jaworski asked Califano to meet him, so Califano walked to the prosecutor's office on K Street. There, Jaworski told him that John Connally, one of Nixon's closest confidants, was in deep trouble and faced indictment for perjury and obstruction of justice. The conversation showed the interlocking relationships between Califano, Jaworski, and their associates. Edward Bennett Williams was Connally's lawyer and Califano's law partner. Connally, a former Texas governor, was a longtime associate of President Lyndon Johnson, Califano's old boss and Jaworski's patron. Haig had used Connally to ask Jaworski if he was interested in being the special prosecutor.[14]

Jaworski told Califano that the case against Connally looked airtight, but Califano said he felt confident that Williams, perhaps the nation's best criminal defense attorney, would get Connally acquitted. But Connally was just the opening for Jaworski's main topic: Haig and the imminent demise of Richard Nixon. "I am convinced that Nixon is guilty of a significant number of crimes: the most obvious, obstruction of justice and subornation of perjury," Jaworski said. He then told Califano of his frequent meetings with Haig and how Haig almost cried when Jaworski delivered him some bad news. "Haig and Nixon are calling every single shot," Jaworski said.

Jaworski told Califano about when he told Haig that the grand jury had named Nixon an unindicted coconspirator and Jaworski had offered to keep the news secret in exchange for eighteen of the sixty-four tapes he wanted. "A few days later," Califano wrote, "Haig called Jaworski back and said that he and Nixon had listened to every one of the eighteen tapes for two full days and nights. 'Haig told me,' Jaworski said, 'there's no way the President will give up those tapes.'"

Jaworski claimed that he had done everything he could to keep the grand jury from indicting Nixon. Only a legal opinion that a sitting president could not be indicted stopped the grand jury. Once Nixon left office, it was only a matter of time before he was indicted.

Califano said that Haig thought he was trying to save the presidency. That could be, Jaworski answered, but he told Haig that he might actually be destroying the presidency by fighting to keep an obviously guilty Nixon in office. Haig, too, could face possible charges, Jaworski said, because it might not be "possible for anyone to serve Nixon at this point without becoming involved in obstruction of justice." Califano realized that Jaworski wanted Califano to pass the word to Haig that he needed to get Nixon to resign before Haig himself "got into criminal trouble."

By this time, Haig had long known that Nixon had obstructed justice with Haldeman thirteen months earlier. He had helped the military spy ring that stole White House secrets and likely leaked them to the press and then given Jaworski a misleading report on the spy ring. He had been a key part of the secret group that supported the FBI wiretaps and passed a fake memo about the taps to Jaworski. Much of what Haig had done as chief of staff was meant to cover his tracks. Now the Watergate special prosecutor, whom Haig had helped through careful releases of White House documents, was telling Haig's longtime mentor that he needed to advise Haig to prepare Nixon to resign. "Joe, let me discuss a hypothetical case with you," Jaworski said. "If we assume that one of the main reasons the President is not resigning is his fear of criminal prosecution and civil lawsuits, then what should I do if he approaches me for a deal in return for his resignation?"

Califano assumed Jaworski really wanted to know if his other clients, the *Washington Post* and the Democratic Party, would support such a deal. He responded that he could not guarantee that no one would sue or keep pushing existing lawsuits. Califano also expressed confidence that the Judiciary Committee would do the right thing and vote for impeachment.

Jaworski worried about younger Americans who could not understand why Nixon still remained president. Many of them, he continued, also thought Spiro Agnew had gotten off too easily when he traded resignation for a no contest plea and no prison time for bribery.

"There are strong arguments for accepting the President's resignation and assuring him he will not be indicted for crimes committed," Califano said. "But the orchestration of any such arrangement is of critical importance." Califano also said he was concerned that Nixon would pardon Haldeman and John Ehrlichman to keep them from spilling Nixon's secrets in court. Congress could prevent that by giving Nixon immunity from prosecution if he resigned.

Jaworski cautioned that they were only discussing a hypothetical situation, but the hypothetical was quickly becoming a reality. Haig would soon start working on what Califano and Jaworski had discussed: getting Nixon to resign with the knowledge that he would not face devastating legal action that could bankrupt him and possibly put him in a prison cell.

In the Judiciary Committee, both sides started their final arguments on July 18. St. Clair argued that no smoking gun existed to warrant impeaching Nixon for the Watergate cover-up and obstruction of justice, which were the core of the first article of impeachment. St. Clair, however, erred when he attempted to introduce part of a March 22, 1973, tape that Nixon had refused to turn over to the committee despite a subpoena. Angry members of both parties complained that Nixon could not refuse to honor a subpoena and then try to defend himself by using information targeted by that subpoena.[15] In California, Nixon thought St. Clair had done a "brilliant job."[16]

Nixon also knew that the odds were leaning against him. He needed three of the committee's southern Democrats—Walter Flowers of Alabama, Ray Thornton of Arkansas, and James Mann of South Carolina—to vote against impeachment with a unified bloc of committee Republicans. That became less likely when John Doar, the majority counsel, presented a detailed "summary of information" and twenty-nine proposed articles of impeachment. Over 306 pages Doar laid out the majority's rationale for impeaching the president, including his multiple campaign abuses, his involvement in the Watergate cover-up, and his abuse of power, which included his use of surveillance tactics, such as the FBI wiretap program, overseen by Kissinger and Haig.[17]

Making matters worse for Nixon was his knowledge that the June 23 tape was on the verge of exposure. If he lost the case in the Supreme Court, that tape would have to be turned over to Judge John Sirica, the committee, and Jaworski. "Of course, how we handle that tape is a very difficult call because I don't know how it could be excerpted properly," Nixon wrote in his diary on June 21.[18]

On July 23, after the closing arguments of all the committee lawyers and St. Clair, the three southern Democrats all said they would support impeachment. Compounding Nixon's woes was the announcement that day by a conservative Republican on the committee, Larry Hogan of Maryland, that he too would support impeachment. Few in the White House considered Hogan at risk of defecting. "I told Haig bitterly that if this was the result of our hands-off strategy, we could hardly have done worse by outright lobbying," Nixon wrote. "I said that we had to do something to try to get at least one of the Southerners back."[19]

Nixon had Haig call Alabama governor George Wallace, a Democrat, but one sometimes sympathetic to Nixon. Just days earlier, a press report had claimed that the CIA, in coordination with Nixon, had been involved in the 1972 assassination attempt against Wallace, so instead of getting through to Wallace, Haig was told by the governor's secretary that Nixon had to call the governor directly. Nixon did, and Wallace told him that he would try to lobby Flowers into supporting Nixon but that he, Wallace, would not support him either. "Well Al," Nixon said, "there goes the presidency."[20]

Nixon knew he faced a choice: Should he keep fighting impeachment in the House and then a trial in the Senate, or should he resign? He had talked more about resigning over the last few weeks with Haig and Ron Ziegler, but Nixon knew that Haig believed that resignation "would mean a dangerously easy victory for the radicals—not just over me but over the system."[21] Haig was already working on a possible resignation, shaped by his talks with Califano, that would enable Nixon to escape prosecution, just like the deal Haig had pressured Spiro Agnew to accept the previous fall.

At 10:00 a.m. in Washington (7:00 a.m. in California), the Supreme Court issued its ruling in the tapes case. All eight justices voting, including three of the Nixon appointees, ruled that Nixon had to turn over the sixty-four tapes that Jaworski wanted. Haig gave the news to Nixon, who cursed the men he had put on the court—Warren Burger, Harry Blackmun, and Lewis Powell—who had voted against him.[22]

Nixon and his team digested the Court's ruling throughout the day on July 24, searching for any way they could possibly disregard the order and keep the tapes, because Nixon knew complying with the order meant his presidency was over. He knew what he had said on June 23, 1972, with Haldeman, knew it had been recorded, and knew that it showed he had authorized the obstruction of justice. "There may be some problems with the June 23 tape, Fred," Nixon told Buzhardt.[23] In Washington, Buzhardt went to the vault that held the tapes and removed the one from June 23. He spent two hours listening to the tape, complete with Nixon's jibes against Jews and gays, and heard what Nixon already knew: the president had ordered the Watergate cover-up. Buzhardt called Haig and St. Clair in California, where it was around 9:30 a.m. "I told them that in my judgment it was all over," Buzhardt said. "The June 23 tape clearly contradicted material we had submitted to the House Judiciary Committee. I told Al that in my opinion the tape was conclusive evidence. It was no longer a question of the President leaving office, but how he was leaving."[24]

Buzhardt and Haig were playacting. They had known for months that Nixon was guilty, perhaps as early as May 8, 1973, when Nixon had first told Haig about the White House tapes. Now came the time for them to determine how the president would leave office, either through an impeachment and Senate trial, which threatened to expose Haig's and Buzhardt's own problems, or through resignation, which would let them avoid the untidy complications of an evidence-producing trial. After all, Haig and Buzhardt had not only concealed their involvement in the military spy ring and its cover-up, as well as Haig's deep ties to the FBI wiretaps, but also covered up their knowledge of the smoking gun tape. They, too, had obstructed justice by not providing the special prosecutor, the Senate Watergate committee, and the House Judiciary Committee the evidence that proved Nixon's guilt. To protect themselves Nixon had to resign, and they had to make it happen.

That conclusion, said White House aide Jerry Jones, was "inescapable." Nixon no longer had the votes in Congress to survive.[25]

Nixon went through the motions of being president, although he knew his early exit from office was inevitable. He traveled north to Los Angeles for a speech before he flew back to Washington in time for the final committee votes on impeachment. On July 27 the panel voted 27–11 for the first article of impeachment. Six Republicans joined all twenty-one Democrats. That included freshman M. Caldwell Butler of Virginia, whose wife read him passages of *All the President's Men* as he considered his vote.[26]

The Judiciary Committee voted 28–10 in favor of the second article of impeachment—abuse of power—on July 29. The article encompassed a range of Nixon's misdeeds, but it particularly included his use of surveillance techniques and the FBI wiretaps, which started in May 1969. After Nixon, only Kissinger, Haig, and Haldeman had more exposure to the legal problems stemming from those taps, and Haldeman had more pressing issues to deal with: his criminal case would soon go to trial. Haig was set to testify before the Senate Foreign Relations Committee on July 30 about Kissinger and the taps. Before that, however, he had to cope with the immediate threat of the Supreme Court's order to produce the tapes to Sirica's court and the committee. Haig asked Buzhardt to create a transcript of Nixon's talks with Haldeman on June 23, 1972, and Buzhardt came upon the section in which Nixon, based on the belief that it was his good friend John Mitchell's recommendation, told Haldeman to ask the CIA's leaders to tell the FBI to stop its investigation of the Watergate break-in. "After reading this document, I knew that the clock had stopped in Richard Nixon's White House," Haig wrote. "What the tape showed was that the President had been aware at a very early stage of a disposition among his subordinates to cover up White House involvement in the burglary, that he had shared in this disposition, and that he had given the order that legitimized, in the minds of his underlings, everything that they subsequently did to cover up the Watergate crimes."[27]

This eloquent description of Haig's discovery of the smoking gun tape is a fanciful lie, one disproved by the White House tapes and Haig's actions. Vernon Walters had come to the White House on May 11, 1973, with written records of his conversations with Haldeman, Ehrlichman, and Dean about the attempts to use the agency to block the FBI's Watergate investigation. Haig already knew about the White House tapes by then, because Nixon had told him. He also knew from sitting with Nixon and Haldeman on May 11 that Nixon had directed Haldeman to meet with Walters to stop the investigation. Haig knew about the cover-up then, knew about the tapes that would prove it, and only professed shock on July 29 that his long-held knowledge was finally going to be public.

Haig sat on his knowledge of Nixon's imminent exposure on July 30 when he went to Capitol Hill to testify before the Foreign Relations Committee about the wiretaps. He had to distance himself from the orders to eavesdrop on members of Nixon's own administration while avoiding any irreparable damage to Kissinger, whom the majority of committee members regarded as the savior of U.S. foreign policy. For three hours, Haig sat with Buzhardt beside him and answered the questions in closed session.[28]

With his testimony before the Senate over, Haig turned his focus to negotiating Nixon's resignation. The trick was persuading Nixon that he could leave office without facing criminal charges that could have him in court for years. Already, Jaworski had set the stage for a combination resignation and pardon that would also eliminate the potential of criminal charges for Haig for obstruction of justice. St. Clair was finally given a copy of a transcript of the June 23 tape, which eliminated any doubt he had about Nixon's guilt. He told Haig and Buzhardt that they could wait no longer to give the tapes to Sirica, because any delay in turning over evidence could put St. Clair at risk of obstruction of justice charges, which Haig and Buzhardt faced, too. Haig and Buzhardt then told Nixon they had to release the tape, and once Sirica got it, the whole world would know about it in days, maybe hours.

Haig was running out of time.

Over the next nine days, Haig would engineer Nixon's removal from office, completing the slow-motion coup that began when Haig returned to the White House on May 3, 1973.

On July 31 Haig told Kissinger about the smoking gun tape, which would force Nixon to quit. Kissinger had long anticipated Nixon's departure.[29] For months he had criticized and undermined Nixon; his catty remarks about a "nonfunctional" president had echoed around Washington for almost a year. Kissinger, Haig told him, had a constitutional role to play, and he needed to help shepherd Nixon through the transition. In his memoirs, Haig denied that he asked Kissinger "to nudge the President toward resignation," but Kissinger was already thinking in those terms.[30] Kissinger also had his own skin to save; the Senate Foreign Relations Committee was still trying to determine if Kissinger had lied about his role in the FBI wiretaps. Kissinger needed little persuading that Nixon had to go.

Haig told other staff members that it was over for Nixon and that impeachment and a criminal trial would damage the democracy and ruin Nixon: "By resigning, he might preserve his health, some fragment of his reputation, and the possibility of winning back the good opinion of his fellow citizens."[31] But Nixon's resignation was even better for Haig. An impeachment proceeding and trial in the Senate, followed by a criminal trial, would expose Haig's role in the military spy ring and how he helped Kissinger pick who would be wiretapped. Haig's career, which now dangled in limbo with Nixon, would truly be over.

Early on the evening of July 31, Haig called Robert Hartmann, Vice President Ford's chief of staff. Stocky and abrasive, Hartmann was a former *Los Angeles Times* reporter who went to work for Ford while he was a House member.[32] Hartmann also considered Haig a legendary brown-noser and opportunist who used Nixon to gain more power. Haig told Hartmann he needed to schedule a private meeting with Ford for the next day. Haig said he would come by Ford's office in the morning. Hartmann suspected something was wrong, so he recommended that Ford have him there as a witness.

Nixon had slightly more than a week left in his presidency. Only his children believed he could withstand what looked like a certain impeachment. He knew he had to resign, but the politician who had risen from rural southern California and overcome such unlikely beginnings resisted simply leaving the White House for an uncertain future filled with criminal trials and civil suits. He needed a graceful escape, which Haig was trying to find.

17 August 1974

Alexander Haig kept the appointment he had made the previous day to see Vice President Ford on August 1, but when he arrived at Ford's office on the second floor of the Old Executive Office Building, he was surprised to see Robert Hartmann, Ford's chief of staff, there, too. Neither chief of staff liked the other. Haig thought Hartmann abrasive and in over his head.[1] Hartmann considered Haig an obsequious schemer who tried to limit Ford's access to the president. Haig wrote in his memoirs that Nixon had told him that morning that he knew he had to resign and that he wanted Haig to give that message to Ford. However, Haig declined to tell Ford about Nixon's declaration with Hartmann in the room. Instead, Haig told them that Nixon's moods changed with each minute, shifting from wanting to fight to accepting that he would be removed from office. Haig said nothing about Nixon's alleged decision to resign and ended the meeting.[2]

Minutes later, as Ford was on his way to the Senate, Haig called back.

Hartmann could only hear Ford's side of the conversation, which was a series of "uh-huhs."[3] Haig said he needed to see Ford privately, and they scheduled a meeting for 3:30 p.m., without Hartmann.

Shortly before the second meeting with Ford, Haig talked to Fred Buzhardt, who told him the president could be pardoned for crimes for which he had not yet been indicted.[4] That meant Nixon could legally be pardoned for anything. Armed with that legal opinion, Haig arrived on time for his second meeting with Ford. Alone, he told the vice president about the contents of the June 23 "smoking gun" tape and that Nixon might resign as early as the next day. There were six options, Haig told Ford, which included Nixon pardoning himself, then resigning; Nixon pardoning all the Watergate defendants, then himself, and then resigning; and finally, Nixon resigning and then being pardoned by his successor. Haig did not tell Ford which White House lawyer had given him the legal opinion. "As I saw it, at this point, the question clearly before me was, under the circumstances, what course of action should I recommend that would be in the best interest of the country?" Ford told the House Judiciary Committee on October 17, 1974.[5]

Neither Ford nor Haig admitted that during that second meeting a deal was struck that Nixon would resign, making Ford president, and then be pardoned by the new president. But Nixon's decision to resign was not absolute. He wavered between fighting to the end, which meant impeachment and conviction in the Senate, which his family wanted him to do, and resigning, which Haig wanted. Also, the contents of the June 23 tape were still known to only a small number of people. There was still no public outcry about the obvious obstruction of justice recorded in that conversation. From his second conversation with Ford, Haig knew that the soon-to-be president understood the stakes, that he had the legal authority to pardon Nixon for crimes for which he had not been indicted, and that Nixon needed some assurance that he would not face ruinous legal battles as a private citizen if he decided to spare the nation the drama of an impeachment and trial by resigning.

Haig wanted to leave no traces of his meeting with Ford, so he told Ford's secretary to write the name of Rogers Morton, the interior secretary, in the appointment calendar instead of his own. During the meeting with Haig, Betty Ford, the vice president's wife, called, looking for her husband. A Ford aide went to the waiting area outside Ford's office and saw a surprised Haig emerge. "What are you doing here?" Haig demanded, as he quickly scurried away. Inside Ford's office, the aide told reporter Seymour Hersh, he encountered a stunned vice president staring out his window at the West Wing of the White House and contemplating the gravity of what Haig had just told him.[6] Haig talked to Ford one more time on August 1, calling him late at night at his home in Virginia to tell him that nothing had changed. "The situation is as fluid as ever," Haig said.

"Well," Ford replied, "I've talked with Betty, and we're prepared, but we can't get involved in the White House decision-making process."

"I understand," Haig said. "I'll be in touch with you tomorrow."[7]

In just a few hours, Haig had received a legal opinion from his collaborator in the White House, Buzhardt; met secretly with Ford and told him he could pardon Nixon before he was even indicted; tried to hide his meeting by using someone else's name in the appointment log; and then left, claiming that he and Ford had not cut a deal for Nixon to resign in exchange for a pardon from Ford.

They had little time in which to act. The House scheduled its impeachment debate for August 19, by which time the details of the June 23 tape were sure to be public.

On the morning of August 2, Ford met with James St. Clair to discuss the likelihood of Nixon's impeachment and conviction in light of the June 23 tape. Ford told St. Clair about Haig's guidance concerning the legal options for a pardon, advice that a surprised St. Clair said did not come from him. Ford told the Judiciary Committee that he then decided that he would not make any recommendations to Nixon about resignation or impeachment.[8]

Hartmann and John Marsh, a former House member from Virginia and a longtime Ford friend, told a different story. They met with Ford after he talked with St. Clair, and the vice president told them that he had called Haig, not that Haig had called him, and that Ford had told Haig, "Betty and I talked it over last night. . . . We felt we were ready. This just has to stop; it's tearing the country to pieces. I decided to go ahead and get it over with, so I called Al Haig and told them they should do whatever they decided to do; it was all right with me."[9]

Hartmann and Marsh jumped all over Ford, telling him he had made a huge mistake in saying anything like that to Haig. They summoned Bryce Harlow, Nixon's longtime aide and also a Ford confidant, who said Ford had to call Haig back and disavow what he had told him earlier. This account differs in meaning from what Ford told the Judiciary Committee in October. "I decided I should call General Haig the afternoon of August 2," Ford testified. "I did make the call late that afternoon, and told him I wanted him to understand that I had no intention of recommending what the President should do about resigning or not resigning, and that nothing we had talked about the previous afternoon should be given any consideration in whatever decision the President might make." Ford said Haig agreed.[10]

Years later, St. Clair told Hersh that he did not recall talking with Ford about the June 23 tape or a presidential pardon. Instead, St. Clair said, they discussed reports that the Nixon White House was involved in the May 1972 shooting of George Wallace. "I couldn't figure out what he was doing," St. Clair said of Ford.[11]

What Ford was doing, whether he meant it or not, was giving Haig the impression that he had reached a deal in which Ford would pardon Nixon if he resigned. Ford certainly did not rule out that possibility.

Also that day, Jaworski's office said it was investigating Alexander Butterfield for possible charges for altering a memorandum related to the FBI wiretaps.[12] Butterfield had testified in July that the altered memorandum excised a reference to Haig and had been turned over to Jaworski by Haig and Buzhardt. When he was shown the memo during the impeachment hearing, Butterfield said he had not altered the memo. He later suspected that his old friend Haig had been behind the alteration.

On August 3 Senator Robert Griffin of Michigan, a Republican ally of Ford and a longtime Nixon supporter, wrote the president to tell him that he would vote to convict Nixon in the Senate if the president failed to honor a subpoena for the tapes.[13] It was another indication of just how much support Nixon had lost among congressional Republicans, and it led him to consider how much money he stood to lose if the House impeached him and the Senate convicted him. By resigning, he could save at least $60,000 in annual pension benefits. Since he had had to borrow money to pay his back taxes, Nixon had lost a considerable part of his net worth in 1974, and he now stood to lose more.

After his meetings with Haig and St. Clair, Ford left Washington for Mississippi and a series of fund-raisers and appearances for Republican candidates, including Trent Lott, a freshman member of the Judiciary Committee. Lott was a solid "no" vote on any of the impeachment articles. Ford said he thought the House would vote to impeach Nixon but that he personally did not think the president had committed impeachable offenses and that he had no idea how a Senate trial would end.[14] Given what he later told the Judiciary Committee in October, Ford had to know that he was not telling the truth. He already knew from Haig and St. Clair that the smoking gun tape would devastate Nixon's defense and force him from office if he did not resign.

Nixon went to Camp David for the weekend and summoned Haig, St. Clair, and other staffers for a five-hour meeting on Sunday, August 4. Resignation hung in the air. By now, the White House insiders all knew about the June 23 tape and what it meant for impeachment in the House. Nixon still remained unsure, wavering in meetings between fighting and resigning. Haig knew fighting meant more problems than it was worth and urged Nixon to resign. Nixon also determined that he would release the June 23 tape transcript to the public and take his chances that the American people would cut him some slack.[15]

Haig had to preserve his deniability. Before the White House released the June 23 transcript on the morning of August 5, Haig called Jaworski, with St. Clair on the line, to let him know what was coming.

"I wanted you to be aware of it before the fact, Leon," Haig said.

"What is it, Al?" Jaworski asked.

"Well, we were reviewing the tape recordings we are going to send you and we found one that's significantly different from the others," Haig said.

"In what way?" Jaworski asked again.

"It's some conversations between the President and Haldeman on June 23, six days after the Watergate break-in," Haig said. "They talk about getting the FBI out of the investigation by using the CIA—having the CIA say it was a national security matter. . . . We didn't know it, Leon," Haig continued. "He didn't tell us about it. He didn't tell anyone. St. Clair and I have been pushing him to come out with a statement saying he was the only one who knew about it. That he didn't tell any of his attorneys and that's why St. Clair made misleading statements to the Judiciary Committee."

"I told him he was going to have to reveal this publicly or I was going to resign," St. Clair interjected. "The advice I've been giving him didn't take any of this into account, Leon. And the positions I took before the Committee didn't either."

Jaworski told St. Clair he would have a problem if Nixon did not disclose the tape right away.

St. Clair said Nixon might be able to explain some of the tape away to minimize some of the damage, "but I have no idea what the full effect will be."

Haig said he did not think Nixon was focused on the importance of the tapes.

"But the President reviewed those conversations on Monday, May 6—after I offered to drop my subpoena if you would deliver just eighteen of the tapes," Jaworski said. "Isn't that true?"

"That's correct," Haig said. St. Clair agreed.

Then, Jaworski said, Nixon had to know what was in the tapes.

St. Clair said he was getting the tapes to Judge John Sirica.

Haig jumped in. "I'm particularly anxious that you believe me, Leon," he said. "I didn't know what was in those conversations."

"I remember, Al, that you told me you couldn't see why I wanted those tapes because there wasn't anything of value in them," Jaworski said.

"That's right," Haig responded. "And that's what I believed!"[16]

Somehow, Haig got word of his ignorance of the tape to the press, too. The *Times* reported that Haig and St. Clair learned about the tape over the weekend, which, of course, was untrue.[17] By his own admission, Haig had known about the tape at least by July 24. In reality, he had known for more than a year, but he, too, would face possible obstruction of justice charges if it was revealed that he knew the truth about Nixon and declined to tell authorities. So he kept up the fiction that he, the architect of Nixon's defense and the de facto president for the last fifteen months, had been in the dark. Jaworski had to be skeptical of Haig's claims of ignorance. In July he told Joseph Califano, Haig's friend and advisor, that Haig's defense of Nixon was pushing him close to obstruction of justice charges. After all, Haig controlled the White House. He had picked an old associate, Buzhardt, as Nixon's chief Watergate defender. He had unfettered access to the tapes and knew they existed two months before Butterfield told the Senate about them. Haig prevented St. Clair and his defense team from access to the tapes. No one had more access to the evidence that would prove Nixon's guilt or innocence. No one had more influence over Nixon's defense.

It is possible that Jaworski knew all along what was on those conversations, given the circumstances under which he was hired. His cooperation with Haig throughout his tenure as special prosecutor focused on Nixon and getting him out of office. No longer did Haig have to worry about the prosecution team ranging far afield and stumbling onto his connection to the wiretaps and the spy ring.

Ford returned to Washington at 2:45 p.m., and Haig went to see him immediately. "He looked more haggard than he had before, and I remember thinking that I'd never seen a man so physically and emotionally drained," Ford wrote of Haig, who told Ford that Nixon was releasing the June 23 transcript. Haig continued, telling Ford that most Nixon aides wanted him to resign, while a core group, mostly his family, wanted him to fight. Nixon, according to Haig, wavered between the two options. "I can't tell you with any certainty what's going to happen in the next seventy-two hours," Haig said. "I don't know myself. It could go either way."[18]

Whatever Nixon had dreamed of when he allowed the release of the smoking gun tape did not happen. His closest allies ran to the exits. Griffin called for Nixon to resign. Charles Wiggins of California, one of

Nixon's staunchest defenders on the Judiciary Committee, said he would vote to impeach him.[19]

Amid the frenzy of August 6, as Nixon convened his cabinet and vowed to remain until the bitter end, the Senate Foreign Relations Committee voted unanimously to clear Kissinger of possible perjury about his role in the FBI wiretaps, declaring, "There are no contradictions between what Dr. Kissinger told the committee last year and the totality of the new information available." "He is needed," said Senator Hubert Humphrey of Minnesota. "His role is good. He's a tremendous national asset."[20] It was almost a willful sense of denial, but in the face of Nixon's inevitable departure and replacement by Ford, Kissinger offered the one source of stability for the future. He had to remain.

Not satisfied with engineering a pardon for Nixon, Haig spent much of August 7 working to get pardons for the president's top aides, who were either in prison already or facing certain conviction and imprisonment. Charles Colson, one of Haig's closest allies on Nixon's staff, received a call from his attorney, who told him Haig was talking to Ford "and getting pardons for everyone."[21] Haig met with Ford early in the morning of August 7, another meeting that went unrecorded in Ford's logs. He told Ford that it was time for him to prepare to be president. They worked out the details of the transition, and the issue of pardoning Nixon, while they said little about it publicly, remained fresh from the discussions on August 1. Just how many pardons would come remained unclear, but Colson and others believed they would get a reprieve. "It was not in the President's personal self-interest to walk out of the White House with his own pardon buttoned up but not that of his aides," Colson told reporter Seymour Hersh. "It wasn't just because the boss wouldn't want to leave the wounded on the battlefield, but also because he was worried about being torn up. They'd walk all over him."[22]

Haldeman thought Haig had engineered a pardon for him and everyone else. Haldeman called his former colleague John Ehrlichman and said it looked like they had a deal for pardons. Later in the day, he called Ehrlichman back and said Haig told him everything had collapsed. Hersh noted Haig's inconsistency. Colson certainly believed Haig was trying to get pardons, while Haig told Jaworski the next day that he had opposed them. Len Garment, one of Nixon's trusted advisors in the final days, argued vehemently against them, saying that pardoning Nixon himself would be acceptable but that leniency for all would be a "bizarre and unacceptable act."[23]

Ford knew his time was coming. He told the *Times* that day that he was prepared for whatever might occur. He declined to say whether he would name former New York governor Nelson Rockefeller as vice president, as his close friend Melvin Laird had already suggested.[24] The wily Laird, who had spied on Nixon while serving as his defense secretary and then covered up his spying with Haig and Buzhardt, was already working on a Ford administration before Nixon was even gone.

As Nixon pondered whether to resign, Washington simmered with speculation about his options for avoiding prosecution. Once he resigned, Congress could pass a resolution granting him immunity from prosecution. Many of Nixon's rivals wanted him out of office far more than they desired seeing him in prison. He could also grant himself a blanket pardon and then resign, or Ford, as the new president, could pardon Nixon. Haig had told Ford about all these options during their second meeting in August 1, but it was the final option—a pardon from Ford—that had the most momentum.

By the night of August 7 Haig knew that Nixon would announce his resignation the following evening. He scheduled a lunch at his home in northwest Washington with Jaworski. Haig told his sparring partner and frequent collaborator that Nixon would resign officially at noon on August 9. Part of the resignation would involve Nixon taking all of his documents to California with him, a deal that Jaworski reported to his subordinates would involve "no hanky-panky." There was no doubt that someone in the White House had tampered with the tapes, Haig told Jaworski, but he identified no suspects. He also said Nixon would not pardon any of his aides and that the president was not asking for any special treatment himself. But Nixon did not have to ask. Haig and Jaworski, either directly or through intermediaries such as Califano, had already done that for him. Haig then returned to the White House and told a nervous Nixon that he had nothing to fear from Jaworski because he could resign without fear of prosecution and could take his documents with him.[25]

As essentially the acting president for fifteen months, Haig knew better than anyone what lay hidden in Nixon's files. He knew what he had told Nixon in private and what others said about him, including in the military spy ring investigation. Those documents, which Haig and Buzhardt had kept from the Watergate defendants for their trials, were in danger of surfacing if they drifted from Nixon's control either to the incoming Ford team or, worse, to Jaworski and his band of ruthless prosecutors.

Nixon went on television from the Oval Office on August 8 and announced his resignation. "I would have preferred to carry through to the finish whatever the personal agony it would have involved," Nixon said, "and my family unanimously urged me to do so." But, he said, he realized he could not stay.[26] In less than twenty-four hours, it would all be over. The constant drama of new revelations, the fears that something new would appear and cast the president into another crisis, and the stress of new threats from outside would end for those remaining inside the White House.

Just hours before Nixon was scheduled to leave at noon on August 9, Jaworski met with his staff. He told them that Nixon would take "some things" with him and that Haig had said "there will be lawyers at San Clemente who will know about" the various requests by prosecutors for documents.[27]

Sweaty and nervous, his family crying as they stood beside him, Nixon addressed his staff in the White House East Room. He then walked through the crowd assembled on the South Lawn, followed his family aboard his military helicopter, turned in the doorway, and raised his arms over his head, making the V for Victory gesture that had become his trademark. He then ducked inside. That image, frozen in time by the legion of photographers capturing the moment, showed the relief on Nixon's face as he ended his turbulent presidency.

Minutes after Nixon flew away, first to Andrews Air Force Base and then aboard what was still Air Force One for a few more minutes, Ford took the oath of office and addressed the nation he now led. "Our Constitution works," he said. "Our great Republic is a government of laws and not of men. Here the people rule."[28] He then walked into what was now his office. Shortly afterward, an anonymous memo appeared asking Ford to acknowledge Haig's role as chief of staff.

Jerry Jones, one of Haig's closest deputies, called Haig an American hero for what he had done during the final days: "He held that government together. And he negotiated the deal with Jaworski. And he negotiated the deal with a somewhat perhaps, majorly incapacitated president. And he kept the train on the tracks. Al Haig, if he never did another thing in the history of the United States, he is absolutely a hero and should have been recognized as the hero he was."[29]

Nixon's final speech as president, a sad and moving talk to his White House staff, did not admit to any wrongdoing, which killed his chances at getting a resolution granting him immunity. Ford's new presidential staff also opposed a pardon. Jerry terHorst, Ford's press secretary, said in his first briefing that he did not see how Ford could pardon Nixon, basing his opinion mostly on what Ford had said during his confirmation hearings the previous winter.[30] But Nixon stepped aboard that helicopter on the White House's South Lawn expecting some kind of deal.

Nixon was gone, but Haig remained chief of staff and determined to shape the new Ford administration. He ordered Jones to write a memorandum for the new president, just hours into the world's most demanding job, that would give Haig the same control in the Ford White House that he had while working for the debilitated Nixon. "Haig had me stay up all night," Jones said, "writing for Ford a document which would outline to him how the White House should work, which was the strong chief of staff White House. Haig took it in the first or second day Ford was there, and ran that at Ford." But Ford was not as pliable as Nixon in his final months as president. "[Haig] went in there and he lost it, and he immediately resigned, and he told me that Ford said to him, 'Now Al, isn't that a little bit hasty?' He thought he had Ford needing him so badly that he could beat him. So what he did, when he did the resign bit that Kissinger always was pulling on Nixon," Jones said.[31]

In California a distressed Nixon, stripped of almost all vestiges of the power once at his disposal, fretted about his future. The initial comments from terHorst about Ford not granting Nixon a pardon worried the now ex-president. "The issue of, one of the things that got Nixon to step down, was that if he was impeached, he would lose his pension," Jones said in a 2009 oral history interview. "And so, if he resigned, he would keep his pension. That was one part of the deal. Then there was the question of would there be a trial post-resignation and would he be sent to jail. And he was sitting there caught on that one. 'Well, God, don't want to do that.' So, if I were guessing, what Haig says is, 'Hey, there's a deal here if you'll pardon him, he'll leave now so we don't have to go through all this.' Now, whether Vice President Ford said 'yes' or 'no,' whether Haig said it in those terms or not, my guess is he led Nixon to believe that Ford would save him. And whether Ford actually said he would do it or whether Haig read from their conversation that he would do it, I think Nixon thought so. Then we began to get the phone calls from San Clemente after Nixon was there and President Ford was in the office about, 'Where in the hell's my pardon?'" Haig received multiple calls, Jones said, because Nixon "was distressed and frantic."[32] In San Clemente, aide Steve Bull watched Nixon try to reach his former chief of staff and be left hanging: "I really lost it with Haig the day after Nixon resigned. It was in California. He put in a call to Al Haig, who was too busy getting ready for Gerald Ford's first social event at the White House to talk to him. Nixon no longer mattered to him."[33]

Haig knew the risks of having Nixon alone in California and facing potential prosecution, Jones said. Shortly after Nixon left, Haig called Jones to his office and asked, "Jerry, what do you think about a pardon?" Jones said Ford could not run the country with Nixon's uncertain fate looming over everything.[34]

Haig's version of the events tied to the pardon in August and September 1974 bears little resemblance to the accounts of the others involved. "Where Nixon's pardon was concerned, I played no role at all," Haig wrote in his memoirs. Like so many other passages in that book, *Inner*

Circles, it is a carefully crafted lie. "Certainly I never discussed the issue with Nixon, on the telephone or otherwise."[35]

While Nixon had gone, his files and tapes remained at the White House, and there was no consensus about what to do with them. Some members of Congress wanted the impeachment process continued, but House Judiciary Committee chairman Peter Rodino declined, saying the committee was not "an investigative body."[36] Others wanted the documents impounded by the National Archives. Nixon had other ideas. He wanted the documents with him in California, and Haig tried to get them. Shortly after Nixon left, Benton Becker, a lawyer who had helped Ford get through the confirmation hearings, saw a large truck being filled with boxes of Nixon's documents. He asked the air force officer supervising the work what was happening and then ordered him to stop. The officer declined, saying he was acting on Haig's orders. Becker confronted Haig and then went to Ford, who told Haig to stop the move.[37] Becker's quick reactions undoubtedly saved a vast trove of documents from destruction and stopped Haig's attempt to hinder future discoveries of his actions.

Nixon remained in San Clemente, but he lacked the papers and tapes he thought were his. He had to wait to see if Ford would follow through on the deal that Ford said he had never explicitly made but that Nixon thought he deserved.

Becker had stopped the loading of papers to be shipped to Nixon, but the issue of what to do with the documents continued to rage. In San Clemente, Nixon fumed, believing he had reached a deal with Jaworski through Haig that he would receive the documents. Nixon knew also that he faced indictment at any moment, and he needed the documents to prepare his defense. Nixon, influenced by Haig and Buzhardt, had denied that right to his subordinates who had been indicted, often by claiming national security. But Haig and Buzhardt wanted Nixon to have the documents in California, because giving the papers to him would get them out of Washington and the hands of people who might look at what Haig really knew, not his false claims to Jaworski. "Al Haig would have been most happy if all those tapes were out of the White House in the hands of Richard Nixon, presumably for some big bonfire in San

Clemente," Becker said. "Because in my view, Al Haig demonstrated, at least to me, in my view, that's what he really wanted."[38] On August 14 terHorst told the White House press corps that the agreement that made Nixon's resignation possible called for him to get his tapes and documents. Democrats and commentators immediately cried foul, demanding that the agreement be changed or killed entirely. The next day, terHorst recanted, saying the deal was off. Buzhardt, whose legal opinion was behind the deal, resigned immediately.[39]

Nixon declined mentally and physical over the next two weeks. The phlebitis that had so worried Haig and others left him weak and vulnerable. Those who saw the exiled president were struck by the thinness of his arms and legs and the depth of his depression. Nixon also knew he faced an imminent indictment from one of the grand juries working with Jaworski. He had narrowly evaded indictment with seven of his closest associates on March 1, and now, stripped of the protection of the presidency, he was exposed and deeply vulnerable.

Nixon kept in close touch with many of his former aides, including Len Garment, a former law partner. On August 27 Garment went to an unlikely advisor—Abe Fortas, the wily Memphis lawyer who was one of Lyndon Johnson's closest advisors, as well as a former Supreme Court justice whom Nixon had forced off the Court in 1969.[40] Fortas, however, knew the law and, even better, how Washington worked on its most fundamental levels. Garment said they needed to put Nixon out of his misery, and Fortas agreed. Garment then called Haig and asked if they could propose to Ford that he grant Nixon a pardon. "Yes," Haig said. "It's time to get something in."[41]

Meanwhile, Jaworski was talking to Nixon's new lawyer, Herbert "Jack" Miller, a former Maryland politician and a Republican, but one close to the Kennedy family and Democrats. His hiring gave the White House and prosecutors a new conduit through which they could deal with Nixon. His other legal advisors, Buzhardt and St. Clair, had remained at the White House with the new president and then left midway through August. Jaworski asked Miller if he would file an argument that Nixon could not receive a fair trial because of overwhelmingly adverse publicity. Jaworski did not want to indict Nixon and be blamed for doing something that would kill him. He knew just how bad Nixon's health was at the time.[42]

Jaworski's request to Miller was a setup. He knew Nixon could not get a fair trial anywhere in the United States. "I knew in my own mind that if an indictment were returned and the court asked me if I believed Nixon could receive a prompt, fair trial as guaranteed by the Constitution, I would have to answer, as an officer of the court, in the negative," Jaworski wrote. "If the question were then asked as to how long it would be before Nixon could be afforded his constitutional rights, I would have to say in fairness that I did not know."[43]

And did it even matter? Jaworski had accomplished what Nixon's enemies and some of the president's own staff wanted. Jaworski had forced Nixon to resign without compromising many of the national security secrets he and Haig valued. He did not feel compelled to put the ex-president in prison, and he certainly did not want him to die there.

By the week of August 28, Ford realized he had to do something. Whether this was part of a preapproved plan made to secure Nixon's resignation or not, Ford knew events were converging in a way that made a pardon inevitable. Jaworski had subpoenaed Nixon to testify in the cases against his seven former aides, but Nixon could not testify without access to his documents back in the White House. Ford thought those documents should belong to the government. His attorney general, William Saxbe, said tradition dictated that the documents were Nixon's property. A bill in the Senate by Birch Bayh, an Indiana Democrat, would deed them to the government if it was passed and signed by Ford in time. The momentum was pushing Ford toward a pardon.

On August 28 Garment passed Ford his memo supporting a pardon. "For President Ford to act on his own now would be strong and admirable, and would be so perceived once the first reaction from the media passed," Garment wrote. "There would be a national sigh of relief."[44]

Haig met with Ford while Garment and Philip Buchen, Ford's attorney, debated their next step. Haig, Ford said, was for the pardon, but he never overtly said so. He told Ford it was his decision, but their earlier meetings had led Ford to believe that Haig believed the pardon was the right thing to do. Haig then told Garment that the lawyers were going over his memo, which would delay any official decision. Garment thought Haig was signaling to him that the pardon was on its way.

Ford took another step to a pardon that evening in his first news conference. Asked if he would consider a pardon, Ford said, "Of course, I make the final decision. And until it gets to me, I make no commitment one way or the other. But I do have the right as president of the United States to make that decision."

Was he ruling it out?

"I am not ruling it out," Ford said. "It is an option and a proper option for any president."[45]

Ford returned to the Oval Office angry that so many questions dealt with Nixon and Watergate. He felt he would never be his own president if he did not resolve Nixon's fate. "The impending criminal prosecution of his predecessor held profound implications not only for Nixon and the cover-up defendants but also for Haig, Buzhardt, Kissinger, and everyone else with whom Nixon worked closely while and after the tape machines were running—including Ford," author Barry Werth wrote.[46] Ford had to find a way out of the worsening dilemma.

He needed his own secret conduit to Jaworski to determine what the special prosecutor had planned, Ford told Buchen. "Well, there is one person you can trust," Buchen answered. "How about my approaching Benton Becker?"[47]

Becker, a former member of the Kennedy Justice Department, had grown up in Washington and practiced law in Maryland. He had helped prepare Ford the previous fall for his vice presidential confirmation hearings, which was when he had first encountered Haig. Becker had told the chief of staff not to pass along to Ford confidential information from the FBI background checks. Becker had a healthy distrust of Haig based on that first encounter and on Haig's attempt earlier in August to hustle Nixon's papers and tapes back to San Clemente without Ford's knowledge or approval.

On August 29 Ford told Haig, Buchen, Hartmann, and Kissinger that he was inclined to offer Nixon a pardon. He swore them all to secrecy and instructed Buchen to tell Becker to find the legal precedents to justify it.

In a memorandum he wrote after Nixon's pardon, Becker said he went to his old law firm's library to start researching.[48] In the books of old Supreme Court decisions, he found a 1915 case, *George Burdick v. United States*, that provided the legal rationale he needed. Burdick, an editor for the *New York Tribune*, had published a series of stories about immigration and bribery in New York. A federal grand jury was investigating whether any Treasury Department officials were leaking information, and they subpoenaed Burdick, who refused to testify, citing his First Amendment free speech rights and Fifth Amendment right against self-incrimination. In order to eliminate the Fifth Amendment concerns, President Woodrow Wilson granted Burdick a pardon so that he would not be prosecuted for anything he said in court. Burdick refused, saying that accepting a pardon would mean acknowledging guilt, and he was not guilty of anything. The judge in the case jailed Burdick for contempt of court, and Burdick sued, taking the case to the Supreme Court, which ruled 8–0 in his favor. To be effective, Justice Joseph McKenna wrote, "a pardon ... must be accepted," because it "carries an imputation of guilt; acceptance a confession of it."[49] To Becker, that meant Nixon did not need to make any statement of contrition for his role in Watergate and the other offenses for which he almost impeached. He needed only to accept the pardon and its implicit acknowledgment that he was guilty.

On Labor Day, September 2, Buchen and Becker met with Ford and told him the legal support for a pardon.[50] Ford was no longer just considering a pardon; he wanted to do it, if he could. Becker and Buchen spent the rest of the day and the next trying to determine what they could do, and then they met on September 4 with Jack Miller, Nixon's new lawyer. In Miller's room in Washington's Jefferson Hotel, about four blocks north of the White House, Buchen told Miller about the pardon. At the top of their list was working out an agreement to give Nixon access to his papers without worrying that he would destroy them once they arrived in California. Meanwhile, Jaworski tasked his deputy, Henry Ruth, to research a pardon, and he produced a memo that showed ten possible violations of the law. But Ruth also concluded, as Jaworski had believed, that it would be more than a year before Nixon could face trial.[51]

Becker met with Ford and Haig around 4:00 p.m. on September 5 and reported the details of his meetings with Miller. Once again, Becker's account contradicts Haig's claim to have had no role in the pardon. "Near the end of the conversation," Becker wrote, "the President advised that the Bird had expressed concern for himself and others with regard to a public disclosure of all tapes." Becker said in 1992 that he referred to Kissinger in the memo as "the Bird" because he was not sure who would read the memo later. "Although not personally incriminating, those tapes were potentially embarrassing to individuals remaining in Washington after the Nixon resignation." Ford also told Becker, contrary to what Buchen had told him earlier, that any agreement with Nixon should keep the tapes secret for fifty years. Becker disagreed. Becker then flew to California, landing after midnight at the marine air base at El Toro. A car drove him to San Clemente, where he met with Ron Ziegler, who had been briefed on Becker's mission by Miller. Later, Becker realized that Haig had also briefed Ziegler by telephone, so Ziegler knew Ford wanted to pardon Nixon.

Armed with that information, Ziegler said, "I can tell you right now that President Nixon will make no statement of admission or complicity in return for a pardon from Jerry Ford."

Becker paused briefly, then said, "Mr. Ziegler, I've never been to San Clemente before and for that matter I don't work for the government, so I'm a bit confused. Can you tell me how to reach the Air Force pilot that brought me here, so that I could instruct him to take me back to Washington?"

A long silence followed.

"I'll also need a car and driver to take me back to El Toro," Becker said.

Miller, who was there with Ziegler, jumped in.

It was too late to talk about such important matters, Miller said. We should talk about them in the morning.

The meetings the following day, September 6, went better. Ziegler lost much of the agitated edge he had displayed the previous night. They neared a deal on the documents and the pardon. At one point that day, a reporter in Washington noticed that Becker was in San Clemente and asked Jerry terHorst why. TerHorst asked Buchen, who told him Becker was negotiating what to do with Nixon's documents.

The three negotiators reached the point of Nixon's statement. Ziegler handed Becker a document that blamed world pressure, Nixon's overreliance on his staff, and his focus on the United States' role in the world. He took no personal responsibility for anything. In response, Becker told Miller and Ziegler that Nixon would be better off with no statement at all. They finally got a statement in which Nixon said, "I was wrong in not dealing with Watergate more forthrightly and directly, particularly when it reached a judicial stage." That, Becker believed, was "an acknowledgment of obstruction of justice by President Nixon."

Ziegler then ushered Becker into Nixon's office. Becker, who had never met Nixon before, was shocked. The president's arms and legs were so thin that they made his head look disproportionately larger than the rest of his body. "He was old," Becker wrote. His jowls were larger than life, his wrinkles like canyons. Nixon's attention focused, then drifted away. Uncomfortable with the pardon, he tried small talk, asking Becker how well he thought the Redskins would do in the upcoming season. Nixon wanted to give Becker a souvenir, but he had none left. Finally, Nixon reached into a drawer and pulled out two small white boxes. One contained a signed presidential tie pin, while the other held two cuff links. "From my personal jewelry box," Nixon told Becker. "I thanked him and took the boxes noting that he was inches away from tears," Becker wrote.

Becker flew back to Washington, arriving there at 5:00 a.m. on Saturday, September 7. He met with Ford that day. Becker also talked to Haig, who read the proposed statement from Nixon and asked Becker if he had "put a gun to President Nixon's head. To Al Haig that acknowledgment by President Nixon represented an admission far beyond any statement of contrition or complicity that he had heretofore made."[52]

At noon on Sunday, September 8, Ford said he would pardon Nixon. "During this long period of delay and potential litigation, ugly passions would again be aroused, our people would again be polarized in their opinions, and the credibility of our free institutions of government would again be challenged at home and abroad," Ford said on television from the White House.[53] He then left the White House to play golf.

The initial reaction was terrible; phone calls to the White House were immediate and outraged. Many Democrats and commentators thought Ford had allowed Nixon to wriggle out of justice. Haig was relieved. So too was Kissinger. TerHorst resigned in protest, no doubt angry that he had been lied to.[54] One month into his presidency, Ford had a crisis.

For Haig, however, it was mission accomplished. He had shepherded Nixon from office, a resolution that Haig had attempted to hasten months earlier but one that left him free of exposure of the criminal problems that had plagued many of his colleagues from the White House. Fifteen months earlier, Haig had left the army to help Nixon at the White House. He knew of Nixon's guilt almost from the beginning and had obstructed justice by not disclosing that guilt to the prosecutors. Haig compounded that obstruction by engineering a continued cover-up of the military spy ring through misleading stories by his collaborator Bob Woodward at the *Washington Post* and with Fred Buzhardt, his hand-picked attorney to handle Watergate issues. He gave false information about the spy ring to Leon Jaworski, who helped him protect alleged national security secrets as he bore down on Nixon. Haig had forced Spiro Agnew to resign as vice president, engineered the selection of Gerald Ford to replace him, worsened Nixon's political problems through the Saturday Night Massacre (disclosures about erased or missing White House tapes), and eventually left Nixon exposed and with no options other than to resign. Jerry Jones, Haig's former aide, was right: Haig had done a masterful job in Nixon's final months in office, but it was all in service of himself and his ambition.

18 After Nixon

After a formal dinner at the British Embassy, the tuxedo-clad Alexander Haig arrived at his northwest Washington home and retired to his office shortly before midnight on September 10, 1974. He soon had two visitors, Bob Woodward and Carl Bernstein of the *Washington Post*, the reporters who had helped fuel the political crisis that forced Nixon to resign the previous month. Their book, *All the President's Men*, had been published a few months earlier to popular acclaim, and they wanted their encore to chronicle the unraveling of the Nixon administration. They looked for guidance to Haig, who had steered the White House through the Watergate scandal and emerged with much of his reputation still intact.

Haig sat lighting his Marlboro Lights with a "zippo-type lighter with large flame," and chain smoking, Woodward wrote in his notes that have never been printed before. Haig's son, Alex, brought the two reporters in to see Haig, who had helped engineer the pardon of Nixon by his successor, new President Gerald Ford, the former Republican House leader Haig had helped pick. It was the first time he had met either man, Haig would claim.

That was a lie.

When Woodward and Bernstein's book, *The Final Days*, was published in 1976, Haig claimed he did not cooperate with them.

That, too, was a lie.

For more than an hour, well past midnight on September 11, Haig spilled forth details of his experience in the Nixon White House, the guilt of the president he had served since 1969, and the need to get Nixon to leave office. He knew "from the beginning . . . the inevitability of Nixon's leaving office prematurely—'from the day I came over.'"[1] Haig actually knew much earlier. As Nixon's deputy national security advisor, he had helped the president spy on members of his own administration through illegal surveillance measures, including wiretaps by the FBI, and had helped Pentagon leaders spy on Nixon, an act that the president would call "a federal offense of the highest order."[2]

Haig, the devoted military man and patriot, had forced the president he had sworn to serve from office. Now, joined by one of the men who had helped him through devastatingly well-timed reports in the press, he was shaping his cover-up. Haig's story, like so much of what he would say or write in the remaining thirty-five years of his life, was a series of interconnected falsehoods designed to hide what he had done and shift the blame to others.

Haig had known Woodward since at least 1969, when the reporter was a navy lieutenant tasked with delivering secret messages from the Pentagon to Haig at the National Security Council offices in the White House basement. Woodward had briefed Haig on military developments and issues critical to the Pentagon, according to three of the people who either sent Woodward there or knew about it: Adm. Thomas Moorer, the chairman of the Joint Chiefs of Staff and Woodward's boss; Defense Secretary Melvin Laird; and Jerry Friedheim, Laird's spokesman. Both Haig and Woodward would deny the relationship at the time, but, as with Haig's claims about *The Final Days*, that was a lie.[3]

Not only did Haig know Woodward well enough to meet with him and Bernstein at his home, he knew Woodward well enough to guide him in putting together their new book, which, Haig told them, "can't deal with only [the] last days, [but] must go back to the last 15 months" specifically Haig's time as chief of staff. That time, Haig said, brought "one shock after another until nothing surprised us."

In what he described as a "self-serving" account, Haig saw his role as preserving the functions of key government institutions as he handled Nixon and coaxed him from office. Haig told of a president consistently at odds with reality, no more so than in the last ten days of his administration, when he and his staff were confronted with the so-called smoking gun tape from June 23, 1972, in which Nixon and his former chief of staff, H. R. "Bob" Haldeman, discussed using the CIA to block the FBI's investigation of the Watergate break-in. "'You only had to read [the transcript] once' to know it was all over," Haig said. But Nixon tried to explain it away, Haig said, by claiming that the details of the tape had been testified to before the Senate and that he had followed up ten days later by telling acting FBI director L. Patrick Gray that he should "conduct a full investigation" of the break-in. Haig said he "really had to push Nixon to get it to sink in. 'I had to say goddamnit'" to the president. That's when, Haig continued, Nixon said he knew he had to resign.

Haig worried about Nixon's mental health during the final two weeks, including the possibility that the president would try to kill himself. "'Yeah, Nixon talked about death, especially in the last week,'" Haig said. "'You fellows in your business have a way of handling problems like this,'" Haig quoted Nixon as saying. "'Somebody leaves a pistol in the drawer. I don't have a pistol.'" Haig had Nixon's doctors remove all of the president's pills in case Nixon decided to check out that way. "I told the doctor, 'no pills,'" Haig said, adding that this was the worst moment and that Nixon's mental state was up and down.[4] Haig's revelation about Nixon and pills proved to be one of the most remarkable revelations in *The Final Days*, and Haig was the sole, although unidentified, source. The quote from the interview with Woodward and Bernstein on September 10, 1974, about the pistol appears verbatim in *The Final Days*.[5]

The man who arrived at the White House in January 1969 as an unheralded colonel and rose to a four-star general in just four years presented his patron as an impatient man who often veered out of control. Haig wanted to distance himself from Nixon. He told the reporters about Nixon's "disciplined" mind, which was "very compartmentalized," although Haig indicated that that was "not the best thing in the world." Nixon, Haig said, often isolated himself in anguish and was very impatient. "Nixon would say 'I want this I want that now,'" Haig said. Virtually every day, Nixon asked Haig to do "immoral or improper things," which Haig said he would either ignore or give lip service to. He would come back to Nixon later in the day and say, "'You didn't mean that.'" Some of that, Haig added, happens in any organization. Did Nixon ever ask Haig to do anything that would have put him in the Watergate conspiracy? Woodward asked. Haig was vague, because, he said, Nixon "probably doesn't think he was guilty of anything." Instead, Haig said, Nixon had a "death wish" that he brought on by tempting fate and his enemies. Haig agreed with the "characterization of almost vindication in the posse finally coming to get him."

Haig came close to saying that Nixon was "crazy outright," but then he pulled back, adding that the most important thing was to "restore confidence in leadership." Some details should not "come out right away" and maybe not for years. Was Haig actually the president for ten months, the reporters asked him? Haig "smiled, put his finger over [his] mouth and said, 'I won't talk about that.'" But Haig made his point without saying anything and guided the reporters to what he hoped would be their conclusion: "'The American people do eventually have a right to know.'"

Throughout the eighty minutes Woodward and Bernstein spent with Haig, ending shortly before 1:00 a.m., Haig did his best to show Nixon's instability while justifying his own actions, such as increasing the nation's nuclear alert during the October 1973 Yom Kippur War between Israel, Egypt, and Syria. "The Mid East alert was very real," Haig told the reporters. They even underplayed the threat from the Soviet Union, Haig said, because the Russians were prepared to move seven divisions of troops into the area, a claim not supported by the facts. He and Henry Kissinger did not usurp control from Nixon, who Haig insisted was informed of each step. Kissinger, Haig claimed, wanted to call a National Security Council meeting at the State Department until Haig stepped in. "I said, 'Henry, it'll be in the situation room of the White House,'" Haig told the two reporters. "Then Henry called the president. We both got guidance from the president." That was an exaggeration, if not an outright lie. Nixon was incapacitated or asleep most of the evening. The threat of a nuclear exchange in October 1973, Haig claimed, surpassed even that of the Cuban Missile Crisis of October 1962.

Haig did not know at the time that the details of the meeting that led to the nuclear alert would become public and contradict virtually everything he told Woodward and Bernstein. No, Haig and Kissinger did not keep Nixon up to speed about the meeting. When Kissinger asked Haig shortly before the principals convened if they should call Nixon, Haig said no. Haig would write in his memoirs that Nixon waited anxiously in the Oval Office for the meeting's outcome. In reality, the president was asleep in his residence at the White House.[6]

The Haig who met with Woodward and Bernstein that night in September 1974 was no reluctant source. Haig spent much of the meeting setting up what would be the premise of *The Final Days*. He repeatedly told Woodward and Bernstein that Nixon resembled Captain Queeg from the World War II classic *The Caine Mutiny*. The political system, Haig insisted, was flawed, and Nixon was a representative of it, not an aberration. He complained that a military man such as himself would not be permitted by the system to run for president. His motivation in becoming chief of staff, Haig claimed, "was to save the office." He was following precedents going back to the Civil War of "military men coming in to help straighten things out in crises."

Bernstein, who knew little about Haig's life before he was chief of staff, theorized that something "truly awful might be buried underneath [Watergate] that nobody ever wants to come out." Haig agreed, adding disingenuously that "'I kept looking for it,'" especially in the international and money areas, but that he could never find it. "'If it's there, I don't know about it,'" Haig claimed. Haig and Woodward knew how bogus that claim was. They had collaborated on some of the events the tuxedo-clad general was now recounting. Woodward had protected Haig when a military spy ring at the White House was first disclosed in January 1974. Woodward had served under Rear Adm. Robert Welander, the Pentagon's liaison with the National Security Council who had been implicated in the spy ring. The real secrets Nixon, Haig, and others were hiding were the unprecedented steps Nixon had taken to consolidate power in the White House, an effort in which Haig was an early and enthusiastic enabler. Haig, however, was not selling that story. He now needed to preserve his reputation, and in Woodward, whom he had used before, he had an ambitious and willing collaborator.

Haig, Woodward's notes show, "kept getting back to the idea in one way or another of how extraordinary the 15 months were and how really out of hand Nixon was, how he had to be watched." There was an implied agreement between Haig, Kissinger, and the White House lawyers to "talk to each other and make sure Nixon didn't do anything crazy." Haig told the two eager reporters that he had "extensive notes" to document his story and "can reconstruct everything."[7]

For the two journalists preparing to write a book about the end of the Nixon presidency, Haig provided a clear direction for how to uncover what had happened and portrayed a White House that threatened to careen out of control if someone, specifically Haig, had not saved the day. Readers of *The Final Days* did not miss Haig's hand; the book presented the general as the one person who maintained stability as Nixon wandered drunkenly around the White House or hid out in Key Biscayne or San Clemente. Haig, however, took great pains to deny helping Woodward and Bernstein. Shortly after the book's publication, he cabled Nixon and said, "I . . . want to reassure you that I have not contributed in any way to the book." Haig wrote another friend that "I have steadfastly declined to contribute to any post mortems which in my view would never be objectively viewed in the current environment." Finally, Haig wrote Victor Lasky, a conservative writer critical of *The Final Days*, to "assure you personally that I did not contribute to the contents of the book despite repeated efforts by the author to get me to do so. Mr. Woodward even traveled to Europe where in the presence of a note-taking witness, I declined any comment in any way on the last days of the Nixon presidency."[8] Following the 1991 publication of *Silent Coup* by Len Colodny and Robert Gettlin, which detailed Woodward's extensive relationship with Haig, the general devoted a section of his 1992 memoirs to denying the relationship with Woodward. "In fact, I met Woodward and Bernstein for the first time in the late summer of 1974, a month or so after Nixon resigned as President," Haig wrote in *Inner Circles*. Haig encountered them outside his home when he arrived there after a dinner; Woodward's notes show that Haig's son greeted them. "They were looking for confirmation of a report that I had issued orders to the White House medical staff in the closing days of the resignation crisis to keep a close watch on the disheartened president in case he should try to harm himself by taking an overdose of prescription pills. I told them I could not provide information for their newspaper, but we chatted in a desultory way for an hour or so. It was a civil encounter." Haig continued by writing that he had talked to Woodward in the days leading up to the publication of his memoirs and that the reporter "assured me that this conversation was helpful to him and his partner in their effort to understand the Watergate affair. From what I remembered of what was said, I was surprised that this should be so."[9]

As he did while he was in the White House and afterward, Haig was covering his tracks. Woodward's notes show that he confirmed the account of Haig limiting Nixon's access to prescription pills, and during the interview Haig did not say that he would not comment for the newspaper. Haig's revelation about the pills was one of the main pieces of news in *The Final Days*. The notes also indicate why Woodward and Bernstein would have found Haig's comments helpful; the general had advised them on the structure of their book, said he had documents that would back up his claims, and promised the reporters access to those documents. And when the book was published, it was Haig, who had steadily pushed the president toward his exile in California, whose reputation was the most intact.

Shortly after the interview, Haig received his chance to leave politics to return to the army. On September 4 Gen. Creighton Abrams, a legendary World War II tank commander and the most successful U.S.

commander in Vietnam, succumbed to cancer. He was the army chief of staff, the service's highest-ranking officer, and if Haig had remained in the army, he would have been the logical choice to succeed Abrams. But Ford realized that the events of the last sixteen months—Haig's tenure as chief of staff for both Nixon and Ford and his prominence at the bitter end of the Nixon presidency—made it virtually impossible for Haig to survive a Senate confirmation battle. Haig knew it, too. The army did not need the politics of a confirmation battle in the wake of Nixon's administration, and neither did the new Ford administration. There was a neat alternative, however, that did not require Senate confirmation. Secretary of State Henry Kissinger and Defense Secretary James Schlesinger had discussed it during one of their breakfast meetings earlier in the year: supreme commander of Allied forces in Europe. Based in Brussels, Belgium, the job meant commanding all the troops that were part of the North Atlantic Treaty Organization force in Europe. While it was not the top spot in the army, it carried tremendous visibility and history— Dwight Eisenhower, before he was elected president, had been the first NATO commander. Ford named Haig to the job on September 15 and replaced him with another young, ambitious player, Donald Rumsfeld, former House member, head of Nixon's Office of Economic Opportunity, and recently departed U.S. ambassador to NATO.[10]

But just before Haig was scheduled to leave in October, Buzhardt called Haig with a warning, Haig wrote in his memoirs. Ford had agreed to testify before the House Judiciary Committee in October about the events leading up to the Nixon pardon amid concerns that he and Nixon had cut a deal. Buzhardt told Haig that Ford's staff had prepared testimony for him that "could very well result in your indictment."

Haig rushed to the White House and confronted White House counsel Philip Buchen and John Marsh, another top Ford aide. He demanded to see Ford immediately. They told him Ford was busy. Haig repeated his demand and threatened to reveal how Ford's associates had worked to push Nixon out, including Senator Robert Griffin's August 3 letter, which mentioned that Nixon had lost support; the appointment of Albert Jenner as the minority counsel to the House Judiciary Committee; and "a good many other things we all know occurred as part of a secret effort by Ford people to hurry Nixon out of the presidency behind Jerry Ford's back."[11] Such a claim by Haig is laughable. His legal advisor, Morris Leibman, had been responsible for the selection of Jenner as the minority counsel, while it was Haig, not Ford's allies, who had pushed Nixon out the door.

Buchen and Marsh let Haig in to see Ford, and Haig told Ford that all he wanted from the president was for him to tell the truth about the pardon. Ford said he would, and Haig later pronounced Ford's testimony to be truthful.[12] Haig went to Brussels unscathed.

Haig's denials about cooperating with Woodward and Bernstein make even less sense when they are compared to another record of Haig's contacts with Woodward during the time he and Bernstein were writing *The Final Days*. On December 18, 1975, the duo had a front-page story in the *Washington Post* challenging Ford's denials that he had cut a deal with Nixon to resign in exchange for a pardon. Haig, then in Brussels, was quoted throughout the report, which referenced an interview on December 17 and another three months earlier. "Until yesterday, Haig had never specifically said publicly whether he and President Ford discussed the question of a pardon for Nixon," the story said.[13] Haig, who had helped Woodward and Bernstein shape *The Final Days*, was still shaping their account of the end of the Nixon administration.

Haig's tenure at NATO came as the military endured its nadir following the end of the Vietnam War in 1975. He maintained a high visibility, and the position enabled him to stay in touch with the world leaders with whom he had developed relationships while serving Nixon. His term ended in 1979, and there were no other jobs open to him. Ford had lost the 1976 election to Democrat Jimmy Carter, and while Carter had kept Haig at NATO, he would not give Haig, a legacy of the deeply troubled Nixon administration, another top post in the military. He retired from the army in 1979 and became the chief executive officer of United Technologies, a giant defense contractor.

Carter's defeat by Republican Ronald Reagan in 1980 presented Haig with a new opportunity. Reagan, the former governor of California, had no foreign policy experience and no real candidates to fill the open job of secretary of state. Richard Allen, the former Nixon foreign policy aide, had counseled Reagan, too, but he was slotted to be Reagan's national security advisor. Henry Kissinger wanted another chance at the job he had held for Nixon and Ford, but he was too tainted by his association with détente for the tastes of the conservative Reagan. Haig, with his years at the NSC, inside the West Wing, and at NATO, presented an appealing choice, and Reagan nominated him in December.

Haig faced Senate confirmation hearings, the same challenge that had kept him from becoming army chief of staff six years earlier. Although the Republicans had captured the Senate in the 1980 elections, he still had to navigate a Senate Foreign Relations Committee filled with potential antagonists. Almost immediately, committee members said they wanted access to Nixon's White House tapes, which Haig had tried to spirit away from the White House just hours after Nixon resigned and fled to California.

To guide him through the confirmation fight, Haig turned to his former boss at the Pentagon during the Kennedy and Johnson administrations: Joseph Califano, who had advised Haig unofficially while Haig was Nixon's chief of staff, helping Haig engineer a claim of executive privilege when called before the Senate Watergate committee, and then greasing a path for Nixon's pardon. Califano was one of Washington's most connected lawyers. He had represented the Democratic Party in its lawsuit against Nixon's campaign following the Watergate break-in and the *Washington Post*. After Carter's election, Califano served as the secretary of health, education, and welfare before leaving in 1979. He prepared Haig thoroughly for his hearings and fought the committee's attempts to get the tapes.[14]

Also helping Haig was a more unlikely defender on the surface: Woodward. One half of the duo riding high for helping to expose Nixon was also, unbeknownst to most Americans, a longtime friend of Haig. Woodward wrote a column in the *Post* arguing that the committee did not need to hear the tapes or read more transcripts. The committee, he wrote, should "forget about obtaining any of the Nixon tapes." Anything Haig said, Woodward continued, was meant to placate Nixon, and if

Haig had to be held to account, "let it happen without the tapes."[15] The committee backed down.

Woodward's intervention was stunning. He gave no indication in his column that he had known Haig since his days as a young navy lieutenant delivering messages to Haig at the NSC for his boss, Adm. Thomas Moorer, the chief of naval operations and then the chairman of the Joint Chiefs of Staff. Woodward also mentioned nothing about his cover-up for another former commander, Welander. Seven years earlier, Woodward's articles for the *Post* about the spy ring also failed to include that he had worked for both Moorer and Welander. His op-ed for Haig followed the same pattern. Woodward had used his journalistic celebrity to protect a source and a patron while keeping his readers in the dark.

Haig's nomination, despite the popularity of the incoming Reagan, would have exploded if the committee had had access to the tapes and performed even the mildest due diligence. Senators could have heard Nixon's correct suspicion that Haig had aided the military spy ring stealing secrets from inside the White House or heard the tape of Nixon, Bob Haldeman, and Haig discussing the White House's attempts to have the CIA block the FBI's Watergate investigation. They would have known that Haig had obstructed justice by sitting on that secret for fifteen months. A legitimate Foreign Relations Committee investigation would have exhumed these and other details embarrassing to not only Haig but also Kissinger. Haig had evaded discovery again, and the full Senate confirmed Haig, 93–6, the day after Reagan was sworn in.[16]

Four years spent watching Kissinger and William Rogers, Nixon's first secretary of state, fight for control of foreign policy had made Haig wary of internal turf battles. He knew that a national security advisor with constant access to the president could sideline any cabinet member, even one at the State Department, so he crafted a plan that would put him at the top of the national security pyramid and presented it to Reagan, whose three top aides—James Baker, Edwin Meese, and Michael Deaver—recoiled. They would not allow Reagan to be boxed in by an outsider, Haig, who was so firmly identified with Nixon and seen as a power grabber. They rejected the plan.[17]

Reagan had also picked some longtime Haig rivals for key cabinet slots. The CIA would be led by William Casey, Nixon's head of the Securities and Exchange Commission, whom Haig had blackballed as a candidate to lead the agency in May 1973. Allen, who had worked with Haig in Nixon's NSC, was Reagan's national security advisor. Haig's deputy at State was William Clark, a longtime Reagan aide from California and a former judge. He would be Reagan's man inside the State Department, watching Haig as only a Reagan loyalist could do.

Haig ran an open shop at State, Clark said, and he was a good boss. But the open-door policy ended when certain visitors came to Foggy Bottom. "While he would be talking to Bob Woodward or the press or someone over breakfast, I always led the staff meetings across the hall," Clark said. "I encouraged him over and over again to come in and at least make an appearance, so they could see that he was alive and well and in command. . . . Al always wanted me to know that his door was open to me at any time and any meeting, and he wanted me to be part of any meeting except Woodward and a few other people, press people, with whom he had developed relationships over the years."[18]

Despite what Haig's associates at State and elsewhere noted as a close relationship with Woodward, neither Haig nor Woodward could get their stories straight about when they first met. They both denied they knew what others such as Melvin Laird and Moorer confirmed—that Woodward and Haig knew each other while Woodward served in the navy. Haig said he did not meet Woodward until he and Bernstein showed up at Haig's home in September 1974, while Woodward put the date some-time in early 1973. Given Woodward's long service on Haig's behalf as a journalist—covering up the spy ring, hiding Woodward's relationship with the military's top officers, masking Haig's identity as a source in *All the President's Men*, and writing a helpful column to push Haig over the hump in the Foreign Relations Committee—their protestations ring hollow. The close relationship between Haig and Woodward that Clark noted at State was no accident and no recent occurrence.

Haig eventually wore out his welcome in Reagan's cabinet. After Haig made one too many threats to resign, Reagan accepted Haig's resignation, before it had been offered, on June 14, 1982. It was the last time Haig would serve in government.

During the last twenty-eight years of his life, Haig would make a failed attempt at the Republican nomination for president in 1988, dropping out before the New Hampshire primary. In the 1990s Haig ran his own consulting company in Washington, where he represented some of the world's rogue regimes. In 1992 he published his memoirs, *Inner Circles: How America Changed the World*. Haig tried to offer a glimpse into his career and the people who influenced him—Gen. Douglas MacArthur, Joseph Califano, Robert McNamara, Henry Kissinger, and Richard Nixon. As has been shown multiple times here, the book is stunning in its attempts to reshape history and mislead readers. Haig lied about when he knew about the White House tapes, how he first tried to help Spiro Agnew and then pushed him to resign, how he covered up what he knew about the FBI wiretaps, and finally his involvement in the military spy ring. Historians who use *Inner Circles* as a guide to what happened during the Nixon administration will be led into a maze of Haig's making that leads far from the truth.

Alexander M. Haig Jr. traced a career arc that stretched from the end of World War II to Korea, Vietnam, the White House, and the State Department. He saw Nixon's restructuring from the inside and witnessed what Attorney General John Mitchell called the "White House horrors." When Nixon was forced to find a replacement for H. R. Haldeman and John Ehrlichman at his side in the White House, Haig was the only logical choice. From that moment on, Nixon's chances for survival, which was an open question on May 3, 1973, became impossible. No one did more to force Nixon from office than Haig. Haig's coup, however, was not made for policy reasons but for self-preservation. Until the day he died on February 20, 2010, Haig succeeded not only in removing Nixon from office but in covering his own tracks.

There is a tremendous trove of available research on the Nixon administration and the activities of Alexander Haig. Most of the White House tapes collected by the Richard Nixon Presidential Library and Museum are available to listen to online, and others are available at the website of the Miller Center at the University of Virginia. They enabled me to listen to and transcribe the taped interviews. In other cases, the tapes were transcribed by historians Douglas Brinkley and Luke Nichter for their two books about the Nixon tapes. I used those transcripts and matched them with the tapes, when available. In some cases, I used the transcripts in Stanley Kutler's *Abuse of Power*, but in many instances, the transcripts were incomplete. As an editor at the *Tampa Tribune* in 1997, I supervised the reporting of an article that demonstrated that Kutler's transcripts were out of order, particularly those about the March 1973 conversations between Richard Nixon and John Dean. Kutler denied that had occurred, but he eventually acknowledged it in a 2009 *New York Times* article. As a result, I have cited his transcripts as a last resort and only in limited instances.

As often as possible, I have include URLs to guide researchers to the online locations of these documents. In the case of interviews with the Colodny Collection at Texas A&M University, the website and search functions are not complete. I obtained those interviews from author Len Colodny personally and have confirmed with Texas A&M officials that they are indeed in his collection. Luke Nichter at Texas A&M is an inexhaustible source of documents through his research. In some cases, he provided me information he obtained through Freedom of Information Act requests.

I accessed the Bob Woodward and Carl Bernstein Papers at the Harry Ransom Center at the University of Texas by using the library's finding aid and then making a written request for the documents in a PDF document sent via email. The same is true for the Lowell Weicker Papers at the University of Virginia Library.

INTRODUCTION

1. Steven Weisman, "Bush Flies Back from Texas Set to Take Charge in Crisis," *New York Times*, March 31, 1981.

2. James Hohmann, "Alexander Haig, 85; Soldier-Statesman Managed Nixon Resignation," *Washington Post*, February 21, 2010.

3. Witcover quoted in Morris, *Haig*, 194–95.

4. Brinkley and Nichter, *The Nixon Tapes*, 327. See also Nixon, Ehrlichman, Haldeman, and Mitchell conversation, December 21, 1971, White House tape 639-30, Nixon Presidential Materials Staff: Tape Subject Log, 36–45, Richard Nixon Presidential Library and Museum (hereafter RNPLM), https://www.nixonlibrary.gov /forresearchers/find/tapes/finding_aids/tapesubjectlogs/oval639.pdf.

5. Alexander Haig, interview by Bob Woodward and Carl Bernstein, September 10, 1974, Series 1, Woodward, Subseries B, *The Final Days*, container 76.5, Woodward and Bernstein Watergate Papers, http://norman.hrc.utexas.edu/fasearch/findingAid .cfm?eadid=00365&kw=woodward.

1. THE MAKING OF ALEXANDER HAIG

1. Morris, *Haig*, 10.

2. Morris, *Haig*, 15, 16.

3. Morris, *Haig*, 28.

4. Morris, *Haig*, 61.

5. Woodward and Bernstein, *Final Days*, 74.

6. Califano, *Inside*, 116.

7. Walter Elder to William Colby, "Special Activities," June 1, 1973, "The Family Jewels," 468, Freedom of Information Act Reading Room, https://www.cia.gov/library /readingroom/collection/family-jewels.

8. Morris Leibman to J. Edgar Hoover, October 6, 1963, vol. 13, American Bar Association FBI Files.

9. Joseph Califano, interview by author, January 22, 2015.

10. William Sullivan to Alan Belmont, "Dr. Fritz G. A. Kraemer, Office of Chief of Staff," May 7, 1963, FBI Records.

11. Rogers, *Vietnam Studies*, 143.

12. Califano, interview by author.

13. Document 11, "National Security Decision Memorandum 2," January 20, 1969, in Humphrey and Miller, *Organization and Management*, 30–33.

14. Document 22, "Memorandum from the President's Military Assistant (Haig) to the President's Assistant for National Security Affairs (Kissinger)," Washington DC, February 7, 1969, in Humphrey and Miller, *Organization and Management*, 50–51.

15. General Earle Wheeler to Melvin Laird, "Japan Policy as Pertains to Okinawa Reversion," March 29, 1969, https://www.nixonlibrary.gov/virtuallibrary/releases /may15/okinawa02.pdf.

16. Charles Colson, interview by Len Colodny, October 2, 1989, transcript, Colodny Collection.

17. Hedrick Smith, "U.S. Perplexed by Okinawa Issue," *New York Times*, March 31, 1969.

18. Hersh, *Price of Power*, 88.

19. William Beecher, "Raids in Cambodia by U.S. Unprotested," *New York Times*, May 9, 1969.

20. Isaacson, *Kissinger*, 213.

21. Haig and McCarry, *Inner Circles*, 215.

22. Document 46, "Memorandum from the Assistant Director (Domestic Intelligence), Federal Bureau of Investigation (Sullivan) to the Director (Hoover), May 20, 1969," in Humphrey and Miller, *Organization and Management*, 134.

23. William Sullivan to C. D. DeLoach, "Black Bag Jobs," July 19, 1966, vol. 14, 77, FBI Surreptitious Entries Files, https://vault.fbi.gov/Surreptitious%20Entries%20 (Black%20Bag%20Jobs)%20/Surreptitious%20Entries%20(Black%20Bag%20Jobs) %20Part%2014%20of%2030.

24. Beverly Gage, "What an Uncensored Letter to M.L.K. Reveals," *New York Times*, November 11, 2014.

25. William Sullivan to Vernon Walters, "Personal and Confidential," February 6, 1973, https://www.cia.gov/library/readingroom/docs/CIA-RDP80R01731R002000050003 -6.pdf.

26. Novak, *The Prince of Darkness*, 208.

27. Hersh, *Price of Power*, 97.

28. E. S. Miller to Alex Rosen, "Sensitive Coverage Placed at Request of the White House," October 20, 1971, vol. 11, FBI William Sullivan Files, https://archive.org /details/foia_Sullivan_William_C._-11.

29. Thomas Moorer, interview by Robert Gettlin, October 4, 1989, transcript, Colodny Collection; Melvin Laird, interview by Robert Gettlin, September 5, 1990, Colodny Collection.

30. Moorer, interview by Gettlin.

31. Laird, interview by Gettlin.

32. Poole, *Joint Chiefs of Staff*, 8.

33. Dobrynin, *In Confidence*, 200.

34. U.S. Congress, Senate, Committee on Armed Services, *Transmittal of Documents, Part 3*, 45.

35. Van Atta, *With Honor*, 298.

36. Elmo Zumwalt, interview by Alfred Goldberg and Maurice Matloff, October 22, 1991, transcript, Historical Office of the Secretary of Defense, http://history.defense.gov/Portals/70/Documents/oral_history/OH_Trans_Zumwalt,%20Elmo%2010-22-1991.pdf?ver=2016-06-20-114138-600.

37. Document 42, "Memorandum of Conversation," Palm Springs, California, May 7, 1971, 2:50–5:45 p.m., in Smith, *South Asia Crisis*, 106–9.

38. Hersh, *Price of Power*, 110.

39. Neil Sheehan, "Vietnam Archive: Pentagon Study Traces 3 Decades of Growing U.S. Involvement," *New York Times*, June 13, 1971.

40. Brinkley and Nichter, *The Nixon Tapes*, 170–71; Haig and Nixon conversation, June 13, 1971, White House tape 5-50, RNPLM, https://millercenter.org/the-presidency/educational-resources/it-s-a-pentagon-study-huh.

41. The details of the contents of the Pentagon Papers, the creation of the White House Plumbers, and their activities were detailed in Lukas, *Nightmare*; Hersh, *Price of Power*; and Colodny and Gettlin, *Silent Coup*.

42. Jack Anderson, "U.S., Soviet Vessels in Bay of Bengal," *Washington Post*, December 14, 1971.

43. Brinkley and Nichter, *The Nixon Tapes*, 327; Nixon, Ehrlichman, Haldeman, and Mitchell conversation, December 21, 1971, White House tape 639-30, RNPLM.

44. Robert Welander, interview by John Ehrlichman and David Young, December 23, 1971, David R. Young, Staff Member and Office Files, box 18, folder 10, White House Special Files, RNPLM.

45. David Young to John Ehrlichman, "Meeting with Admiral Welander re Anderson Leak of December 14 and Subsequent Investigation," December 22, 1971, box 18, David R. Young Files, RNPLM, https://www.nixonlibrary.gov/forresearchers/find/textual/special/smof/young.php.

46. John Ehrlichman, interview by Len Colodny, September 18, 1990, transcript, Colodny Collection.

47. Laird, interview by Gettlin.

48. John Ehrlichman and Melvin Laird, telephone call, December 23, 1971, transcript, Colodny Collection.

49. W. Donald Stewart, interview with Len Colodny, October 28, 1986, transcript, Colodny Collection.

50. Clodfelter, *Vietnam in Military Statistics*, 224.

51. Lukas, *Nightmare*, 227–28.

52. Lukas, *Nightmare*, 252–56.

2. MAY 1973

1. Robert Semple Jr., "End of an Era in Nixon Presidency," *New York Times*, May 1, 1973.

2. Nixon and Haldeman conversation, May 2, 1973, White House tape 910-3, RNPLM, https://www.nixonlibrary.gov/forresearchers/find/tapes/tape910/910-003.mp3.

3. Haig and McCarry, *Inner Circles*, 332.

4. Haig and McCarry, *Inner Circles*, 286.

5. Nixon and Kissinger conversation, May 3, 1973, White House tape 911-1, RNPLM, https://www.nixonlibrary.gov/forresearchers/find/tapes/tape911/911-003.mp3.

6. Haig and McCarry, *Inner Circles*, 334.

7. Nixon and Haig conversation, May 3, 1973, White House tape 911-31, RNPLM, https://www.nixonlibrary.gov/forresearchers/find/tapes/tape9 11/911-031.mp3.

8. Bob Woodward and Carl Bernstein, "Wiretaps Put on Phones of 2 Reporters," *Washington Post*, May 3, 1973.

9. Woodward, *Secret Man*, 12.

10. Holland, *Leak*, 31.

11. Martin Arnold, "Ellsberg Judge Wants Hunt Data," *New York Times*, May 4, 1973.

12. Daniel Ellsberg was a former Pentagon consultant who worked at the RAND Corporation when it had a copy of a secret military history of the Vietnam War that detailed the multiple lies behind U.S. policy. With his colleague Anthony Russo, Ellsberg stole the documents from RAND, copied them, and gave them to the *New York Times*. The documents, which first appeared in June 1971, became known as the Pentagon Papers.

13. Bill Kovach, "Interim Choice," *New York Times*, May 5, 1973.

14. Nixon, *RN*, 857.

15. Haig and McCarry, *Inner Circles*, 338.

16. Kovach, "Interim Choice."

17. Marjorie Hunter, "4-Star Diplomat in White House," *New York Times*, May 5, 1973.

18. William Ruckelshaus to Mark Felt, "Wiretaps on Newspapermen," May 4, 1973, in "FBI Files," 11. http://www.paperlessarchives.com/FreeTitles/NixonJournalistsWiretapsFBIFiles.pdf.

19. O. T. Jacobson to Bucky Walters, "Wiretaps on Newspapermen," Robert Mardian interview, May 11, 1973, in "FBI Files."

20. Nixon and Haldeman conversation, October 19, 1972, White House tape 370-5, RNPLM, https://www.nixonlibrary.gov/forresearchers/find/tapes/tape370/370-009a.mp3.

21. Nixon and Colson conversation, February 13, 1973, White House tape 854-17, RNPLM, https://www.nixonlibrary.gov/forresearchers/find/tapes/tape854/854-017a.mp3.

22. Nixon, Ehrlichman, and Gray conversation, February 16, 1973, White House tape 858-3, RNPLM, https://www.nixonlibrary.gov/forresearchers/find/tapes/tape858/858-003.mp3.

23. Nixon and Dean conversation, February 27, 1973, White House tape 864-4, RNPLM, https://www.nixonlibrary.gov/forresearchers/find/tapes/tape864/864-004.mp3.

24. "John Dean Points a Finger," *Newsweek*, May 5, 1973.

25. Haig and McCarry, *Inner Circles*, 339.

26. Nick Thimmesch, "The Iron Mentor of the Pentagon," *Washington Post*, March 2, 1975.

27. Seymour Hersh, "Cushman Named," *New York Times*, May 7, 1973.

28. Haig and McCarry, *Inner Circles*, 345.

29. Nixon and Haig conversation, May 8, 1973, White House tape 913-8, RNPLM, https://www.nixonlibrary.gov/forresearchers/find/tapes/tape913/913-008.mp3.

30. Nixon and Haig conversation, May 8, 1973, White House tape 913-8.

31. Haig and McCarry, *Inner Circles*, 340.

32. Haig and McCarry, *Inner Circles*, 346.

33. Leonard Garment, interview by Robert Gettlin, October 4, 1989, transcript, Colodny Collection.

34. Nixon and Haig conversation, May 8, 1973, White House tape 433-73, RNPLM, https://www.nixonlibrary.gov/forresearchers/find/tapes/tape433/433-073.mp3.

35. Woodward, *The Last of the President's Men*, 77–78.

36. Nixon and Haig conversation, May 8, 1973, White House tape 433-73, RNPLM, https://www.nixonlibrary.gov/forresearchers/find/tapes/tape433/433-073.mp3.

37. Nixon and Dean conversation, March 13, 1973, White House tape 878-14, RNPLM, https://www.nixonlibrary.gov/forresearchers/find/tapes/tape878/878-014.mp3.

38. Haig, interview by Woodward and Bernstein, September 10, 1974.

39. Haig and McCarry, *Inner Circles*, 373.

40. Alexander Haig to Rembrandt Robinson, March 27, 1971, in U.S. Congress, Senate, Committee on Armed Services, *Transmittal of Documents, Part 2*, 81.

41. Nixon and Haig conversation, May 8, 1973, White House tape 433-73.

42. Holland, *Leak*, 6.

43. Marjorie Hunter, "CIA Head Admits 'Ill-Advised' Act," *New York Times*, May 10, 1973.

44. Colby and Forbath, *Honorable Men*, 338.

45. Elder to Colby, "Special Activities," June 1, 1973, 465. https://www.cia.gov/library/readingroom/collection/family-jewels.

46. Colby and Forbath, *Honorable Men*, 343.

47. Nixon, Buzhardt, and Haig conversation, May 9, 1973, White House tape 434-9, RNPLM, https://www.nixonlibrary.gov/forresearchers/find/tapes/tape434/434-009a.mp3.

48. Document 256, "Transcript of Telephone Conversation between President Nixon, His Assistant for National Security Affairs (Kissinger) and the Chairman of the Senate Armed Services Committee (Stennis)," April 24, 1970, 876-77, https://history.state.gov/historicaldocuments/frus1969-76v06/d256.

49. Nixon, Buzhardt, and Haig conversation, May 9, 1973, White House tape 434-9.

50. David E. Rosenbaum, "Senate Panel Contends Cox and Courts Have No Authority to Restrict Its Hearing," *New York Times*, June 8, 1973.

51. Nixon, Buzhardt, and Haig conversation, May 9, 1973, White House tape 434-9.

52. Nixon and Haig conversation, May 9, 1973, White House tape 45-185, https://www.nixonlibrary.gov/sites/default/files/forresearchers/find/tapes/tape045/045-185.mp3.

53. Colby and Forbath, *Honorable Men*, 344.

54. "Same Men, New Jobs," *New York Times*, May 12, 1973.

55. David E. Rosenbaum, "Richardson Feels He Was Betrayed," *New York Times*, May 11, 1973.

56. Nixon and Haig conversation, May 11, 1973, White House tape 916-11, RNPLM, https://www.nixonlibrary.gov/forresearchers/find/tapes/tape916/916-011.mp3.

57. Martin Arnold, "FBI Tap Picked Up Calls Ellsberg Made in 1969–70," *New York Times*, May 11, 1973.

58. Nixon and Haig conversation, May 11, 1973, White House tape 916-11.

59. John M. Crewdson, "'69 Phone Taps Reported on Newsmen at 3 Papers," *New York Times*, May 11, 1973.

60. Nixon and Haig conversation, May 11, 1973, White House tape 916-11.

61. Nixon and Kissinger conversation, May 11, 1973, White House tape 916-14, https://www.nixonlibrary.gov/forresearchers/find/tapes/tape916/916-014.mp3.

62. Nixon and Haig conversation, May 11, 1973, White House tape 916-6, RNPLM, https://www.nixonlibrary.gov/forresearchers/find/tapes/tape916/916-006.mp3.

63. Nixon and Haldeman conversation, June 23, 1972, White House tape 343-36, transcript, RNPLM, https://www.nixonlibrary.gov/forresearchers/find/tapes/watergate/trial/exhibit_01.pdf.

64. Nixon and Haig conversation, May 11, 1973, White House tape 916-11.

65. Nixon, Haldeman, and Haig conversation, May 11, 1973, White House tape 916-19, RNPLM, https://www.nixonlibrary.gov/forresearchers/find/tapes/tape916/916-019.mp3.

66. Nixon and Haig conversation, May 11, 1973, White House tape 916-11.

67. Marjorie Hunter, "Cushman Says Helms 'Assented' to CIA Aid to Hunt for Break-In on Coast," *New York Times*, May 12, 1973.

68. Martin Arnold, "New Trial Barred," *New York Times*, May 13, 1973.

69. Jacobson to Walters, "Wiretaps on Newspapermen," John Mitchell interview, 54, http://www.paperlessarchives.com/FreeTitles/NixonJournalistsWiretapsFBIFiles.pdf.

70. Jacobson to Walters, "Wiretaps on Newspapermen," Robert Mardian interview, 53, http://www.paperlessarchives.com/FreeTitles/NixonJournalistsWiretapsFBIFiles.pdf.

71. William C. Sullivan to William Ruckelshaus, "Sensitive Coverage Placed at Request of the White House," May 11, 1973, in "FBI Files," 50, http://www.paperlessarchives.com/FreeTitles/NixonJournalistsWiretapsFBIFiles.pdf.

72. O. T. Jacobson to Bucky Walters, "Wiretaps on Newspapermen," Alexander Haig interview, May 12, 1973, in "FBI Files," 76, http://www.paperlessarchives.com/FreeTitles/NixonJournalistsWiretapsFBIFiles.pdf.

73. Nixon and Haig conversation, May 11, 1973, White House tape 165-4, RNPLM, https://www.nixonlibrary.gov/forresearchers/find/tapes/tape165/165-004.mp3.

74. Nixon and Haig conversation, May 11, 1973, White House tape 165-4.

75. Nixon and Haig conversation, May 12, 1973, White House tape 165-19, RNPLM, https://www.nixonlibrary.gov/forresearchers/find/tapes/tape165/165-019.mp3.

76. Hersh, *Price of Power*, 400.

77. Seymour Hersh, "Dean Tied to Plan for Ring to Spy on 1972 Protests," *New York Times*, May 14, 1973.

78. Nixon and Haig conversation, May 13, 1973, White House tape 165-40, RNPLM, https://www.nixonlibrary.gov/forresearchers/find/tapes/tape165/165-040.mp3.

79. Nixon and Haig conversation, May 13, 1973, White House tape 165-40.

80. Holland, *Leak*, 6.

81. William Ruckelshaus, interview by Timothy Naftali, April 12, 2007, RNPLM, https://www.nixonlibrary.gov/virtuallibrary/documents/histories/ruckelshaus -2007-04-12.pdf.

82. Bob Woodward and Carl Bernstein, "FBI Officials Warned Gray of Cover-Up," *Washington Post*, May 14, 1973.

83. Nixon and Haig conversation, May 14, 1973, White House tape 917-2, RNPLM, https://www.nixonlibrary.gov/forresearchers/find/tapes/tape917/917-002.mp3.

84. William Ruckelshaus, interview by Timothy Naftali.

85. John Crewdson, "Ruckelshaus Says FBI Tap File, Including the Data on Ellsberg, Was Found in Ehrlichman's Safe," *New York Times*, May 15, 1973.

86. Colodny and Gettlin, *Silent Coup*, 308.

87. "Sirica Holds Dean Papers Brought from Bank Vault," *New York Times*, May 15, 1973.

88. Marjorie Hunter, "Bid to CIA Cited," *New York Times*, May 15, 1973.

89. Nixon and Haig conversation, May 14, 1973, White House tape 426-15, RNPLM, https://www.nixonlibrary.gov/forresearchers/find/tapes/tape426/426-015.mp3.

90. Laurence Stern, "CIA Resisted Lengthy Cover-Up Attempt by White House, Hill Account Reveals," *Washington Post*, May 16, 1973.

91. T. J. Smith to E. S. Miller, "Interagency Committee on Intelligence (ad hoc)," May 22, 1973, FBI Files, Luke Nichter private collection.

92. Nixon, Haig, Ziegler, and Buzhardt conversation, May 17, 1973, White House tape 921-8, RNPLM, https://www.nixonlibrary.gov/forresearchers/find/tapes/tape921/921 -008.mp3.

93. Hersh, *Price of Power*, 400.

94. Seymour Hersh, "President Linked to Taps on Aides," *New York Times*, May 16, 1973.

95. Stern, "CIA Resisted Lengthy Cover-Up."

96. Smith to Miller, "Interagency Committee."

97. Nixon, Haig, and Buzhardt conversation, May 16, 1973, White House tape 919- 32, RNPLM, https://www.nixonlibrary.gov/forresearchers/find/tapes/tape919/919 -032.mp3.

98. Nixon, Haig, and Buzhardt conversation, May 16, 1973, White House tape 919-32.

99. Nixon, Haig, and Buzhardt conversation, May 16, 1973, White House tape 920-13, RNPLM, https://www.nixonlibrary.gov/forresearchers/find/tapes/tape920/920-013.mp3.

100. Woodward and Bernstein, *All the President's Men*, 318.

101. Downie, *New Muckrakers*, 44.

102. Carl Bernstein and Bob Woodward, "Vast GOP Undercover Operation Originated in 1969," *Washington Post*, May 17, 1973.

103. Nixon, Haig, Buzhardt, and Ziegler conversation, May 17, 1973, White House tape 921-8, RNPLM, https://www.nixonlibrary.gov/forresearchers/find/tapes/tape921/921-008.mp3.

104. Nixon, Haig, and Buzhardt conversation, May 17, 1973, White House tape 921-3, RNPLM, https://www.nixonlibrary.gov/forresearchers/find/tapes/tape921/921-003.mp3.

105. Woodward and Bernstein, *All the President's Men*, 330.

106. Nixon and Haig conversation, May 17, 1973, White House tape 438-22, RNPLM, https://www.nixonlibrary.gov/forresearchers/find/tapes/tape438/438-022.mp3.

107. Haldeman, *Haldeman Diaries*, 768.

108. Nixon, Haldeman, and Ehrlichman conversation, April 14, 1973, White House tape 428-19, RNPLM, https://www.nixonlibrary.gov/forresearchers/find/tapes/tape428/428-019.mp3.

109. Nixon, Kissinger, and Rogers conversation, May 11, 1973, White House tape 916-14, RNPLM, https://www.nixonlibrary.gov/forresearchers/find/tapes/tape916/916-014.mp3.

110. Colodny and Shachtman, *Forty Years War*, 172.

111. Cohen and Witcover, *A Heartbeat Away*, 78.

112. Spiro Agnew collection, FBI Records, https://vault.fbi.gov/Spiro%20Agnew.

113. James Naughton, "A Low-Key Beginning," *New York Times*, May 18, 1973.

114. Nixon, Haig, and Buzhardt conversation, May 17, 1973, White House tape 921-3.

115. Nixon and Buzhardt conversation, May 17, 1973, White House tape 921-3, RNPLM, https://www.nixonlibrary.gov/forresearchers/find/tapes/tape921/921-003.mp3.

116. Marjorie Hunter, "Symington Cites New Data by CIA," *New York Times*, May 19, 1973.

117. Seymour Hersh, "Broad Role Cited," *New York Times*, May 17, 1973.

118. Nixon and Haig conversation, May 18, 1973, White House tape 922-7, RNPLM, https://www.nixonlibrary.gov/forresearchers/find/tapes/tape922/922-007.mp3.

119. Robert Welander, interview with Len Colodny, March 28, 1987, transcript, Colodny Collection.

120. Welander, interview with Colodny.

121. Nixon and Haig conversation, May 18, 1973, White House tape 46-116, RNPLM, https://www.nixonlibrary.gov/forresearchers/find/tapes/tape046/046-116.mp3.

122. Nixon and Haldeman conversation, May 18, 1973, White House tape 46-116, RNPLM, https://www.nixonlibrary.gov/forresearchers/find/tapes/tape046/046-116.mp3.

123. Leonard Garment, interview by Timothy Naftali, April 6, 2007, RNPLM, https://www.nixonlibrary.gov/virtuallibrary/documents/histories/garment-2007-04-06.pdf.

124. Presidential daily diary, May 21, 1973, RNPLM, https://www.nixonlibrary.gov/virtuallibrary/documents/PDD/1973/100%20May%2016-31%201973.pdf.

125. Nixon and Haig conversation, May 21, 1973, White House tape 439-2, RNPLM, https://www.nixonlibrary.gov/forresearchers/find/tapes/tape439/439-002.mp3.

126. William Claiborne, "Nixon Aide Proposed Espionage, Burglaries," *Washington Post*, May 22, 1973.

127. Smith to Miller, "Interagency Committee."

128. "Text of a Statement by the President on Allegations Surrounding Watergate Inquiry," *New York Times*, May 23, 1973.

129. "More of the Truth," *New York Times*, May 23, 1973.

130. Nixon, *RN*, 871.

131. Nixon and Haig conversation, May 23, 1973, White House tape 926-4, RNPLM, https://www.nixonlibrary.gov/forresearchers/find/tapes/tape926/926-004a.mp3.

132. Nixon and Haig conversation, May 24, 1973, White House tape 39-16, RNPLM, https://www.nixonlibrary.gov/forresearchers/find/tapes/tape039/039-016.mp3.

133. Nixon and Richardson conversation, May 25, 1973, White House tape 928-12, RNPLM, https://www.nixonlibrary.gov/forresearchers/find/tapes/tape928/928-012.mp3.

3. JUNE 1973

1. Van Atta, *With Honor*, 441.

2. Linda Charlton, "Symington Presses Challenge on Haig," *New York Times*, June 3, 1973.

3. Seymour Hersh, "Offers to Talk," *New York Times*, June 3, 1973; Carl Bernstein and Bob Woodward, "Dean Alleges Nixon Knew of Cover-up Plan," *Washington Post*, June 3, 1973.

4. Nixon, *RN*, 874.

5. Nixon and Ziegler conversation, June 3, 1973, White House tape 168-24, RNPLM, https://www.nixonlibrary.gov/forresearchers/find/tapes/tape168/168-024.mp3.

6. Nixon and Haig conversation, June 3, 1973, White House tape 168-36, RNPLM, https://www.nixonlibrary.gov/forresearchers/find/tapes/tape168/168-036.mp3.

7. Nixon and Dean conversation, March 16, 1973, White House tape 37-134, RNPLM, https://www.nixonlibrary.gov/sites/default/files/forresearchers/find/tapes/tape037/037-134.mp3.

8. Nixon and Haig conversation, June 3, 1973, White House tape 168-36, RNPLM, https://www.nixonlibrary.gov/forresearchers/find/tapes/tape168/168-036.mp3.

9. Haig and McCarry, *Inner Circles*, 348.

10. Haig and McCarry, *Inner Circles*, 349.

11. Nixon and Bull conversation, June 4, 1973, White House tape 441-9, RNPLM, https://www.nixonlibrary.gov/forresearchers/find/tapes/tape441/441-009.mp3.

12. Nixon and Haig conversation, June 4, 1973, White House tape 931-1, RNPLM, https://www.nixonlibrary.gov/forresearchers/find/tapes/tape931/931-001.mp3.

13. Nixon and Haig conversation, June 4, 1973, White House tape 931-1.

14. John Crewdson, "Richardson Bars Security as Issue," *New York Times*, June 5, 1973.

15. Senator Lowell Weicker to William Ruckelshaus, June 4, 1973, box 1671, folder 1, Weicker Papers, https://ead.lib.virginia.edu/vivaxtf/view?docId=uva-sc/viu04106.xml.

16. Haig and McCarry, *Inner Circles*, 350.

17. Haig and McCarry, *Inner Circles*, 350.

18. Presidential daily diary, June 11, 1973, RNPLM, https://www.nixonlibrary.gov /virtuallibrary/documents/PDD/1973/101%20June%201-15%201973.pdf.

19. Nixon, Agnew, and Haig conversation, June 14, 1973, White House tape 940-2, RNPLM, https://www.nixonlibrary.gov/forresearchers/find/tapes/tape940/940 -002.mp3.

20. Nixon and Haig conversation, June 18, 1973, White House tape 943-2, RNPLM, https://www.nixonlibrary.gov/forresearchers/find/tapes/tape943/943-002.mp3.

21. U.S. Congress, Senate, *Hearings, Book 3*, 914.

22. U.S. Congress, Senate, *Hearings, Book 3*, 916.

23. U.S. Congress, Senate, Select Committee to Study Governmental Operations, *Book 3*, 974.

24. U.S. Congress, Senate, *Hearings, Book 3*, 929.

25. U.S. Congress, Senate, *Hearings, Book 3*, 947.

26. U.S. Congress, Senate, *Hearings, Book 3*, 998.

27. Nixon and Dean conversation, March 21, 1973, White House tape 886-8, RNPLM, https://www.nixonlibrary.gov/forresearchers/find/tapes/tape886/886-008.mp3.

28. Nixon, *RN*, 890.

29. Colodny and Gettlin, *Silent Coup*, 307.

30. U.S. Congress, Senate, *Hearings, Book 3*, 1071.

31. U.S. Congress, Senate, *Hearings, Book 4*, 1368.

32. Colodny and Gettlin, *Silent Coup*, 308.

33. Nixon, *RN*, 893.

34. Colodny and Gettlin, *Silent Coup*, 119.

35. Len Garment to Elliot Richardson, June 29, 1973, Len Colodny private collection.

36. Van Atta, *With Honor*, 445.

37. Van Atta, *With Honor*, 445.

38. Presidential daily diaries, June 21–July 13, 1973, RNPLM, https://www.nixonlibrary .gov/virtuallibrary/documents/PDD/1973/102%20June%2016-30%201973.pdf, https:// www.nixonlibrary.gov/virtuallibrary/documents/PDD/1973/103%20July%201-15 %201973.pdf.

4. JULY 1973

1. "Cox Probes Nixon House Purchase," *Los Angeles Times*, July 3, 1973.

2. Cohen and Witcover, *Heartbeat Away*, 110–12.

3. Larry Higby, interview by Len Colodny, March 26, 1987, transcript, Colodny Collection.

4. Higby, interview by Colodny.

5. Higby, interview by Colodny.

6. Lukas, *Nightmare*, 410.

7. Thompson, *At That Point*, 68.

8. William Sullivan interview notes, July 9, 1973, box 1671, folder 1, Weicker Papers.

9. Scott Armstrong to Terry Lenzner, William Sullivan interview notes, July 12, 1973, container B68, U.S. Senate, Select Committee on Presidential Campaign Activities.

10. Colodny and Gettlin, *Silent Coup*, 309.

11. U.S. Congress, Senate, *Hearings, Book 5*, 1823.

12. Nixon, *RN*, 898.

13. Nixon, *RN*, 898.

14. Nixon and Haig conversation, July 12, 1973, White House tape 949-12, RNPLM, https://www.nixonlibrary.gov/forresearchers/find/tapes/tape949/949-012.mp3.

15. U.S. Congress, Senate, *Hearings, Book 5*, 1945.

16. Nixon and Haig conversation, July 12, 1973, White House tape 949-17, RNPLM, https://www.nixonlibrary.gov/forresearchers/find/tapes/tape949/949-017.mp3.

17. Nixon, Haig, Ziegler, and Tkach conversation, July 12, 1973, White House tape 949-12, RNPLM, https://www.nixonlibrary.gov/forresearchers/find/tapes/tape949/949-012.mp3.

18. Presidential daily diary, June 11, 1973, RNPLM, https://www.nixonlibrary.gov/virtuallibrary/documents/PDD/1973/103%20July%201-15%201973.pdf.

19. U.S. Congress, Senate, *Hearings, Book 5*, 2066.

20. Colodny and Gettlin, *Silent Coup*, 326.

21. Woodward and Bernstein, *All the President's Men*, 214.

22. Woodward, *Last of the President's Men*, 149.

23. Author's notes on Scott Armstrong and James Hamilton remarks, June 17, 2017, fortieth anniversary of Watergate panel discussion, Washington DC.

24. Alexander Butterfield, interview with Senate committee staff, transcript, July 13, 1973, container B305, U.S. Senate, Select Committee on Presidential Campaign Activities.

25. U.S. Congress, Senate, *Hearings, Book 3*, 1016.

26. Butterfield, interview with Senate committee staff.

27. Dash, *Chief Counsel*, 180.

28. Presidential daily diary, July 13, 1973.

29. Dash, *Chief Counsel*, 180.

30. Woodward and Bernstein, *All the President's Men*, 331.

31. Woodward and Bernstein, *All the President's Men*, 331.

32. Nixon and Haig conversation, May 11, 1973, White House tape 916-11, RNPLM, https://www.nixonlibrary.gov/forresearchers/find/tapes/tape916/916-011.mp3.

33. Haig and McCarry, *Inner Circles*, 391.

34. Alexander Butterfield, pretestimony notes, container C12, U.S. Senate, Select Committee on Presidential Campaign Activities.

35. Alexander Butterfield, interview by Timothy Naftali, June 12, 2008, RNPLM, https://www.nixonlibrary.gov/virtuallibrary/documents/histories/butterfield-2008-06-12.pdf.

36. Dash, *Chief Counsel*, 180.

37. Thompson, *At That Point*, 87.

38. Colodny and Gettlin, *Silent Coup*, 331.

39. Colodny and Gettlin, *Silent Coup*, 333.

40. Presidential daily diary, July 15, 1973, RNPLM, https://www.nixonlibrary.gov /virtuallibrary/documents/PDD/1973/104%20July%2016-31%201973.pdf.

41. Nixon, *RN*, 899.

42. Presidential daily diary, July 16, 1973, RNPLM, https://www.nixonlibrary.gov /virtuallibrary/documents/PDD/1973/104%20July%2016-31%201973.pdf.

43. Dash, *Chief Counsel*, 181.

44. Califano, *Inside*, 288.

45. U.S. Congress, Senate, *Hearings, Book 5*, 2074.

46. U.S. Congress, Senate, *Hearings, Book 5*, 2090.

47. Haig and McCarry, *Inner Circles*, 374.

48. Lukas, *Nightmare*, 420.

49. W. Donald Stewart to Martin Hoffmann, July 16, 1973, Colodny Collection.

50. James Naughton, "Surprise Witness," *New York Times*, July 17, 1973.

51. U.S. Congress, Senate, *Hearings, Book 5*, 2136.

52. Lukas, *Nightmare*, 420.

53. Haig and McCarry, *Inner Circles*, 380; Agnew, *Go Quietly*, 87.

54. Nixon, *RN*, 901.

55. Haig and McCarry, *Inner Circles*, 375.

56. Presidential daily diary, July 18, 1973, RNPLM, https://www.nixonlibrary.gov /virtuallibrary/documents/PDD/1973/104%20July%2016-31%201973.pdf.

57. Haig and McCarry, *Inner Circles*, 379.

58. Lukas, *Nightmare*, 420.

59. Lukas, *Nightmare*, 420.

60. Nixon, *RN*, 901.

61. R. W. Apple Jr., "Aide Declares President Won't Turn Over Tapes," *New York Times*, July 20, 1973.

62. Nixon, *RN*, 902.

63. Anthony Ripley, "Special Prosecutor Decides to Take Legal Action Rather Than Resign over Move to Block His Inquiry," *New York Times*, July 24, 1973.

64. Colodny and Gettlin, *Silent Coup*, 340.

65. Sirica, *To Set the Record Straight*, 138.

66. Sirica, *To Set the Record Straight*, 138.

67. Jack Anderson, "My Journal on Watergate," *Parade*, July 22, 1973.

68. W. Donald Stewart, memorandum for the record, July 22, 1973, Colodny Collection.

69. Stewart, memorandum for the record.

70. Colodny and Gettlin, *Silent Coup*, 340.

71. U.S. Congress, Senate, *Hearings, Book 7*, 2708.

72. U.S. Congress, Senate, *Hearings, Book 7*, 2708.

73. U.S. Congress, Senate, *Hearings, Book 7*, 2708.

74. Colodny and Gettlin, *Silent Coup*, 314.

75. Colodny and Gettlin, *Silent Coup*, 314.

76. Cohen and Witcover, *Heartbeat Away*, 134.

5. AUGUST 1973

1. Cohen and Witcover, *Heartbeat Away*, 134–35.

2. Agnew, *Go Quietly*, 94.

3. Agnew, *Go Quietly*, 95.

4. Cohen and Witcover, *Heartbeat Away*, 146.

5. Alfred Hantman to Carl Belcher, "Letter from Leonard Garment Recommending Investigation of W. Donald Stewart," August 2, 1973, Colodny Collection.

6. Colodny and Gettlin, *Silent Coup*, 310.

7. Van Atta, *With Honor*, 454.

8. Van Atta, *With Honor*, 454.

9. Ford, *A Time to Heal*, 101.

10. Agnew, *Go Quietly*, 96.

11. Haig and McCarry, *Inner Circles*, 355.

12. Cohen and Witcover, *Heartbeat Away*, 142.

13. Copaken, *Target Culebra*, 162.

14. Copaken, *Target Culebra*, 162.

15. Presidential daily diary, August 6, 1973, RNPLM, https://www.nixonlibrary.gov /virtuallibrary/documents/PDD/1973/105%20August%201-15%201973.pdf.

16. Agnew, *Go Quietly*, 103.

17. Presidential daily diary, August 6, 1973.

18. Presidential daily diary, August 7, 1973, https://www.nixonlibrary.gov/virtuallibrary /documents/PDD/1973/105%20August%201-15%201973.pdf.

19. Haig and McCarry, *Inner Circles*, 358.

20. Agnew, *Go Quietly*, 108; Nixon, *RN*, 914.

21. Agnew, *Go Quietly*, 108.

22. Agnew, *Go Quietly*, 109.

23. Spiro Agnew, interview by Len Colodny, July 28, 1986, transcript, Colodny Collection.

24. Christopher Lydon, "Agnew Says 'Damned Lies' to Report of Kickbacks; Doubts He'll Be Indicted," *New York Times*, August 9, 1973.

25. Haig and McCarry, *Inner Circles*, 355.

26. Haig and McCarry, *Inner Circles*, 358.

27. Haig and McCarry, *Inner Circles*, 358.

28. Nixon, Agnew, and Haig conversation, June 14, 1973, White House tape 940-2, RNPLM, https://www.nixonlibrary.gov/forresearchers/find/tapes/tape940/940 -002.mp3.

29. Haig and McCarry, *Inner Circles*, 358.

30. Seymour Hersh, "Laird Approved False Reporting of Secret Raids," *New York Times*, August 10, 1973.

31. Seymour Hersh, "Secret 1969 Foray into Laos Reported," *New York Times*, August 12, 1973.

32. Dave Philipps, "Secrets, Denial, and Decades Later, a Medal of Honor for a Vietnam Medic," *New York Times*, July 30, 2016.

33. Lukas, *Nightmare*, 420.

34. "Haig's Job—Officially, Is Illegal," *San Francisco Examiner*, July 22, 1973.

35. John Herbers, "Nixon's Mood Stirs Anxiety; Some Find Him Distraught, Others Say His Spirits Are High," *New York Times*, August 14, 1973.

36. Haig and McCarry, *Inner Circles*, 360.

37. R. W. Apple Jr., "Nixon Asks Watergate Be Left to Courts and Nation," *New York Times*, August 16, 1973.

38. William Sullivan, interview by Donald Sanders, August 18, 1973, notes, container B105, U.S. Senate, Select Committee on Presidential Campaign Activities.

39. Agnew, *Go Quietly*, 132.

40. Cohen and Witcover, *Heartbeat Away*, 197.

41. Haig and McCarry, *Inner Circles*, 385.

42. Nixon, *RN*, 910.

43. *Public Papers of the Presidents of the United States, Richard Nixon, 1973*, 722, https://quod.lib.umich.edu/p/ppotpus/4731942.1973.001/776?rgn=full+text;view=image.

44. Lukas, *Nightmare*, 434.

45. Sirica, *To Set the Record Straight*, 159.

6. SEPTEMBER 1973

1. Presidential daily diary, September 1, 1973, RNPLM, https://www.nixonlibrary.gov/virtuallibrary/documents/PDD/1973/107%20September%201-15%201973.pdf.

2. Nixon, *RN*, 915.

3. "Transcript of President News Conference on Foreign and Domestic Matters," *New York Times*, September 6, 1973.

4. Haig and McCarry, *Inner Circles*, 361.

5. Haig and McCarry, *Inner Circles*, 360.

6. Haig and McCarry, *Inner Circles*, 360.

7. Nixon, *RN*, 102.

8. Haig and McCarry, *Inner Circles*, 360.

9. Lukas, *Nightmare*, 447.

10. Cohen and Witcover, *Heartbeat Away*, 220.

11. Agnew, *Go Quietly*, 142.

12. Cohen and Witcover, *Heartbeat Away*, 220.

13. Cohen and Witcover, *Heartbeat Away*, 222; Agnew, *Go Quietly*, 145; Haig and McCarry, *Inner Circles*, 358.

14. Agnew, *Go Quietly*, 146.

15. Bernard Gwertzman, "Kissinger's Role in Wiretaps Told to Senate Panel," *New York Times*, September 11, 1973.

16. Agnew, *Go Quietly*, 158.

17. Agnew, *Go Quietly*, 150.

18. Agnew, *Go Quietly*, 151.

19. Haig and McCarry, *Inner Circles*, 363.

20. Cohen and Witcover, *Heartbeat Away*, 231.

21. Cohen and Witcover, *Heartbeat Away*, 236.

22. Lukas, *Nightmare*, 456.

23. Bernard Gwertzman, "Wiretaps Termed No Bar to Approval of Kissinger," *New York Times*, September 18, 1973.

24. Carroll Kilpatrick and Lou Cannon, "Agnew Pressure Denied," *Washington Post*, September 20, 1973.

25. Kilpatrick and Cannon, "Agnew Pressure Denied."

26. Agnew, *Go Quietly*, 155.

27. Agnew, *Go Quietly*, 157.

28. Agnew, *Go Quietly*, 158.

29. Presidential daily diary, September 20, 1973, RNPLM, https://www.nixonlibrary.gov/virtuallibrary/documents/PDD/1973/108%20September%2016-30%201973.pdf.

30. Cohen and Witcover, *Heartbeat Away*, 244.

31. Lukas, *Nightmare*, 456.

32. Presidential daily diary, September 21, 1973, RNPLM, https://www.nixonlibrary.gov/virtuallibrary/documents/PDD/1973/108%20September%2016-30%201973.pdf.

33. Cohen and Witcover, *Heartbeat Away*, 248.

34. Agnew, *Go Quietly*, 163.

35. Presidential daily diary, September 25, 1973, RNPLM, https://www.nixonlibrary.gov/virtuallibrary/documents/PDD/1973/108%20September%2016-30%201973.pdf.

36. Nixon, *RN*, 915.

37. Nixon, *RN*, 917; Cohen and Witcover, *Heartbeat Away*, 256.

38. Haig and McCarry, *Inner Circles*, 365.

39. Clare Crawford, "Carl Albert Doesn't Want to Be President, but He's Next in Line," *People*, November 18, 1974.

40. Haig and McCarry, *Inner Circles*, 361.

41. Steven Roberts, "Agnew Declares He Will Not Quit; Attacks Inquiry," *New York Times*, September 30, 1973.

42. Agnew, *Go Quietly*, 181.

43. Haig and McCarry, *Inner Circles*, 365.

44. Lukas, *Nightmare*, 503.

7. OCTOBER 1973

1. Nixon, *RN*, 920.

2. Lukas, *Nightmare*, 503; quote in Nixon, *RN*, 918; Haig and McCarry, *Inner Circles*, 428.

3. Agnew, *Go Quietly*, 182.

4. James Naughton, "President Backs Agnew's Refusal to Resign Office," *New York Times*, October 4, 1973.

5. Agnew, *Go Quietly*, 189.

6. Haig, *Inner Circles*, 366.

7. Agnew, *Go Quietly*, 190.

8. Agnew, *Go Quietly*, 190.

9. Haig and McCarry, *Inner Circles*, 360.

10. Haig, interview by Woodward and Bernstein, September 10, 1974.

11. Document 112, "Minutes of Washington Special Actions Group Meeting," Washington DC, October 6, 1973, 7:22–8:27 p.m., in Howland and Daigle, *Arab-Israeli Crisis*, 324.

12. Haig and McCarry, *Inner Circles*, 411.

13. Presidential daily diary, October 6, 1973, https://www.nixonlibrary.gov/sites/default/files/virtuallibrary/documents/PDD/1973/109%20October%201-15%201973.pdf.

14. Document 106, "Transcript of Telephone Conversation between Secretary of State Kissinger and the White House Chief of Staff (Haig)," October 6, 1973, 10:35 a.m., in Howland and Daigle, *Arab-Israeli Crisis*, 309–12.

15. Document 107, "Transcript of Telephone Conversation between Secretary of State Kissinger and the White House Chief of Staff (Haig)," October 6, 1973, 12:45 p.m., in Howland and Daigle, *Arab-Israeli Crisis*, 313.

16. Agnew, *Go Quietly*, 194.

17. Cohen and Witcover, *Heartbeat Away*, 322.

18. Cohen and Witcover, *Heartbeat Away*, 293.

19. Document 107, in Howland and Daigle, *Arab-Israeli Crisis*, 314.

20. Document 107, in Howland and Daigle, *Arab-Israeli Crisis*, 314.

21. Agnew, *Go Quietly*, 194.

22. Agnew, *Go Quietly*, 195.

23. Bob Woodward and Carl Bernstein, "Military Aide Phone Was Tapped," *Washington Post*, October 10, 1973.

24. Haig and McCarry, *Inner Circles*, 392.

25. Ervin, *Whole Truth*, 241.

26. Haig and McCarry, *Inner Circles*, 368.

27. Nixon, *RN*, 926.

28. Haig and McCarry, *Inner Circles*, 368.

29. Haig and McCarry, *Inner Circles*, 370.

30. Presidential daily diary, October 10, 1973, RNPLM, https://www.nixonlibrary.gov/virtuallibrary/documents/PDD/1973/109%20October%201-15%201973.pdf.

31. Haig and McCarry, *Inner Circles*, 392.
32. Document 134, "Memorandum of Conversation," Washington DC, October 9, 1973, 8:20–8:40 a.m., in Howland and Daigle, *Arab-Israeli Crisis*, 392–96.
33. Presidential daily diary, October 11, 1973, RNPLM, https://www.nixonlibrary.gov/virtuallibrary/documents/PDD/1973/109%20October%201-15%201973.pdf.
34. Kissinger and Scowcroft telcon, October 11, 1973, Henry A. Kissinger Telephone Conversation Transcripts, box 22, RNPLM, https://www.nixonlibrary.gov/forresearchers/find/textual/kissinger/telcons.pdf.
35. Lukas, *Nightmare*, 463.
36. Stephen Bull, interview by author, July 2, 2017.
37. Agnew, *Go Quietly*, 202.
38. Presidential daily diary, October 14, 1973, RNPLM, https://www.nixonlibrary.gov/virtuallibrary/documents/PDD/1973/109%20October%201-15%201973.pdf.
39. Lukas, *Nightmare*, 475.
40. Lukas, *Nightmare*, 465.
41. Nixon, *RN*, 932; Lukas, *Nightmare*, 465.
42. Lukas, *Nightmare*, 466.
43. Lukas, *Nightmare*, 466.
44. Haig and McCarry, *Inner Circles*, 396.
45. Frank Van Riper, "FBI and Political Spying," *New York Daily News*, October 14, 1973.
46. Richard McGowan to Lowell Weicker, undated, box 1671, folder 1, Weicker Papers.
47. Locker, *Nixon's Gamble*, 200.
48. William Sullivan to Lowell Weicker, October 16, 1973, box 1671, folder 1, Weicker Papers.
49. William Sullivan to *New York Daily News*, October 16, 1973, box 1671, folder 1, Weicker Papers.
50. Lukas, *Nightmare*, 468.
51. "Ervin Panel Loses in Suit for Tapes," *New York Times*, October 18, 1973.
52. Lukas, *Nightmare*, 469.
53. Haig and McCarry, *Inner Circles*, 399; Lukas, *Nightmare*, 470.
54. Nixon, *RN*, 929.
55. Lukas, *Nightmare*, 471; Colodny and Gettlin, *Silent Coup*, 345.
56. Lukas, *Nightmare*, 473.
57. Lukas, *Nightmare*, 473.
58. Lukas, *Nightmare*, 474.
59. Nixon, *RN*, 931.
60. Lukas, *Nightmare*, 478.
61. Nixon, *RN*, 931.
62. Document 214, "Backchannel Message from Secretary of State Kissinger to the Egyptian Presidential Adviser for National Security Affairs (Ismail)," Washington DC, undated, in Howland and Daigle, *Arab-Israeli Crisis*, 622–23.

63. Lukas, *Nightmare*, 478.

64. Lukas, *Nightmare*, 476; Colodny and Gettlin, *Silent Coup*, 353.

65. Lukas, *Nightmare*, 477.

66. Haig and McCarry, *Inner Circles*, 402.

67. Presidential daily diary, October 19, 1973, RNPLM, https://www.nixonlibrary.gov/virtuallibrary/documents/PDD/1973/109%20October%201-15%201973.pdf.

68. Haig and McCarry, *Inner Circles*, 404.

69. Lukas, *Nightmare*, 478.

70. Lukas, *Nightmare*, 480.

71. William Ruckelshaus, interview by Timothy Naftali, April 12, 2007, RNPLM, 26, https://www.nixonlibrary.gov/sites/default/files/forresearchers/find/histories/ruckelshaus-2007-04-12.pdf.

72. Presidential daily diary, October 20, 1973, RNPLM, https://www.nixonlibrary.gov/virtuallibrary/documents/PDD/1973/109%20October%201-15%201973.pdf.

73. "Ziegler Statement and Texts of Letters," *New York Times*, October 21, 1973.

74. Douglas Kneeland, "Bork Takes Over," *New York Times*, October 21, 1973.

75. Haig and McCarry, *Inner Circles*, 407.

76. Document 218, "Telegram from the President's Deputy Assistant for National Security Affairs (Scowcroft) to Secretary of State Kissinger," October 20, 1973, in Howland and Daigle, *Arab-Israeli Crisis*, 628.

77. Document 220, "Telegram from Secretary of State Kissinger to the President's Deputy Assistant for National Security Affairs (Scowcroft)," October 21, 1973, in Howland and Daigle, *Arab-Israeli Crisis*, 633.

78. Document 223, "Telegram from the President's Deputy Assistant for National Security Affairs (Scowcroft) to Secretary of State Kissinger," Washington DC, October 21, 1973, 1538Z, in Howland and Daigle, *Arab-Israeli Crisis*, 643–44.

79. Document 234, "Telegram from the White House Chief of Staff (Haig) to Secretary of State Kissinger in Tel Aviv," Washington DC, October 22, 1973, 1754Z, in Howland and Daigle, *Arab-Israeli Crisis*, 668–69.

80. Alexander Haig, interview by Bob Woodward, October 22, 1973, Series 1, Woodward, Subseries B, *The Final Days*, container 76.5, Woodward and Bernstein Watergate Papers, http://norman.hrc.utexas.edu/fasearch/findingAid.cfm?eadid=00365&kw=woodward.

81. Bob Woodward and Carl Bernstein, "Richardson Felt Nixon Curbed Probe," *Washington Post*, October 23, 1973.

82. Haig, interview by Woodward.

83. Haig, *Inner Circles*, 323.

84. Benton Becker, interview by Richard Norton Smith, June 9, 2009, Gerald R. Ford Presidential Library and Museum (hereafter GRFPLM), https://geraldrford-foundation.org/centennial-docs/oralhistory/wp-content/uploads/2013/05/Benton-Becker.pdf.

85. John Crewdson, "Richardson Says White House Aides Suggested Ousting Cox before He Balked," *New York Times*, October 24, 1973.

86. John Herbers, "President Talks to Press Tonight," *New York Times*, October 25, 1973.

87. Lesley Oelsner, "Abrupt Reversal," *New York Times*, October 24, 1973.

88. Nixon, *RN*, 936.

89. Document 259, "Minutes of Washington Special Actions Group Meeting," Washington DC, October 24, 1973, 10:21–11:11 a.m., in Howland and Daigle, *Arab-Israeli Crisis*, 711–19.

90. Document 262, "Message from Soviet General Secretary Brezhnev to President Nixon," Moscow, October 24, 1973, in Howland and Daigle, *Arab-Israeli Crisis*, 727–28.

91. Nixon, *RN*, 938.

92. Haig and McCarry, *Inner Circles*, 415.

93. Document 268, "Transcript of Telephone Conversation between Secretary of State Kissinger and the White House Chief of Staff (Haig)," in Howland and Daigle, *Arab-Israeli Crisis*, 736–37.

94. Document 267, "Message from Soviet General Secretary Brezhnev to President Nixon," Moscow, undated, in Howland and Daigle, *Arab-Israeli Crisis*, 734–35.

95. Kissinger, *Crisis*, 346; presidential daily diary, October 24, 1973, RNPLM, https://www.nixonlibrary.gov/virtuallibrary/documents/PDD/1973/109%20October%201-15%201973.pdf.

96. Document 269, "Memorandum for the Record," CJCS Memo M-88-73, Washington DC, October 24/25, 1973, 10:30 p.m.–3:30 a.m., in Howland and Daigle, *Arab-Israeli Crisis*, 737–42.

97. Document 269, in Howland and Daigle, *Arab-Israeli Crisis*, 737–42.

98. Document 269, in Howland and Daigle, *Arab-Israeli Crisis*, 741.

99. John Herbers, "Nixon's Motives Questioned and Defended," *New York Times*, October 26, 1973.

100. John Herbers, "A Fatigued Nixon Asserts He Will Not Quit His Post," *New York Times*, October 27, 1973.

101. Document 285, "Transcript of Telephone Conversation between Secretary of State Kissinger and the White House Chief of Staff (Haig)," Washington DC, October 26, 1973, 7:55 p.m., in Howland and Daigle, *Arab-Israeli Crisis*, 764–65.

102. Kissinger, *Crisis*, 384.

103. Document 285, in Howland and Daigle, *Arab-Israeli Crisis*, 764–65.

104. Presidential daily diary, October 26, 1973, RNPLM, https://www.nixonlibrary.gov/virtuallibrary/documents/PDD/1973/109%20October%201-15%201973.pdf.

105. Document 285, in Howland and Daigle, *Arab-Israeli Crisis*, 765.

106. Document 293, "Transcript of Telephone Conversation between Secretary of State Kissinger and the White House Chief of Staff (Haig)," Washington DC, October 27, 1973, 12:28 p.m., in Howland and Daigle, *Arab-Israeli Crisis*, 778.

107. John Crewdson, "Bork Asserts He'd Press White House for Evidence," *New York Times*, October 25, 1973.

108. Morris Leibman to J. Edgar Hoover, October 6, 1961, vol. 9, 167, American Bar Association FBI Files, https://ia800504.us.archive.org/22/items/ABA-FBI/ABA-HQ-34.pdf.

109. Garrow, *FBI and Martin Luther King*, 36.

110. Beverly Gage, "What an Uncensored Letter to M.L.K. Reveals," *New York Times*, November 11, 2014.

111. H. L. Edwards to Mr. Malone, "American Bar Association Standing Committee on Education against Communism Committee Meeting, Washington, D.C., 9/30/62," vol. 12, 145, American Bar Association FBI Files, https://archive.org/stream/ABA-FBI/ABA-HQ-37#page/n0.

112. Edwards to Malone, "American Bar Association," 146.

113. Lyndon Johnson news conference, September 9, 1964, in *Public Papers of the President, Lyndon B. Johnson, 1963–1964: Book 2*, http://www.presidency.ucsb.edu/ws/index.php?pid=26491.

114. Morris Leibman to J. Edgar Hoover, January 10, 1966, vol. 17, 212, American Bar Association FBI Files, https://archive.org/stream/ABA-FBI/ABA-HQ-42#page/n1.

115. Presidential daily diary, December 5, 1973, RNPLM, https://www.nixonlibrary.gov/virtuallibrary/documents/PDD/1969/019%20December%201-15%201969.pdf.

116. Donald Marshall to Vernon Walters, July 19, 1973, https://www.cia.gov/library/readingroom/docs/CIA-RDP80R01731R001900060019-0.pdf.

117. Woodward and Bernstein, *Final Days*, 75.

118. Harry Hurt III, "Have Conscience, Will Travel," *Texas Monthly*, November 1977.

119. Haig and McCarry, *Inner Circles*, 438.

120. Oral Memoirs of Leon Jaworski, vol. 2, interviews 7–9, March 13, 1979–May 23, 1979, 504, 498.

121. Warren Weaver Jr., "Court Informed," *New York Times*, November 1, 1973.

122. Nixon, *RN*, 945.

123. Oral Memoirs of Leon Jaworski, vol. 2, 514.

124. Oral Memoirs of Leon Jaworski, vol. 2, 504.

125. Lukas, *Nightmare*, 494.

126. United States v. Egil Krogh Jr., motion for discovery, October 31, 1973, Colodny Collection.

127. "Where the Cox Probe Left Off," *Time*, November 5, 1973.

8. NOVEMBER 1973

1. "The Strange Case of the Missing Tapes," *Washington Post*, November 1, 1973.

2. Nixon, *RN*, 945.

3. Drew, *Washington Journal*, 94.

4. Douglas Kneeland, "White House Says Nixon Doesn't Intend to Resign," *New York Times*, November 3, 1973.

5. Warren Weaver Jr., "Aide Says Nixon Knew on Sept. 29 of Lack of Tapes," *New York Times*, November 2, 1973.

6. Drew, *Washington Journal*, 98.

7. Woodward and Bernstein, *Final Days*, 22.

8. Nixon, *RN*, 946.

9. Nixon, *RN*, 946.

10. Haig and McCarry, *Inner Circles*, 426.

11. Haig and McCarry, *Inner Circles*, 427.

12. Clare Crawford, "Carl Albert Doesn't Want to Be President, but He's Next in Line," *People*, November 18, 1974.

13. Haig and McCarry, *Inner Circles*, 427.

14. Woodward and Bernstein, *All the President's Men*, 333.

15. Colodny and Gettlin, *Silent Coup*, 374.

16. Warren Weaver Jr., "Sirica Calls Nixon's Secretary to Testify in the Tapes Inquiry," *New York Times*, November 7, 1973.

17. John Herbers, "Fewer Aides See Nixon as Haig's Role Increases," *New York Times*, November 8, 1973.

18. Douglas Kneeland, "Nixon Has No Intention of Leaving White House," *New York Times*, November 8, 1973.

19. George Lardner Jr., "Nixon Aide Testifies," *Washington Post*, November 8, 1973.

20. Carl Bernstein and Bob Woodward, "Tapes Have Puzzling 'Gap,' Parts 'Inaudible,'" *Washington Post*, November 8, 1973.

21. Warren Weaver Jr., "Miss Woods Says Tapes Contain Inaudible Parts," *New York Times*, November 9, 1973.

22. Sam Powers, interview by Len Colodny, January 21, 1988, transcript, Colodny Collection.

23. Morris Leibman to J. Edgar Hoover, January 10, 1966, vol. 17, American Bar Association FBI Files.

24. Document 325, "Telegram from the White House Chief of Staff (Haig) to Secretary of State Kissinger in Amman," Washington DC, November 8, 1973, 0423Z, in Howland and Daigle, *Arab-Israeli Crisis*, 910–11.

25. Warren Weaver Jr., "Nixon Offers Sirica Data on the Two Conversations," *New York Times*, November 13, 1973.

26. Leon Jaworski notes of November 11, 1973, meeting with Alexander Haig and J. Fred Buzhardt, Leon Jaworski File, Records of the Watergate Special Prosecution Force.

27. Jaworski notes with Haig and Buzhardt.

28. Jaworski, *Right and the Power*, 36.

29. Hersh, "The Pardon."

30. Powers, interview by Colodny.

31. Geoffrey C. Shepard, interview by Terry Good, September 11, 1974, transcript, Nixon Presidential Materials Staff, National Archives and Records Administration,

RNPLM, https://www.nixonlibrary.gov/virtuallibrary/documents/exitinterviews/shepard-exit.pdf.

32. Bill Kovach, "St. Clair Control of Case Doubted," *New York Times*, April 16, 1974.

33. Richard Nixon, Question-and-Answer Session at the Annual Convention of the Associated Press Managing Editors Association, Orlando, Florida, November 17, 1973, in *Public Papers of the Presidents, Richard Nixon: 1973*, 334, http://www.presidency.ucsb.edu/ws/index.php?pid=4046.

34. Nixon, *RN*, 957.

35. Haig, *Inner Circles*, 433.

36. Nixon, *RN*, 957.

37. Nixon, *RN*, 950.

38. David Rosenbaum, "Another Section of Tapes Is Blank," *New York Times*, November 22, 1973.

39. Haig and McCarry, *Inner Circles*, 434.

40. W. Donald Stewart to Donald Sanders, December 1, 1973, Colodny Collection.

9. DECEMBER 1973

1. John Herbers, "State of Nixon's Health Is a Dimension of Watergate Affair Constantly Being Gauged," *New York Times*, December 4, 1973.

2. Bob Woodward and Carl Bernstein, "Stennis Denial," *Washington Post*, December 5, 1973.

3. Lesley Oelsner, "Haig Says Gap in Tape Disturbed Nixon," *New York Times*, December 6, 1973.

4. Woodward and Bernstein, *Final Days*, 82.

5. Lesley Oelsner, "Haig Says White House Feared 'Sinister Force' Ruined Tapes but Now Feels Miss Woods Is to Blame," *New York Times*, December 6, 1973.

6. Oelsner, "Haig Says White House."

7. James Naughton, "A Watershed for Nixon," *New York Times*, December 7, 1973.

8. Haig and McCarry, *Inner Circles*, 441.

9. Tom Wicker, "Nixon and Ford," *New York Times*, December 8, 1973.

10. Marjorie Hunter, "Ford Says Nixon Told Him He Won't Resign Presidency," *New York Times*, December 9, 1973.

11. Shenon, *Cruel and Shocking Act*, 79.

12. Ford, *A Time to Heal*, 77.

13. Seymour Hersh, "Nixon's Role on Plumbers: His Talks with Leaders Recalled," *New York Times*, December 10, 1973.

14. Hersh, "Nixon's Role."

15. Dobrynin, *In Confidence*, 303.

16. Document 389, "Backchannel Message from Secretary of State Kissinger to the President's Deputy Assistant for National Security Affairs (Scowcroft)," Cairo, December 14, 1973, 0045Z, in Howland and Daigle, *Arab-Israeli Crisis*, 1056–59.

17. Woodward and Bernstein, *Final Days*, 103.

18. Haig and McCarry, *Inner Circles*, 441.

19. Document 389, in Howland and Daigle, *Arab-Israeli Crisis*, 1056–59.

20. Dan Thomasson, interview by Len Colodny, August 21, 1990, transcript, Colodny Collection.

21. Dash, *Chief Counsel*, 224.

22. Woodward and Bernstein, *Final Days*, 75.

23. Alexander Haig, interview by Martha Kumar, December 22, 1999, transcript, White House interview program, RNPLM, https://www.archives.gov/files/presidential -libraries/research/transition-interviews/pdf/haig.pdf.

24. Jaworski, *Right and the Power*, 47.

25. Oral Memoirs of Leon Jaworski, vol. 2, 555.

26. Elmo Zumwalt interview with Alfred Goldberg and Maurice Matloff, October 22, 1991, transcript, Historical Office of the Secretary of Defense, 43, http://history .defense.gov/Portals/70/Documents/oral_history/OH_Trans_Zumwalt,%20Elmo %2010-22-1991.pdf?ver=2016-06-20-114138-600.

27. Hersh, "The Pardon."

28. Zumwalt, interview with Goldberg and Matloff.

29. R. W. Apple Jr., "Nixon Feels Trip 'Scored Points,'" *New York Times*, December 28, 1973.

30. Jaworski, *Right and the Power*, 55.

31. Nixon, *RN*, 973.

10. JANUARY 1974

1. Lukas, *Nightmare*, 572.

2. Dan Thomasson, interview by Len Colodny, August 21, 1990, transcript, Colodny Collection.

3. Charles Radford, interview by Robert Gettlin, March 11, 1989, transcript, Colodny Collection.

4. W. Donald Stewart, memorandum for the record, January 7, 1974, Colodny Collection.

5. Colodny and Gettlin, *Silent Coup*, 380; Donald Stewart, memorandum for the record, January 7, 1974, Colodny Collection.

6. Colodny and Gettlin, *Silent Coup*, 57.

7. Stewart, memorandum for the record.

8. Woodward and Bernstein, *Final Days*, 75.

9. Haig and McCarry, *Inner Circles*, 445.

10. Woodward and Bernstein, *Final Days*, 115.

11. Jaworski, *Right and the Power*, 56.

12. Nixon, *RN*, 978.

13. Robert Welander, interview with Len Colodny, transcript, March 28, 1987, Colodny Collection.

14. Jim Squires, "Probers Charge Pentagon Spied on Kissinger in 1971," *Chicago Tribune*, January 11, 1974.

15. Seymour Hersh, "A Military 'Ring' Linked to Spying on White House," *New York Times*, January 12, 1974.

16. Bob Woodward and Carl Bernstein, "Pentagon Got Secret Data of Kissinger's," *Washington Post*, January 12, 1974.

17. Seymour Hersh, "Blackmail Laid to Official in Pentagon 'Spy' Inquiry," *New York Times*, January 13, 1974.

18. Seymour Hersh, interview by Len Colodny, February 4, 1987, transcript, Colodny Collection.

19. Hersh, interview by Colodny.

20. Bob Woodward and Carl Bernstein, "The Plumbers," *Washington Post*, January 13, 1974.

21. Document 234, "Minutes of Secretary of Defense Laird's Armed Forces Policy Council Meeting," Washington DC, December 6, 1971, 9:37–10:40 a.m., in Smith, *South Asia Crisis*, 652–55.

22. Document 274, "Memorandum of Conversation," New York, December 10, 1971, 6:05–7:55 p.m., in Smith, *South Asia Crisis*, 751–63.

23. Van Atta, *With Honor*, 298.

24. Seymour Hersh, "Report on Data Leak Said to Have Named Moorer," *New York Times*, January 14, 1974.

25. Seymour Hersh, "Officials Dispute Military Spy Plan," *New York Times*, January 16, 1974.

26. Michael Getler, "Alleged Pentagon Spying Probed," *Washington Post*, January 16, 1974.

27. Seymour Hersh, "Stennis to Examine 'Spying' by Military," *New York Times*, January 15, 1974.

28. Getler, "Alleged Pentagon Spying Probed."

29. Getler, "Alleged Pentagon Spying Probed."

30. Lesley Oelsner, "White House Vows Full Cooperation on Tape," *New York Times*, January 17, 1974.

31. Jack Anderson, "Pentagon Spied Out of Frustration," *Washington Post*, January 17, 1974.

32. W. Donald Stewart to Martin Hoffmann, January 21, 1974, Colodny Collection.

33. Seymour Hersh, "Kissinger Says He Heard Tape of 'Plumbers' Inquiry," *New York Times*, January 23, 1974.

34. Stewart to Hoffmann, January 21, 1974.

35. "Pentagon Aide Cited in Plot to Lead FBI," *New York Times*, January 25, 1974.

36. Seymour Hersh, "Defense Official Denies Pressure," *New York Times*, January 25, 1974.

37. Melvin Laird, interview by Len Colodny, October 28, 1986, Colodny Collection.

38. Stewart to Hoffmann, January 21, 1974.

39. Document 292, Editorial Note, in Qaimmaqami, *Energy Crisis*, 820.

40. Document 242, in Qaimmaqami, *Energy Crisis*, 821.

41. David Rosenbaum, "A Pledge to Stay," *New York Times*, January 31, 1974.

42. Seymour Hersh, "Kissinger Called on Alleged Spying," *New York Times*, February 1, 1974.

11. FEBRUARY 1974

1. Jaworski, *Right and the Power*, 87.

2. Kissinger, Schlesinger, Scowcroft, and Wickham, memorandum of conversation, February 1, 1974, GRFPLM, https://www.fordlibrarymuseum.gov/library/document /0314/1552657.pdf.

3. Kissinger, Schlesinger, Scowcroft, Wickham, memorandum of conversation.

4. Seymour Hersh, "Spying in the White House Said to Have Begun in '70," *New York Times*, February 3, 1974.

5. Seymour Hersh, "Senator Hughes Asks Public Military Spy Hearings; Breaks with Stennis on Closed Kissinger Session," *New York Times*, February 4, 1974.

6. Seymour Hersh, "Moorer Concedes He Got Documents," *New York Times*, February 6, 1974.

7. U.S. Congress, Senate, Committee on Armed Services, *Transmittal of Documents, Part 1*, 28.

8. U.S. Congress, Senate, Committee on Armed Services, *Transmittal of Documents, Part 1*, 46.

9. Seymour Hersh, "Kissinger Scores Military Spying," *New York Times*, February 7, 1974.

10. "Yeoman Quoted as Saying Admirals Asked Files," *New York Times*, February 8, 1974.

11. W. Donald Stewart to Martin Hoffmann, "Moorer-Welander-Radford Matter," February 8, 1974, Colodny Collection.

12. Document 308, "Draft Telegram from the President's Deputy Assistant for National Security Affairs (Scowcroft) to Secretary of State Kissinger in Panama," February 7, 1974, in Qaimmaqami, *Energy Crisis*, 865.

13. Presidential daily diary, February 7, 1974, RNPLM, https://www.nixonlibrary.gov /virtuallibrary/documents/PDD/1974/117%20February%201-15%201974.pdf.

14. Nixon, Ambassador Al Sowayel, Scowcroft, memorandum of conversation, February 7, 1974, GRFPLM, https://www.fordlibrarymuseum.gov/library/document /0314/1552659.pdf.

15. Colodny and Gettlin, *Silent Coup*, 393.

16. Stewart to Hoffmann, "Moorer-Welander-Radford."

17. "Stennis Hears Yeoman's Story; Praises Him for Forthrightness," *New York Times*, February 10, 1974.

18. W. Donald Stewart, memorandum for the record, February 12, 1974, Colodny Collection.

19. Document 319, "Transcript of a Telephone Conversation between Secretary of State Kissinger and the White House Chief of Staff (Haig)," February 11, 1974, in Qaimmaqami, *Energy Crisis*, 895.

20. Document 323, "Transcript of a Telephone Conversation between Secretary of State Kissinger and the White House Chief of Staff (Haig)," February 14, 1974, in Qaimmaqami, *Energy Crisis*, 903.

21. W. Donald Stewart, interview by Senator Howard Baker, February 19, 1974, container CII2, U.S. Senate, Select Committee on Presidential Campaign Activities.

22. U.S. Congress, Senate, Committee on Armed Services, *Transmittal of Documents, Part 2*, 6.

23. U.S. Congress, Senate, Committee on Armed Services, *Transmittal of Documents, Part 2*, 12.

24. U.S. Congress, Senate, Committee on Armed Services, *Transmittal of Documents, Part 2*, 12.

25. U.S. Congress, Senate, Committee on Armed Services, *Transmittal of Documents, Part 2*, 221.

26. Elmo Zumwalt interview with Alfred Goldberg and Maurice Matloff, October 22, 1991, transcript, Historical Office of the Secretary of Defense, http://history.defense .gov/Portals/70/Documents/oral_history/OH_Trans_Zumwalt,%20Elmo%2010-22 -1991.pdf?ver=2016-06-20-114138-600.

27. U.S. Congress, Senate, Committee on Armed Services, *Transmittal of Documents, Part 2*, 148.

28. U.S. Congress, Senate, Committee on Armed Services, *Transmittal of Documents, Part 2*, 162.

29. U.S. Congress, Senate, Committee on Armed Services, *Transmittal of Documents, Part 2*, 159.

30. U.S. Congress, Senate, Committee on Armed Services, *Transmittal of Documents, Part 2*, 210.

31. U.S. Congress, Senate, Committee on Armed Services, *Transmittal of Documents, Part 2*, 231.

32. Seymour Hersh, "Nixon Said to Have Balked at Charges in Secrets Theft," *New York Times*, February 24, 1974.

33. Oral Memoirs of Leon Jaworski, vol. 2, interviews 7–9, March 13, 1979–May 23, 1979, 555.

34. Haig and McCarry, *Inner Circles*, 449.

35. John Herbers, "Nixon Asserts a Criminal Charge Is Required for Impeachment; He Does Not Expect House to Act," *New York Times*, February 26, 1974.

12. MARCH 1974

1. Anthony Ripley, "Federal Grand Jury Indicts 7 Nixon Aides on Charges of Conspiracy on Watergate: Haldeman, Ehrlichman, Mitchell on List," *New York Times*, March 1, 1974.

2. Lukas, *Nightmare*, 522.

3. James Naughton, "A Legal Question," *New York Times*, March 3, 1974.

4. John Herbers, "Haig, a Strong Right Arm, Replaces 2 Indicted Men," *New York Times*, March 3, 1974.

5. "Admiral Says Ehrlichman Asked His Confession in Spying Case," *New York Times*, March 3, 1974.

6. Michael Getler, "White House Had Channel to Pentagon," *Washington Post*, March 3, 1974.

7. Kissinger, Schlesinger, Scowcroft, and Wickham, memorandum of conversation, March 6, 1974, GRFPLM, https://www.fordlibrarymuseum.gov/library/document /0314/1552666.pdf.

8. John Herbers, "Nixon Insists He Didn't Authorize Hush Money in Watergate Cases; Offers Testimony to Rodino Unit," *New York Times*, March 7, 1974.

9. Marjorie Hunter, "GOP Begins to Rally around Ford; Growing Crowds Hail New Boldness," *New York Times*, March 9, 1974.

10. "2 on Judiciary Panel Criticize Nixon for Not Disclosing Tapes," *New York Times*, March 11, 1974.

11. Bernard Nussbaum, interview by Timothy Naftali, October 1, 2011, RNPLM, https:// www.nixonlibrary.gov/virtuallibrary/documents/histories/nussbaum-2011-10-01.pdf.

12. William Weld, interview by Timothy Naftali, September 28, 2011, RNPLM, https:// www.nixonlibrary.gov/virtuallibrary/documents/histories/weld-2011-09-28.pdf.

13. Evan Davis, interview by Timothy Naftali, September 29, 2011, RNPLM, https://www .nixonlibrary.gov/virtuallibrary/documents/histories/davis-2011-09-29.pdf.

14. U.S. Congress, Senate, Committee on Armed Services, *Transmittal of Documents, Part 3*, 9.

15. U.S. Congress, Senate, Committee on Armed Services, *Transmittal of Documents, Part 3*, 13.

16. U.S. Congress, Senate, Committee on Armed Services, *Transmittal of Documents, Part 3*, 27.

17. U.S. Congress, Senate, Committee on Armed Services, *Transmittal of Documents, Part 3*, 38.

18. U.S. Congress, Senate, Committee on Armed Services, *Transmittal of Documents, Part 3*, 40.

19. "Ford Bars Plea That Nixon Quit," *New York Times*, March 12, 1974.

20. Jerry Jones, interview by Len Colodny, January 23, 1988, transcript, Colodny Collection.

21. Jones, interview by Colodny.

22. Susanna McBee, "Officials Must Report a Crime," *Washington Post*, March 13, 1974.

23. Bob Woodward and Carl Bernstein, "Last Payoff in Cover-Up Pinpointed," *Washington Post*, March 15, 1974.

24. Kissinger, Schlesinger, Scowcroft, memorandum of conversation, March 19, 1974, GRFPLM, https://www.fordlibrarymuseum.gov/library/document/0314/1552671.pdf.

25. Jack Nelson, "Hush Money Tape Held 'Explosive' in Backing Dean Story," *Los Angeles Times*, March 23, 1974.

26. John Herbers, "White House Says Court Was Told 10 of Nixon's Talks Aren't on Tape," *New York Times*, March 29, 1974.

13. APRIL 1974

1. Bill Kovach, "House Judiciary Staff on Impeachment Begins," *New York Times*, April 4, 1974.

2. Lesley Oelsner, "Nixon Lawyer Argues Against Release of Dean Tapes," *New York Times*, April 3, 1974.

3. Marjorie Hunter, "Tape Compromise Favored by Ford," *New York Times*, April 6, 1974.

4. Woodward and Bernstein, *All the President's Men*, 270.

5. John D. O'Connor, "I'm the Guy They Called Deep Throat," *Vanity Fair*, July 2005.

6. "Nixon Fares Better in Ratings," *Times-News* (Burlington NC), April 8, 1974.

7. Bill Kovach, "House Subpoena Bids President Turn Over Tapes, Other Material; White House May Yield Some Data," *New York Times*, April 12, 1974.

8. Christopher Lydon, "A Passive Electorate," *New York Times*, April 14, 1974.

9. Haig, *Inner Circles*, 447.

10. Bill Kovach, "St. Clair Control of Case Doubted," *New York Times*, April 16, 1974.

11. John J. Chester, interview by Sam Rushay and Sam McClure, July 3, 2002, RNPLM, https://www.nixonlibrary.gov/virtuallibrary/documents/histories/chester-2002-07-30.pdf.

12. William Saxbe, interview by Karl Weissenbach and Sam Rushay, July 30, 2002, RNPLM, https://www.nixonlibrary.gov/virtuallibrary/documents/histories/saxbe-2002-09-27.pdf.

13. Dick Polman, "Al Haig, the Long Goodbye," *Philadelphia Inquirer*, February 22, 2010.

14. Jaworski, *Right and the Power*, 134.

15. Haig and McCarry, *Inner Circles*, 451.

16. Kissinger, Schlesinger, Scowcroft, memorandum of conversation, April 23, 1974, GRFPLM, https://www.fordlibrarymuseum.gov/library/document/0314/1552698.pdf.

17. Document 82, "Memorandum from the President's Deputy Assistant for National Security Affairs (Scowcroft) to President Ford," October 25, 1974, in Mahan, *SALT II*, 398.

18. Kissinger, Schlesinger, Scowcroft, memorandum of conversation, April 23, 1974.

19. Document 64, "Minutes of a Meeting of the Verification Panel," in Mahan, *SALT II*, 243.

20. Martin Arnold, "Mitchell and Stans Are Acquitted on All Counts," *New York Times*, April 29, 1974.

21. Jaworski, *Right and the Power*, 131.

22. Haig, St. Clair, Cabinet, memorandum of conversation, April 29, 1974, GRFPLM, https://www.fordlibrarymuseum.gov/library/document/0314/1552700.pdf.

23. John Herbers, "Nixon Will Give Edited Transcripts on Watergate to House and the Public; Notes Ambiguities, Insists He Is Innocent," *New York Times*, April 30, 1974.

24. Haig and McCarry, *Inner Circles*, 452.

25. Haig and McCarry, *Inner Circles*, 453.

26. R. W. Apple Jr., "White House Accuses Dean of Attempting to Blackmail Nixon to Gain Immunity," *New York Times*, April 30, 1974.

14. MAY 1974

1. James Naughton, "Nixon Depicted in Transcripts as Having Searched for Ways to Hide Details of Watergate," *New York Times*, May 1, 1974.

2. John Herbers, "House Faces Bar on Nixon Material," *New York Times*, May 2, 1974.

3. Califano, *Inside*, 299.

4. "Haig, on Nixon's Order, Refuses Questions of Watergate Panel," *New York Times*, May 3, 1974.

5. James Naughton, "Rodino Aides Find Their Transcripts Vary from Nixon," *New York Times*, May 2, 1974.

6. Drew, *Washington Journal*, 261.

7. John Herbers, "Move Is Surprise," *New York Times*, May 6, 1974.

8. Jaworski, *Right and the Power*, 135.

9. Haig and McCarry, *Inner Circles*, 455.

10. Presidential daily diary, May 6, 1974, RNPLM, https://www.nixonlibrary.gov/virtuallibrary/documents/PDD/1974/123%20May%201-15%201974.pdf.

11. Nixon, *RN*, 1001.

12. Nixon, *RN*, 1001.

13. Presidential daily diary, May 6, 1974.

14. Haig and McCarry, *Inner Circles*, 455.

15. Jaworski, *Right and the Power*, 136.

16. Drew, *Washington Journal*, 270.

17. George Lardner Jr., "Sirica Seals Memo Seeking More Tapes," *Washington Post*, May 12, 1974.

18. Drew, *Washington Journal*, 274.

19. Seymour Hersh, "Nixon Use of Ethnic Epithets Is Reported," *New York Times*, May 12, 1974.

20. Document 56, "Telegram from Secretary of State Kissinger to the President's Deputy Assistant for National Security Affairs (Scowcroft)," May 14, 1974, 0840Z, in Howard, *Arab-Israeli Dispute*, 277.

21. Nixon, *RN*, 1001.

22. Kutler, *The Wars of Watergate*, 536.

23. Document 66, "Telegram from the President's Deputy Assistant for National Security Affairs (Scowcroft) to Secretary of State Kissinger," Washington DC, May 21, 1974, 1431Z, in Howard, *Arab-Israeli Dispute*, 290–91.

24. Seymour Hersh, "Judge Denies US Security Justified Ellsberg Break-In," *New York Times*, May 25, 1974.

25. Marjorie Hunter, "Nixon-Ford Friendship Seems Strained," *New York Times*, May 28, 1974.

26. Presidential daily diary, May 23, 1974, RNPLM, https://www.nixonlibrary.gov/virtuallibrary/documents/PDD/1974/124%20May%2016-31%201974.pdf.

27. Hunter, "Nixon-Ford Friendship."

28. Lukas, *Nightmare*, 610.

29. Nixon, *RN*, 1006.

30. Seymour Hersh, "'Plumbers' Case Dismissal Opposed," *New York Times*, June 1, 1974; Colodny and Gettlin, *Silent Coup*, 408.

15. JUNE 1974

1. Drew, *Washington Journal*, 283.

2. Doris Kearns Goodwin, review of *All the President's Men*, *New York Times*, June 9, 1974.

3. Richard Whalen, "Putting It All Together," *Washington Post*, June 3, 1974.

4. Seymour Hersh, "Colson Pleads Guilty to Charge in Ellsberg Case and Is Expected to Aid Jaworski and Rodino Panel," *New York Times*, June 4, 1974.

5. Lesley Oelsner, "'Pushing of Keys' Caused Tape Gap, Experts Assert," *New York Times*, June 5, 1974.

6. Laurence Stern, "Nixon Attributed Taps to Kissinger," *Washington Post*, June 5, 1974.

7. Haig and McCarry, *Inner Circles*, 457.

8. Lukas, *Nightmare*, 552.

9. Anthony Ripley, "Jury Named Nixon a Co-conspirator but Didn't Indict," *New York Times*, June 7, 1974.

10. Seymour Hersh, "Kissinger Linked to Order to FBI Ending Wiretaps," *New York Times*, June 9, 1974.

11. Hersh, *Price of Power*, 400.

12. Haig and McCarry, *Inner Circles*, 457.

13. Stephen Bull, interview by author, July 2, 2017.

14. Haig and McCarry, *Inner Circles*, 458.

15. Bernard Gwertzman, "Kissinger Threat Culminates Long Dispute," *New York Times*, June 12, 1974.

16. Haig and McCarry, *Inner Circles*, 458.

17. John Crewdson, "FBI Tied Tap Requests to Kissinger or Gen. Haig," *New York Times*, June 12, 1974.

18. John Crewdson, "Wiretap Inquiry Is Said Not to Aim at Kissinger Role," *New York Times*, June 14, 1974.

19. Bernard Gwertzman, "Capital Rallying Round Kissinger; Vindication Asked," *New York Times*, June 14, 1974.

20. Gwertzman, "Capital Rallying."

21. Bull, interview by author.

22. David Rosenbaum, "An Explanation: Cox Ouster Spurred House Inquiry," *New York Times*, June 19, 1974.

23. "Kissinger Quoted on Ordering Taps," *New York Times*, June 20, 1974.

24. Nixon, *RN*, 1014.

25. Document 68, "Minutes of a Meeting of the National Security Council," Washington DC, June 20, 1974, 3:10–5:10 p.m., in Mahan, *SALT II*, 266–75.

26. Haig and McCarry, *Inner Circles*, 462.

27. Nixon, *RN*, 1024.

28. Nixon, *RN*, 1027.

16. JULY 1974

1. U.S. Congress, House, Committee on the Judiciary, *A Resolution, Book 1*, 55.

2. U.S. Congress, House, Committee on the Judiciary, *A Resolution, Book 1*, 58.

3. U.S. Congress, House, Committee on the Judiciary, *A Resolution, Book 1*, 58.

4. U.S. Congress, House, Committee on the Judiciary, *A Resolution, Book 1*, 59.

5. U.S. Congress, House, Committee on the Judiciary, *A Resolution, Book 1*, 61.

6. Alexander Butterfield, interview by Len Colodny, March 26, 1987, transcript, Colodny Collection.

7. Presidential daily diary, July 4, 1974, RNPLM, https://www.nixonlibrary.gov /virtuallibrary/documents/PDD/1974/127%20July%201974.pdf.

8. Nixon, *RN*, 1042.

9. Lukas, *Nightmare*, 563.

10. Warren Weaver Jr., "High Court Hears 3 Hours of Debate in Nixon Cases and Reserves Its Decision," *New York Times*, July 9, 1974.

11. John Herbers, "President Withheld Part of Tape on Cover-Up Talk," *New York Times*, July 11, 1974.

12. Haig and McCarry, *Inner Circles*, 470.

13. Nixon, *RN*, 1045.

14. Califano, *Inside*, 299–303.

15. James Naughton, "St. Clair Quotes a Withheld Tape to Support Nixon," *New York Times*, July 19, 1974.

16. Nixon, *RN*, 1047.

17. "The Summation," *New York Times*, July 21, 1974.

18. Nixon, *RN*, 1052.

19. Nixon, *RN*, 1049.

20. Haig and McCarry, *Inner Circles*, 471.

21. Nixon, *RN*, 1051.

22. Haig and McCarry, *Inner Circles*, 472.

23. Nixon, *RN*, 1052; Lukas, *Nightmare*, 573; Woodward and Bernstein, *Final Days*, 263.

24. Hersh, "The Pardon."

25. Jerry Jones, interview by Richard Norton Smith, January 26, 2009, GRFPLM, https:// geraldrfordfoundation.org/centennial-docs/oralhistory/wp-content/uploads/2013 /05/Jerry-Jones.pdf.

26. Lukas, *Nightmare*, 584.

27. Haig and McCarry, *Inner Circles*, 476.

28. Haig and McCarry, *Inner Circles*, 491.

29. Lukas, *Nightmare*, 615.

30. Haig and McCarry, *Inner Circles*, 493.

31. Haig and McCarry, *Inner Circles*, 493.

32. Hersh, "The Pardon."

17. AUGUST 1974

1. Hersh, "The Pardon."

2. Haig and McCarry, *Inner Circles*, 480.

3. Hartmann, *Palace Politics*, 124.

4. Hersh, "The Pardon."

5. Gerald R. Ford, Statement and Responses to Questions from Members of the House Judiciary Committee Concerning the Pardon of Richard Nixon, in *Public Papers of the Presidents: Gerald R. Ford, 1974*, http://www.presidency.ucsb.edu/ws/?pid=4471.

6. Hersh, "The Pardon."

7. Ford, *A Time to Heal*, 1.

8. Hersh, "The Pardon."

9. Ford, *A Time to Heal*, 10.

10. Ford, Statement and Responses.

11. Hersh, "The Pardon."

12. "Jaworski Studies 2 Altered Memos," *New York Times*, August 3, 1974.

13. Lukas, *Nightmare*, 603.

14. Douglas Kneeland, "Ford Sees Odds in House Shifting to Impeachment," *New York Times*, August 3, 1974.

15. John Herbers, "Nixon Calls Aides in Possible Move on Impeachment," *New York Times*, August 5, 1974.

16. Jaworski, *Right and the Power*, 208.

17. "President Considered Resigning but Rejected Idea, Aides Assert," *New York Times*, August 5, 1974.

18. Ford, *A Time to Heal*, 16.

19. John Herbers, "Top Aides Rally," *New York Times*, August 7, 1974.

20. Bernard Gwertzman, "Fulbright Panel Clears Kissinger on Wiretap Role," *New York Times*, August 7, 1974.

21. Colodny and Gettlin, *Silent Coup*, 423.

22. Hersh, "The Pardon."

23. Hersh, "The Pardon."

24. Bernard Gwertzman, "Ford Promises That He and Kissinger Will Continue Nixon's Foreign Policy," *New York Times*, August 9, 1974.

25. Jaworski, *Right and the Power*, 217.

26. John Herbers, "The 37th President Is First to Quit Post," *New York Times*, August 9, 1974.

27. Jaworski, *Right and the Power*, 217; Hersh, "The Pardon."

28. Marjorie Hunter, "A Plea to Bind Up Watergate Wounds," *New York Times*, August 10, 1974.

29. Jerry Jones, interview by Richard Norton Smith, January 26, 2009, GRFPLM, https://geraldrfordfoundation.org/centennial-docs/oralhistory/wp-content/uploads/2013/05/Jerry-Jones.pdf.

30. Lesley Oelsner, "Aide Doubtful That Ford Would Give Nixon Pardon," *New York Times*, August 10, 1974.

31. Jones, interview by Smith.

32. Jones, interview by Smith.

33. Stephen Bull, interview by author, July 2, 2017.

34. Jones, interview by Smith.

35. Haig and McCarry, *Inner Circles*, 513.

36. John Crewdson, "Scott Says Capitol Leaders Oppose Nixon Prosecution," *New York Times*, August 12, 1974.

37. Benton Becker, interview by Richard Norton Smith, June 9, 2009, GRFPLM, https://geraldrfordfoundation.org/centennial-docs/oralhistory/wp-content/uploads/2013/05/Benton-Becker.pdf.

38. Becker, interview by Smith.

39. John Crewdson, "White House Says Tapes Are Nixon's Own Property," *New York Times*, August 15, 1973.

40. Hersh, "The Pardon."

41. Hersh, "The Pardon."

42. Jaworski, *Right and the Power*, 231.

43. Jaworski, *Right and the Power*, 231.

44. Werth, *31 Days*, 213.

45. John Herbers, "Decision Put Off," *New York Times*, August 29, 1974.

46. Werth, *31 Days*, 222.

47. Werth, *31 Days*, 222.

48. Benton L. Becker, "History and Background of Nixon Pardon," box 2, Nixon Pardon—Becker's Memorandum folder, Benton L. Becker Papers, GRFPLM, https://www.fordlibrarymuseum.gov/library/document/0238/1126646.pdf.

49. Burdick v. United States, https://supreme.justia.com/cases/federal/us/236/79/.

50. Becker, "History and Background."

51. Jaworski, *Right and the Power*, 228–30.

52. Becker, "History and Background."

53. John Herbers, "No Conditions Set," *New York Times*, September 9, 1974.

54. Herbers, "No Conditions Set."

18. AFTER NIXON

1. Haig, interview by Woodward and Bernstein, September 10, 1974.
2. Brinkley and Nichter, *The Nixon Tapes*, 335.
3. Colodny and Gettlin, *Silent Coup*, 82.
4. Haig, interview by Woodward and Bernstein.
5. Woodward and Bernstein, *Final Days*, 403.
6. Document 268, "Transcript of Telephone Conversation between Secretary of State Kissinger and the White House Chief of Staff (Haig)," in Howland and Daigle, *Arab-Israeli Crisis*, 737.
7. Haig, interview by Woodward and Bernstein.
8. Lasky, "The Woodstein Ripoff," https://aim.org/publications/aim_report/1976/10a.html.
9. Haig and McCarry, *Inner Circles*, 323.
10. Leslie Gelb, "Successor to Haig," *New York Times*, September 25, 1974.
11. Haig and McCarry, *Inner Circles*, 518.
12. Haig and McCarry, *Inner Circles*, 519.
13. Bob Woodward and Carl Bernstein, "Ford Disputed on Events Preceding Nixon Pardon," *Washington Post*, December 8, 1975.
14. Califano, *Inside*, 388.
15. Bob Woodward, "Don't Subpoena the Tapes," *Washington Post*, January 15, 1981.
16. Steven Roberts, "Haig Is Confirmed by Senate, 93 to 6," *New York Times*, January 22, 1981.
17. Colodny and Shachtman, *The Forty Years War*, 295.
18. William Clark, interview by Stephen F. Knott, Ronald Reagan Oral History Project, https://millercenter.org/the-presidency/presidential-oral-histories/william-p-clark-oral-history-assistant-president.

BIBLIOGRAPHY

ARCHIVAL SOURCES

American Bar Association FBI Files. https://archive.org/details/ABA-FBI.

Colodny Collection. Texas A&M University, Waco, Texas. http://www.watergate.com/Colodny-Collection/Colodny-Collection.aspx.

FBI Records: The Vault. https://vault.fbi.gov/.

Gerald R. Ford Presidential Library and Museum (GRFPLM). Grand Rapids, Michigan. https://www.fordlibrarymuseum.gov/library.

Freedom of Information Act Electronic Reading Room. https://www.cia.gov/library/readingroom/.

Historical Office of the Secretary of Defense. https://history.defense.gov.

Oral Memoirs of Leon Jaworski. Baylor University Program for Oral History, Waco, Texas. http://digitalcollections.baylor.edu/cdm/ref/collection/buioh/id/1591.

Richard Nixon Presidential Library and Museum (RNPLM). Yorba Linda, California. https://www.nixonlibrary.gov/forresearchers/find/tapes/finding_aids/tapesubjectlogs/oval639.pdf.

Ronald Reagan Oral History Project. Miller Center of Public Affairs, Charlottesville, Virginia. https://millercenter.org/the-presidency/presidential-oral-histories/ronald-reagan.

Records of the Watergate Special Prosecution Force. National Archives and Records Administration, Washington DC. https://www.archives.gov/research/investigations/watergate.

U.S. Senate. Select Committee on Presidential Campaign Activities. Library of Congress, Washington DC.

Lowell P. Weicker Jr. Papers. Special Collections, University of Virginia Library, University of Virginia, Charlottesville. http://ead.lib.virginia.edu/vivaxtf/view?docId=uva-sc/viu04106.xml;query=weicker%20papers;brand=default.

Woodward and Bernstein Watergate Papers. Harry Ransom Center, University of Texas at Austin. http://norman.hrc.utexas.edu/fasearch/findingAid.cfm?eadid=00365.

PUBLISHED SOURCES

Agnew, Spiro. *Go Quietly . . . or Else: His Own Story of the Events Leading to His Resigna-tion*. New York: Morrow, 1986.

Ahlberg, Kristine L., and Alexander Wieland, eds. *Foundations of Foreign Policy, 1973–1976*. Vol. 38, pt. 1 of *Foreign Relations of the United States, 1969–1976*, edited by Edward C. Keefer. Washington DC: U.S. Government Printing Office, 2011.

Baker, Russ. *Family of Secrets: The Bush Dynasty, the Powerful Forces That Put It in the White House, and What Their Influence Means for America*. New York: Bloomsbury, 2009.

Barry, James A. "Managing Covert Political Action." *Orbis: A Journal of World Affairs*, Summer 1993.

Bass, Gary J. *The Blood Telegram: Nixon, Kissinger, and a Forgotten Genocide*. New York: Knopf, 2013.

Bennett, M. Todd, ed. *National Security Policy, 1969–1972*. Vol. 34 of *Foreign Relations of the United States, 1969–1976*, edited by Edward C. Keefer. Washington DC: U.S. Government Printing Office, 2011.

———, ed. *National Security Policy, 1973–1976*. Vol. 35 of *Foreign Relations of the United States, 1969–1976*, edited by Adam M. Howard. Washington DC: U.S. Government Printing Office, 2014.

Berman, Larry. *No Peace, No Honor: Nixon, Kissinger, and Betrayal in Vietnam*. New York: Free Press, 2001.

———. *Zumwalt: The Life and Times of Admiral Elmo Russell "Bud" Zumwalt, Jr.* New York: HarperCollins, 2012.

Best, Richard A., Jr. *The National Security Council: An Organizational Assessment*. Congressional Research Service, December 28, 2011.

Bird, Kai. *The Chairman: John J. McCloy; The Making of the American Establishment*. New York: Simon & Schuster, 1992.

———. *The Color of Truth: McGeorge Bundy and William Bundy, Brothers in Arms*. New York: Simon & Schuster, 1998.

Bohning, Don. *The Castro Obsession: U.S. Covert Actions against Cuba, 1959–1965*. Washington DC: Potomac Books, 2005.

Bradlee, Ben. *A Good Life: Newspapering and Other Adventures*. New York: Simon & Schuster, 1995.

Branch, Taylor. *At Canaan's Edge: America in the King Years, 1965–68*. New York: Simon & Schuster, 2006.

———. *Parting the Waters: America in the King Years 1954–63*. New York: Simon & Schuster, 1988.

———. *Pillar of Fire: America in the King Years, 1963–65*. New York: Simon & Schuster, 1998.

Branch, Taylor, with Eugene M. Propper. *Labyrinth*. New York: Viking, 1982.

Brinkley, Douglas, and Luke A. Nichter. *The Nixon Tapes*. New York: Houghton Mifflin Harcourt, 2014.

————. *The Nixon Tapes: 1973*. New York: Houghton Mifflin Harcourt, 2015.

Brower, Brock. "Agnew on the Warpath." *Life*, October 16, 1970.

Buchanan, Patrick J. *Nixon's White House Wars: The Battles That Made and Broke a President and Divided America Forever*. New York: Crown Forum, 2017.

Bundy, William. *A Tangled Web: The Making of Foreign Policy in the Nixon Presidency*. New York: Hill & Wang, 1998.

Califano, Joseph A., Jr. *Inside: A Public and Private Life*. New York: PublicAffairs, 2004.

Carland, John M., ed. *Vietnam, January–October 1972*. Vol. 8 of *Foreign Relations of the United States, 1969–1976*, edited by Edward C. Keefer. Washington DC: U.S. Government Printing Office, 2010.

————, ed. *Vietnam, October 1972–January 1973*. Vol. 9 of *Foreign Relations of the United States, 1969–1976*, edited by Edward C. Keefer. Washington DC: U.S. Government Printing Office, 2010.

Clifford, Clark, with Richard Holbrooke. *Counsel to the President: A Memoir*. New York: Random House, 1991.

Cohen, Richard M., and Jules Witcover. *A Heartbeat Away: The Investigation and Resignation of Vice President Spiro T. Agnew*. New York: Viking, 1974.

Colby, William, and Peter Forbath. *Honorable Men: My Life in the* CIA. New York: Simon & Schuster, 1978.

Coleman, Bradley Lynn, ed. *Vietnam, January 1973–July 1975*. Vol. 10 of *Foreign Relations of the United States, 1969–1976*, edited by Edward C. Keefer. Washington DC: U.S. Government Printing Office, 2010.

Colodny, Len, and Robert Gettlin. *Silent Coup: The Removal of a President*. New York: St. Martin's, 1991.

Colodny, Len, and Tom Shachtman. *The Forty Years War: The Rise and Fall of the Neocons, from Nixon to Obama*. New York: HarperCollins, 2009.

Copaken, Richard D. *Target Culebra: How 743 Islanders Took on the Entire U.S. Navy and Won*. San Juan: University of Puerto Rico Press, 2008.

Cronin, John. *The Problem of American Communism in 1945: Facts and Recommendations*. https://msa.maryland.gov/megafile/msa/speccol/sc5300/sc5339/000030/000000/000004/restricted/hiss_research/hiss/cronin-report.pdf.

Crouse, Timothy. *The Boys on the Bus: Riding with the Campaign Press Corps*. New York: Random House, 1973.

Cullen, Leslie Julian. *Brown Water Admiral: Elmo R. Zumwalt Jr. and United States Naval Forces Vietnam, 1968–1970*. Lubbock: Texas Tech University, 1998.

Dallek, Robert. *Nixon and Kissinger: Partners in Power*. New York: HarperCollins, 2007.

Daly, Chris. "The Inside Story." *Harvard Crimson*, April 19, 1976.

Dash, Samuel. *Chief Counsel: Inside the Ervin Committee—the Untold Story of Watergate*. New York: Random House, 1976.

Dean, John W. *Blind Ambition: The White House Years*. New York: Simon & Schuster, 1976.

Dobrynin, Anatoly. *In Confidence*. New York: Times Books, 1995.

Downie, Leonard. *The New Muckrakers: An Inside Look at America's Investigative Reporters.* Washington DC: New Republic, 1976.

Drea, Edward J. *McNamara, Clifford, and the Burdens of Vietnam, 1965–1969.* Washington DC: Office of the Secretary of Defense, 2011.

Drew, Elizabeth. *Washington Journal: Reporting Watergate and Richard Nixon's Downfall.* New York: Random House, 2014.

Ellsberg, Daniel. *Secrets: A Memoir of Vietnam and the Pentagon Papers.* New York: Viking, 2002.

Emery, Fred. *Watergate: The Corruption of American Politics and the Fall of Richard Nixon.* New York: Simon & Schuster, 1994.

Farrell, John A. *Nixon: The Life.* New York: Doubleday, 2017.

"FBI Files: Investigation of Nixon Administration Ordering of Wiretaping [*sic*] of Newspapermen and Others." FBI Serial: 65-HQ-75085, October 1971–May 1973. http://www.paperlessarchives.com/FreeTitles/NixonJournalistsWiretapsFBIFiles.pdf.

Feldstein, Mark. *Poisoning the Press: Richard Nixon, Jack Anderson, and the Rise of Washington's Scandal Culture.* New York: Farrar, Straus and Giroux, 2010.

Felt, Mark. *The FBI Pyramid: From the Inside.* New York: G. P. Putnam & Sons, 1979.

Ford, Gerald. *A Time to Heal: The Autobiography of Gerald Ford.* New York: Harper & Row, 1979.

Gardner, Lloyd C. *Pay Any Price: Lyndon Johnson and the Wars for Vietnam.* Chicago: Ivan R. Dee, 1995.

Garrow, David. *The FBI and Martin Luther King, Jr.: From "Solo" to Memphis.* New York: Norton, 1981.

Gentry, Curt. *J. Edgar Hoover: The Man and the Secrets.* New York: W. W. Norton, 1991.

Geyer, David C., ed. *Germany and Berlin, 1969–1972.* Vol. 40 of *Foreign Relations of the United States, 1969–1976,* edited by Edward C. Keefer. Washington DC: U.S. Government Printing Office, 2007.

———, ed. *Soviet Union, October 1970–October 1971.* Vol. 13 of *Foreign Relations of the United States, 1969–1976,* edited by Edward C. Keefer. Washington DC: U.S. Government Printing Office, 2011.

Geyer, David C., Nina D. Howland, and Kent Sieg, eds. *Soviet Union, October 1971–May 1972.* Vol. 14 of *Foreign Relations of the United States, 1969–1976,* edited by Edward C. Keefer. Washington DC: U.S. Government Printing Office, 2006.

Glass, Andrew. "House Denies Vice President Agnew's Impeachment Request." *Politico,* September 26, 2016.

Goldman, David, and Erin Mahan, eds. *Vietnam, July 1970–January 1972.* Vol. 7 of *Foreign Relations of the United States, 1969–1976,* edited by Edward C. Keefer. Washington DC: U.S. Government Printing Office, 2010.

Gray, L. Patrick, III, and Ed Gray. *In Nixon's Web: A Year in the Crosshairs of Watergate.* New York: Henry Holt, 2008.

Greenberg, David. "Throat Clearing." *Slate,* June 1, 2005.

Grose, Peter. *Gentleman Spy: The Life of Allen Dulles*. Boston: Houghton Mifflin, 1994.

Gulley, Bill, with Mary Ellen Reese. *Breaking Cover*. New York: Simon & Schuster, 1980.

Haig, Alexander M., Jr., and Charles McCarry. *Inner Circles: How America Changed the World; A Memoir*. New York: Warner, 1992.

Haldeman, H. R. *The Haldeman Diaries: Inside the Nixon White House*. New York: G. P. Putnam's Sons, 1994.

Hartmann, Robert T. *Palace Politics: An Inside Account of the Ford Years*. New York: McGraw-Hill, 1980.

Helms, Richard, and William Hood. *A Look over My Shoulder*. New York: Random House, 2003.

Hersh, Seymour. "The Pardon." *Atlantic*, August 1983.

———. *The Price of Power: Kissinger in the Nixon White House*. New York: Summit, 1983.

Himmelman, Jeff. *Yours in Truth: A Personal Portrait of Ben Bradlee*. New York: Random House, 2012.

Holland, Max. *Leak: Why Mark Felt Became Deep Throat*. Lawrence: University Press of Kansas, 2012.

Hougan, Jim. "The McCord File." *Harper's*, January 1980.

———. *Secret Agenda: Watergate, Deep Throat and the CIA*. New York: Random House, 1984.

Howard, Adam, ed. *Arab-Israeli Dispute, 1974–1976*. Vol. 26 of *Foreign Relations of the United States, 1969–1976*, edited by Edward C. Keefer. Washington DC: U.S. Government Printing Office, 2012.

Howland, Nina, and Craig Daigle, eds. *Arab-Israeli Crisis and War, 1973*. Vol. 25 of *Foreign Relations of the United States, 1969–1976*, edited by Edward C. Keefer. Washington DC: U.S. Government Printing Office, 2011.

Hughes, Ken. *Chasing Shadows: The Nixon Tapes, the Chennault Affair and the Origins of Watergate*. Charlottesville: University of Virginia Press, 2014.

Humphrey, David C., ed. *Organization and Management of U.S. Foreign Policy, 1969–1972*. Vol. 2 of *Foreign Relations of the United States, 1969–1976*, edited by Edward C. Keefer. Washington DC: U.S. Government Printing Office, 2006.

Humphrey, David C., and James E. Miller, eds. *Organization and Management of U.S. Foreign Policy: United Nations*. Vol. 33 of *Foreign Relations of the United States, 1964–1968*, edited by Edward C. Keefer. Washington DC: U.S. Government Printing Office, 2004.

Hurt, Harry, III. "Have Conscience, Will Travel." *Texas Monthly*, November 1977.

Isaacson, Walter. *Kissinger: A Biography*. New York: Simon & Schuster, 1992.

Jaworski, Leon. *The Right and the Power: The Prosecution of Watergate*. New York: Reader's Digest, 1976.

Johnson, U. Alexis, with J. O. McAllister. *The Right Hand of Power*. Englewood Cliffs NJ: Prentice-Hall, 1984.

Karnow, Stanley. *Vietnam: A History*. New York: Viking, 1983.

Keefer, Edward C., and Carolyn Yee, eds. *Vietnam, January 1969–July 1970*. Vol. 6 of *Foreign Relations of the United States, 1969–1976*, edited by Edward C. Keefer. Washington DC: U.S. Government Printing Office, 2006.

Kissinger, Henry A. *Crisis*. New York: Simon & Schuster, 2003.

———. *Diplomacy*. New York: Simon & Schuster, 1994.

———. *White House Years*. Boston: Little, Brown, 1979.

———. *Years of Renewal*. New York: Simon & Schuster, 1999.

———. *Years of Upheaval*. Boston: Little, Brown, 1982.

Kraemer, Fritz G. A. "U.S. Propaganda: What It Can and Can't Be." *Readings in Counter-Guerrilla Operations*. Fort Bragg NC: U.S. Army Special Warfare School, 1961. http://www.dtic.mil/dtic/tr/fulltext/u2/661045.pdf.

Krogh, Egil, with Matthew Krogh. *Integrity: Good People, Bad Choices and Life Lessons from the White House*. New York: PublicAffairs, 2007.

Kutler, Stanley I. *Abuse of Power: The New Nixon Tapes*. New York: Free Press, 1997.

———. *The Wars of Watergate: The Last Crisis of Richard Nixon*. New York: Knopf, 1990.

Lasky, Victor. "The Woodstein Ripoff." *Accuracy in Media,* October 1976.

Lawler, Daniel J., ed. *Southeast Asia, 1969–1972*. Vol. 20 of *Foreign Relations of the United States, 1969–1976*, edited by Edward C. Keefer. Washington DC: U.S. Government Printing Office, 2006.

Lawler, Daniel J., and Erin R. Mahan, eds. *Korea, 1969–1972*. Vol. 19, pt. 1 of *Foreign Relations of the United States, 1969–1976*, edited by Edward C. Keefer. Washington DC: U.S. Government Printing Office, 2009.

Leibman, Morris I. "Civil Disobedience: A Threat to Our Society under Law." *Freeman*, December 1963.

Lenzner, Terry. *The Investigator: Fifty Years of Uncovering the Truth*. New York: Blue Rider Press, 2013.

Liddy, G. Gordon. *Will: The Autobiography of G. Gordon Liddy*. New York: St. Martin's, 1980.

Locker, Ray. *Nixon's Gamble: How a President's Own Secret Government Destroyed His Administration*. Guilford CT: Lyons Press, 2016.

Lukas, J. Anthony. *Nightmare: The Underside of the Nixon Years*. New York: Viking, 1976.

Maas, Peter. *Manhunt: The Incredible Pursuit of a CIA Agent Turned Terrorist*. New York: Random House, 1986.

Mahan, Erin R., ed. *SALT I, 1969–1972*. Vol. 32 of *Foreign Relations of the United States, 1969–1976*, edited by Edward C. Keefer. Washington DC: U.S. Government Printing Office, 2010.

———, ed. *SALT II, 1972–1980*. Vol. 33 of *Foreign Relations of the United States, 1969–1976*, edited by Adam M. Howard. Washington DC: U.S. Government Printing Office, 2013.

———, ed. *Soviet Union, January 1969–October 1970*. Vol. 12 of *Foreign Relations of the United States, 1969–1976*, edited by Edward C. Keefer. Washington DC: U.S. Government Printing Office, 2006.

McElveen, James, and James Siekmeier, eds. *Chile, 1969–1973*. Vol. 21 of *Foreign Relations of the United States, 1969–1976*, edited by Adam Howard. Washington DC: U.S. Government Printing Office, 2014.

McGowan, Richard J. "Watergate Revisited." *Barnes Review*, March/April 2003.

Menges, Constantine. *Inside the National Security Council: The True Story of the Making and Unmaking of Reagan's Foreign Policy*. New York: Simon & Schuster, 1988.

Merrill, William H. *Watergate Prosecutor*. East Lansing: Michigan State University Press, 2008.

Miller, James E., and Laurie Van Hook, eds. *Western Europe; NATO, 1969–1972*. Vol. 41 of *Foreign Relations of the United States, 1969–1976*, edited by David S. Patterson. Washington DC: U.S. Government Printing Office, 2012.

Morris, Roger. *Haig: The General's Progress*. Chicago: Playboy Press, 1982.

———. *Richard Milhous Nixon: The Rise of an American Politician*. New York: Henry Holt, 1990.

———. *Uncertain Greatness: Henry Kissinger & American Foreign Policy*. New York: Harper & Row, 1977.

Newhouse, John. *Cold Dawn: The Story of SALT*. Washington DC: Pergamon-Brassey's, 1989.

Nixon, Richard. *RN: The Memoirs of Richard Nixon*. New York: Grosset & Dunlap, 1978.

Noah, Timothy. "John Dean Says Deep Throat Was Not a G-Man." *Slate*, June 17, 2002.

———. "Yes, Virginia, There Is a Deep Throat." *Slate*, May 8, 2002.

Novak, Robert. *The Prince of Darkness: 50 Years Reporting in Washington*. New York: Crown, 2007.

O'Connor, John D. "I'm the Guy They Called Deep Throat." *Vanity Fair*, July 2005.

Official History of the Bay of Pigs Operation, Volume 1, Air Operations, March 1960–April 1961. N.p.: Central Intelligence Agency, September 1979. https://www.cia.gov/library/readingroom/collection/bay-pigs-release.

Official History of the Bay of Pigs Operation, Volume 2, Participation in the Conduct of Foreign Policy. N.p.: Central Intelligence Agency, October 1979. https://www.cia.gov/library/readingroom/collection/bay-pigs-release.

Official History of the Bay of Pigs Operation, Volume 3, Evolution of CIA's Anti-Castro Policies, 1959–January 1961. N.p.: Central Intelligence Agency, December 1979. https://www.cia.gov/library/readingroom/collection/bay-pigs-release.

Perry, Mark. *Four Stars: The Inside Story of the Forty-Year Battle between the Joint Chiefs of Staff and America's Civilian Leaders*. Boston: Houghton Mifflin, 1989.

Phillips, Steven E., ed. *China, 1969–1972*. Vol. 17 of *Foreign Relations of the United States, 1969–1972*, edited by Edward C. Keefer. Washington DC: U.S. Government Printing Office, 2006.

Poole, Walter. *The Joint Chiefs of Staff and National Policy, 1969–1972*. Washington DC: Office of the Chairman of the Joint Chiefs of Staff, 2013.

Powers, Richard Gid. *Secrecy and Power: The Life of J. Edgar Hoover*. New York: Free Press, 1987.

Powers, Thomas. *The Man Who Kept the Secrets: Richard Helms and the* CIA. New York: Knopf, 1979.

Prados, John. *Keepers of the Keys: The National Security Council from Truman to Bush*. New York: Morrow, 1991.

President Nixon and the Role of Intelligence in the 1973 Arab-Israeli War. Center for the Study of Intelligence, January 30, 2013. https://www.cia.gov/library/readingroom /collection/president-nixon-and-role-intelligence-1973-arab-israeli-war.

Public Papers of the Presidents: Gerald R. Ford, 1974. http://www.presidency.ucsb.edu /ws/?pid=4471.

Public Papers of the President, Lyndon B. Johnson, 1963–1964: Book 2. http://www.presidency .ucsb.edu/ws/index.php?pid=26491.

Public Papers of the Presidents of the United States, Richard Nixon, 1973. https://quod.lib .umich.edu/p/ppotpus/4731942.1973.001/776?rgn=full+text;view=image.

Qaimmaqami, Linda W., and Adam M. Howard, eds. *Middle East Region and Arabian Peninsula, 1969–1972; Jordan, September 1970*. Vol. 24 of *Foreign Relations of the United States, 1969–1976*, edited by Edward C. Keefer. Washington DC: U.S. Government Printing Office, 2008.

Rhodes, Richard. *Arsenals of Folly: The Making of the Nuclear Arms Race*. New York: Knopf, 2007.

Riebling, Mark. *Wedge: The Secret War between the* FBI *and* CIA. New York: Knopf, 1994.

Rodriguez, Felix, and John Weisman. *Shadow Warrior: The* CIA *Hero of a Hundred Unknown Battles*. New York: Simon & Schuster, 1989.

Rogers, Lt. Gen. Bernard William. *Vietnam Studies: Cedar Falls–Junction City: A Turning Point*. Washington DC: Department of the Army, 1989.

Rosen, James. *The Strong Man: The Life of John N. Mitchell*. Garden City NY: Doubleday, 2008.

Selvage, Douglas E., and Melissa Jane Taylor, eds. *Soviet Union, June 1972–August 1974*. Vol. 15 of *Foreign Relations of the United States, 1969–1972*, edited by Edward C. Keefer. Washington DC: U.S. Government Printing Office, 2011.

Shawcross, William. *Sideshow: Kissinger, Nixon and the Destruction of Cambodia*. New York: Simon & Schuster, 1979.

Sheehan, Neil. *A Bright Shining Lie: John Paul Vann and America in Vietnam*. New York: Random House, 1988.

Shenon, Philip. *A Cruel and Shocking Act: The Secret History of the Kennedy Assassination*. New York: Henry Holt, 2013.

Shepard, Alicia. *Woodward and Bernstein: Life in the Shadow of Watergate*. Hoboken NJ: John Wiley & Sons, 2007.

Shepard, Geoff. *The Real Watergate Scandal: Collusion, Conspiracy, and the Plot That Brought Nixon Down*. New York: Regnery History, 2015.

Silverstein, Ken. "Alexander Haig's Last Years." *Mother Jones*, September/October 1999.

Sirica, John J. *To Set the Record Straight: The Break-in, the Tapes, the Conspirators, the Pardon*. New York: Norton, 1979.

Smith, Louis J., ed. *South Asia Crisis, 1971.* Vol. II of *Foreign Relations of the United States, 1969–1976,* edited by Edward C. Keefer. Washington DC: U.S. Government Printing Office, 2005.

Snepp, Frank. *Decent Interval: An Insider's Account of Saigon's Indecent End Told by the CIA's Chief Strategy Analyst in Vietnam.* New York: Random House, 1978.

Snider, L. Britt. *The Agency and the Hill: CIA's Relationship with Congress, 1946–2004.* Washington DC: Center for the Study of Intelligence, 2008.

Sorley, Lewis. *Thunderbolt: From the Battle of the Bulge to Vietnam and Beyond: General Creighton Abrams and the Army of His Times.* Herndon VA: Brassey's, 1992.

Stanford, Phil. *White House Call Girl: The Real Watergate Story.* Port Townsend WA: Feral House, 2013.

Stayton, Richard. "Fade In." *Written By,* April/May 2011.

Stone, Roger, with Mike Colapietro. *Nixon's Secrets: The Rise, Fall, and Untold Truth about the President, Watergate, and the Pardon.* New York: Skyhorse, 2014.

Strober, Gerald, and Deborah Hart Strober. *Nixon: An Oral History of His Presidency.* New York: HarperCollins, 1994.

Sullivan, William C., with Bill Brown. *The Bureau: My Thirty Years in Hoover's FBI.* New York: W. W. Norton, 1979.

"A Telltale Tape Deepens Nixon's Dilemma." *Time,* January 22, 1974.

Thelen, Sarah. "Helping Them Along: Astroturf, Public Opinion, and Nixon's Vietnam War." *49th Parallel,* 2015. https://fortyninthparalleljournal.files.wordpress.com/2015/11/thelen-49thparallel-formatted3.pdf.

Thomas, Evan. *Being Nixon: A Man Divided.* New York: Random House, 2015.

———. *The Man to See: The Life of Edward Bennett Williams.* New York: Simon & Shuster, 1992.

Thompson, Fred. *At That Point in Time.* New York: Quadrangle / New York Times Book Co., 1975.

"Unauthorized Disclosure of Classified Defense Information Appearing in the Jack Anderson Columns in *The Washington Post* dated December 14 and December 16, 1971." https://www.nixonlibrary.gov/virtuallibrary/releases/jan10/094.pdf.

Ungar, Sanford. *FBI: An Uncensored Look behind the Walls.* Boston: Little, Brown, 1976.

U.S. Congress, House, Committee on the Judiciary. *A Resolution Authorizing and Directing the Committee on the Judiciary to Investigate Whether Sufficient Grounds Exist for the House of Representatives to Exercise Its Constitutional Power to Impeach Richard M. Nixon, President of the United States of America, White House Surveillance Activities and Campaign Activities, Book 1, Alexander Butterfield, Paul O'Brien, and Fred C. LaRue.* 93rd Cong., 2nd sess., 1974. https://archive.org/details/WatergateHearingsBeforeTheHouseCommitteeOnTheJudiciary.

U.S. Congress, Senate. *Hearings before the Select Committee on Presidential Campaign Activities: Watergate and Related Activities, Book 3.* 93rd Cong., 1st sess., 1973. https://archive.org/search.php?query=presidential%20campaign%20activities.

———. *Hearings before the Select Committee on Presidential Campaign Activities: Watergate and Related Activities, Book 4.* 93rd Cong., 1st sess., 1973. https://archive.org/search .php?query=presidential%20campaign%20activities.

———. *Hearings before the Select Committee on Presidential Campaign Activities: Watergate and Related Activities, Book 5.* 93rd Cong., 1st sess., 1973. https://archive.org/search .php?query=presidential%20campaign%20activities.

———. *Hearings before the Select Committee on Presidential Campaign Activities: Watergate and Related Activities, Book 7.* 93rd Cong., 1st sess., 1973. https://archive.org/search .php?query=presidential%20campaign%20activities.

———. *Hearings before the Select Committee on Presidential Campaign Activities: Watergate and Related Activities, Book 9.* 93rd Cong., 1st sess., 1973. https://archive.org/search .php?query=presidential%20campaign%20activities.

U.S. Congress, Senate, Committee on Armed Services. *Transmittal of Documents from the National Security Council to the Chairman of the Joint Chiefs of Staff. Hearing before the Committee on Armed Services, Part 1.* 93rd Cong., 1st sess., February 6, 1974. https://babel.hathitrust.org/cgi/pt?id=mdp.39015078167940.

———. *Transmittal of Documents from the National Security Council to the Chairman of the Joint Chiefs of Staff. Hearing before the Committee on Armed Services, Part 2.* 93rd Cong., 2nd sess., February 20, 21, 1974. https://babel.hathitrust.org/cgi/pt?id =mdp.39015078167908.

———. *Transmittal of Documents from the National Security Council to the Chairman of the Joint Chiefs of Staff. Hearing before the Committee on Armed Services, Part 3.* 93rd Cong., 2nd sess., March 7, 1974. https://babel.hathitrust.org/cgi/pt?id=mdp .39015078168062.

U.S. Congress, Senate, Select Committee to Study Governmental Operations with Respect to Intelligence Activities. S. Rep. No. 94-755. *Book 1, Foreign and Military Intelligence.* Washington DC: U.S. Government Printing Office, 1976. https://archive .org/search.php?query=church%20committee.

———. S. Rep. No. 94-755. *Book 2, Intelligence Activities and the Rights of Americans.* Washington DC: U.S. Government Printing Office, 1976. https://archive.org/search .php?query=church%20committee.

———. S. Rep. No. 94-755. *Book 3, Supplementary Detailed Staff Reports on Intelligence Activities and the Rights of Americans.* Washington DC: U.S. Government Printing Office, 1976. https://archive.org/search.php?query=church%20committee.

———. S. Rep. No. 94-755. *Book 4, Supplementary Detailed Staff Reports on Foreign and Military Intelligence.* Washington DC: U.S. Government Printing Office, 1976. https://archive.org/search.php?query=church%20committee.

———. S. Rep. No. 94-755. *Book 5, The Investigation of the Assassination of President John F. Kennedy: Performance of the Intelligence Agencies.* Washington DC: U.S. Government Printing Office, 1976. https://archive.org/search.php?query=church%20committee.

————. S. Rep. No. 94-755. *Book 5, Supplementary Reports on Intelligence Activities*. Washington DC: U.S. Government Printing Office, 1976. https://archive.org/search.php ?query=church%20committee.

Van Atta, Dale. *With Honor: Melvin Laird in War, Peace, and Politics*. Madison: University of Wisconsin Press, 2008.

Walters, Vernon A. *Silent Missions*. Garden City NY: Doubleday, 1978.

Webb, William J. *The Joint Chiefs of Staff and the War in Vietnam 1969–1970*. Washington DC: Office of the Chairman of the Joint Chiefs of Staff, 2002.

Webb, William J., and Walter Poole. *The Joint Chiefs of Staff and the War in Vietnam 1971–1973*. Washington DC: Office of the Chairman of the Joint Chiefs of Staff, 2007.

Weiner, Tim. *Enemies: A History of the FBI*. New York: Random House, 2012.

————. *Legacy of Ashes: The History of the CIA*. New York: Random House, 2007.

————. *One Man against the World: The Tragedy of Richard Nixon*. New York: Henry Holt, 2015.

Weinstein, Allen. *Perjury: The Hiss-Chambers Case*. New York: Random House, 1978.

Werth, Barry. *31 Days: The Crisis That Gave Us the Government We Have Today*. New York: Doubleday, 2006.

Witcover, Jules. *Very Strange Bedfellows: The Short and Unhappy Marriage of Richard Nixon & Spiro Agnew*. New York: Public Affairs, 2007.

Woodward, Bob. *Bush at War*. New York: Simon & Schuster, 2002.

————. *The Commanders*. New York: Simon & Schuster, 1991.

————. *The Last of the President's Men*. New York: Simon & Schuster, 2015.

————. *Plan of Attack*. New York: Simon & Schuster, 2004.

————. *The Secret Man: The Story of Watergate's Deep Throat*. New York: Simon & Schuster, 2005.

————. *State of Denial*. New York: Simon & Schuster, 2006.

————. *Veil*. New York: Simon & Schuster, 1987.

Woodward, Bob, and Carl Bernstein. *All the President's Men*. New York: Simon & Schuster, 1974.

————. *The Final Days*. New York: Simon & Schuster, 1976.

Worley, D. Robert. *Orchestrating the Instruments of Power: A Critical Examination of the U.S. National Security System*. Raleigh NC: Lulu Press, 2012.

Zumwalt, Elmo R., Jr. *On Watch: A Memoir*. New York: Quadrangle, 1976.

INDEX